# MONEY

Since the publication of Georg Simmel's *Philosophy of Money* more than a century ago, social science has primarily considered money a medium of exchange. This new book treats money as a more inclusive social concept that has profoundly influenced the emergence of modern society. Money is also a *moral and political category*. It communicates prices and thus embodies innumerable evaluations and judgments of objects and services, of social relationships and associations.

At the same time, modern societies are undergoing fundamental transformations in which money assumes an ever-important role, while banking and financial services constitute the new primary sector of modern service economies. In this book, the authors trace the transformational scope of monetarization and financialization along the four classical productive forces—land, capital, labor, and knowledge—and evaluate the consequences of an irrepressible urge to quantify and monetarize almost everything social. What happens to a society in which the tangible products of the real economy lose their preeminent status, and everything is judged purely according to its *economic* value? The authors identify an increasing disconnect between market prices and social values with serious social, political, economic, and environmental consequences.

**Nico Stehr** was until the summer of 2018 Karl Mannheim Professor of Cultural Studies at the Zeppelin University, Friedrichshafen, Germany. He is a fellow of the Royal Society (Canada) and a fellow of the European Academy of Sciences and Arts. His research interests center on the transformation of modern societies into knowledge societies and developments associated with this transformation in different major social institutions of modern society (e.g. science, politics, governance, the economy, inequality, and globalization); in addition, his research interests concern the societal consequences of climate change. He is one of the authors of the *Hartwell Paper* on climate policy. Among his recent book publications are: *Information, Power and Democracy* (Cambridge University Press, 2016), *Knowledge: Is Knowledge Power?* (with Marian Adolf, Routledge, 2016) and *Society and Climate* (with Amanda Machin, World Scientific Publishers, 2019).

**Dustin Voss** is a PhD candidate in Political Economy at the European Institute of the London School of Economics and Political Science. His dissertation is concerned with the turn to neoliberalism and the rise of economic orthodoxy in social democratic policy making. His research interests include comparative political economy, monetary and fiscal policy, financialization, and the relationship of democracy and capitalism in advanced nations. He holds an MSc in Political Economy of Europe (with Distinction) from the LSE as well as a BA in Sociology, Politics, and Economics from Zeppelin University, Germany.

Not since Georg Simmel's *Philosophy of Money* has there been a book that so persuasively examines money—hence also, capitalism—from the point of view of culture and knowledge. In *Money: A Theory of Modern Society* Nico Stehr and Dustin Voss have made an important contribution—not just to social theory but to our understanding of the current world order.

—*Charles Lemert*, *University Professor and John C. Andrus*
*Professor of Social Theory Emeritus, Wesleyan University, USA*

This new masterpiece explores the mysterious existence of money—a myth without intrinsic value. Stehr and Voss carefully disclose how and why money (and economic relations in general) "disguise" social processes and what putting prices on land, capital, labor, and knowledge means for societies. A must read for any scholar in sociology.

—*Lucia Reisch*, *Professor, Copenhagen Business School, Department*
*of Management, Society and Communication, Denmark*

This is a very ambitious and interesting volume on the many different roles that money plays in the modern world. Perhaps it can be characterized as something that Georg Simmel, the author of *The Philosophy of Money*, would have written if he had lived today. Read and enjoy!

—*Richard Swedberg*, *Professor of Sociology, Cornell University, USA*

Social theory is in need of renewal, in a world in which the past is recognizable but no longer informative in terms of the old categories. Nico Stehr and Dustin Voss go to the heart of the problem: the role of money and the problematic relation of the fact of price to the puzzlingly elusive facts of value, such as the value of knowledge, and indeed of work itself. This book is an excellent inventory of, and introduction to, the intellectual resources we have for this renewal, and a contribution to it.

—*Stephen Turner*, *Distinguished Professor, University of*
*South Florida, USA*

Money has been at the center of social theory in its different attempts to understand modern society and to disclose its dynamics from the classics up to our time. The study of Nico Stehr and Dustin Voss is an extraordinary enrichment of this tradition. It starts from what we know and leads us systematically step by step far beyond the state of the art to help us understand and explain how money in its contemporary form of the financialization of everything penetrates every sphere of human action to transform modern society fundamentally. This is social theory at its best. The study features all qualities to make it a classic.

—*Richard Münch*, *Emeritus of Excellence, Department of Sociology,*
*University of Bamberg, Germany*

# MONEY

## A Theory of Modern Society

*Nico Stehr and Dustin Voss*

Routledge
Taylor & Francis Group

NEW YORK AND LONDON

First published 2020
by Routledge
52 Vanderbilt Avenue, New York, NY 10017

and by Routledge
2 Park Square, Milton Park, Abingdon, Oxon, OX14 4RN

*Routledge is an imprint of the Taylor & Francis Group, an informa business*

*Library of Congress Cataloging-in-Publication Data*
A catalog record for this book has been requested

ISBN: 978-0-367-35462-6 (hbk)
ISBN: 978-0-367-35465-7 (pbk)
ISBN: 978-0-429-33156-5 (ebk)

Typeset in Bembo
by Apex CoVantage, LLC

Printed and bound by CPI Group (UK) Ltd, Croydon, CR0 4YY

# CONTENTS

# ILLUSTRATIONS

## Figures

## Table

# PREFACE

For some time now, modern societies have been undergoing a profound process of change, one that is not necessarily obvious, tangible or, let alone, measurable, but nevertheless of immense social significance. A new master narrative has shifted the attention of most observers of modern transformation processes from the social to a mixture of technology and finance. More precisely, what we are witnessing may also be described as a reversal in the traditional hierarchy of the real (primary) economy and finance as the secondary economy. Finance takes on the characteristics of a self-sufficient socio-economic system that supports the formation of an immaterial economy. Its points of reference are increasingly financial matters, meaning that money is increasingly applied to money itself. International financial markets become something akin to the inaccessible center of world society. However, at the same time the exact relationship between finance, the real economy, and society in its many facets, for example its volatility, crisis moments and potential for inequality formation, remain an empirical and theoretical desideratum.

Money is not only present, condemned and prominent in various forms and ways in modern societies: As in the past, it continues to be desirous, chastised, hidden or openly displayed, it generates conflicts or becomes the means of consensus formation. The interest among *social scientists* in money, in the broad sense of the term—money as a social process—has been significant as well and has produced some of the field's most remarkable studies. In the tradition of an expansive analysis that anchors its knowledge-guiding interest in an examination of the relevant *societal context*, we analyze money using the perspective of French sociologist and anthropologist Marcel Mauss ([1925] 1990), that is, money as a *fait social total* (total social fact).

We realize when we employ the term "price" of capital, labor, land and knowledge that this may be misunderstood to merely refer to its common everyday usage or its narrow conventional or "rational" meaning in economics, money as something that itself is beyond dispute and understood simply as a number or as a technical means of exchange. But the fact that in reality, for many people in modern societies "the possession of money is the actual and ultimate aspiration in life" (Simmel, [1915] 2000: 118) becomes the triggering moment of cultural-critical reflections on the super-elevated role of money in the simultaneous loss of what bears value but lacks a market price. Against such notions, our reference to money and the price of the means of production is far more extensive. Where appropriate, we attend to justice and equity (just income, fair prices), wages (as a function of multiple attributes of the wage earner and the institution of the world of work with its changing circumstances of working; unemployment; automation; burdens and wages; social inequality), human capital, patents and public goods (as proxies for the price of knowledge), the environment (land grabbing; the economic appropriation of nature) and financialization (the growing dominance of the immaterial economy; globalization; social crises; the marketization of the self). In short, money and, more generally, economic relations "disguise" social processes. Those very processes we try to reveal and explore.

In the course of our enquiry, we agree with the observation of Niklas Luhmann (1997: 1120), who points out that a structural change of society and its inclusion in theoretical considerations do not necessarily need to coincide in time. The same delay occurs with respect to expectations. Expectations tend to stick around even though social realities may well have changed. The societal realities are in collision with expectations that belong to a previous era. In both instances, at the theoretical and empirical level, the social law of the *simultaneity of the non-simultaneous* applies. The simultaneity of the non-simultaneous refers to distinct social facts or circumstances such as dialects, religions, political parties or economic forms that are not mutually exclusive. On a historical axis, one of the multiple social forms tends to be in terms of its influence on the decline and another on the ascent (cf. Ferguson, 2017).

In this sense, the social transformation processes analyzed by us under the heading of a social theory of modernity include social, political and cultural changes in modern societies that have been materializing for some time, both in synchronous and asynchronous fashion, and not necessarily just since the financial crisis at the beginning of the 21st century.

## GEORG SIMMEL ON MONEY AND FOOD (1915)

Our investigation resonates with Georg Simmel's observations on value and money in the context of a deeply impoverished society at the beginning of World War I. Simmel (1915) notes that since the replacement of the medieval natural economy, "for most people of the present, anything that can be bought is worth just as much as it costs" (our translation). The social penetration of money as universal medium and thus as highest aspiration in life led to the fact that the socially recognized value of a commodity manifested itself not through its objective functionality, but exclusively through its market price. The contradictoriness of the "exceptional social function" of money became particularly apparent in the context of economic scarcity. In light of the general level of poverty in 1915, the dominant view demanded that the wealthier classes should save money, tighten their belts and do without luxury and splendor. In practical terms, lobsters were spared for cabbage. As a result, however, simpler and more affordable diets became scarcer and thus more expensive and the famine continued to spread. This illustrates the eminent paradox of monetized values: the *economic* price of cabbage may be much lower than that of a lobster, but its *intrinsic* (real) value is based on its affordable nutritious qualities in the event of a crisis. Due to the cultural dominance of monetary value, however, the primacy of saving in need does not refer to objective means, but to money itself and, consequentially, misses its purpose entirely. In this respect, Simmel emphatically underlines the importance of the relativity of values, which inevitably is disregarded in a society dominated by money. The natural value of goods measured by their individual (and context-dependent) utility is not only disguised by expression in aggregated monetary market value, but essentially turned into the opposite. How the social dominance of money, which has undoubtedly increased exponentially since the beginning of the 20th century, affects modern societies and their value systems is the fundamental subject of our study.

All of the social processes we are examining in our enquiry are constitutive of the fundamental social fact of the simultaneity of the non-simultaneous. Put more simply, we are constantly encountering, contesting and struggling with the presence of more or less tangible social phenomena that define individual and collective change, ascent and descent. Hence, the simultaneity of the non-simultaneous quite obviously represents a significant aspect of the complexity of our social world, which our analysis both reveals and is similarly subjected to and constrained by.

Karl Mannheim's ([1928] 1993) classical analysis of generations forms a well-known example of social collectivities that are linked in distinct ways to the past, present and future. The immaterial economy that we sketch in the first chapter as the general economic context of our enquiry into the price of knowledge, land, capital and labor is not alone among existing forms of economic relations. More traditional economic relations familiar to us from capitalism's past, which transcend the immaterial economy, are still present as (largely indeterminable) indications that neither will the immaterial economy represent the end of the history of economic relations. Path dependencies determine the nature of social change. Hence, it would be foolish to assume that we are able to anticipate what form of economic relation may transcend the immaterial economy. Nor are monies available in but one form and function. Money has strong moral attributions (e.g. money in politics is evil) that constantly define, deconstruct and reshape social values simply by its everyday use. Identifying and understanding the transformative nature of these social processes is the aim of our study.

Of course, an ambitious study of this scale poses an immense challenge that we could never have met without the invaluable support of many helpful friends and colleagues. We would like to express special gratitude to Marian Adolf, Susanne Schara and Barbara Stehr for their substantive assistance with content development and editing. Furthermore, we are indebted to a number of distinguished friends and colleagues who have generously made their scarce time available to us and shared innumerable critical and helpful comments and remarks: Patrick Aspers, Friederike Döbbe, Ottmar Edenhofer, Bruno Frey, Steve Fuller, Fred Gault, Reiner Grundmann, Dieter Haselbach, Arne Kalleberg, Susan McDaniel, Scott McNall, Guy Peters, Birger Priddat, Lord Robert Skidelsky, Steven Vallas, Rainer Voss, Ansgar Weymann and Helmut Willke. All remaining errors and interpretive flaws are ours.

## References

Ferguson, Niall (2017), *The Square and the Tower. Networks and Power, from the Freemasons to Facebook*. New York: Penguin.

Luhmann, Niklas (1997), *Die Gesellschaft der Gesellschaft*. Frankfurt am Main: Suhrkamp.

Mannheim. Karl ([1928] 1993), "The problem of generations," pp. 351–395 in Kurt H. Wolff (ed.), *From Karl Mannheim*. New Brunswick, NJ: Transaction Books.

Mauss, Marcel ([1925] 1990), *The Gift. The Form and Reason for Exchange in Archaic Societies*. London: Routledge.

Simmel, Georg ([1915] 2000), "Geld und Nahrung," pp. 117–122 in Georg Simmel (ed.), *Aufsätze und Abhandlungen 1909–1918. Georg Simmel Collected Works: Volume 11*. Frankfurt am Main: Suhrkamp.

# INTRODUCTION

Finances of the state are one of the best points of the investigation of the social, especially, but not exclusively, of the political.

—*Joseph Schumpeter (1918: 7)*

Money leads an apparently carefree life and, here and there, a mysterious existence. You shouldn't talk about money.[1] Nevertheless, this is exactly what we intend to do in this volume.[2]

## Money, Price and Value as Social Phenomena

Money was created many times in many places. Its development required no technological breakthroughs—it was a purely mental revolution. It involved the creation of a new inter-subjective reality that exists solely in people's shared imagination.

—*Yuval Noah Harari ([2011] 2014: 177)*

Modern money (coins, notes[3] and bank deposits) as a general medium of exchange has no intrinsic value.[4] The value of money stems from its use and operation in *social exchanges*,[5] in activities, for example, by generating social conflicts or exchange opportunities[6] that constitute value:[7] "In exchange, value becomes supra-subjective, supra-individual" (Simmel, [1907] 2005: 75).[8] Money conveys information. There is no private money.[9]

The issue then is to explain how money can have value, what kind of value it may have and on what bases it acquires value (in our case, the value of the means of production land, labor, capital and knowledge). Values reflect the moral budget of a society. At least in modern societies, hardly anyone buys a product for reasons of pure usefulness (cf. Stehr, 2008).[10] Value systems in a society are interpretative adaptations to the characteristic societal circumstances of action, for example, the structural realities of society and, more specifically, the prevailing production conditions.

But the ambivalence of values does not apply to prices. Prices signal definitive market outcomes. Prices indicate the *value* of something, which means the socially anchored and differentiated assessment, evaluation and appreciation of something (cf. Priddat, 2015; Morris, 2015).[11] Almost everything has a price in our societies. There are prices for baseball players, information, bank accounts, books and a ton of carbon dioxide. Economic activities are about uncertain future prices. In a market economy[12] "order in the production and distribution of goods is ensured by prices alone" (Polanyi, [1944] 2001: 72; Luhmann, 1995: 461).[13] Indeed, the oldest and most persistent problem of economics is that of price determination.[14]

Prices represent or form *income*. Rent is the price for real estate, wages are the price for labor, interest is the price for money (capital), and receipts are the price for knowledge. However, to be informed about the price of something is not sufficient to understand what makes the economy or the market work.[15] Prices live a precarious existence between uncertainty and risk.

The secular and durable societal trend of financialization, which we are examining in our subsequent analysis, revolves around finance, money and technology but more precisely is linked to value (cf. Heilbronner, 1983).[16] Money is an efficient, neutral, generalized medium of exchange, and a means of compensating for the inefficiency of barter or, for that matter, of reducing the transaction cost of doing business. Money is more than a mute background noise or silent currency. Money facilitates social interaction. It reduces the complications of interacting with strangers.

Money is about prices. And prices are, as indicated, about *value*. But the value of something may be distinct from its price. Valuation can occur through prices. Valuation cannot be reduced to prices (Dewey, 1939; Hall, 2011; Brighenti, 2018).[17] As Oscar Wilde in *Lady Windermere's Fan* had Lord Darlington quip: a cynic is "a man who knows the price of everything and the value of nothing."

Values are always essentially contested phenomena while prices only appear to be objective entities. Economics should not merely be a science of prices. Prices are not a neutral signifier of value. There is a two-way relationship between values and prices. At times, objects are valued or devalued because of their high or even exorbitant price (cf. Boltanski and Esquerre, 2016); at other times, objects are devalued or valued because of their "ridiculously" low or high prices.

Indeed, despite the progressive diffusion of trends toward monetary quantification and financialization throughout society, money/finance remains a puzzle, as does the *value* of knowledge, capital, land and labor. Contemporary economics does not excel at explanation. This puzzle extends with particular force to a notion that occupies the doghouse of economics or has been banished to the attic of economic discourse: The idea of a fair or just price of the means of production. Despite its dubious status, the notion of ethically unfair prices is of interest to us (see Frey and Pommerehne, 1993).[18] The fair price may be above or below the market price as it is first and foremost a function of dominant social values.

But why should a sociological analysis *itself* or, better, an interdisciplinary rather than an economic account of the development toward a financialization of society or the transformation of the economy of production into a financial economy (Touraine, 1998: 144) *be of value*? One of the key mistakes in many of the growing number of economic discussions of the modern financial world has been to frame the issue too narrowly. A more inclusive but also flexible and multidimensional view is needed in order to capture the complexity and dynamics of the "wicked" problem of financialization. Such an approach is crucial for a productive examination of both the adverse and the potentially beneficial impact of the contemporary financial world on modern social relations.

Economists excel at discovering differences based on large data sets (including the use of raw data) pertaining for instance to social inequality across social strata and nations (cf. Alvaredo et al., 2017; Piketty, Saez and Zucman, 2018).[19] However, discovering, often with great precision, differences and trends is considered to be an end in itself, the fundamental objective economists assign to their research efforts. But merely discovering differences and trends fails to attend to the underlying processes that make these observations possible in the first instance. *Understanding* the origin of economic trends and how they mold our thought is important not only for social science but also for policy purposes and, ultimately, for cohabitation in modern societies.

The requirement of a socio-economic and sociological analysis of value draws attention to the fact that value does not embody an intrinsic God-given worth but that the conditions for the possibility of value are dependent on social relations. Hence, the idea or phenomenon, for example, of a "market price" as something that travels unimpededly and with the speed of light, and which can be extracted unproblematically or communicated without constraints is an illusion (cf. Burrell and Oreglia, 2015). Various operations such as ascribing beneficial or negative attributes to a process result in the emergence of value not least, of course, in monetary form. Conversely, prices can also be a source of value. As a result, specific values invariably are a highly contentious matter. In other terms, we do not subscribe to the idea that markets are intrinsically *inhabited* by values (if such is even possible to imagine) that are less idiosyncratic and diffuse, easier to calculate and compare than values found in non-market contexts.[20]

Given the sum of often highly contentious attributes assigned to knowledge, land, labor and capital, how would it be possible to find a commensurate calculus that integrates, for example, the sum of the symbolic features into a common currency? Among other things, such a commensurate formula would require, as Morgan Adamson (2009: 273) notes, an equation that perfectly calculated the value of human capital and therefore "would be able to measure the value of all layers of socialization, which occur over the span of an individual life, that add to productive capacity, including such immeasurables as 'luck' and other factors." An entirely unlikely undertaking.

## The Mystery of Money

> Profit arises out of the inherent, absolute unpredictability of things, out of the sheer brute fact that the results of human activity cannot be anticipated and then only in so far as even a probability calculation in regard to them is impossible and meaningless.
>
> —*Frank Knight ([1921] 2000: 141)*

Despite the persistent trend toward monetary quantification and financialization of society as a whole, money remains a mystery. Money is taken as a common denominator of value.[21] Money is a store of value, a unit of account, or a standard of deferred payment. Money is an economic entity. It is scarce. But processes that do not apply to other objects that are or become economic entities govern its scarcity or the creation of money, for example, limits that are governed by physical restrictions. It is an often taken-for-granted but also contested view that in market societies the market price of a purchase is synonymous with the value/worth of the acquisition. Money as such, as we have noted, is most often without intrinsic value.[22] But money is a form of relief or constitutes a shortcut. Money offers a convenient form of orientation.[23] In modern societies, money is an instrument devised by the state that must be acceptable, however. The state cannot escape the consequences of its own action on money.

All economic activity (and not only economic activity) is oriented toward expectations regarding prices,[24] the change of prices (cf. Keynes, 1936: 294; Weber, [1956] 1978: 92),[25] and therefore the *value* of commodities and services prices come to signal.[26] Individuals and groups define economic goods and services as commodities and services that they value. The classical economy is largely confined in its horizon to determining the price of the means of production, goods and services and hopes, at least indirectly, to establish something like a homogeneity and objectification of economic activity. However, such objectification is vigorously opposed by an elementary insight from cultural studies thought. For example, Hans Blumenberg (2006: 606; our translation) draws attention to relevant premises of the cultural-scientific approach by emphasizing that "the survival capacity of mankind . . . is to a large extent based on the fact that its needs and thus its possibilities of happiness are not objective, i.e. not determined by the nature of mankind and thus homogeneous" and, as we may add, free from all circumstances whatsoever.

The value of money and the price of the production factors—in their dual function as sources of income and production costs—are only the "indirect objectification of the absolute subjective" (Blumenberg, 2006: 606). We will attempt to determine how the (non-homogeneous) values of the production factors, such as their age, may either enhance or diminish the constitution of its prices. The values of the production factors are not fixed objective phenomena. The meaning of the means of production and relation to each other, as well as their social relevance, changes in the course of economic development and societal transformation. Currently, an almost uncontested observation asserts that the importance of knowledge and skills as means of production in the economy and society is growing in significance. As a result, the distribution of skills and knowledge in society increasingly determines patterns of social inequality (Piketty, ([2013] 2014: 22).

We aim to determine how values are constituted. Valuation does not occur in splendid isolation nor does it merely rest on the "possibility of comparison and competition" (Aspers, 2009: 113). Valuation is, drawing on a term coined by Marcel Mauss (1925: 3), a *total social fact*.[27] Valuation in the sense of a total social fact brings into view the whole of society and each of its institutions. The notion of a total social fact extends and includes reference to the moral force behind economic transactions (Appadurai, 2011; earlier Weber, [1956] 1978: 110). And quite independently of the economic formation, be it "pre-capitalism, capitalism or post-capitalism," value continues to be valued, implicating moral considerations (cf. Stehr, 2008).

## Money as Driver of Societal Change

> The test of money measurement constantly tends to widen the area where we weigh concrete goods against abstract money.
> —*John Maynard Keynes ([1925] 2010)*[28]

Our treatise on money and its power carries the ambitious subtitle "A social theory of modern society." This is to say, our aspiration is to identify and reflect on a significant structural and cultural long-term trend that, despite considerable resistance by social movements, for example, in the streets of Seattle, New York, Berlin or Hamburg, is underway within modern society in general and in the economy in particular.[29] Put differently, the new master narrative abandons the societal for a hybrid of the technical and financial narration.

What we are witnessing may also be described as a reversal in the traditional hierarchy of the real (primary) economy and finance as a secondary economy. From the mid-20th century onwards, finance more and more takes on the characteristics of a self-sufficient socio-economic system. Its points of reference are increasingly financial matters, meaning that money is increasingly applied to money itself (cf. Willke, 2006: 46–53; Preda, 2009). International financial markets become, as Niklas Luhmann (1997: 808) stresses, something akin to the center of world society. However, the exact relationship between finance and the real economy, markets and value in its many facets, for example, its fluctuations, remains an empirical and theoretical desideratum. Already Joseph Schumpeter (1954: 289) was convinced that "views on money are as difficult to describe as are shifting clouds."

What is different today? The practical societal transformations under investigation represent a shift toward the growing monetarization, financialization and hence expanding quantification of a host of social phenomena while enhancing the differentiation of ownership and income. Recognizing different, often traditional ways in which modern capitalism is organized (Hollingsworth and Boyer, 1997; Nelson, 2011), capitalism nonetheless becomes more and more *financial*.[30] What is new is that massive financial transactions are realized without the detour of real production. However, what does not change therefore is the core regulating mechanism of capitalism, namely the value placed on the profit motive and the expansionary expectation of investors. Money invested is expected to generate surplus money. In other terms, a large proportion of money currently in circulation is simply and only covered by money (cf. Paul, 2002: 254). The simultaneous presence of different phases of the development of capitalism remains characteristic as an attribute of the ruling form of capitalism. The simultaneity of the non-simultaneous allows a look into the future as well as into the past of the social relations of capitalism.[31]

What is also not new is the deep curiosity of sociology into the workings of the economy. Such inquisitiveness was not always sustained in the history of its thought. Since the late-19th century in Europe, sociologists have examined the nature and the transformation of the economy as the center of social life. Classical sociologists studied and participated in economic discourse. Similarly, economists and their debates saw the contribution of the classical sociologist as relevant to their concerns. The growing intellectual differentiation among the social sciences disciplines in subsequent decades meant that economics and sociology went their distinctive intellectual paths. The current societal and economic changes that are at the center of our investigation represent a curious occasion for the renewal of a mutually beneficial relationship that should not go wasted.

Whether the growing significance of finance is in the context of modern society a virtuous savior or a dark curse is a highly contentious matter.[32] The adjectives attributed to and associated with the world of finance therefore range across the entire spectrum from despairing and skeptical to enthusiastic forms of endorsement: from epiphenomenal to unreal, from false to fictitious, from parasitical to merely speculative, from ghostly to connecting.[33] The early euphoria of the 1980s, when it was more common to refer to a win–win situation, assuming that the good of investors equals the good for society (cf. Welch, 1981), has long since given way to more sober, doubtful diagnoses; for instance, with respect to the impact of financialization on the competition and control of natural resources around the globe (cf. Tricarico and Löschmann, 2012). It is easy to see who is on which side of this contested assessment of financialization. But skeptical evaluations of the social consequences of financialization and the discontent with financialization that is widespread do not rule out the possibility that its growing importance has a noticeable influence on the world in general and its livelihood in particular, for example, on what is understood to be a good life (see Mehrling, 2017).

An increasingly contested assessment pertains also the core business model of many corporations in the world of symbolic commodities. The big "tech" companies such as Google, Facebook, and Apple that would not exist without the internet have enormous market presence and market power. Increasingly, these social media corporations are criticized for producing the opposite effects on their consumers of what they actually promise in their name: addiction, depression, loneliness, social exclusion and less engagement with the "real" world (see Twenge, 2017). Still, the internet would not be the same without Amazon, Apple and Alphabet (Google).

In any event, and in a similar manner, finance becomes a dominant and at times irritating driver of the economy and society.[34] Financial markets govern other markets; and acquire a considerable measure of systemic independence as well as fragility. Financial markets are characterized by high degrees of uncertainty (Benhabib, Liu and Wang, 2018); decision-making under incertitude is the norm (Kraemer, 2010). Although not new (Carlos and Lewis, 1995; Davis, 2017), financial markets in turn are affected by the accelerated flow of information and knowledge provided by the internet. It follows that an increasing number of problems of social action are problems of knowledge and information.

Modern capitalism experiences and has to cope with new forms of money. New financial instruments, for example, collateralized debt obligations (CDOs), trading in options, and complex packages of securitization are examples of novel forms of money originating in global financial markets.[35] The flood of daily financial transactions around the world far exceeds the value of transactions of commodities and traditional services.

Financial transactions are much more difficult to monitor, to control, and to regulate and easier to manipulate and hide (cf. Lewis, 2015; Reurink, 2016).[36] The development of financialization is uneven across different countries and regions of the world. A measure of variation of socio-structural changes across societies and regions of the world is always the case. Socio-historical contexts differ and respond in different ways to social changes. Financialization processes are no exception. Country-level statistics using different proxies for financialization indicate that Anglo-Saxon countries at the present show higher levels of financialization (Darcillon, 2015: 487; Lapavitsas and Powell, 2013).

New actors appear on the stage. Among these are also (established) central banks employing novel strategies. Central banks have an impact on the course of economic cycles not merely *ex post facto* as has been typical of the past but also *ex ante*. However, it is necessary to ask whether economics and financial theory has adjusted to the new realities, for example, "can a market be efficient, or properly balance risk and reward, if the dominant players are central banks, who are not interested in maximising their profits?" (Buttonwood, 2015; Best, 2018). Innovative forms of money quicken the pace of life. Financial crises that produce major economic crises are a symptom of the new economic and political order.[37] Financial crises are of varying duration and changing social consequences, but the biggest victims are often the poorest segments of the population.

Our theoretical framework challenges alternative approaches for the understanding of advanced capitalism, including the notion of the emergence of what sometimes is called in the literature "digital capitalism" (e.g. Nachtwey and Staab, 2015).[38] The challenge extends to a rejection of the distance of the semantics of political economy from the other social science phenomena.[39] A significant part of the societal trend we are investigating is the dissolution of the once fateful conflictual link between *labor and capital* of the classical political economy (the ownership of the means of production is no longer class-based) and the suspension of the iron dichotomy of marginalist theory of exchange and use-value based on the discovery of new values, for example, a moralization of goods and services (see Stehr, 2008). The use-value and consumption of immaterial goods and services are non-rival.

The motives that would appear to govern financial processes, at least with respect to the motives that tend to dominate transactions and innovations, are far removed from those that Max Weber identified as the "spirit" of capitalism. In this sense, the motive structure also reached a new phase of capitalist development. As Arjun Appadurai (2011: 524) notes "the typical 'master' of the financial universe is not a dull or nerdy accountant or lawyer but a gaudy, adventurous, reckless, amoral type, who embodies just the sort of avarice, adventurism, and charismatic self-motivation that Weber saw as the absolute enemy of systematic capitalist profit making."

In his theory of the modern *aesthetic economy*, Gernot Böhme ([2001] 2003: 72) develops the concept of the *staging value* (*Inszenierungswert*):

> aesthetic qualities of the commodity . . . develop into an autonomous value, because they play a role for the customer not just in the context of exchange but also in that of use. They are certainly not classical use values, for they have nothing to do with utility and purposiveness, but they form, as it were, a new type of use value, which derives from their exchange value in so far as use is made of their attractiveness, their aura, their atmosphere. They serve to stage, costume and intensify life.

The aesthetic economy produces values that are not really "needed"—and may possibly never be satisfied (e.g. fame). These values remain scarce. As a result, the question of the limits to growth of the "immaterial economy" compared to the so-called "real economy" takes on an entirely new meaning.[40]

In a similar vein, John Maynard Keynes considers the "love of money" in contrast to the "love for goods" as distinct motive forces. The disposition to value money over things postponed "enoughness" (cf. Skildelsky and Skidelsky, 2012) into a distant future: "for whereas one might convince oneself that one had enough goods, it was much harder to persuade oneself that one had enough money" (Skidelsky, 2010: 139). Money remains scarce in an economy that no longer is merely a commodities-producing machine but a sophisticated monetary engine. A determining factor of outmost relevance in this context is climate change and its effects, as well as the question of the conditions for maintaining and extending access to affordable and reliable modern energy services in an environmentally sustainable and responsible manner. Without energy, no economic growth.

Value constitutes the core phenomenon of the modern economy (cf. Orléan, [2011] 2014: 3). Up to now, the analysis of modern economy and characteristic long-term structural shifts has to a large extent relied on the tracing of changes in *employment* patterns in its importance for different sectors of the economy (see Clark, 1940; Bell, 1973) and the satisfaction of *material needs*. These are by no means bygone trends. However, our observations about money pertain to more recent changes in the nature of the economy, its impact on social relations and the discourse about the economy. By the same token, our interest is in the effect that the discourse about the new economy has on the economy and society. Empirical evidence, for example in the form of national and international statistics about financialization and monetarization, is lagging behind the developments we are describing. It is, for example, no longer adequate to describe the financialization of the economy as just another manifestation of the trend toward an extension of the service sector (Krippner, 2005: 176). Our focus is on prices and values. Money facilitates exchange, but money is also a moral and a political category.[41] Money embodies civilizational progress. With the introduction of money, the dominance of exchange in form of presents, theft, violence, and ferocious misappropriation of goods retreated (see Orleans, [2011] 2014: 10). Money stands for a range of social relations and is itself a social relation *sui generis* (cf. Ingham, 1996; Kirshner, 2003). As such it stands for interpretative (cultural) activities and not so much for calculative rationalities. Money signifies power or the lack thereof—but only if others are ready to acknowledge its presence or absence.

Following Marcel Mauss, total social facts, for example gifts, are features of society that permeate *every* institution of society: "all kinds of institutions are given expression at one and the same time [in gifts]—religious, juridical, and moral . . . economic ones" (Mauss, 1925: 3; also Mitchell, 1998). The origins of money can therefore be traced not to law or a state institution but to a specific form of social or economic action. For instance, for Max Weber (1923: 238), "the function of money as a general medium of exchange originated in foreign trade."

Our observation that money is a total social phenomenon must be extended to all economic processes. Hence, the proper function of a firm, for instance, should not be restricted to maximizing its market value but incorporate the pursuit of strictly non-economic objectives such as sustainability or the wellbeing of the local community.[42]

However, our study should not be dubbed a sociology of money. Rather, it is a sociology of modern society in which the financial world assumes an increasingly important function that penetrates many forms of social action and social institutions.[43] A cautionary note about the persuasiveness and social power of particular social facts stresses that we are not about to identify new laws of modern society or its capitalist economic order.[44] As a matter of fact, we follow the advice of an astute economist who in his examination of the idea of just wages made it clear to his readers that his intention was "to clarify issues rather than to give direct and explicit answers to questions" (Knight, 1950: 463) let alone elucidating laws that cannot but curtail our freedom of action and inquiry.

From an *analytical* point of view, the value of the means of production constitutes a "wicked" problem. In contrast to "tame" analytical problems (complicated, but with defined and achievable end-states and simple causal relations), the determination of the price or value of labor, capital, land and knowledge represents a wicked problem that comprises open, complex, and imperfectly understood systems. Wicked problems are embedded in various social systems (not only in the economic system) as might be the case upon initial sight of the issue of the price of labor, for example. Originally described by C. West Churchman (1967) and later explicated more comprehensively by Horst Rittel and Melvin Webber (1973) in the context of urban planning, wicked problems are issues that are often formulated as if they were susceptible to a simple, unilinear solution when in fact they are not (cf. also Prins et al., 2010; Bisin and Verdier, 2017).[45]

Immediate, unequivocal and unambiguous answers to the question of the value of the means of production in the modern economy are impossible to provide. But we hope to clarify the issues and advance preliminary answers. In fact, we do live in a time of upheaval. But was there ever a time in modern history when this observation did not appear to be true? In any case, the question of how the economy will continue to develop is a crucial factor in the current period of rapid and seemingly inexorable change. With this book, we aim to find a preliminary answer to this captivating enigma.

## Notes

1. We can only speculate as to whether the modern taboo on talking about money and consideration of money as contemptible is but a distant echo of the strong biblical condemnation of the love for money: "the love of money is the root of all evil" (I Timothy 6:10). A strong loathing for money is repeatedly affirmed as a kind of *Leitmotiv* in the work of Jean Jacques Rousseau (see Pignol, 2010).
2. On how to avoid the taboo on talking about money problems in everyday life, see "We're All Afraid to Talk About Money. Here's How to Break the Taboo," *New York Times*. August 28, 2018.
3. "The British North American colonies were the first Western economies that issued sizeable amounts of paper money—called *bills of credit*" (Cutsail and Grubb, 2018: 1).

4. It will become evident in the course of our analysis that we use the term "value" in a broad economic sense and with a conceptual link to the virtues of good living (cf. Lübbe, 2014: 205–220).

5. Our assertion is strengthened by the following observation about the value of money by Philip Mirowski (1990: 712), "in a social theory of value money is the embodiment of value; but precisely because it is socially instituted, its invariance cannot be predicated on any 'natural' ground, and must continually be shored up and reconstituted by further social institutions, such as accountants and banks and governments."

6. The observation about the exchangeability or exchange opportunities of money refers, in other words, to the inherent reflexivity of money (see also Luhmann, 1970: 216).

7. Aside from more recent sociological discussions of the social facts of money (cf. Zelizer, 1997), our thesis of the social constitution or embeddedness of money may also refer to multiple classical theoretical perspectives in the history of ideas, importantly for example to Ludwig Wittgenstein's philosophical investigations of language or Max Weber's elementary sociological categories. Ludwig Wittgenstein (1945: app. 340) stresses in his *Philosophical Investigations*: "One cannot guess how a word functions. One has to *look* at its use and learn from that." In *Economy and Society*, Max Weber ([1956] 1978: 30) emphasizes with particular regard to pricing on markets: "Many of the especially notable uniformities in the course of social action are not determined by orientation to any sort of norm which is held to be valid, nor do they rest on custom, but entirely on the fact that the corresponding type of social action is in the nature of the case best adapted to the normal interests of the actors as they themselves are aware of them. This is above all true of economic action, for example, the uniformities of price determination in a 'free' market, but is by no means confined to such cases. The dealers in a market thus treat their own actions as means for obtaining the satisfaction of the ends denned by what they realize to be their own typical economic interests, and similarly treat as conditions the corresponding typical expectations as to the prospective behavior of others. . . . This phenomenon—the fact that orientation to the situation in terms of the pure self-interest of the individual and of the others to whom he is related can bring about results comparable to those which imposed norms prescribe, very often in vain—has aroused a lively interest, especially in economic affairs. Observation of this has, in fact, been one of the important sources of economics as a science."

8. Georg Simmel ([1907] 2005: 77) explains his observation about the significance of exchange processes as a condition for the possibility of an intersubjective value of a commodity as follows: "The specific characteristic of the economy as a particular form of behaviour and communication consists not only in exchanging *values* but in the *exchange* of values."

9. For an opposing view from an economic perspective see Pingle and Mukhopadhyay (2010) and Friedrich Hayek's (1990) proposal for a denationalization of money. Pablo Paniagua (2018: 115) raises the intriguing question whether a market economy could exist without money. His answer is in the negative: "Eradicating money would eliminate the only mechanism beside of language by which novel social relations are extended into wider realms of the social life, and thus would severely curtail our social intelligence. Without money, the higher order phenomena built upon our tacit knowledge, skills, and organized relations—which we call the market economy—would never exist."

10. This is precisely the thesis Thorstein Veblen ([1899] 1992) advances in his classic treatise of the "Theory of the Leisure Class." Veblen's statement about the value of a commodity with which we concur is at the same time a critique of the classical theory of marginal utility (William Jevons, Carl Menger and Leon Walras) in which the value of a commodity is determined by the market based on its subjective *utility* to the consumer; and that utility decreases with the extent of consumption (cf. Kaldor, 2018).

11. Compare also Max Weber's ([1956] 1978: 85–86) definition of "substantial rationality" as a term with close affinity to our use of the term "value," both full of ambiguities and with possible references to a multitude of specific "value postulates."
12. Our reference to markets throughout the book is for the most part a reference to price-setting markets.
13. In Niklas Luhmann's (1995: 462) words, "whereas prices are expectational programs, the value of money regulates the system's autopoetic reproduction."
14. With respect to the problem of determining prices, John Kenneth Galbraith (1958: 144) in his influential monograph *The Affluent Society* notes "nothing [in the history of economics] originally proved more troublesome in the explanation of prices, i.e., exchange values, than the indigestible fact that some of the most useful things [such as water] had the least value in exchange and some of the least useful had the most."
15. This is a controversial statement, since economists have argued that all one needs to "know" as an economic actor in order to make decisions are the prices of goods and services. Prices coordinate all economic activities. Prices insure efficient allocation of resources; central planning is not required. All the information that is required is communicated by prices. But this model, as Stiglitz (2017: 5) points out "made extraordinarily string assumptions" about market actors, for example, the absence of asymmetric information "where a well-informed individual could take advantage of a less informed one."
16. We are aware of the lack of value the issue of value has in modern economics. But the lack of esteem of the matter of value in economics will deter us from treating it as a researchable issue. Our theory of value is a theory of prices and vice versa. Robert Heilbroner (1983: 254; also Mirowski, 1990: 691) stresses, the "general problematic of value [refers to] the effort to tie the surface phenomena of economic life to some inner structure or order . . . an inquiry directed not at the 'facts' of economic life but at some structure or principle 'behind' the facts."
17. John Dewey's theory of valuation is formulated in protest against an authoritative and absolute standard of value or against the idea of a fixed and eternal notion of value. It follows, as David Hall (2011) formulates it that *value* is always linked to *values*.
18. Georg Simmel ([1907] 2005: 124) emphasizes in his *Philosophy of Money* that there can be no fair price beyond the exchange: "Medieval theory regarded value as something objective. It required the seller to ask the 'just price' for his commodity and occasionally attempted to fix this price by regulation. Value was considered to inhere in the object as a quality of its isolated existence, with which it entered the act of exchange, regardless of the relations between buyer and seller."
19. Compare the numerous recent empirical studies by economists published by the *National Bureau of Economic Research*—quite a few will be cited in this study.
20. Paul DiMaggio and Amir Goldberg (2018: 153), based on the 1996 General Social Survey, examine the diverse understanding of markets among the American public. Their findings suggest, not surprisingly, "that people who benefit most from markets are most likely to support them. But first, most adapt their understanding of the market to their religious and political convictions, in effect constructing versions of the market they find morally tolerable." The main finding, however, is that few Americans support an "extreme" (highly rational) neoclassical conception of the role of markets in economic life.
21. For an extensive and informative discussion of the social origins of value and the differences between value and prices see Birger Priddat (2015: 309–341).
22. The elimination of cash (hand-to-hand currency), of course, does not eliminate money from the economy (for a position advocating the elimination of cash see Rogoff, 2017).
23. Joseph Stieglitz (1987: 2–3) refers to the following example to describe the "relief function" of prices: "the price serves as a signal or as a screening device. The fact that an

employee is willing to work for $1 an hour suggests that she knows of no better offers; others who have looked at her have evidently decided that she is worth no more than $1 an hour."

24. As Vaclav Smil (2017: 344) points out, "every economic activity is fundamentally nothing but a conversion of one kind of energy to another." Money based on this hypothesis becomes a proxy for the valuation of energy flows.

25. John Maynard Keynes (1936: 269) summarizes the function of the clasp of present and future money represents as follows: "Money in its significant attributes is, above all, a subtle device for linking the present to the future; we cannot even begin to discuss the effect of vanishing expectations on current activities except in monetary terms. We cannot get rid of money by abolishing gold and silver and legal tender instruments. So long as there exists any durable asset, it is capable of possessing monetary attributes and, therefore, of giving rise the characteristic problems of a monetary economy."

26. In other words, in an affluent society, what counts are not always what can be counted but what is valued. Therefore, money as such is not the agent let alone the director of social change (Carruthers, 2005: 355), but the social appreciation of money is partly and indirectly contributing to social change.

27. Recently, social scientists are (re-)discovering the oeuvre of Marcel Mauss as germane to socio-economic discourse (cf. Graeber, 2014; Hart, 2014; McGoey, 2018).

28. As cited in Robert Skidelsky (2010: 139).

29. The focus of our analysis is clearly on *society's* economic life. For this reason, the beginning of modern society, in contrast to all past forms of society, can best be determined by means of a single economic indicator and the social significance assigned to that indicator: the modern epoch of mankind differs from all other periods of world history through constant economic growth (Lukas, 2017) and the privilege attributed to economic growth in politics in particular and society in general. Our mode of differentiation between modern and pre-modern is of course silent about the societal organization of economic growth (see North, 1991 or Perotti, 2014; these authors stress the role of legal, cultural and political institutions as the foundation for the emergence and development of the economy). The emergence of capitalism occurs under different institutional conditions therefore the distinction between pre-modern and modern based on sustained economic growth provides a clearer and "universal" indicator of the separation of modern from pre-modern societies.

30. William Goetzmann (2016) presents a contrarian thesis in his recent book *Money Changes Everything*. For Goetzmann as well as Niall Ferguson (2008: 342) the transformative power of money has to be located much earlier in human history. The observation about the importance of finance for transforming the world and the peculiar character of human civilization is not new, both note. For Goetzmann, it is not the development of the real economy that is responsible for the economic rise of humankind in the past centuries, but the responsibility rests with the financial economy. Without interest, without debts and without money our civilization would not have been possible. In elevating the historical role of finance in the emergence of civilizations, Goetzmann is not silent about the dark side of finance, for example slave trade, opium trades or various financial manias such as the Great Depression. In general, Goetzmann is however upbeat about the societal role of the world of finance.

31. As far as we can see, the metaphor was first introduced into sociology by Karl Mannheim ([1928] 1993). He used the concept to describe existing social phenomena, particularly in the context of his by now classical essay on the social phenomenon of generations. In his analysis of the simultaneity of the non-simultaneous, Mannheim drew on an idea that was first developed by art historian Wilhelm Pinder (1926). Another relevant example is Ernst Bloch's ([1918] 2000) theory of the simultaneity of the non-simultaneous art forms as elaborated in his work *Geist der Utopie*; as well as William F. Ogburns' ([1922] 1950) thesis of the cultural retardation of social

phenomena, and Arnold Gehlen's ([1957] 2004: 35) "law of differential development." The observation of the simultaneity of distinct social processes—for instance, within the global society—shows that the simultaneous presence of global interdependencies and discrepancies is not necessarily contradictory; on the contrary, divergent processes like these are mutually interdependent (cf. Luhmann, 1988: 170).

32. Cf. Zingales (2015); Buttonwood (2015). Cecchetti and Kharrouibi (2012, 2015) investigated the impact of a growing financial sector on economic growth for a sample of developed and emerging economies; they conclude that "the level of financial development is good only up to a point, after which it becomes a drag on growth. Second, focusing on advanced economies, we show that a fast-growing financial sector can be detrimental to aggregate productivity growth. Finally, looking at industry-level data, we show that financial sector growth disproportionately harms industries that are either financially dependent or R&D-intensive."

33. The number and range of normative assessments of the rapid expansion of the financial markets and its speculative nature is far too long to even list its major contributors. But here are references of recent evaluations of the societal role of the expanding work of finance: Streeck (2014), Keen (2017), Konings (2018).

34. A linguistic study of the contents of World Bank Annual Reports (Moretti and Pestre, 2015: 76) also finds evidence for the shift underway; the "key discontinuity, as we shall see, falls mostly between the first three decades and the last two, the turn of the 1990s, when the style of the Reports becomes much more codified, self-referential and detached from everyday language. From the early 1990s on, the change in the dominant language of the Annual Reports of the World Bank occur in stride with the growing financialization of the global economy, the first—and most important [shift]—has to do with finance: here, alongside a few predictable adjectives (*financial, fiscal, economic*) and nouns (*loans, investment, growth, interest, lending, debt*), we find a landslide of *fair value, portfolio, derivative, accrual, guarantees, losses, accounting, assets*; a little further down the list, *equity, hedging, liquidity, liabilities, creditworthiness, default, swaps, clients, deficit, replenishment, repurchase, cash*" (Moretti and Pestre, 2015: 79).

35. Renate Mayntz (2010: 7–8) describes the changing role of banks in the world of financialization: "Banks do not orient their operations towards the world of finance. This is no longer primarily due to the fulfillment of their traditional functions, such as the safekeeping of money, lending and the organization of payment transactions, but also because they themselves trade profit-oriented and can be measured against indicators such as the return on equity. As a result, transactions between financial institutions increase in proportion to their transactions with investors and borrowers outside the financial system" (our translation). In other words, the traditional banking business is "boring" and not particularly profitable.

36. See also the study by Jesse Eisinger (2017) of what accounts within the legal system for the limited legal pursuit of US managers.

37. For an examination of various indicators of financial fragility, the nature of financial crises and shocks, see Pryor, 2002: 54–81; Reinhart and Rogoff, 2009; Bougrine and Rochon, 2016. Babecký et al. (2012) examine multiple financial crises between 1970–2010.

38. The idea of "digital capitalism" is based, quite similar to Castell's theory of the network society, on the emphasis on a "*technological push*" (Nachtwey and Staab, 2015: 1; our emphasis), that is, investments in digital technologies as the specificity of modern economics and society. Indications mount, as Nachtwey and Staab (2015: 1) concretize their thesis of the emergence of a digital capitalism, that "we are in the middle of a technological advance of new quality. Revolutions in data storage, processing and availability (big data), the increasing proliferation and networking of digital devices among producers and consumers, as well as intelligent algorithms enable the transformation of work organizations, labor supply and demand on digital marketplaces,

inexpensive, flexible and quickly programmable service and industrial robots, as well as new production processes and a reorganization of supply and service chains between customers, producers and suppliers (our translation)."

39. We concur with Emile Durkheim's ([1908] 1982: 230–231) rejection of the idea that economics deals with a unique set of phenomena and occupies a special place within the social sciences, for example, the notion it dealt with objective constraints and values faced by and imposed on all agents while sociology or history study highly flexible and variable socially constructed opinions. As Durkheim stresses, "wealth, which is the object of political economy, consists of things which are apparently essentially objective and seemingly independent of opinion [however], the relationship between the sciences of economics and the other social sciences presents themselves to us in a different light. Both deal with phenomena which, at least, when considered under certain aspects, are homogeneous, because in some respects they are all matters of opinion." Durkheim's views cited here are a summary of his intervention in a debate on political economy and sociology written by an observer of the discussion.

40. We are deliberately abstaining from calling the phenomena we are describing in our analysis of the modern economy and society as some might expect as a manifestation of "late capitalism." Late capitalism in its current usage is a "catchall phrase for the indignities and absurdities of our contemporary, with its yawning inequality and superpowered corporations and shrinking middle class" (Lowrey, 2017: 1). The analytical benefit of the inflated term has shrunk immeasurably, as a result.

41. In an editorial, the staff of *Nature* offers the bold assertion "one of the many innovations that enabled humanity's rise to global dominance is the development of money, which is a measure of relative value" ("Pricing the planet," Volume 541, January 119, 2017, p. 260).

42. Economic phenomena are never *merely economic* phenomena although frequently economists, politician or managers treat them as a plain economic data. Employment or unemployment to mention but one obvious example is such a total societal phenomenon. Declining employment tends to affect particular categories of individuals and their social environment, for example those with lower levels of accumulated schooling which in turn impacts the local wellbeing. As Charles, Hurst and Schwartz (2018: 62) document "declining manufacturing employment is associated with increased prescription opioid use and increased death rates from drug overdoses."

43. The history of the sociology of money proper begins in Europe and is associated with the names of the sociologists Georg Simmel and Max Weber and the theorists of classical economics. The history of a sociology of the financial world, which is often overlooked in the Anglo-Saxon world (see Keister, 2002), also began in Europe, and is linked to names like Rudolf Hilferding ([1910] 2006), Ludwig Goldscheid (1917), Joseph Schumpeter (1918) and Fritz Karl Mann (1937). Early financial sociology focused far and foremost on the financial economy and fiscal policy of the state. Joseph Schumpeter (1918: 7) emphasizes the generally prominent role of the "financial regulations of states, even where not actively intended, that created and destroyed industrial branches, forms, and districts and thus directly contributed to the construction of modern economy and, by extension, of the modern spirit." For a correction of the amnesia of the discipline see Reinhard Blomert (2001).

44. We agree with the instructive cautionary note issued by Daron Acemoglu and James Robinson (2015: 3): "The quest for general laws of capitalism is misguided because it ignores the key forces shaping how an economy functions: the endogenous evolution of technology and of the institutions and the political equilibrium that influence not only technology but also how markets function and how the gains from various different economic arrangements are distributed."

45. We are grateful to B. Guy Peters for the reference to C. West Churchman's initially published discussion of the issue of "wicked problems." Churchman (1967: B141) draws attention in his contribution to the fact that the first reference to "wicked

problems" goes back to an oral publication by Horst Rittel in an architecture seminar at the University of California, Berkeley.

## References

Acemoglu, Daron and James A. Robinson (2015), "The rise and decline of general laws of capitalism," *Journal of Economic Perspectives* 29: 3–28.
Adamson, Morgan (2009), "The human capital theory," *Ephemera* 9: 271–284.
Alvaredo, Facundo, Lucas Chancel, Thomas Piketty, Emmanuel Saez and Gabriel Zucman (2017), "Global inequality dynamics: New findings from WID.world," *NEWR Working Paper* No. 23119.
Appadurai, Arjun (2011), "The ghost in the financial machine," *Public Culture* 23: 517–539.
Aspers, Patrick (2009), "Knowledge and valuation in markets," *Theory and Society* 38: 111–131.
Babecký, Jan, Tomáš Havránek, Jakub Matějů, Marek Rusnák, Kateřina Šmídková and Bořek Vašíček (2012), "Banking, debt, and currency crises: Early warning indicators for developed countries," *IES Working Paper* No. 20/2012.
Bell, Daniel ([1973] 1975), *Die nachindustrielle Gesellschaft*. Frankfurt am Main: Campus.
Bell, Daniel (1973), *The Coming of Post-Industrial Society. A Venture in Social Forecasting*. New York: Basis Books.
Benhabib, Jess, Xuewen Liu and Pengfei Wang (2018), "Financial markets, the real; economy, and self-fulfilling uncertainties," *NBER Working Paper* No. 24984.
Best, Jacqueline (2018), "Technocratic exceptionalism: Monetary policy and the fear of democracy," *International Political Sociology*, DOI:10.1093/ips/oly017
Bisin, Alberto and Thierry Verdier (2017), "On the joint evolution of culture and institutions," *NBER Working Paper* No. 23375.
Bloch, Ernst ([1918] 2000), *The Spirit of Utopia*. Stanford, CA: Stanford University Press.
Blomert, Reinhard (2001), "Sociology of finance—Old and new perspectives," *Economic Sociology: European Electronic Newsletter* 2: 9–14.
Blumenberg, Hans (2006), *Beschreibung des Menschen*. Frankfurt am Main: Suhrkamp.
Böhme, Gernot ([2001] 2016), "Zur Kritik der ästhetischen Ökonomie," pp. 25–46 in Gernot Böhme (ed.), *Ästhetischer Kapitalismus*. Berlin: Suhrkamp.
Boltanski, Luc and Arnaud Esquerre (2016), "The economic life of things," *New Left Review* 98: 31–54.
Bougrine, Hassan and Louis-Phillippe Rochon (2016), "Financialization, crisis and economic policy," pp. 143–158 in Naomi Levy and Etelberto Ortiz (eds.), *The Financialization Response to Economic Disequilibria. European and Latin American Experiences*. Cheltenham: E. Elgar.
Brighenti, Andrea Mubi (2018), "The social life of measures: Conceptualizing measure-value environments," *Theory Culture & Society* 35: 23–44.
Burrell, Jenna and Elisa Oreglia (2015), "The myth of market price information: Mobile phones and the application of economic knowledge in ICTD," *Economy and Society* 44: 271–292.
Buttonwood (2015), "What's wrong with finance," *Economist*, 1 May. URL: www.economist.com/blogs/buttonwood/2015/05/finance-and-economic (accessed 14 March 2019).
Carlos, Ann M. and Frank D. Lewis (1995), "Foreign financing of Canadian railroads. The role information," pp. 383–423 in Michael D. Bordo and Richard Sylla (eds.), *Anglo-American Financial Systems: Institutions and Markets in the Twentieth Century*. New York: Irwin.

Carruthers, Bruce G. (2005), "The sociology of money and credit," pp. 355–378 in Neil J. Smelser and Richard Swedberg (eds.), *The Handbook of Economic Sociology*. Princeton, NJ: Princeton University Press.

Cecchetti, Stephen G. and Enisse Kharroubi (2015), "Why does financial sector growth crowd out real economic growth?" *CEPR Discussion Paper* No. DP10642.

Cecchetti, Stephen G. and Enisse Kharroubi (2012), "Reassessing the impact of finance on growth," *Conference draft*.

Charles, Kerwin Kofi, Erik Hurst and Mariel Schwartz (2018), "The transformation of manufacturing and the decline in U.S. employment," *BFI Working Paper 2018–20*. Becker Friedman Institute for Research in Economics.

Churchman, C. West (1967), "Wicked problems," *Management Science* 14: B141–B142.

Clark, Colin (1940), *The Conditions of Economic Progress*. London: Macmillan.

Cory Cutsail, Cory and Farley Grubb (2018), "The paper money of colonial North Carolina, 1712–74 – Reconstructing the evidence," *NBER Working Paper* No. w25260.

Darcillon, Thibault (2015), "The political economy of financialisation in an age of growing inequality," *SSFA*, Papier de recherche.

Davis, Leila E. (2017), "Financialization and investment: A survey of the empirical literature," *The Journal of Economic Surveys* 31: 1332–1358.

Dewey, John (1939), *Theory of Valuation*. Chicago, IL: University of Chicago Press.

DiMaggio, Paul and Amir Goldberg (2018), "Searching for *homo economicus*: Variation in Americans' construals of and attitudes toward markets," *European Journal of Sociology* 59: 151–189.

Durkheim, Emile ([1908] 1982), "Debate on political economy and sociology," pp. 229–235 in Emile Durkheim, *The Rules of Sociological Method*, edited by Steven Lukes. New York: Free Press.

Eisinger, Jesse (2017), *The Chickenshit Club: Why the Justice Department Fails to Prosecute Executives*. New York: Simon & Schuster.

Ferguson, Niall (2008), *The Ascent of Money. A Financial History of the World*. New York: Allen Lane.

Frey, Bruno and Werner W. Pommerehne (1993), "On the fairness of pricing—An empirical survey among the general population," *Journal of Economic Behavior and Organization* 20: 295–307.

Galbraith, John Kenneth (1958), *The Affluent Society*. Boston, MA: Houghton Mifflin.

Gehlen, Arnold ([1957] 2004), "Die Seele im technischen Zeitalter," pp. 1–137 in Arnold Gehlen (ed.), *Die Seele im technischen Zeitalter und andere soziologische Schriften und Kulturanalysen. Gesamtausgabe Band 6*. Frankfurt am Main: Vittorio Klostermann.

Goetzmann, William N. (2016), *Money Changes Everything. How Finance Made Civilization Possible*. Princeton, NJ: Princeton University Press.

Goldscheid, Rudolf (1917), *Staatssozialismus oder Staatskapitalismus? Ein finanzsoziologischer Beitrag zur Lösung der Staatsschulden*. Wien: Anzengruber.

Graeber, David (2014), "On the moral grounds of economic relations: A Maussian approach," *Journal of Classical Sociology* 14: 65–77.

Hall, David (2011), "What's valuable?" in Patrick Aspers and Jens Beckert (eds.), *The Worth of Goods: Valuation and Pricing in the Economy*. Oxford: Oxford University Press.

Harari, Yuval Noah ([2011] 2014), *Sapiens. A Brief History of Humankind*. Toronto, ON: McClelland & Stewart.

Hart, Keith (2014), "Marcel Mauss' economic vision, 1920–1925: Anthropology, politics, journalism," *Journal of Classical Sociology* 14: 34–44.

Hayek, Fredrich (1990), *The Denationalisation of Money*. London: Institute of Economic Affairs.

Heilbroner, Robert L. (1983), "The problem of value in the constitution of economic thought," *Social Research* 50: 253–277.

Hilferding, Rudolf ([1910] 2006), *Finance Capital: A Study in the Latest Phase of Capitalist Development*. London: Routledge.

Hollingsworth, J. Rogers and Robert Boyer (1997), *Contemporary Capitalism: The Embeddedness of Institutions*. Cambridge: Cambridge University Press.

Ingham, Geffrey (1996), "Money is a social relation," *Review of Social Economy* 54: 507–529.

Kaldor, Yair (2018), "The cultural foundation of economic categories: Finance and class in the marginalist revolution," *Socio-Economic Review*. DOI:10.1093/soceco/mwy043.

Keen, Steve (2017), *Can We Avoid Another Financial Crisis?* Cambridge: Polity.

Keister, Lisa A. (2002), "Financial markets, money, and banking," *Annual Review of Sociology* 28: 39–61.

Keynes, John M. (1936), *The General Theory of Employment, Interest and Money*. London: MacMillan.

Kirshner, Jonathan (2003), "Money is politics," *Review of International Political Economy* 10: 645–660.

Knight, F.H. (1950), "The determination of just wages," pp. 467–511 in G. Hoover (ed.), *Twentieth Century Economic Thought*. New York: Philosophical Library.

Konings, Martijn (2018), "How finance is governed: Reconnecting cultural and political economy," *Distinktion: Journal of Social Theory*, DOI:10.1080/1600910X.2018.1430045

Kraemer, Klaus (2010), "Propheten der Finanzmärkte. Zur Rolle charismatischer Ideen im Börsengeschehen," *Berliner Journal für Soziologie* 20: 179–201.

Krippner, Greta R. (2005), "The financialization of the American economy," *Socio-Economic Review* 3: 173–208.

Lapavitsas, Costas and Jeff Powell (2013), "Financialization varied: A comparative analysis of advanced economies," *Cambridge Journal of Regions, Economy and Society* 6: 359–379.

Lewis, Mervyn K. (2015), *Understanding Ponzi Schemes. Can Better Financial Regulation Prevent Investors from Being Defrauded?* Cheltenham: Edward Elgar.

Lowrey, Annie (2017), "Why the phrase 'late capitalims' is suddenly everywhere," *The Atlantic*. URL: www.theatlantic.com/business/archive/2017/05/late-capitalism/524943/ (accessed 10 June 2019).

Lübbe, Hermann (2014), *Zivilisationsdynamik. Ernüchterter Fortschritt politisch und kulturell*. Basel: Schwabe Verlag.

Luhmann, Niklas (1997), *Die Gesellschaft der Gesellschaft. Erster Teilband*. Frankfurt am Main: Suhrkamp.

Luhmann, Niklas (1995), "Self-reference and rationality," pp. 437–477 in Niklas Luhman (ed.), *Social Systems*. Stanford, CA: Stanford University Press.

Luhmann, Niklas (1988), *Die Wirtschaft der Gesellschaft*. Frankfurt am Main: Suhrkamp.

Luhmann, Niklas (1983), "Das sind Preise: Ein soziologisch-systemtheoretischer Klärungsversuch," *Soziale Welt* 34: 153–170.

Luhmann, Niklas (1970), "Wirtschaft als soziales System," pp. 204–231 in Niklas Luhmann, *Soziologische Aufklärung. Aufsätze zur Theorie sozialer Systeme*. Wiesbaden: Westdeutscher Verlag.

Lukas Jr., Robert E. (2017), "What was the industrial revolution?" *NBER Working Paper* No. 23547.

Mann, Fritz K. (1937), *Steuerpolitische Ideale. Vergleichende Studien zur Geschichte der ökonomischen und politischen Ideen und ihres Wirkens in der öffentlichen Meinung 1600–1935*. Jena: Gustav Fischer.

Mannheim. Karl ([1928] 1993), "The problem of generations," pp. 351–395 in Kurt H. Wolff (ed.), *From Karl Mannheim*. New Brunswick, NJ: Transaction Books.

Mauss, Marcel ([1925] 2013), *Die Gabe. Form und Funktion des Austauschs in archaischen Gesellschaften*. 10. Auflage. Frankfurt am Main: Suhrkamp.

Mayntz, Renate (2010), "Die transnationale Ordnung globalisierter Finanzmärkte. Was lehrt uns die Krise?" *MPIfG Working Paper* No. 10/8. Köln: Max-Planck-Institut für Gesellschaftsforschung.

McGoey, Linsey (2018), "Bataille and the sociology of abundance: Reassessing gifts, debt and economic excess," *Theory, Culture & Society* 35: 69–91.

Mehrling, Perry (2017), "Financialization and its discontents," *Finance and Society* 3: 1–10.

Mirowski, Philip (2009), "Why there is (as yet) no such thing as an economics of knowledge," pp. 99–156 in Don Ross and Harold Kincaid (eds.), *The Oxford Handbook of Philosophy of Economics*. Oxford: Oxford University Press.

Mirowski, Philip (1990), "Learning the meaning of a dollar: Conservation principle and the social theory of value in economic theory," *Social Research* 57: 689–717.

Mitchell, Timothy (1998), "Fixing the economy," *Cultural Studies* 12: 82–101.

Moretti, Franco and Dominique Pestre (2015), "Bankspeak. The language of World Bank reports," *New Left Review* 92: 75–99.

Morris, Ian (2015), *Foragers, Farmers, and Fossil Fuels: How Human Values Evolve*. Edited and with an introduction by Stephen Macedo. Princeton, NJ: Princeton University Press.

Nachtwey, Oliver and Philipp Staab (2015), "Die Avantgarde des digitalen Kapitalismus," *Mittelweg* 36.

Nelson, Richard R. (2011), "The complex economic organization of capitalist economies," *Capitalism and Society* 6.

North, Douglas C. (1991), "Institutions," *Journal of Economic Perspectives* 5: 97–112.

Ogburn, William F. ([1922] 1950), *Social Change. With Respect to Culture and Original Nature*. New 1950 Edition with Supplementary Chapter. New York: Viking Press.

Orléan, André ([2011] 2014), *The Empire of Value. A New Foundation for Economics*. Cambridge, MA: MIT Press.

Paniagua, Pablo (2018), "Money and the emergence of knowledge in society," *Review of Social Economy* 76: 95–118.

Paul, Axel T. (2002), "Money makes the world go around. Über die Dynamik des Geldes und die Grenzen der Systemtheorie," *Berliner Journal für Soziologie* 12: 243–262.

Perotti, Enrico (2014), "The political economy of finance," *Capitalism and Society* 9: 1–44.

Pignol, Claire (2010), "Money, exchange and division of labour in Rousseau's economic philosophy," *The European Journal of the History of Economic Thought* 7: 199–228.

Piketty, Thomas ([2013] 2014), *Das Kapital im 21. Jahrhundert*. München: Verlag C.H. Beck.

Piketty, Thomas, Emmanuel Saez and Gabriel Zucman (2018), "Distributional national accounts: Methods and estimates for the United States," *Quarterly Journal of Economics* 133: 553–609.

Pinder, Wilhelm (1926), *Das Problem der Generationen in der Kunstgeschichte Europas*. Berlin: Frankfurter Verlagsanstalt.

Pingle, Mark and Sankar Mukhopadhyay (2010), "Private money as a competing medium of exchange," *Journal of Macroeconomics* 32: 541–554.

Polanyi, Karl ([1944] 2001), *The Great Transformation. The Political and Economic Origins of Our Time*. Boston, MA: Beacon Press.

Preda, A. (2009), *Framing Finance. The Boundaries of Markets and Modern Capitalism*. Chicago, IL: University of Chicago Press.

Priddat, Birger (2015), *Economics of Persuasion. Ökonomie zwischen Markt, Kommunikation und Überredung.* Marburg: Metropolis-Verlag.

Prins, Gwythian, Isabel Galiana, Christopher Green, Reiner Grundmann, Mike Hulme, Atte Korhola, Frank Laird, Ted Nordhaus, Roger Pielke Jr., Steve Rayner, Daniel Sarewitz, Michael Shellenberger, Nico Stehr and Hiroyuki Tezuka (2010), *The Hartwell-Paper. A New Direction for Climate Policy after the Crash of 2009.* URL: https://eprints.lse.ac.uk/27939/1/HartwellPaper_English_version.pdf (accessed 2 January 2019).

Pryor, Frederic L. (2002), *The Future of U.S. Capitalism.* Cambridge: Cambridge University Press.

Rayner, Steve (2006), "Wicked problems: Clumsy solutions—Diagnoses and prescriptions for environmental ills," Jack Beale Memorial Lecture, UNSW. URL: http://eureka.sbs.ox.ac.uk/93/1/Steve%20Rayner%2C%20Jack%20Beale%20Lecture%20Wicked%20Problems.pdf (accessed 29 February 2019).

Reinhart, Carmen M. and Kenneth S. Rogoff (2009), *This Time Is Different. Eight Centuries of Financial Folly.* Princeton, NJ: Princeton University Press.

Reurink, Arjan (2016), "From elite lawbreaking to financial crime: The evolution of the concept of white-collar crime," *MPIfG Discussion Paper* No. 16/10. Köln: Max-Planck-Institut für Gesellschaftsforschung.

Richta, Radovan (1971), *Richta-Report, Politische Ökonomie des 20. Jahrhunderts: die Auswirkungen der technisch-wissenschaftlichen Revolution auf die Produktionsverhältnisse.* Frankfurt am Main: Makol Verlag.

Rittel, Horst and Melvin M. Webber (1973), "Dilemmas in the general theory of planning," *Policy Sciences* 4: 154–59.

Rogoff, Kenneth (2017), "Dealing with monetary paralysis at the zero bound," *Journal of Economic Perspectives* 31: 47–66.

Schumpeter, Joseph A. (1954), *History of Economic Analysis.* New York: Oxford University Press.

Schumpeter, Joseph A. (1918), *Die Krise des Steuerstaates. Zeitfragen aus dem Gebiete der Soziologie.* Graz, Leipzig: Leuschner & Lubensky.

Simmel, Georg ([1915] 2000), "Geld und Nahrung," pp. 117–122 in Georg Simmel, *Aufsätze und Abhandlungen 1909–1918. Georg Simmel Gesamtausgabe Band 11.* Frankfurt am Main: Suhrkamp.

Simmel, Georg ([1907] 2005), *The Philosophy of Money,* 3rd enlarged ed. Edited by David Frisby. London: Routledge.

Skidelsky, Robert and Edward Skidelsky (2012), *How Much Is Enough? Money and the Good Life.* New York: Other Press.

Skidelsky, Robert (2010), *Keynes. The Return of the Master.* Philadelphia, PA: Perseus Books Group.

Smil, Vaclav (2017), *Energy and Civilization. A History.* Cambridge, MA: MIT Press.

Stehr, Nico (2008), *Moral Markets.* New York: Routledge.

Stiglitz, Joseph E. (2017), "The revolution of information economics—The past and the future," *NBER Working Paper* No. 23780.

Stiglitz, Joseph E. (1987), "The causes and consequences of the dependence of quality on price," *Journal of Economic Literature* 25: 1–48.

Streeck, Wolfgang (2014), *Buying Time: The Delayed Crisis of Democratic Capitalism.* London: Verso.

Touraine, Alain (1998), "Culture without society," *Cultural Values* 2: 140–157.

Tricarico, Antonio and Heike Löschmann (2012), "Finanzialisierung—ein Hebel zur Einengung der Commos," pp. 184–195 in Silke Helfrich and Heinrich-Böll-Stiftung (eds.), *Commons. Für eine neue Politik jenseits von Markt und Staat.* Bielefeld: Transcript.

Twenge, Jean M. (2017), *iGen: Why Today's Super-Connected Kids Are Growing Up Less Rebellious, More Tolerant, Less Happy—and Completely Unprepared for Adulthood—and What That Means for the Rest of Us*. New York: Atria Books.

Veblen, Thorstein ([1899] 1992), *The Theory of the Leisure Class*. With an Introduction by C. Wright Mills. New Brunswick, NJ: Transaction Books.

Weber, Max ([1921] 1972), *Wirtschaft und Gesellschaft: Grundriss der Verstehenden Soziologie*, 5th ed. Tübingen: J.C.B. Mohr

Weber, Max ([1956] 1978), *Economy and Society*. Edited by Guenther Roth and Claus Wittich. Berkeley: University of California Press.

Weber, Max (1923), *Wirtschaftsgeschichte*. München and Leipzig: Duncker & Humblot.

Welch, Jack (1981), "Growing fast in a slow-growth economy," Lecture in the Hotel Pierre, 8 December. New York.

Willke, Helmut (2006), "The autonomy of the financial system: Symbolic coupling and the language of capital," pp. 46–53 in Thorsten Strulik and Helmut Willke (eds.), *Toward a Cognitive Mode in Global Financing. The Governance of a Knowledge-Based Financial System*. Frankfurt am Main: Campus.

Wittgenstein, Ludwig (1945), *Philosophische Untersuchungen*. Frankfurt am Main: Suhrkamp.

Zelizer, Viviana A. (1997), *The Social Meaning of Money: Pin Money, Paychecks, Poor Relief, and Other Currencies*. Princeton, NJ: Princeton University Press.

Zingales, Luigi (2015), "Presidential address: Does finance benefit society?" *The Journal of Finance* 70: 1327–1363.

# 1

# THE IMMATERIAL ECONOMY

Semantic changes follow the structural changes at a considerable distance.
—*Niklas Luhmann (1997: 1142)*[1]

At the heart of our inquiry is a systemic transformation of economic conduct and the conditions of economic relations that comes with the emergence of an internationalized and interdependent[2] economic structure[3] increasingly devoted to the exchange of monetary and non-monetary *symbolic* "commodities" and services.[4] Money and finance are now at the heart of capitalism and economic policies. The transformation of the industrial into an immaterial economy also implies a significant *acceleration* of economic activities.[5]

Following Niklas Luhmann's observation about the time elapse between structural changes in society and their theoretical uptake, we agree that the socioeconomic developments we are trying to capture under the heading of a social theory of modernity reflect social, political and cultural changes in modern societies that have been underway for some time and not necessarily only since the financial crisis during the early 21st century.

The observation that economic exchanges do not revolve around material products and their substantive value alone is not a historical novelty. It is no longer sufficient to convert a material resource into a material substance or product. It is crucial for the success of products and services to endow them with meaning (cf. Bourdieu, [1979] 1984), for example, aesthetic, moral, altruistic or sustainable attributes that make products desirable and valuable. Books, CDs, cars, furniture and so forth all aspire by their producers to have immaterial qualities that are not merely directly related to any functional improvement of the service or product. Material products can become hybrid commodities, for instance, cars, jet engines or ovens can generate and return data that in turn become the foundation for a business in the immaterial economy and that can be utilized and exploited independent of the location of their material substance.

It follows that businesses will attempt to differentiate themselves from their competitors based on the values of the company and their services and commodities, instead of just their products. Socially constructed immaterial/symbolic qualities, for example because other individuals value them, are not fixed desires or preferences (cf. Keynes, 1936: 156).[6] And what may be of worth in one social context may be valueless or of small value in another age or society.

Our focus is the transformation of the economy into an primarily immaterial/symbolic/digital economy,[7] an economy that is not linked to a specific location and has impacts reaching far beyond the boundaries of the economy and economics (that is, knowledge about the knowledge economy),[8] that also affects for example policy prescriptions, changes in the nature of educational perspectives or the biography of individuals and families;[9] in short, the immaterial economy is multifunctional.[10] The impact of the financial crash of 2008 in North America and Europe may have been more political than economic although the monetary impact has enormous leading and amplifying to a persistent wave of cultural and political nationalism, protectionism and populism throughout most of the West (cf. Goodhart, 2017; Tooze, 2018: 20). In many countries a growing backlash against the political *status quo* is in evidence and perhaps only beginning. The backlash, in our view, represents a response to the broad sentiment of losing out in a giant zero-sum game. More than ever, the conviction that the winners appear to take it all is growing and supported by naked economic data about robust forms of social inequality in many societies.

The influence of the immaterial economy on the world of production and work is significant. Industrial production linked to a specific location does not cease but retains much of its economic importance. The socially necessary labor to produce things continues to decline. Instead of making new things, the working population much more often incrementally enhances the value of material and immaterial products and frequently is paid to serve others.

A concomitant manifestation of the immaterial economy is a shift in the rate of investment toward intangible assets or the digital infrastructure/platforms of the immaterial economy (R&D, information and knowledge, software, brands, and other resources) compared to investments in tangible assets. Inventions and innovations in firms are to a large extent fueled by investments in intangible capital in order to generate additional intangible assets (for example, computer designed services, management consulting services, marketing campaigns, online platforms, apps, advertising campaigns) and novel tangible commodities.[11] The trend toward investments in intangible assets is supported by the trends in financialization such as the emphasis on shareholder value that depress physical investment (cf. Davis, 2017: 1352).

A further significant development of the immaterial economy that can at least be observed until this day is the rapid and extensive *concentration* of intangible business activities in the hands of but a few corporations or even super-corporations, including software companies, airlines, banks, pharmaceuticals, car rental, credit rating, and many more economic activities, in fact, in some instances amounting to the global control of activities by just one or two corporations.[12] The winner-takes-all future scenarios are not scarce (Haskel and Westlake, 2017: 68). Apple and Google now control and provide a combined 99% of the software on which smartphones are run.

A representative example of applicable corporations would include U.S. companies such Starbucks, Google, Amazon, Facebook, Microsoft, and Apple. We emphasize the possibly temporary market dominance of corporations even though they are not very old—Apple was founded 21 years ago—but have ascended to dominance quickly because there is, of course, the distinct possibility that countries and multinational bodies rein into the degree to which they are able to operate without subject to severe state regulations.[13] For the time being, a profound shift toward a concentration of now massive corporate profits among the super-companies can be observed. In the United States, in 1975, "109 companies collected half of the profits produced by all publicly traded companies. Today, those winnings are captured by just 30 companies" (Phillips, 2018).

Given the rapid growth of corporations that depend on few tangible investments, there is no need for sophisticated laboratories or experimental settings. It is reasonable to assume that their success rests on their ability to develop and control intangible assets. Given the lack of tangible investment for the creation of innovative services, the tendency toward monopolization and winner-take-it-all dynamics finds its counterpart in easy access to markets. This process is exemplified by the "app economy" (cf. Guellec and Paunov, 2017).

As is well known, an important aspect of this developmental pattern of the modern economy is the almost revolutionary expansion in the scale and rate of the growth of international financial transactions. At the same time, with the rise of the intangible economy, there is a need to rethink the limits of growth as well as the relation between nature (the environment) and the economy.

The boundaries between the social system of the economy and other social systems in modern society have become increasingly porous, if not eroded, and easier to cross, and so have the cognitive boundaries between economics and the other social sciences. Real changes and cognitive changes act on society as a whole. These changes will not be neglected in our analysis.

The transformation we investigate represents a significant change of the economic structure of both, industrial economies and modern societies that are assumed to have a knowledge-based economy.[14] A knowledge-based economy is, of course, an economy characterized by the fact that knowledge (and information)[15]

> has become the main productive force; that as a consequence, the products of social activity are no longer chiefly crystallized labour but crystallized

knowledge; and that the exchange value of commodities, material or otherwise, is no longer determined in the last instance by the quantity of general social labour they contain but mainly by their content in terms of general information, knowledge and intelligence.

*(Gorz, [2003] 2010: 34–35)*[16]

From our more skeptical as well as more realistic point of view, we deem that André Gorz's definition[17] of the foundation of a modern knowledge economy, shared by many other observers, is far too knowledge-centered.[18]

Knowledge-centeredness means that knowledge *as such* and its core components, for example, its methodological (knowledge) apparatus is assigned a much too powerful direct and immediately productive and efficient role.[19] Knowledge alone does not generate a profit or score goals. Knowledge is all too often portrayed as a set of ideas, coded instructions and/or methods that will somehow, for example, allow for the immediate exploitation of a given technology; or, as another erroneous implicit assertion has it, knowledge will diffuse almost on its own. Knowledge obviously "has to be transmitted and received, and there are barriers at both ends" (Stiglitz and Greenwald, 2014: 74).[20]

Our cautious reaction is also seen in response to the emphasis on information or information technology as the defining factor of the modern economy. Although this is a rather common assertion, more information is not more knowledge.[21] The theorist of the network society,[22] Manuel Castells ([1996] 2000: 219), emphasizes for example that the decisive difference "between the economic structures of the first half and of the second half of the twentieth century [industrial and post-industrial economy] is the revolution in information technology, and its diffusion in all spheres of social and economic activity." Manuel Castells' (2000: 10) theoretical perspective, its singular focus on "what is new in our age is a new set of information technologies," can be properly criticized as an idea based to the history of technocratic ideas (cf. Stehr, 2000). The conception of information or knowledge in such an abbreviated manner easily results in a triumph of instrumental reason.

Knowledge is not a production factor that can simply be assimilated into a chain with the traditional production factors land, labor and capital. This also applies to information. Knowledge lacks a number of the characteristics of traditional production factors: for example, it is not necessarily scarce; it does not disappear or is destroyed as one „consumes" it;[23] the use of knowledge does not exclude its use by other actors; it is difficult, as we shall show in detail, to attribute the costs and returns of knowledge to individual producers of knowledge; the expansion of our knowledge is often linked to non-economic motives and, as we have indicated, knowledge has no direct instrumental qualities (see also Vazquez and Gonzalez, 2016: 147–148).[24]

Our knowledge about the knowledge-based economy is precarious and limited. The same deficit applies to ways of quantifying the outstanding characteristics of the knowledge-based economy on the level of both national economies and individual corporations (cf. van Eekelen, 2015), for example knowledge-adjusted GDP (see McCulla, Holden and Smith, 2013) or new corporate accounting standards that would be needed for a knowledge-based economy.[25] There is no economic theory that accounts for exactly what benefits accrue from the investment in and utilization of knowledge in the corporate world (cf. Forey, 2004). Moreover, Gorz and other observers of the knowledge-based economy fail to critically raise, let alone arrive at robust results on, the issue of how such knowledge-based commodities and services come to be priced/valued in market transactions. We will appraise the economic value of knowledge in a separate chapter.

It would appear that at least on the surface, the concept of immaterial economy, as it will be explicated here, competes with terms and perspectives of the modern economy (and democracy) such as *Supercapitalism* (Reich, 2007) connecting the triumph of capitalism with the decline of democracy (also Crouch, 2004), *Post-Capitalism* (e.g. Mason, 2016; Srnicek and Williams, 2016),[26] *third capitalism*, where accumulation is based on knowledge and creativity (Boutang, [2008] 2011),[27] or *post-industrial society* (e.g. Bell, 1973).[28]

The major drawback of the competing concepts, however, is that they fail to propose, from the very beginning, a theory of society and of the economy that would give an idea of what "post" constitutes. The terms "PostCapitalism" and "post-industrial" mainly signify an absence (cf. Hatherly, 2016),[29] for example the decline of the economic importance of material production or shifts in the importance of economic sectors.

The theory of post-industrial society as developed by Daniel Bell, and some of his successors, not only underestimates the persistent role of the industrial sector as a value-adding sector of the economy even in so-called de-industrializing societies (that is, of course, the simultaneity of the non-simultaneous) but also neglects the emerging shift of industrial type production into countries with a low wage regime (cf. Boltanski and Esquerre, 2016: 31).

In the late eighties of the last century, Peter Drucker (1989: 127) assumed that in the form of money flows, the symbolic economy already shapes and rivals the transnational material economy.[30] The dynamics of the global economy are no longer driven by trade in wheat, oil, cars and steel, but rather by traffic in currencies, stocks, bonds, and—increasingly—derivatives of the former. The trade in derived assets does not require one to actually own the underlying assets (or "underlyings"). The underlying assets are less important than is their measurement. The underlyings could be coffee, mortgages or oil. Derivatives now represent the lion-share of global financial transactions. Though derivatives were invented centuries ago, for example in agricultural markets in the 17th century, the dominance of present-day derivatives in financials dates back to the 1960s (cf. Wigan, 2009; Arvidsson, 2016).[31]

Similarly, the symbolic form of wealth is rapidly expanding with the result that, for example, during the financial crisis in the spring of 1999 a "15 percent drop in the market erases wealth equivalent to the entire annual output of all U.S. factories" (*New York Times*, February 15, 1999).[32] The decision of voters in the United Kingdom on June 23, 2016 to leave the European Union (*Brexit*) erased some three trillion dollars on worldwide stock markets on two consecutive work-days, June 25 and June 27, 2016.[33] The loss refers to what is commonly known as paper wealth. Paper wealth refers to what can only be characterized as a category of symbolic wealth. The paper wealth loss was in turn erased within the next few days on most of the stock markets around the world.

The available volume, patterns of creation, complexity, for example, in assessing the value of immaterial goods, the distribution of its returns, the societal influence and the speed at which paper wealth travels across national boundaries and time zones have given rise to many concerns. The combined effect of these attributes of monetary goods is to make economic conduct riskier, more precarious, une-qual and uncertain not only due to the strong influence of non-economic factors but also due to difficulties in the political control of the financial system. How-ever, this does not amount to a complete uncoupling of the immaterial economy from the flow of real economic relations and asset streams.

## Symbolic Products and Processes

For the time being, the term "symbolic commodities" should be put in quota-tion marks to preclude the simple assumption that the full range of symbolic commodities carries the *economic, legal, and practical* attributes of conventional commodities. Commodities such as, for example, durable manufactured goods that have a certain utility independent of the specific context in which they are produced, exchanged, or consumed, typically have a legal status, and especially property rights, attached to them.

None of these attributes apply, at least in the strict sense, to a number of sym-bolic commodities. The distinction between symbolic products and durable or material products or their material reality should, however, not be interpreted to imply that these products belong *in toto* to different realms—one virtual, the other real—that will never congregate. Real commodities increasingly have intangi-ble dimensions. The exchange value of intangible elements such as, for example, embedded software often exceeds that of the material components. Digital plat-forms, data flows, patents, brand names and other forms of abstract capital tend to be highly contested. Among the additional salient attributes of symbolic or immaterial commodities is the incredibly low cost of transporting and storing these goods in comparison to traditional commodities.

Widely contested, however, is whether derivatives are merely an extension of tradable products whose exchange tends to approach what is considered to be a complete market and thereby turn uncertainties into manageable risks, or, if derivatives actually enhance systematic societal risks of repeated financial and economic crisis that destabilize entire societies and regions of the world.

An important attribute of symbolic commodities is that the identity and utility of intangible items is their often highly context-sensitive character and that they cannot be "understood" or assessed disregarding the context in which they originated and were "consumed." With symbolic commodities, their contexts of production and utilization often have a close proximity to each other; their life expectancy is fairly limited. Property rights to symbolic commodities are virtually absent. Symbolic products are not subject to a natural interpretation of scarcity. Limitations of the quantity of symbolic goods are only to a very minor degree influenced by nature. The production of symbolic goods is not directly linked to the natural environment of the company and its boundaries. The regulative principles that govern market exchanges and intervention into the market do not apply in full force to exchange processes that involve symbolic commodities. Symbolic products have their very own logic of rationality, form of scarcity, mobility, life expectancy and utility.

## Monetary Symbolic Products

Symbolic "commodities" of *monetary* nature are disembodied, in particular capital movements, cross-rates, exchange rates, interest rate differentials, and credit flows are, as indicated, to a considerable extent "unconnected to trade—and indeed largely independent of it" and "greatly exceed trade finance" (Drucker, 1986: 782). The importance of monetary symbolic products for the world economy now exceeds that of the traditional flows of manufactured goods and services.[34] The gold exchange standard that operated industrial societies for the most parts of their existence has been replaced by the electronic information system of today.

There then is a close conceptual relation between what we have described as the symbolic economy and extensive financialization of the modern economy.[35] The evolution of the financialization of the economy and societal relations more generally is enhanced by the spread of neoliberal policies. The term neoliberalism is more than a political (rhetorical) weapon. In contrast to classical liberalism, neoliberalism rejects the passive notion of a *laissez faire* state by arguing for the need to politically construct the conditions for the possibility of economic success including financialization, of course. In one sentence, "the market could not be depended upon to naturally conjure up the conditions for its own continued flourishing" (Mirowski, 1990: 108).

Neoliberal policies in many countries and regional political blocks differ (see Fourcade, 2009) but, in most instances, push for deregulation of the economy. Neoliberal agendas argue for the opening of national and international markets for capital and goods. Although the state is supposed to withdraw and shrink via austerity and privatization, yet governments are to provide the foundation, for example, the legal framework for the possibility of sustainable free markets. Neoliberal economics and policies not only enhance financialization but also are seen to be responsible for recent economic crises, perhaps even with built in boom-and-bust-cycles as well as the growth of social inequality (see Ostry, Loungani and

Furceri, 2016; Davis and Walsh, 2017) and its eventual push back from those who see themselves as the losers of the spread of neoliberalism. In short, neoliberalism and financialization differ (emphasis on production and consumption as opposed to transactions) but also have similarities (global perspective and emphasis on the role of the market). Among economists, both Rudolf Hilferding ([1910] 2006: 283) in his book *Finance Capital* and Joseph Alois Schumpeter ([1911] 1934: 165) in his classical study *The Theory of Economic Development* draw attention to the economic importance of monetary capital and meta-capital. Hilferding identifies a specific stage in the development of capitalist economies as the financial capital stage (organizes capitalism), that is, as the stage at which, due to the huge capital required for the financing of production in the entire industrial sector, *banking houses* become central actors in economic affairs. Bank capital and industrial capital merge, allowing for an enormous expansion of economic activities including oversea regions in a permanent search for profits.

Symbolic products of a *monetary* nature are expenditures for research and development (R&D), health care, education and the production and dissemination of knowledge. Symbolic commodities of a *non-monetary* nature are, for example, data ("sets of numbers"), technological trajectories, organizational structures and processes, statistics, fashion regimes, programs/software, training, R&D, product marketing, advice and organizational "knowledge" capital (that is, specialists and experts) as well as the growing flow of information within and across national boundaries. Another symbolic but non-monetary commodity that ought to be added to this category is the varied activity of the largest and fastest growing segment of the modern economy, namely tourism.[36]

In the course of the development of the modern economy, investments in *intangible* assets will gain considerable importance compared to investments in tangible assets, such as production property or equipment, and will surpass tangible investments in the future. The major obstacle in gaining insights into the volume of intangibles and therefore its overall economic importance is their absence in national income accounting (GDP) figures. Investments in intangibles from software codes to business processes in the form of platforms are treated as costs rather than investments (Haskel and Westlake, 2017).

Other significant symbolic factors that have a decisive effect on the performance of the modern economy but are rarely taken into consideration by conventional economic thinking are moral, philosophical, and political events and other factors that reflect normative objectives, but also rumors, the social and political construction of climate change as well as the social construction of other natural processes. In the world of economics, words do matter. Quantifying immaterial commodities and services is a highly complicated and controversial task. As Bergje van Eekelen (2015: 456) stresses, "the work of measuring and mapping intangible goods is . . . a conceptual practice—it is a form of attribution, recognition and figuring out." In other words: socio-cultural work[37] that will never be able to completely eliminate the essentially contested nature of its results.

The ever-accelerating flow of information increases uncertainty; more pre-cisely, it reduces the duration of those moments in which certainty seems to prevail. The rapid dissemination of symbolic goods accelerates their obsolescence. In the manufacturing industry, for example, the growing importance of sym-bolic commodities for the provision and production of products raises costs and requires larger markets for these expenditures to be absorbed. Commodities and services, to a growing extent, embody knowledge.

Georg Simmel ([1907] 1989: 180) could still describe the net asset value of money in the early days of extensive worldwide trade relations in terms of the distance it had to (physically) travel:

> The spread of trade relations, however, requires a valuable currency, if only because the transportation of money over long distances makes it desirable that the value should be concentrated in a small volume. Thus, the historical empires and the trading states with extensive markets were always driven towards money with a high material value.

The greater the intrinsic value of money, the larger the number of individuals and groups generally prepared to accept the value of the money. The intrinsic value of money ensures that its value cannot fall to zero: "Money performs its services best when it is not simply money, but represents the value of things in pure abstraction" (Simmel, [1907] 1989: 163; cf. Smit, Buekens and Plessis, 2016). This theory of money as intrinsic value, or a metal theory of money, was well established until far into the 19th century if not later (cf. Schumpeter, 1954: 63). In the era of financialization, however, there no longer is such a thing as capital preservation of the value of money.[38]

Developments of the monetary symbolic economy, changes in its trends, and abrupt shifts often occur in response to anticipated political events or are driven by unanticipated crises in various parts of the world. Indeed, it is not only trade in goods and services that is strongly affected by the symbolic economy; the dynam-ics of the symbolic economy often have political repercussions, as well. Moreover, in the traditional realm of international trade and services, the flow of *symbolic commodities*, that is, knowledge, has become a much more salient factor in the world economy (cf. Dickson, 1984: 163–216).

## Productive Processes

> That knowledge has become *the* resource, rather than *a* resource, is what makes our society "post-capitalist." This fact changes—fundamentally—the structure of society. It created new social and economic dynamics. It creates new politics.
> —*Peter Drucker (1993: 40–41)*

Modern society and its economy have, until recently, been understood pri-marily in terms of tangible assets (or property: land, equipment, structures that house the equipment, inventories) and labor. Peter Drucker, one of the pioneers of a modern theory of society, is convinced in the classical sense of social theory that even a *post-capitalist society* is a society in which a transformation of the economy has societal consequences much beyond the boundaries of the economic system and leaves nothing as it was.[39] Labor and property[40] have had a long association in social, economic and political theory.[41] Work is seen as a source of current and emerging property. Adam Smith ([1776] 2001: 586) explains:

> Land and capital stock are the two original sources of all revenue both private and public. Capital stock pays the wages of productive labour, whether employed in agriculture, manufacturing, or commerce. The management of the two original sources of revenue belongs to two different sets of people; the proprietors of land, and the owners or employers of capital stock.

In Marxist tradition, capital is objectified and encapsulated labor. On the basis of these attributes, individuals and groups were able, or constrained, to define their membership in society. With their declining importance in the productive process, especially in terms of their conventional economic attributes and manifestations (e.g. as "corporeal" property such as land and manual work), the social constructs of labor and property themselves are changing.[42]

While the traditional features of labor and property certainly have not disappeared entirely, the new principle of "knowledge" has been added. To some extent, this challenges and transforms the classical forces of production—property, capital and labor—as the constitutive mechanisms of society.[43] Our focus, therefore, is not on the classical role of labor, capital and property in generating added economic value; nor are we concerned with exclusivity as the distinguishing attribute of property (Durkheim, [1950] 1991), or with the extent to which only labor may be viewed as a source of value.

Different theoretical classifications of society are based on what is seen as a society's core principles. These core principles symbolize the constitutive mechanisms of societies and their replacement by new constitutive processes. Thus, bourgeois society was originally a society of owners. It later became a "working society" (*Arbeitsgesellschaft*), and it is now transforming into a knowledge society. It is doubtful whether it is possible to specifically date the emergence or decline of a particular type of society.

Radovan Richta (1969: 276) and his colleagues date the beginning of the profound transformation of modern society brought about by the scientific and technological revolution (as they call it) back to the 1950s. Daniel Bell (1973: 346), while noting that it is indeed foolhardy to propose precise dates for social processes, nevertheless argues that the "symbolic" onset of the post-industrial society can be traced to the period since the end of World War II as it was during this era that a new consciousness of time and social change began to emerge.

In contrast, Block and Hirschhorn (1979: 368) suggest that it is the 1920s that mark the emergence of the new productive forces typical of post-industrial society (namely information, knowledge, science and technology), and in particular the period when these began to make a decisive difference in the production sphere. In the 1920s, at least in the United States, the input of labor, time and capital was constant or had begun to decrease, while output had begun to rise. Be that as it may, in modern society, as all of these observers concur, "knowledge" has become—in economic terms—the *crucial* source of (added) value.[44] Knowledge has of course always been an indispensable part of production and consumption.

The reason why the knowledge structure in modern society is being analyzed, in the first place, is the heightened social significance of knowledge in this society, which in turn is the result of the tremendous increase in the overall fund of knowledge. Of course, shared knowledge has always had a function in social life and knowledge has of course always been an indispensable part of production and consumption. In fact, one could justifiably speak of an anthropological constant: human action is knowledge-based. This also applies, of course, to economic conduct (cf. Veblen, [1908] 1919: 324–351; Arrow, 1994; David and Forey, 2003, among others). Social *groups* and social roles of all types depend on and are mediated by knowledge.[45] All relations among *individuals* are based on knowledge of each other, as Georg Simmel ([1908] 1992) so appropriately noted.[46] And, without such knowledge, social interaction would be impossible; but "in many fields, reciprocal knowledge does not have to be equal on both sides or is not permitted to be" (Simmel, [1906] 1950: 308; see also the well-known analysis of asymmetric knowledge by the economist George Akerlof, 1970).

Similarly, power has frequently been based not only on physical strength but also on advantages in knowledge. And, last but not least, societal reproduction is not merely a physical but, in the case of humans, always a cultural process, i.e. the reproduction of knowledge (see also Elias, 1991).[47]

In retrospect, a variety of ancient societies can be described as knowledge societies. For example, ancient Israel was a society structured by its religious-legalistic knowledge of the Torah. Ancient Egypt was a society in which religious, astronomical and agrarian knowledge served as the organizing principle and the basis of authority.[48] Contemporary society may be described as a knowledge society based on the extensive penetration of all its spheres of life and institutions by scientific and technical knowledge. Although only a minority of social theories has explicitly defined knowledge as problematic, most of them have always considered it to be a determinant of social order. Marxist theories of society have always attributed a crucial importance, for social development, to the forces or means of production since "man's understanding of nature and his mastery over it by virtue of his presence as a social body ... appears as the great foundation-stone (*Grundpfeiler*) of production and of wealth" (Marx, [1939–1941] 1973: 705).

As a result, scientific and technical knowledge has become a direct though not independent force of production (cf. Rosenberg, 1976: 126–138). Contemporary

Marxist theories, especially those relying on the notion of scientific-technological revolution developed by Radovan Richta and others, have analyzed scientific and technical knowledge as the principal motor of change. Max Weber's seminal inquiry into the unique features of Western civilization stresses the pervasive use of reason to secure the methodical efficiency of social action. The source of rational action and, therefore, of rationalization is located in specific intellectual constructs.

Raymond Aron's (1962) theory of industrial society, which encompasses both socialist and capitalist forms of economic organization, stresses the extent to which science and technology shape the social organization of productive activities and, consequently, other forms of life in society. More recent theories of post-industrial society and similar efforts to forecast the course of social evolution in industrial society, in particular the efforts of Daniel Bell, have elevated theoretical knowledge to the axial principle of society. That is, codified theoretical knowledge becomes, as Bell (1979: 164) describes it, "the director of social change." In the economy, instrumental knowledge replaces labor as the source of added value. The strata of the producers of scientific and technological knowledge therefore become the key agency and actors of future social and economic development.

Daniel Bell acknowledges, of course, that every society has been dependent on knowledge. But, as he emphatically stresses, this knowledge has very rarely been theoretical knowledge. It is the "codification of theoretical knowledge that now becomes the source of advances and change in society" (Bell, 1973: 25), and it is only in the last half century that we have seen "a fusion of science and engineering" (Bell, 1979: 164) that has transformed the nature of technology itself. In post-industrial society, the emphasis is evidently on the *instrumental mode of rational action*. It therefore seems to be almost self-evident to some observers that knowledge and human capital provide the foundation not only as new basis for economic power and but also for an entirely new social class who advantage no longer rest on their ownership of physical capital (cf. Milner Jr., 2015: 91). But what conception of knowledge forms the foundation for such conclusions?

In the context of Bell's theory of post-industrial society, and of theoretical concepts that resonate with his theory of modern society, knowledge—and the groups of individuals that acquire influence and control through knowledge—tend to be conceptualized rather narrowly as exemplifying the status of objective scientific knowledge and of what Bell calls "intellectual technology" (see Bell, 1979: 167). That is, the producers of knowledge claims in the natural and the social sciences generate more and more axiomatically structured assertions that employ formal languages as their medium of communication and have thus become increasingly distanced from empiricism (cp. Bell, 1973: 25), on the one hand, and embedded in "automatic machines" or computers, on the other.

However, Daniel Bell (1979: 46) argues, the social change that can be observed in post-industrial societies is not confined to the socio-technical attributes of the society nor to other societal institutions such as, for instance, the political system.

More precisely, Daniel Bell (1979: 46) suggested a "post-industrial society is basically an information society." In contrast, the immaterial economy is based on knowledge and knowledge skills, with consequences for society as a whole.

Theories of modern society often display too much deference toward orthodox theories of science and therefore lack sufficient detail and scope in their conceptualization of the "knowledge" supplied and in their awareness of the embeddedness of the fabrication of knowledge; the reasons for the societal demand for more and more knowledge; the ways in which knowledge travels; the rapidly expanding groups of individuals in society who, in one of many ways, live off knowledge;[49] the many forms of knowledge which are considered as pragmatically useful; the various effects which knowledge may have on social relations, and, last but not least, the question of determining how to deploy knowledge efficiently (see Garicano and Rossi-Hansberg, 2014) if one abstracts for the moment from the many unsuccessful efforts to establish the idea of knowledge management.

Although knowledge has always been an indispensable resource of production, with an increase in the significance of knowledge for economic relations comes a growing importance of social circumstances, networks and constraints of "knowledge relations" up to now considered, by economic discourse, to be extraneous to economic conduct. Any transfer of financial capital, materials, commodities or even labor can be affected with greater ease than the transfer of knowledge (cf. Landes, 1980). In spite of many efforts to move knowledge closer to those attributes that are seen to be the essential attributes of commodities, when it comes to knowledge, "market failure is the rule rather than the exception" (Lundvall, 1992: 18).

As we will have occasion to stress again, the transformations outlined above that are underway in modern society and in the economy are only marginally reflected in economic theory today.[50] For classical economists, from Adam Smith to David Ricardo, John Stuart Mill and, above all, Karl Marx, economic change induced by technical developments was one of the salient and taken-for-granted sources of the dynamics of the economic system. Technological change affects the somewhat static world of economic affairs, as reconstructed by neo-classical economic theory, only in peripheral ways, namely as a change "in its assumed schedules of unit cost against production" (Schwartz, 1992: 142). But since the very transformations that alter major production schedules have been rarely examined, the impact of technological change remains marginal to the concerns of economic theory.

One of the perhaps more salient transformation processes of the economy is not linked to technological development but to what makes technological development possible in the first instance: knowledge. Given the central importance of knowledge in the immaterial economy, an initial examination of the peculiar means of production of the resource knowledge is in order. Within the confines of the common, perhaps even common-sense definition, the concept of knowledge is anything but peculiar. The customary definition of knowledge refers to accounts that claim or are seen to be able to cognitively grasp or explain some-thing (Smith, 2015: 15). Our definition differs. Our conception is concerned with what knowledge may accomplish in practice, that is, with the answers knowledge is able to offer.

## The Peculiarities of Knowledge

> Human cognition and thought are, . . . actually or virtually directed to the external . . . the structure of skills reveals that these invariably involve an inte-gration of perception and action to form an *ability*.
> —*Arnold Gehlen ([1940] 1988: 54)*

On a number of occasions in our examination of the immaterial economy we have already referred to knowledge as a *productive* force in modern societies. But among those observers of the modern economy—as well as of earlier economic formations—who recognize that knowledge is a crucial resource of economic activities and relations, there is no agreement as to *what is actually meant* when speaking of knowledge. Arnold Gehlen's reference above to the constitutive link between reflection and action is a first helpful starting point, however, toward an analysis of the peculiarities of knowledge that does not, as one can often observe, insist on certain philosophical attributes of the nature of knowledge.

In addition, there is no agreement assuming this matter is considered at all, *how much and what kind* of knowledge is needed to carry out any economic action aiming to reach a particular outcome. What is characteristic of the literature are references to wide array of philosophical definitions and sociological categories of knowledge that can range from tacit knowledge, to everyday knowledge and formal scientific knowledge.

For these confusing reasons, we put the question of the relationship between knowledge and scientific knowledge in brackets. As soon as the idea is put forward that scientific knowledge is a special class of knowledge, we are confronted with new and difficult questions. These include primarily the question of the reasons for the boundaries between different classes of knowledge and scientific knowl-edge. This difficulty also applies to the problem of the simultaneity of conflicting forms of knowledge from different historical epochs. We reject any *a priori* defi-nition of the boundaries between different classes of knowledge, wherever they may be drawn.

Often, and independently of the definition of knowledge chosen, the immedi-ate practical efficacy/power/competence of knowledge is not only overstated but also simply assumed to be the case (cf. Milner Jr., 2015: 91), and frequently seen to derive more or less directly from science.[51] According to Daniel Bell's influential theory of the post-industrial society, social change extends not only to the socio-technical attributes of society but to other social institutions such as the political system. More specifically, a post-industrial society is, according to Bell, essentially an *information society* (Bell, 1976: 46). In contrast, the immaterial economy is based on broad range of knowledges, knowledge about knowledge and knowledge skills of the workforce and their impact on society as a whole. Most forms of knowledge tend to grow as knowledge is employed. This is one of the reasons why those who control knowledge like to have regulations in place to fence knowledge in rather than have it made readily available especially to competitors.

Theories of modern society as well as canonical economic models display too much deference toward orthodox theories and philosophies of science and therefore lack sufficient detail and scope or pay attention to their conceptualization of the "knowledge" implicated in their design and in their awareness of the embeddedness of the fabrication of knowledge; the reasons for the societal demand for more and more knowledge;[52] the ways in which knowledge travels; the rapidly expanding groups of individuals in society who, in one of many ways, live off knowledge; the many forms of knowledge which are considered as pragmatically useful; the extent to which knowledge is pregnant with inconsistencies (Smith, 2015: 16); the various effects which knowledge may have on social relations, and, last but not least, the question of determining how to deploy knowledge efficiently (see Garicano and Rossi-Hansberg, 2014).

If we are to critically address the role of knowledge in society at large and in the economy in particular it is necessary and only fair, in contrast to other, competing conceptions—especially the epistemological idea that knowledge represents justified "true belief" and authorized belief (cf. Kitcher, 1993; Goldman and McGrath, 2015; McGinn, 2017)—to address in some detail the basic question of how we conceive knowledge. In the sense of knowledge as true belief, knowledge is a subset of belief. Belief for which the believer has good reason to belief: whether "it's because we've done experiments, because we've proved logically; or, because God has revealed them to our people" (Weinberger, 2011: 43). Knowledge extends to forms of knowledge that are not limited to (individual or collective) *true* belief.

We define knowledge as a *capacity for social action* (not as a capacity to formulate what then aspires to be is true or right), thus temporarily—that is analytically—suspending the linkage between knowledge and social action.[53] Every human has enabling abilities and can find answers to more or less pressing problems. In this sense, knowledge is a universal phenomenon, or an anthropological constant.[54] Knowledge as an anthropological phenomenon "works" even though it may be rather deficient in terms of those attributes that often are seen to privilege certain forms of knowledge over common ways of thinking and formulating knowledge claims. Everyday forms of knowledge, for example, have the ability to enable an actor to make a decision under pressure to act that is often typical of everyday life.

In contrast to what is constitutive of everyday life, the *suspension* of the constraint to act within scientific discourse may be described, on the one hand, as a virtue of intellectual activity taking place under privileged conditions which moderate the effect of the pressing interests, rapidly passing opportunities and ambiguous dependencies of everyday contexts on the production of scientific knowledge claims. On the other hand, the result of this suspension of the pressure to act is that scientific knowledge takes on qualities of incompleteness, provisionality, fragmentariness or expansiveness that reduce its effectiveness as knowledge in circumstances in which social action, decision-making is the foremost requirement. In everyday life in particular, we are forced to act; for as Durkheim ([1912] 1981: 479) observed so well: "Life cannot wait" (cf. also Gehlen, [1940] 1993: 296–297).[55]

In most social contexts, the need to act takes precedence over the need to know. Not only in cases of inordinate circumstances, acting, for example, by providing an account of what has happened re-establishes a sense of security or normality. It does not matter whether such accounts may later prove to be factually and logically inaccurate. Perhaps there exists, as Georg Simmel (1890: 1) surmises, an anthropological constant in the form of a general and widespread preference among humans to "do" something rather than merely to know about something. Knowing, in turn, may require prior doing.[56]

In 1948, Claude Shannon published a small volume entitled *The Mathematical Theory of Communication*. In it he explained how words, sounds and images could be converted into blips and sent electronically. While Shannon's communication model has been surpassed by ever more complex models in communication theory, it might be argued that he foretold the digital revolution in communications. Shannon's formulation of information theory was driven by a purely technical, non-semantic interest. He was interested in showing how to best transfer a digital signal.[57]

Knowledge as a symbolic "system" enables people to act on the world. Based on the same general definition of knowledge, a *software program* as a protocol for organizing "information" constitutes a form of knowledge. A *metaphor* may have the capacity to enable us to act on the world. How to capture water power, how to smelt iron and craft tools, how to increase the output of heavy soils, how to structure a state and markets or how to generate a narrative (cf. Goldstone, 2006: 276–279), all of these phenomena constitute knowledge that made up the core of the emergence of modernizing societies. Consistent with our sociological view of the function of knowledge, capacities to act are socially constructed, sustained and interpreted. The world does not classify itself for itself (cf. Barnes, 1995: 94–103).

Our choice of terms derives from Francis Bacon's famous observation "*scientia est potentia*"—or, as it has often been translated in a somewhat misleading fashion: *knowledge is power*. Bacon suggests that knowledge derives its utility from its capacity to set something in motion.[58] The term *potentia*, or *capacity*, is employed to describe this power of knowing. More specifically, Bacon asserts at the outset of his *Novum Organum* (first published in 1620) that "human knowledge and human power meet in one; for where the cause is not known the effect cannot be produced. Nature to be commanded must be obeyed; and that which in contemplation is the cause is in operation the rule" (Francis Bacon, *Novum Organum* I, Aph. 3). Knowledge and power join forces when human knowledge is knowledge about the causes of events in nature. If human action follows rules—the rules that bring about a thing or event—it follows that human knowledge represents the capacity to act, to set the process in question in motion or to produce something. In other terms, humans engage with the world through acquired capacities to act. The success of human action can be gauged from changes that have taken place in reality or from the reproduction of society (Krohn, 1981, 1987: 87–89).[59]

Within the narrower semantic confines of economic discourse, knowledge may be defined "as the ability to solve the problems that naturally arise in any production process" (Garicano and Rossi-Hansberg, 2014: 2). If we conceive of the production process as a process mainly driven by technical contingencies and technical objects (for example, means of transportation, energy), then the kind of knowledge as capacity to act become in a narrower sense the special ability to produce something (Popitz, 1986: 115: *Fähigkeit zum Herstellen*). The human ability to produce something is, as Heinrich Popitz (1986: 116) emphasizes, subject to greater efficiency and progress, it can be enlarged and improved; "we can increase the efficiency of artifact production in several ways: by increasing the *variety* of products, product *quantity*, product *quality* and reducing the effort involved in the manufacturing process (increasing *productivity*)."

## Knowledge Skills (and Machines)

> There is nothing more intricate nor more exciting to the student of history than to watch how the process of a new age gradually dismisses its old concepts, and how together with the changes in the social structure new axioms and hypotheses clear the ground for new types of experiences.
>
> —*Karl Mannheim ([1938] 1953: 262)*[60]

Knowledge as generalized capacity for action acquires an "active" role in the course of social action *only* under circumstances where such action does not follow purely stereotypical patterns (Max Weber) or is otherwise strictly regulated.[61] Knowledge gains significance under conditions where social action is, for whatever reasons, based on a certain degree of freedom with respect to the courses of action that can be chosen. In much the same sense, Karl Mannheim ([1929] 1936) defines the range of social conduct in general, and therefore the contexts in which knowledge plays a role, as restricted to spheres of social life that have not been completely routinized and regulated. For, as he observes, "conduct, in the sense in which we use it, does not begin until we reach the area where rationalization has not yet penetrated, and where we are forced to make decisions in situations which have as yet not been subjected to regulation" (Mannheim, [1929] 1936: 102).[62] More precisely,

> the action of a petty official who disposes of a file of documents in the prescribed manner or of a judge who finds that a case falls under the provisions of a certain paragraph in the law and disposes of it accordingly, or finally of a factory worker who produces a screw by following the prescribed technique, would not fall under our definition of "conduct." Nor for that matter would the action of a technician who, in achieving a given end, combined certain general laws of nature. All these modes of behavior would be considered as merely "reproductive" because they are executed in a rational framework, according to a definite prescription entailing no personal decision whatsoever.

In line with Mannheim's observation, our definition of knowledge as capacity to act does not imply that knowledge is immediately performative or persuasive.[63] Knowledge is deployed, if used at all, in *specific social contexts*. Knowledge does not enjoy—as kind of an immanent or intrinsic attribute, for instance as the result of the "truthfulness" or "logicality" of its propositions—practical competence and hence general applicability. Problems we are confronted with, for example environmental problems, *are not directly* "scientific or technological, but social, political, and cultural" (Lowe, 1971: 569). In other words, knowledge—and be it technical or scientific knowledge—"does not contain its consequences and potential within itself. . . . Clients' use *defines* success" (Bozeman and Rogers, 2002: 773).[64]

For example, climate scientists and other impatient observers concerned with the impact of global warming on society fail to see that "decisions of public concern have to be made according to a time table established within the political sphere, not the scientific or technical sphere" (Collins and Evans, 2002: 241). Knowledge does not "cause" future conditions, it *enables* some futures and *prevents* others and does so in conjunction with relevant conditions of action (cf. Koppl et al., 2015: 13).[65]

Our cautionary note about the immediate "power" or direct persuasiveness of scientific knowledge does not imply, however that one cannot in fact observe the capacity of science "to authorize and certify certain facts and pictures of reality [as] a potent source of political influence" (Ezrahi, 1971: 121). Scientific narratives may for example be deployed as means of defending, in an apparently rational manner the legitimacy of political decisions (cf. Nelkin, 1975: 36). Yet, access to such knowledge itself often becomes a source of political contests.

Put differently, the realization and implementation of discoveries based on new knowledge may for example require an entrepreneur, as Joseph Schumpeter ([1911] 1934) argued: an entrepreneur who has an idea or purpose to pursue,[66] is capable of raising the financial capital, perhaps create a company, find the necessary personnel and develop the new commodity in order "to get the job done" (cf. Phelps, 2013). More generally, what actors need—independently from the knowledge available to them—is power, for example (Schumpeter, 1916/17: 14),[67] or specific social, intellectual and cognitive skills that allow them to convert a capacity for into a practice of social action. The societal distribution of knowledge and the societal distribution of power do not necessarily coincide. There is power without knowledge and knowledge without power.

The tendency to overestimate and overreach in assigning a crucial role to the singularity of knowledge (and information) in social conduct is evident, also as one considers the question of *how much knowledge* is needed to carry a specific task, let alone how deeply and subtly one needs to know it. A curiosity about the question of how much we need to know also extends to the question on what we do not need to know. In the first instance, this happens to be an issue that is rarely systematically examined. Second, the inclination is prevalent to assume that the resource of knowledge is somehow sufficient to carry out a specific transaction. A more adequate conjecture would be to expect that most decisions and actions are carried out with rather limited knowledge and information (cf. Akerlof, 1970; Smith, 2015) about future conditions of action and that actors are cognizant of how little knowledge one typically is able to mobilize in many situations: Speculation, for example, takes its cue from speculation (Luhmann, 2002: 184). The pressures characteristic of everyday life to act assure that decisions are arrived at and action is carried despite of most actors' knowledge of the limited knowledge and information.[68]

A cluster of societal developments are responsible for limiting the power of knowledge and information that are not connected with the lack of performance and persuasion of knowledge described by us. These social changes include the growing equality of the distribution of knowledge and information. The growing equality of the possession knowledge is a function of different but interrelated developments: the once privileged access to knowledge is less unevenly distributed in present-day societies. The basic access to knowledge and the growing difficulties of limiting knowledge is linked to the historically unique degree of education of the members of society. Access to knowledge beyond the borders of social and national systems is, of course, facilitated by the new media. The growing number of people involved in the production of knowledge is contributing to the social diffusion of knowledge. As well as the growing number of experts, counselors and consultants, whose primary function is to mediate and interpret knowledge, overall facilitates access to knowledge. Experts reduce the transaction costs of access to knowledge. The central role that knowledge plays as an economic resource also ensures that an interest in the dissemination and capture of knowledge is of great importance and receives appropriate support. The incentive to locate and to bind knowledge is extraordinarily significant not only for companies, but also for other social institutions such as the state. Knowledge about knowledge provides further incentives and opportunities to appropriate knowledge. Knowledge skills are not only helpful in order to acquire knowledge about knowledge but also in the production of knowledge and in finding shortcuts in the search for knowledge.

What counts, therefore, as competitive advantages in the social context of an immaterial economy are *knowledge skills* because these foundational skills define an employee's creativity and productivity, her ability to shoulder responsibility, to work in teams and, more generally, to get things done.[69] Therefore, what matters, rather than merely information, knowledge, knowledge about knowledge and so-called technical skills,[70] are knowledge skills that create added economic value.[71] Knowledge skills *complement* technological changes.

A number of recent studies have documented that the collective share of the gross domestic product that is paid to labor has declined. Setting aside the issue of income inequality among workers or the sector of the economy with which we will deal in the chapter on labor, explanations for the decline of the share of labor have stressed technical change displacing labor, offshoring, demographic changes in the labor force or the degree of concentration. If it were possible to detect a common denominator among the different explanations for the labor share decline, we would point to the differential skill ratio among jobs and firms. Our explanation would expect that the labor share decline is distributed unequally across occupations. In jobs with a high-skill ratio, the labor share should increase while in jobs with a low-skill ratio the share should decline or stagnate.[72]

Knowledge skills have at least one property in common with economic phenomena. They are scarce. Knowledge skills constitute *resources* that influence whether an individual or collectivity will thrive or fall behind. Knowledge skills can be put to tactical and strategic use. Knowledge skills represent the ability to deal with economic disequilibria in order to regain equilibrium; specifically, as Theodore Schultz (1975: 827) notes, the extent to which individuals and collectivities are capable "to undertake action that will appropriately reallocate their resources." Allocative abilities are mainly cultural traits. The capacity to cope with disequilibria or the skill to persevere through frustration involve the ability to correctly interpret looming changes or changes that have already taken place in order to initiate appropriate action adjusting to changing circumstances.[73]

Knowledge skills strengthen and sharpen our sense of possibilities (Robert Musil) and help to generate scenarios and thought images (Walter Benjamin).[74] However, these cognitive and social resources defy orthodox forms of economic knowledge and theoretical reflection—and, so far, quantification.[75] Knowledge skills represent complimentary human abilities to computers that cannot be effectively replicated by machines.

An *empirical* analysis of actual knowledge skills practiced in companies should observe start-ups. Their employees are typically self-recruited and did not achieve their employment status because their abilities corresponded to the requirement profile of the management of existing enterprises, that is, a management claiming to know exactly which competences are needed as a basis for economic success in the developing world of digital work. It is this point of view that resembles the trust in demand-determined competences, which overestimates the own ability to anticipate the future.

For André Gorz ([2003] 2010: 35–36) knowledge skills are an essential part of his definition of the nature of knowledge. It is useful to quote his extensive and deviant—as compared to many more conventional definitions of knowledge especially within the philosophy of science—conception in detail since here we find a helpful notion of the range of social and cognitive abilities that are part of knowledge skills. Knowledge

> covers—refers to—a wide diversity of *heterogeneous* capacities, including judgment, intuition, aesthetic sense, level of education and information, ability to learn, and to adapt to unforeseen situations, which are capacities themselves brought into play by heterogeneous activities ranging from mathematical calculation to rhetoric and the art of persuasion, from techno-scientific research to the invention of aesthetic norms.

The importance of knowledge skills for the economy is not new. Knowledge skills were always a potent, if often latent, resource for economic institutions, employment and the value of labor. Hence the conclusion drawn by Thomas Piketty ([2013] 2014: 313): "the best way to increase wages and reduce wage inequalities in the long run is to invest in education and skills." However, the nature of the skills in demand is changing; we can easily be mistaken about the (abstract) skills (see Autor, Levy and Murnane, 2003) that are not subject to automation, for example.[76]

Initial empirical studies about the payoff to skills in the "third industrial revolution" (through mounting technical change such as computerization) indicate that the increasing in between-occupation inequality is accounted for in terms of differential skills brought to the work tasks at hand. What kinds of skills are increasingly in demand? Our hypothesis is of course that knowledge skills play a central role in the observed shifts in the world of work and that manual task-intensive occupational activities are not complemented by knowledge capacities. That thesis resembles Lui and Grusky's (2013: 1332) conclusion that "the defining feature . . . of the last 30 years has been a precipitous increase in the wage payoff to jobs requiring synthesis, critical thinking, and deductive and inductive reasoning."

The authors distinguish between general skills, measured conventionally based on schooling and experience and a more differentiated set of eight workplace nonmanual skills identifying cognitive (verbal, quantitative, analytic), creative, technical (computer and science and engineering) and social skills (managerial, nurturing). The further assumption is that multiple nonmanual skills are acquired on the job as incumbents carry out their work. Earnings are measured based on hourly wages. The findings indicate that a clear job skill upgrading can be observed as the third industrial revolution evolves (over the period 1979–2001 covered in the study) and that the rate of upgrading is quite variable (cf. Lui and

Grusky, 2013: 1349). Computer and managerial skills increase most rapidly. This in turn leads to the conclusion consistent with our knowledge skills hypothesis that the third industrial revolution is as much a social revolution as a technical one (Lui and Grusky, 2013: 1351). As far as the payoff to skills is concerned, the rising return to analytic skills far outpaces that of other nonmanual skills. The most striking result Lui and Grusky (2013: 1368) report is that "rewards are increasingly going to those who engage in critical thinking, problem solving, and deductive reasoning . . . The evidence from our models suggests that, contrary to [the] . . . view [that technical change is crucial], the real driving force is skill-biased institutional change rather than skill-biased technical change."

And as we will have occasion to observe in more detail in the context of our discussion of digitalization and automation, perhaps also as the result of the anticipated dissemination of artificial intelligence (AI) in the world of work,[77] there is a shift toward skills that *complement* the technologization of routine and codifiable tasks; a shift that we tend describe as an increasing utility of *knowledge skills* and hence the comparative advantage of workers that are capable of *supplying* such competences. The growing deployment of computers and efforts to make AI part of work *complements* rather than drives the function served by knowledge skills.[78]

With the growth and extension of the "financialization" of economic conduct, that is, the growing weight of finance in the economy and society based on a massive technologization, the roles of knowledge in general and knowledge skills in particular are growing in tandem and, as we argue, are gaining a much more pervasive influence. The returns from labor, capital, knowledge and land—be it in the form of profits, capital gains, interests, wages or income—have increasingly become a function of financial transactions rather than commodity production, trade or the performance of basic services.

## Financialization

> The concentration of money affected by the big investors (pension funds, insurance companies, investment funds) have become an autonomous force, controlled solely by bankers, who increasingly favor speculation—financial operations for ends that are purely financial—over productive investment.
> —*Pierre Bourdieu (2005: 229)*

The concept of "financialization" refers—in line with Pierre Bourdieu's observation—to the importance of the rapidly growing *volume* of autonomous monetary resources—embedded in international finance regimes that are controlled by large, internationally operating financial institutions, huge corporations, state-controlled investment funds (sovereign wealth funds),[79] pension funds, big (and small) investors or a growing number of wealthy individuals and, as a consequence, financial movements, financial firms and financial markets that have gained a central part in the dynamics of the economy and of modern society in general (cf. Tomaskovic-Devey and Lin, 2015).

The latter is true, for example, for growing levels of social inequality in developed countries or the acceleration of indebtedness (cf. Alvaredo et al., 2017; Hein and Mundt, 2011: 4–13; Van Arnum and Naples, 2013: 1165–1168; Kwon and Roberts, 2015; Roberts and Kwon, 2017).[80] The benefits gained with the aid of financial products come of course in the form of capital gains, interests, asset-management fees and dividends. At least a parallel development is the decline of labor's share of national income. In the leading economies of the world, United States, Japan, China and Germany, the *labor share* "specifically, the share of corporate gross value-added paid to labor—declined by roughly 2 to 4 percentage points per decade during the 1975–2010 period, with the precise time window differing by country according to data availability" (Autor, 2015: 7). Dominique Guellec and Caroline Paunov (2017: 1) attribute the widening income gap between the upper one percent of the income hierarchy compared to the large remaining number of employees in the OECD countries to the expansion of *digital infrastructure* in the immaterial economy: "the growing importance of digital innovation . . . has increased market rents, which benefit disproportionally the top income groups."[81]

Thomas Piketty and his colleagues (Piketty, Saez and Zucman, 2018) in an effort to recalibrate the way the *Gross National Product* (GDP), now almost a century old, is calculated propose a new statistic to compute the distribution of the national income of the United States that combines tax data, survey findings and national accounts data. The accumulated data enable the authors to capture 100% of national income and its stratification over time; the data thereby capture much better the reality of economic life among different social strata more accurately in an era of the growing immaterial economy than the conventional method still in use of arriving at the GDP. The results of their recalibration of the GDP statistic for the United States are remarkable. The distribution of pretax real national income for the years 1980 to 2014 indicate that incomes on average per adult have risen by 60%. However, it has stagnated for the bottom 50 per cent of the distribution at about US\$ 16,000 a year (Piketty, Saez and Zucman, 2018: 553). The rise in inequality is mainly a function of the significant increase in capital rather than labor income.[82]

Moreover, financialization transforms the *power structure* of society and of corporations. The managerial "class" and managerial knowledge give way to the control of corporations by financiers, activist shareholders and financial knowledge. Managerial *compensation* in an increasing number of corporations relies on financial accomplishments such as profits realized, stock prices, and return on equity (cf. Admati, 2017). In other terms, managers are seen to have the fiduciary responsibility to make profits their central, at times only obligation. The *companies* that rise to the top of the hierarchy of profitability, stock market valuations, R&D, and in public appeal as investment opportunities are corporations who design and live off *platforms* on which tangible and intangible goods and services are traded (for instance, Facebook, Uber, Lyft, Airbnb, Amazon):

> The world's largest taxi firm, Uber, owns no cars. The world's most popular media company, Facebook, creates no content. The world's most valuable retailer, Alibaba, carries no stock. And the world's largest accommodation provider, Airbnb, owns no property.
>
> *(cited in Kornberger, Pflueger and Mouritsen, 2017: 82)*

As is in the case of other historically significant changes in society, not all members of society benefit equally from these developments. As inequalities rise, frustrated ambitions and resentment not surprisingly becomes a common feature of the canvas of modern society especially among the young and well educated and among those strata of society that feel they are the victims of a huge zero-sum game in society.

But financialization refers not only and perhaps not even primarily to the growing volume of financial products and the extent to which their turnover far exceeds the value of the transactions of material products as part of the modern economy but to their "qualitative" impact on society at large, for example, as Thibault Darcillon (2015) has determined in a comparative analysis of OECD data on employment protection legislation and worker's bargaining power, financialization tends to reduce worker's bargaining efficacy and the strictness of employment protections.

The origins of financialization can perhaps best be traced to the initial establishment of a company pension fund for the work force of General Motors (GM) in October of 1950 by Charles Wilson, the chief executive officer of the then largest manufacturing company in the United States. GM's pension fund intended to invest in private equities only rather than government securities of the public sector as labor union funds of the day tended to do. For this good reason, the fear of a general loss of influence, for example, by strengthening management, the main labor union of GM, the United Automobile Workers Union (UAW) was skeptical in its assessment of the management proposal. As a matter of fact, the UAW was not supposed to have any influence in the investment decisions of the pension fund: "Instead, the company was to be responsible for the fund, which could be entrusted to professional 'asset managers'. . . . Wilson's major invention was a pension fund investing in the 'American economy'" (Drucker, 1976: 5).

Within a short time after the establishment of the GM pension fund, thousands of new plans had been replicated by corporations copying the plans of GM. Peter Drucker (1976: 4) calls these financial developments the dawn of "Pension Fund Socialism" in the United States where "employees through their pension funds also [become] the legal owners, the suppliers of capital, and the controlling force in the capital market." The outcome of these developments not only is an enormous accumulation of finance capital in search for investment opportunities but

**TABLE 1.1** Total Pension Fund Assets in 2015 in Selected Countries (in US$ Billion)

| | Total Assets 2015 (US$ Billion) | Assets/BIP Ratio (%) |
| --- | --- | --- |
| Australia | 1686 | 113.1 |
| Brazil | 250 | 12.0 |
| Canada | 1304 | 74.7 |
| Chile | 165 | 68.3 |
| France | 12.5 | 0.5 |
| Germany | 234 | 6.6 |
| Hong Kong | 110 | 38.1 |
| India | 11.4 | 0.6 |
| Ireland | 132 | 58.6 |
| Japan | 1221 | 30.2 |
| Mexico | 161 | 13.9 |
| Netherlands | 1282 | 161.1 |
| South Korea | 98.7 | 7.3 |
| Spain | 122 | 9.5 |
| Switzerland | 823 | 125.6 |
| UK | 2685 | 96.0 |
| USA | 14734 | 84.6 |

*Source:* OECD (www.oecd.org/finance/Pension-funds-pre-data-2015.pdf)

also, as Drucker (1976: 71) anticipates that capital market decisions are "effectively shifting from the 'entrepreneurs' to the 'trustees'."

OECD estimates for the year 2014 show that pension fund assets exceeded US$ 25 trillion in member countries. Most of the pension fund allocations are in shares, bonds and real estate assets.[83] In some countries, for example Australia and the United States, almost half of the assets are in equities. In a number of OECD countries, the size of the pension funds exceeds the Gross National Product of the country; this is for example the case for Australia (113.1%), Iceland (146.3%), Netherlands (161.1%) and Switzerland (125.6%). According to OECD figures, the total investment of the pension funds in the United States in 2014 amounted to US$ 14,733,946 million.[84] The United States is the country with the most assets in pension funds. Pensions fund assets tend to be concentrated in a few countries.

More recently, these developments are facilitated by institutional reforms that lead to a thorough liberalization of financial markets in many countries as well as technological developments that ensure the increasing irrelevance of time and place for financial transactions and the speed at which they take place.[85] New forms of money[86] and financial products quicken the pace of life, as Georg Simmel already noted in his seminal *Philosophy of Money*,[87] and do so even more intensely under contemporary circumstances. The larger the number of financial products the larger the number of transactions carried out by a growing number of actors. In the course of the development and growth of the financial markets "the machinery for measuring, modeling, managing, predicting, commoditizing, and *exploiting risk* has become the central diacritic of modern capitalism" (Appadurai, 2011: 522; our emphasis).[88] This means that the incentive to identify risks in the world of financialization is no longer risk avoidance but the opportunity of actively exploiting and profiting from them.

Our succinct definition of financialization as a total social fact does not yet reach deep enough into its multiple impacts, direct and indirect, on social institutions throughout modern society, for example, the importance of new computer and communication technologies or the impact of financial markets on the markets of real goods and services. Financialization also has an impact on state policies, education, sports, wage disparities, social inequality patterns, wealth polarization, and international political and economic relations. Households, governments, corporations, labor unions, political parties, and voters are constrained to make choices depending on the movements of financial markets. Nor does the brief concept of financialization take into account the fact that important social elements of past economic relations are retained under the new regime; for example, without trust, financial transactions[89] would collapse just as quickly as money transactions do (cf. Simmel, [1907] 1989: 178).[90] Last but not least, as one observer insists, financialization and with it "the increasingly autonomous realm of global finance. . . [alters] the inner workings of democracy" (van der Zwan, 2014: 100).

Financialization refers to economic relations that are not bound to and driven by conventional production, the trade and consumption of commodities, or scarcity constraints in the spheres of production and services. Borrowing and lending operations increasingly take place outside the traditional banking system (shadow banks). The importance of traditional credits granted to corporations by banks declines under the growing regime of financialization and the involvement of (large) corporations in the financial world. Immaterial capital relies on less credit than investments in the material economy.

Financialization involves the transfer of income and wealth from the real sectors of the economy to the financial sector. Derived monetary benefits or losses (money from money—but in the sense of interests) such as, for example, increasing or declining asset values, are money from money even if the money is fictitious.[91] Losses and gains are not driven by the price of goods and services. The rise and the decline of asset values are based on intangible or symbolic phenomena such as confidence, fear, desire, greed or trust, even belief, magic and faith. Markets may well tend toward and be about efficiency but not so individual actors on financial markets (Appadurai, 2011: 525).[92]

Shifts in economic and monetary policies often respond to changes in financialization processes rather than to transformations of the "real" economy such as, for example, productivity trends or income distribution. This reversal is one of the significant features of the immaterial economy. An additional significant attribute of financialization and hence of the immaterial economy is its limited impact on employment. The share of employment accounted for by the financial sector as compared to other economic sectors is fairly insignificant and hardly grows over time.[93]

It follows that a growing portion of profits, losses, or income of individuals and corporations "accrue primarily through financial channels rather than through trade and commodity production" (Krippner, 2005: 174). Unsurprisingly, therefore, many corporations seek to enhance their activities in the financial markets, favoring investments in finance rather than production (cf. Epstein, 2005). A growing number of industrial corporations are transformed into "hollow corporations" characterized "by declining production levels, a high share of financial income relative to total income, increased financial assets to total assets ratio, and increased shareholder compensation schemes (through dividend payments, stock buy backs or mergers, acquisitions and corporate restructuring)" (Lagoarde-Segot, 2017: 122–123). The shift of investment from production to finance has led to the poor performance of the real economy.

Figure 1.1 shows that the profitability of the industrial sector in the course of the financial crisis of 2008, arguably so far, the most influential event of the 21st century along with terrorist attacks of 9/11, recovered a little, while the economic share of financial sector profits fell behind. However, original profitability could be re-established quickly in the following years.[94]

Further phenomena to be included under the term of financialization are the deregulation, at least in some countries, of the financial sector, the liberalization of financial flows across national boundaries, new financial instruments (credit default swaps, collateralized debt obligations), the expansion of the role of central banks in gaining independence from governments, the rise of non-banks and hybrid lenders, the creation of financial corporations of non-financial firms in response

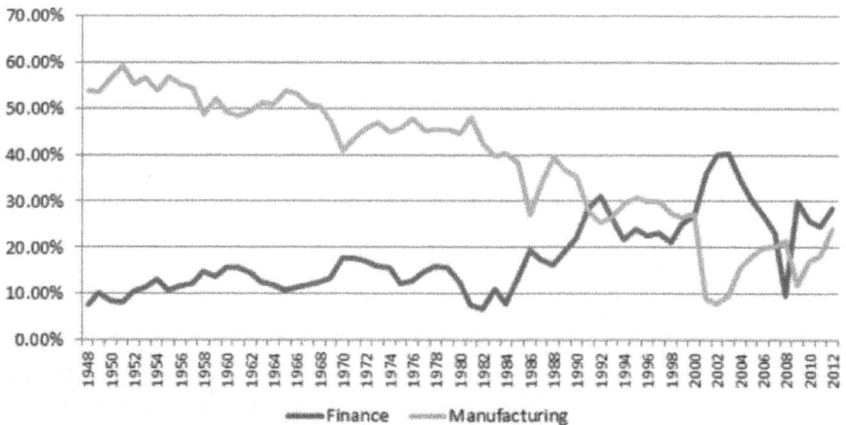

**FIGURE 1.1**   Finance and Manufacturing: Share of All Domestic Corporate Profits

*Source:* Roose 2013

to declining profits in the material economy (Markham, 2002; Orhangazi, 2008; Krippner, 2005), the narrowing-down of financial policies to the maintenance of price stability, the emphasis on the shareholder value (e.g. Ho, 2009; Fligstein, 1990, 2001; Dore, 2008; van der Zwan, 2014: 107–110), the change in power relations within companies (e.g. Zorn, 2004), the impact of financialization on everyday life (e.g. Pryke and Allen, 2000; Pryke and du Gay, 2007; Langley, 2008) and, last but not least, the enhanced fragility of modern societies, for example in the form of severe social crises most recently the financial and economic calamity that started in 2007 (cf. Hein and Mundt, 2011) demonstrating that markets in fact failed to regulate themselves.

Quantifying the consequences of financialization for the economy and society in terms of exact statistical measures remains, for the time being, very difficult. Any adequate quantitative account of the volume of financialization activities would have to cover not only the activities of the financial sector as such (for example, the activities of banks, brokers, hedge funds, finance companies, insurance companies) but also the financial actions of corporations in the traditional economic sector that attempt to make profits from financial transactions rather than productive activities (cf. Krippner, 2005: 186–188).[95]

Whether the transformation of the economy and society in terms of financialization represents a gravitational shift and a new stage in the evolution of capitalism (or in what Frank Knight, [1950: 470] calls an "entrepreneurial economy") is a controversial matter (cf. Foster, 2007). One point the many studies on financialization are unanimous about, however, is the observation that the finance sector is taking on a life of its own while losing a large part of its traditional function as a provider of capital for the real economy. Moreover, there is growing agreement that financialization is a societal force and a complex subject matter (a total social fact) that in its level of impact resembles globalization and neo-liberalism in terms of power, scale, speed and complexity.[96]

With growing financialization, criticism of the profound social consequences of financialization is growing, just as condemnation of globalization is rising louder and louder with its increasingly clear implications, and the once dominant narrative of the economists, which emphasized its positive consequences, is becoming quieter and quieter.

However, the agreement about the trend toward financialization has from the very beginning been accompanied by distinctive warnings, for example about the sustainability of the process, global imbalances, the stability or instability of financial markets, the limited ability to intervene into the process of financialization, a propensity for overconsumption (see Hein and Mundt, 2011: 27–28)[97] and the possibility of detrimental as well as unintended consequences for the society and the economy (cf. Schiller, 2003). James Tobin (1984: 14–15), for example, explicitly admits

> to an uneasy Physiocratic suspicion . . . that we are throwing more and more of our resources . . . into financial activities remote from the production of

goods and services, to activities that generate high private rewards disproportionate to their social productivity. . . . I fear, as Keynes saw even in his
day, the advantages of the liquidity and negotiability of financial instruments come at the cost of facilitating nth-degree speculation which is short
sighted and inefficient.

Given that the umbrella concept of financialization covers a wide range of phenomena as well as their peculiar consequences, different authors have emphasized
different aspects, from the growing influence of a rentier class[98] (resonating with
discussions in the first part of the last century, for example Hilferding ([1910] 2006),
but also with Keynes' [1936] analysis of mature capitalism)[99] to the increasing inequality regarding incomes, wealth and social security to the shift of talent into financial institutions to the creation and proliferation of new financial instruments.[100]

The financial sector share of income grows over time.[101] However, as Thomas
Philippon and Ariell Reshef (2013: 17) have documented "even within high-
income countries finance reaches very different sizes and represents very different
shares of the economy. In particular, the United States financial sector experiences
the largest rise in the share of its financial sector." Moreover, there is no established correlation between the increase of the share of the financial sector in an
economy and economic growth in a country.

A couple of largely unexamined but looming questions about the impact of
financialization (and its preferred digital infrastructure) concern, first, the future
growth of the economy and the uneven development of economies within countries and across regions around the globe or, as this question can also be framed,
will (capitalist) economies continue to grow? A necessary part of our set of questions is the extent to which financialization is capable to obliterate the so-called
"real" economy. Or whether it has to reply on the real economy as its foundation,
for example, a "circuitous link between stable income sources and financial speculation" (Leyshon and Thrift, 2007: 98).

Second, a related issue is, of course, the extent to which future economic
development will be compatible with environmental constraints. Is financialization perhaps even the lever that will bring about the convergence of economic
and ecological goals? In any case, the production of new ideas, symbolic capital,
financialization and comparable elements of the developing symbolic economy
requires much less energy than was still the case for the conditions and products of
the world of industrial society. This fact explains the disparity between economic
growth and energy consumption in recent decades (cf. Smil, 2017: 345).

The optimistic outlook Keynes ([1930] 1963: 365–366)[102] communicated in
the early thirties of the last century made no reference to environmental limitations and was rarely seconded in later decades. On the contrary, pessimism about
the future of an economy and society that stick to the path of business-as-usual
kept growing, resurrecting Thomas Malthus' famous argument and culminating in
the 1970 Club of Rome Report *The Limits to Growth*.

Among the few optimistic voices, albeit not from the world of politics but from a professional perspective, is Harry Saunders (2016: 28), known as an international expert on energy efficiency and consumption who argues that a reconciliation of ecological and economic aspirations is possible, and that economic growth will end. Saunders claims to be able to demonstrate echoing Keynes that "both neo-classical growth theory and empirical evidence suggest that capitalist economies do not require endless growth but are rather much more likely to evolve toward a steady state once consumption demands of the global population have been satisfied. Those demands demonstrably saturate once economies achieve a certain level of affluence. For these reasons, a capitalist economy is as likely as any other to see stable and declining demands on natural resources and ecological services." However, Harry Saunders is silent about the role of financialization and the shift toward an immaterial economy underway in the process he forecasts.

But even in a world of an immaterial economy, driven to a significant extent by the advance of financialization, the consumption of finite material resources and its contribution to the depletion of the very environmental conditions that sustain and enable this kind of economy is unlikely to cease. Even without major wars, radical societal transformations and significant technological break-throughs (to borrow the terms of the Keynesian perspective) growing finan-cialization will at best be capable of postponing the clash of economic and ecological goals.

Since financial resources and financial stability and instability have always been part of economic and social relations, we will, first, examine how financialization has emerged and spread as a potent force in economic relations. A number of observers date the onset of the era of financialization at about 1980 (e.g. Aglietta and Breton, 2001; Krippner, 2005). In the wake of the financial crisis (2007–2009) prompted by speculative mortgage lending in the United States and spreading globally, the ascendancy of financial processes has increased significantly, as has the scholarly interest in and the public awareness of financialization.

Prior to the mid-1970s, the financial sector was heavily regulated and subject to control by banks. Since the mid-1970s, however, financial indicators such as the indices of the leading stock exchanges around the world have become more decisive for economic conduct than the more tangible indicators of economic hardship or well-being such as the growth or decline of employment, or, for that matter, wages that selectively rise, stagnate or even decrease. In a second step, we will examine the influence of financialization on the money value of labor, capital, land and knowledge.

Gerald Davis and Suntae Kim (2015: 204) see the reasons for the extension of financial markets in a combination of political, technological and ideological factors: "The spread of financial markets was enabled by the confluence of sup-portive ideology and historical circumstance, economic theories that allowed the creation of financial instruments, and information technology that sped up their valuation."

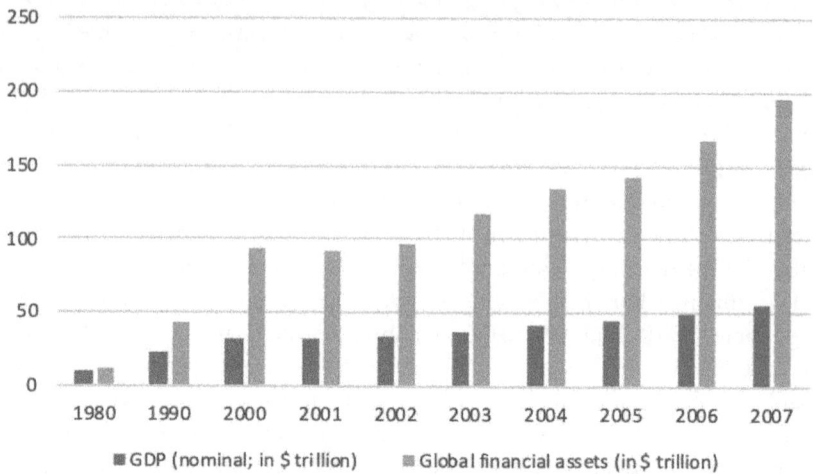

**FIGURE 1.2**   Nominal GDP and Global Financial Assets, 1980–2007

*Source:* Bone 2015: 888

Not surprisingly for a sociological analysis of major societal transformations, a central role in the emergence and development of financialization is assigned to a new social class. In this case, this role is obtained by the global class as Ralf Dahrendorf, one of the most astute observers of social inequality in the post-war era, aptly proposes.

## The Global Class

The emergence of the global class, described by Ralf Dahrendorf (2000a) as a social class in the classic sense of the concept, can be traced back to the far-reaching social, political and economic consequences of the end of the Cold War in the last decade of the 20th century. However, it is not the end of the Cold War or its consequences as such that allowed for the emergence of the new global class (see also Sklair, 2002). Rather, the end of the bipolar world accelerated and made manifest the processes that led to this emergence. The transformation Dahrendorf has in mind is, of course, usually described as the globalization process. The global class operates independently of national boundaries and nation states.[103] The economic activities of the global class encompass both those of the industrial age, that is, the production and trade of commodities, and those of the world of financialization.[104] It is in this sense that Thomas Piketty ([2013] 2014: 424), too, notes the growing gap between the "classes" who make their income from financial products or from labor, respectively: "The growing sophistication of capital markets and financial intermediation tends to separate owners from managers more and more and thus to sharpen the distinction between pure capital income and labor income."

Dahrendorf, in line with his reputation as a conflict theorist—as he himself emphasizes—(Dahrendorf, 2000b: 5), stresses the contradictions and antagonisms of the economic and social forces brought about by globalization.[105] What is described as globalization are new economic and social forces that, however, cannot be conceptualized as productive forces: "Even 'services' in the old sense in which Colin Clark and Jean Fourastier used the term is not an appropriate description" (Dahrendorf, 2000b: 5).

The decisive new forces are *informational assets* or skills as well as informational technologies (computerization, digitization, miniaturization, satellite communication, internet, and fiber optics) that "in principle" ensure simultaneous and worldwide access to these informational assets (whether relevant or irrelevant). The proper name for the society that is evolving is, therefore, *information society*. The information society is a social reality, as real as the power of the elite or global class that controls it.

New forces create new interests. The globalization process brings about the new global class with its unique class-specific consciousness, its optimistic outlook and message of hope. Members of the global class are, for example, inventors and investors, users and owners, media professionals and professors, who expect benefits from their affiliation to the new class and represent around one percent of the population.[106] Ruling classes do *not* have to control everything. Their rule is based on their access to "invisible [intangible] treasures." The members of the global class set the tone and control values and behaviors; in addition, "the global class has a train of people who are dependent on them. They range from technicians and other direct helpers, secretaries, security guards, agents for this and agents for that, to those who provide private comforts" (Dahrendorf, 2000b: 7).

However, "[t]he global class does not need all the work which in principle is available. It needs computers but not workers. When I write my planned book about this class and the new conflicts, I shall call it *Capital Without Labour*." (Dahrendorf, 2000b: 12). The fateful link between labor and capital once described particularly by Marx, but also by many other observers and analysts, is severed. Capital and labor under auspices of the global class are no longer locked in a common destiny. The global class, as we have seen, "can do without the work of many . . . a large portion of the 40 percent without higher education remain not needed by the rest" (Dahrendorf, 2000b: 12).

Although the dominance and victory of the global class is not assured, neoliberal economic policies with their distinct emphasis on deregulation define and promote the interests of the global class. Without the deregulation of the financial markets no information society would have been possible. The public emphasis is on personality traits such as creativity, flexibility, initiative, education and innovation as well as on the praise of the virtues of entrepreneurship. In short,

> [m]eritocracy, the availability of opportunities to all who seek merit, is part of the global class consciousness. So is the construction of a life world that can last. The global class is quite young. . . . It also wants sustainable social conditions, that is, a welfare state that endures.
>
> *(Dahrendorf, 2000b: 8–9)*

Due to the control they exert over the resources of the information society, the power of the global class is colossal. Our society is a slave to the global class. Although the ruling class is not omnipotent, they are definitely setting the tone in many areas of the world community since 1989 (Dahrendorf, 2000b: 6). The rise of the global class and the dominance it has gained in the knowledge economy will bring about a momentous change in the amount of socially necessary labor (see also Stehr, 2002).

This is what Dahrendorf (2000b: 12) calls the age of *capital without work*. The working society (*Arbeitsgesellschaft*) crumbles and is about to disappear. What is becoming visible is not only new forms of inequality that will be central to the emerging forms of social conflict in a society that runs out of labor but also the weakening of social control as a result of the transformation of the nature of work. The key problem faced by the new society, however, is that work has lost its role as an agent of societal control.

As Ralf Dahrendorf (2000b: 15) resignedly concludes: "Since the disadvantaged, as we have seen, are already disinclined to participate in associations either political or general, they tend towards apathy, and the apathy of the many is always the other side of the unchecked power of the few." Dahrendorf fears that new forms of authoritarianism will take hold in place of democracy. "If work fails to bring about the social control of the disadvantaged, that objective has to be achieved in some other way."

The pessimistic assessment concerning a significant decrease in the volume of socially necessary work is echoed almost two decades later by observers predicting the disappearance of a significant portion of the jobs that today are performed by humans, on the one hand, and wondering what the impact on the political order is likely to be if a large proportion of the benefits accrue to machines that are physically stronger and intellectually quicker than human workers, on the other. The prospects for democracy, as Dahrendorf also feared, might be quite limited. "A small upper class will largely rely on technology to serve its needs. Meanwhile, a large lower class will have very little of value to offer a shrinking labor market" (Mounk and Drutman, 2016). Decreased material well-being constrains individual liberty. The lack of the requisite cognitive skills in a world where the robots rise is the basis for a rise in apathy and skepticism toward a democratic political order.

## Conclusion: The Price (and Value) of Land, Capital, Labor and Knowledge

> Scientific knowledge like land, labor, and capital, is a resource—indeed a commodity—and the ability to manipulate and control this resource has profound implications for the distribution of political power in democratic societies.
>
> —*Dorothy Nelkin, 1979: 118*

In the course of our reflections on the modern immaterial economy and the role and price of four productive forces, which will be further elaborated in the following chapters of our study, we seem to have come to an initial, preliminary conclusion: We no longer live in a society where the products of the real economy obtain a key role; where the conventional social classes compete for the benefits of the productive process; where the nation state is a crucial actor and arbitrator in the lives of its members; where the population is convinced that the cultural and national borders are not porous; and where the future is more or less an extension of the past.

The world of financialization and, more generally, any process determining prices and values can be described as a *wicked* issue where consequences are uncertain and stakes are high. In contrast, a *tame* topic refers to problems that are complicated but characterized by defined and achievable final states. Originally described by Rittel and Webber (1973) in the context of urban planning, *wicked* problems are issues that are often formulated as being susceptible to (simple) solutions when in fact they are not. In other words, translating the price and value of the means of production into simple abstract and context-free units is not only a laborious but also a risky process, as we will show in detail in the following chapters.

## Notes

1. Our translation.
2. This means that only a few "countries, if any, are able to control their own currency. There is a loss of one of the main levers of power and influence" (Bell, 1987: 9).
3. Alain Touraine ([1984] 1988: 104) describes the transition to a post-industrial society in an analogous sense as a transformation of the economy that occurs "when investment results in the production of symbolic goods that modify values, needs, representations, far more than in the production of material goods or even of 'services.' Industrial society had transformed the means of production; postindustrial society changes the ends of production, that is, culture."
4. Our understanding of the symbolic economy transcends the idea of a "data-intensive information" economy or an informational economy in which digital networks of communication, computation, data infrastructures, digital content such as the aggregation of information and other mostly (sophisticated) technical devices are seen to dominate economic processes.
5. Although the issue of the (geographic) mobility of the means of economic production is not part of the core of our analysis of the immaterial economy, it should be noted

that the mobility of the means of production and the mobility of their combination (corporations) is not in most instances enhanced in the immaterial economy. For example, large (modern) corporations attract and are attracted to specific locations because of a centering of a high skilled labor force.

6. Georg Simmel (1904: 134) in his sociological analysis of fashion already refers to the split of markets in the case of the transitive fashion: "The absolute indifference of fashion to the material standards of life is well illustrated by the way in which it recommends something appropriate in one instance, something abstruse in another, and something materially and aesthetically quite different in a third. The only motivation with which fashion is concerned are formal social norms."

7. We prefer the term immaterial/symbolic economy to alternative concepts that may be found in the literature or in policy discussions that describe some of the same phenomena and socio-economic transformations that are of interest to us. The idea that we are on the verge of heading toward a "*digital economy*" could be such an example for an apparently alternative term. However, digitalization or digital technology merely means the representation of information in bits. Our position would be that the concept of an immaterial/symbolic economy is broader and more inclusive than digital economy by incorporating social phenomena that originated and were a part of the industrial or post-industrial economy, for example, the motives that drive economic action, the categories of actors that are part of the economy, the employment patterns or the indicators employed to assess the nature or the failure of economic life.

8. This is not a novel observation. We concur for example with Michel Foucault's (2007: 95) observations in his lectures Collége de France lectures on „security, territory, population" that the political economy is a key to political power in as much as governance is executed "in the form, and according to the model, of economy." Economic reasoning provides the foundation for the assessment of the adequacy and efficacy of modern governance. This continues to be the case today. For an interpretation of the engagement of Foucault with (ordo-)liberal political economic thought (see Guala, 2006).

9. One specific demand that recurs from time to time is to introduce "financial literacy programs" as part of the curriculum. A study on the level of financial information among the general public in the United States suggests that a considerable confidence in and lack of knowledge about financial matters indeed co-exist (see Jeff Sommer, "What you think you know about money, but don't, can hurt you," *New York Times*, July 23, 2016.

10. For a substantive critique, shared by us, of the theory of the emerging "knowledge economy" and especially narrow notions of knowledge as widely employed in the economics literature see Mirowski (1990).

11. Efforts to measure the shift in investment patterns are only at its beginnings (see McGrattan, 2017; Davis, 2017).

12. Since the early 1980s, when the US Administration decided to stop collecting data on market share that companies held within their industries, the exact market share companies hold within each industry is, at least in the United States, not transparent.

13. In the summer of 2018, Google was fined five billion euros by the European Commission. The fine is being appealed by Google.

14. Greta Krippner (2005: 177) defines a highly monetized symbolic economy as an "accumulation-centered" economy as opposed to the "activity-centered" idea of a post-industrial society. An accumulation-centered view of economic change focuses on the sites where profits are made (which excludes the public sector since the latter has no equivalent to the concept of profit that defines the private sector of the economy; it also tends to exclude income from self-employment).

15. Economists have frequently taken the undemanding approach and treated knowledge and information as fully interchangeable phenomena; or, at least, economists see no

meaningful distinction between information and knowledge (Nelson, 1959 or Arrow, 1962) and, more recently, Stiglitz (2017: 14) who suggests „knowledge can be thought of as a particular form of information." For the frequent and often careless conflation of the concepts of information and knowledge also: Castells ([1996] 2000: 218), Urry (2003: 64–65), Ungar (2008: 311–312), Proctor and Schiebinger (2008: 2–3), Drew et al. (2013: 50–51) and Rimes, Welch, and Bozeman (2014: 156–157). The frequent assertion that knowledge and information are virtually equivalent prompts us to add the concept information to the discussion of the knowledge-based economy in an effort to advance the point that it is helpful to distinguish between information and knowledge (Machlup, 1979; Ancori, Bureth and Cohendt, 2000: 259–265; Adolf and Stehr, 2017).

16. For social theorists committed to a Marxist perspective it is beyond dispute that Karl Marx anticipates the formation of the modern knowledge-based economy in his critique of the classical political economy published as the *Grundrisse* in 1939. In the literature, the origins of or the "tipping point" toward a knowledge-centered economy are a highly contested matter. One such example in addition to the position attributed to Marx is the definition of a "genuine" knowledge-based economy by Manuel Castells ([1996] 2000: 219). Knowledge, according to Castells, was already the basis of productivity growth in the economy of modern societies as industrial employment reached its climax in the first half of the 20th century.

17. It is important to note that André Gorz' ([2003] 2010: 35) conception of knowledge is much more comprehensive than most definitions of knowledge usually found in observations about the knowledge that defines the knowledge economy. The definition is often restricted to knowledge in terms of strictly scientific or technical knowledge. Gorz's definition covers a heterogeneity of social and intellectual capacities that are associated with knowledge and therefore has a considerable affinity to our notion of *knowledge skills*. Nonetheless, Gorz attributes a considerable measure of immediate power to knowledge as such.

18. Our skepticism about the time and place of knowledge-based economies does not extend to the a-historical assertion that knowledge-based economies have been and are universal, as W. Edward Steinmüller (2006: 211) for instance claims: "There is no immediately obvious reason to believe that that contemporary economic activities are inherently more knowledge-intensive than those of the past . . . manufacturing and service activities have always involved knowledge inputs." If one defines knowledge as an anthropological constant then the inference that knowledge-based economic activities of course are universal. But his is not the claim made by most theorists with an interest in knowledge-based economies. Their claim is a relational claim. The claim is about a changing and not a fixed role of knowledge in economic processes, for example, in the development of technology.

19. Our critique of the orthodox treatment of knowledge also applies to notion that the power of knowledge as derivative or in concert with its place at the top of a hierarchical image of data, information, knowledge and—even superior to knowledge—wisdom (Rowley, 2007). Within the confines of this hierarchy, the transformation of information into knowledge, for example, represents a person's use of information. But how the separation is achieved remains a mystery.

20. Michel Foucault ([1997] 2003: 27–34) can be interpreted to embrace a notion of knowledge that moves it close to a conception convinced of the immediacy with which knowledge confers power. But it is the knowledge apparatus that forms the immediate dagger of knowledge. Foucault assigns particular relevance not to intentions or decisions but to study power from within its field of application, its target or object. In its field of application, it is "the actual instruments that form and accumulate knowledge, the observational methods, the recording techniques, the investigative research procedures, the verification mechanism" constitute power leverage. The

"delicate mechanism of power cannot function unless knowledge, or rather knowledge apparatuses are formed, organized, and put into circulation, and those apparatuses are not ideological trimmings or edifices" (Foucault, [1997] 2003: 33–34).

21. One recent example of what we have described as a rather common assertion in the literature about the close linkage between information and knowledge may be sufficient in as much as Jonathan Haskel and Stan Westlake (2017: 64) only reiterate a point almost consistently made in past observations on knowledge and information: "We define knowledge as connections made between pieces of information supported by evidence." "Pieces" of information—in a modernized definition—refer to "anything that can be digitized thereby implicitly defining information as digitized data" (Haskel and Westlake, 2017: 64). If such a (intangible?) thing as a piece of information might indeed the identified, the task of naming the value of information would advance measurably. However, where a piece of information begins and ends remains a mystery.

22. The concept of modern society as a network society can already be found in a *Wall Street Journal* article by Peter Drucker (1995; March 29, page A12) entitled "The Network Society."

23. Georg Simmel ([1900] 2004: 415) formulates the same idea in his *Philosophy of Money* as follows "once expressed, the thought remains indivisibly bound up with the personality as a constantly reproducible content in a manner that has no analogy in the economic sphere." Robert K. Merton's ([1949] 1968: 27–28, 35–37) metaphor "incorporation by obliteration" reminds us that such a link can be rather fragile and not only in the scientific community to which Merton's observation originally applies.

24. Our observation on the lack of instrumental characteristics of (scientific) knowledge is a controversial observation: in an editorial of the journal *Nature*, for example, there is the demand that science, not politics, should determine the price of: "any useful assessment of the carbon price must take into account the full range of scientific and economic research, and not bend to the political proclivities of those in charge" ("Pricing the planet," Volume 541, 19. January 2017, p. 260). The statement of the lead article undoubtedly leaves some room for interpretation when it comes to the question of *who exactly* sets the price of carbon.

25. It is important to alert, at this early stage, to the essential difficulties faced by organizations such as the OECD that are trying to measure knowledge and its economic consequences. Fred Gault (2006) highlights these difficulties and emphasizes the need to address the methodological and theoretical challenges bound up with measurement methods for knowledge-intensive economies. The historical origins of measuring the value of all economic activities in a country (Gross National Product) are an equally complicated story well documented for instance in Ehsan Masood's *The Great Invention. The Story of the GPD and the Making (and Unmaking) of the Modern World* (2016).

26. See also Paul Mason, "The end of capitalism has begun," in *The Guardian*, URL: www.theguardian.com/books/2015/jul/17/postcapitalism-end-of-capitalism-begun. (accessed 14 July 2019).

27. Yann Moulier Boutang ([2008] 2011: 57) defines third, or cognitive, capitalism in contrast to earlier forms of capitalism (mercantile and industrial) as based on an "accumulation in which the object of accumulation consists mainly of knowledge, which becomes the basic source of value, as well as the principal location of the process of valorisation. Issues such as property rights, positioning in networks, alliances and project management become the major institutional and organizational factors." Boutang's conception of a third capitalism formation therefore conforms to most definitions of the foundations of the modern knowledge economy.

28. Without even referring to the so-called work of post-modernity, for instance Lyotard, ([1979] 1994); critique Luhmann, 1997: 1143–1149; Adolf and Stehr, 2017: 199–204.

29. The same conceptual vacuum may be observed in many discussions surrounding the notion of a post-growth society.

30. In the wake of the "currency crisis" in the third week of September 1992, the *New York Times* (September 23, 1992, Section C1) was prompted to observe that "on a dull day, hundreds of billions of dollars worth of marks, yen, dollars and other currencies change hands, as speculators bet on the direction of currency markets and money managers seek opportunities overseas. On a busy day, volume can top a trillion dollars. That is a lot of money. And as last week proved, the combined power of all these traders can overwhelm the power of governments, even when all of Europe is trying to act in concert. The events provided a bitter reminder to central bankers and finance ministers around the world that the power of Governments to control economies and currencies has eroded."

31. Arjun Appadurai (2012: 9) comments on the proximity of derivative trading and discourse about derivatives to magical thinking.

32. Financial crises of different magnitude are not a new phenomenon. Charles Kindleberger (1989) lists some twenty financial dislocations during the 19th and 20th centuries.

33. "Worldwide markets *hemorrhaged more than $3 trillion in paper wealth* on Friday and Monday, according to data from S&P Global, even worse than in the 2008 financial crisis. About $1.3 trillion of those Brexit-inspired losses came from U.S. markets alone" (CNBC).

34. In 1986, Peter Drucker (1986: 782) provides the following figures to illustrate this claim: "World trade in goods is larger, much larger, than it has ever been before. And so is the 'invisible trade,' the trade in services. Together, the two amount to around $2.5 trillion to $3.0 trillion a year. But the London Eurodollar market, in which the world's financial institutions borrow and lend to each other, turns over $300 billion each working day, or $75 trillion a year, a volume at least 25 times that of world trade." In 2013, the daily average exchange transactions in US$ reached 6,671,446 Million (Source: Bank for International Settlement, 2014).

35. We will discuss the idea of financialization at greater length later in this chapter. For a basic definition we can turn at this point to Aalbers (2015): "the increasing dominance of financial actors, markets, practices, measurements and narratives at various scales, resulting in a structural transformation of economies, firms (including financial institutions), states and households."

36. The distinction between *tangible* and *intangible* capital resonates to a degree with our differentiation between monetary and non-monetary commodities: "Intangible capital largely falls into two main categories: on the one hand, investment geared to the production and dissemination of knowledge (i.e. in training, education, R & D, information and coordination); on the other, investment geared to sustaining the physical state of human capital (healthcare expenditures). In the USA, the current value of the stock of intangible capital (devoted to knowledge creation and human capital) began to outweigh that of tangible capital (physical infrastructure and equipment, inventories, natural resources) at the end of the 1960s" (David and Forey, 2003: 21; Brynjolfsson, Hitt and Yang, 2002).

37. A helpful definition of the use of the term "culture" in this context is offered by Alain Touraine's (1998: 140) notion that it refers "to the voluntaristic construction of set of norms and practices" (also Swidler, 1995). The cultural norms and practices are different in different societies.

38. Georg Simmel ([1907] 1989: 181) also correctly describes why money that has no intrinsic value is still bound up with trust or confidence in modern societies: "The association and unification of constantly expanding social groups, supported by laws, customs and interests, is the basis for the diminishing intrinsic value of money and its replacement by functional value."

39. As we will have occasion to stress in our discussion of knowledge about knowledge, we feel that Peter Drucker overestimates the *immediate* societal power of knowledge. Our interpretation is based on, for example, Drucker's (1993: 46) observation about the power of knowledge: "The shift from knowledge to [specialized] knowledges has given knowledge *the power to create a new society*" [our emphasis].

40. As Albert Borgmann (1992: 61) notes—and as every (small) bank customer is also well aware of: "Capital is less real than land; it is relatively mobile and, as financial capital, quite intangible. But the latter is always within hailing distance on being properly balanced with material goods."

41. As is well known, 19th-century social theory, for example Emile Durkheim, was particularly concerned with the phenomena of property and labor. Social scientists were convinced that humanity was about to enter an era where property would become obsolete and labor would have a very different social, political and economic status. Our immediate focus here, however, is not on the nature of the totality of changes in these social constructs conceived of as independent entities, nor on the ways in which labor and property can be used to identify major social formations in modern society. We will be more concerned with the reduced economic and, therefore, societal relevance of these constructs as productive forces. Of course, the social, legal, and political conceptions and predominant symbolic functions of these phenomena are likely to be transformed as a consequence of their less prominent status in the production process (cf. Luhmann's [1988: 151–176] discussion of the cognitive significance and decline of capital and work as salient categories of social theory).

42. In his examination of the economy as a social system (*Die Wirtschaft der Gesellschaft*), Niklas Luhmann (1988: 164–166) attributes the decline of the theoretical and practical relevance of capital and labor to their neglect of the demand and consumption side of modern economic activity. Patterns of social inequality (*Lebenslagen*) among workers, for example, are much more strongly determined by consumption activities than by wage differentials.

43. In the course of past economic successes and failures, the transformation of nature by man in the last two centuries has reached the point where the prevailing natural landscape is a man-made landscape. From an economic point of view, therefore, it has become almost impossible to distinguish between the rent that may accrue to property due to its natural advantage and the quasi-rent of the same property that is due to its transformation by man (see also the discussion of the change in the meaning of the term "rent" in Piketty, [2013] 2014: 422–424).

44. The essentially contested nature or ambivalence of the concept of knowledge economy can easily be documented by reference to historians who posit a link between the beginning of the knowledge economy and the beginning and development of the industrial revolution between 1750 and 1850: see, for example, the work of Margaret Jacob (2014) who emphasizes the role of education as the foundation of the industrial revolution.

45. Florian Znaniecki (1940: 23), for example, emphasizes "every individual who performs any social role is supposed by his social circle to possess and believes himself to possess the knowledge indispensable for its normal performance."

46. Cf. Georg Simmel's ([1908] 1992: 383–455) analysis of secrets and secret societies.

47. By the same token, and as Anthony Giddens (1990: 21) observed, "modernity has not just recently become an 'information society': it was such from its very beginnings. Indeed, the control and dissemination of information, as facilitated through the invention of printing, was one of the main conditions making possible modernity's rise."

48. Taking into consideration the entire range and history of human societies, it is, as Thorstein Veblen ([1908] 1919: 334) notes, not until late "in the life-history of material civilisation that ownership of the industrial equipment, in the narrower sense in which that phrase is commonly employed, comes to be the dominant and typical method

engrossing the immaterial equipment," that is, the intangible assets or stocks of knowledge (as well as the practice of ways and means) of a community or society. Even in the industrial age, capital goods are not made such by their material constituents. Rather, as Veblen ([1908] 1919: 349–350) also notes, such assets are turned into capital goods by the way human agents deal with the means at their disposal and by the way "human technology" relates to material goods.

49. As Daniel Bell (1968: 160) argues, "post-industrial society, necessarily, becomes a meritocracy." Nico Stehr showed that knowledge may indeed become the basis for inequality regimes in modern society, displacing the more traditional bases for the formation of inequality (Stehr, 1999); however, such a theory of inequality, and therefore the future of inequality, is not necessarily in line with the discussion of inequality that is based on a narrow conception of knowledge—as mirrored, for example, in different degrees of formal education.

50. A critique of the concept of modern economy as a knowledge economy may be found in Bregje van Eekelen's (2014: 1) essay where he insists that the idea of the knowledge economy is mobilized by its proponents "to redraw the map so that endangered economies can regain their challenged sense of centrality in a world economy." Could it be that van Eekelen's critique is itself another overestimation of the immediate power of ideas?

51. One of the "necessary conditions of rationality" of economic action becomes, as Talcott Parsons ([1938] 1964: 22) for example stresses "the knowledge should be scientifically valid. Valid empirical knowledge in this sense . . . consists of concepts and propositions and their logical interrelations."

52. A theory of modern society as a knowledge society does not begin with, or somehow rely on, Steve Fuller's premise that the supply of knowledge creates its own demand, in the sense of Say's Theorem. More precisely, Steve Fuller's (1992: 174) argument is that no knowledge is supposed to be "useless and unassailable, though determining its many uses may require the generation of still more knowledge." As we will try to show, the demand for additional or incremental knowledge is, on the contrary, based—although by no means solely—on economic motives.

53. Compare the affinity of our definition of knowledge as a capacity to act to Gilbert Ryle's ([1945] 1971) distinction between knowledge-how, in contrast to knowledge-that. As Ryle ([1945] 1971: 215) argues, philosophers "assume that intelligence equates with the contemplation of propositions and is exhausted in this contemplation. I want to turn the tables and to prove that knowledge-how cannot be defined in terms of knowledge-that." It follows that it is a fallacy to suppose "that the primary exercise of minds consists in finding the answers to questions and that their other occupations are merely applications of considered truths or even regrettable distractions from their consideration" (Ryle, 1949: 30). Also, Pierre Bourdieu's (2015: 250) notion of knowledge mediating between habitus and the world has an affinity to our conception of knowledge as a capacity to act: "to strike with a hammer is an act of knowledge."

54. In some instances, the discussion of the role of knowledge in social action is quite restricted to this rather elementary undifferentiated observation. But in such a case, knowledge hardly lends itself to sociological or economic analysis. For example, sociological inquiry requires some idea of the extent to which knowledge operates not merely as a condition *for* social action but as a stratified phenomenon *in* social action.

55. Tolerance for the incompleteness of knowledge in the scientific community (a.k.a. "research takes time") is linked to the missing impetus to action as constitutive for scientific knowledge. The probability that myths and half-truths are employed by large segments of the population in "advanced" societies may well be even more characteristic of crisis situations in which various dangers appear to be imminent, as Norbert Elias (1989: 500–501) for example notes. In this respect, present-day societies do not differ from so-called "primitive" societies in which similar responses were elicited by the

dangers brought about by illness, draught, thunderstorms or floods. However, Elias is convinced that this state of affairs can be corrected in principle as adequate knowledge is diffused more widely throughout society.

56. Georg Simmel's observations may have been inspired by Goethe's dictum "Im Anfang war die Tat" ("in the beginning was the deed").

57. For an informative account of the "information age" and the role of Claude Shannon and Norbert Wiener in originating "cybernetics" and the more narrow "information theory" that became part of everyday engineering and computer science while Norbert Wiener's cybernetics had a philosophical bent, more interested in analog signals (see Kline, 2015).

58. As Hans Blumenberg ([1966] 1982: 239–240) stresses, Francis Bacon thereby advances "a concept of human happiness . . . that separated theory from existential fulfillment by reducing the necessary knowledge to the amount fixed by the requirements of domination over natural reality. . . . The subject of theory and the subject of the successful life no longer needed to be identical."

59. The conception of knowledge proposed here resonates with Ludwig von Mises' (1922: 14) *sociological* definition of *property*. Von Mises suggests that as a sociological category, "property represents the capacity to determine the use of economic goods." The ownership of knowledge and, thus, the control over knowledge are not as a rule exclusive. Juridically, however, this exclusivity is stipulated as a definition of property, or of the institution of property. Formal law, as is well known, recognizes owners and proprietors; it in particular recognizes individuals that should have, but have not. From a legal point of view, property is indivisible. Also, the nature of the concrete—material or immaterial—"things" at issue is irrelevant. The sociological meaning of knowledge is also primarily defined by the actual ability to dispose of knowledge as an asset.

60. The Karl Mannheim citation originates with a 1930 lecture series (here first lecture) at Manchester College, Oxford entitled "Planned society and the problem of human personality: A sociological analysis." We have changed the citation slightly based on the original manuscript.

61. Proceeding from the basic idea that knowledge constitutes a capacity for action, one can, of course, develop distinctive categories or forms of knowledge depending on the enabling *function* knowledge is supposed to fulfill. We assume that Jean-Francois Lyotard's ([1979] 1984: 6) attempt to differentiate between "payment knowledge" and "investment knowledge" (in analogy to the distinction between expenditures for consumption and expenditures for investment) is an example of such a functional differentiation between more or less distinctive forms of knowledge.

62. Similar conceptions may be found in Friedrich Hayek's 1945 examination of the "use of knowledge in society," written well before his embarrassing admiration for the government of Augusto Pinochet which in fact is a treatise in praise of decentralization, the importance, for action, of knowledge about local circumstances, and the price system as an agent that communicates information and constitutes the answer to the question of coordinating local knowledges. Hayek (1945: 523) emphasizes that "as long as things continue as before, or at least as they were expected to, there arise no new problems requiring a decision, no need to form a new plan."

63. As we have discussed elsewhere, reducing the knowledge produced by the scientific community to instrumental or technical knowledge is far too restrictive. Scientists are also meaning producers. Especially social science knowledge is of value because it generates meaning. Literary talents are not a lost art in the sciences. The model of the usefulness of the social sciences in terms of meaning production does not focus on the practical choices made by actors but on processes of meaning that may subsequently engender choices (cf. Stehr and Ruser, 2017).

64. An example of the misleading assumption that knowledge is immediately productive may be found in Gary Becker and Kevin Murphy's (1992: 1138) discussion of the

benefits of the division of labor in organizations; the authors, in an effort to specify the ideas of the productivity of the division of labor proposed by Adam Smith, stress that "the productivity of specialists at particular tasks depends on how much knowledge they have." In Becker and Murphy's discussion, the causation does not go as in Smith from the division of labor to greater knowledge but from greater "general" knowledge to a more extensive division of labor and to more task-specific knowledge. Knowledge is however defined very much as human capital such as years of schooling and thereby remains treated as a black box.

65. Knowledge that lacks some of the attributes philosophy of science perspectives specify in order to distinguish or highlight knowledge that is not faulty knowledge, based on its factual accurateness for instance, does not assure that such knowledge may not offer consensual answers in everyday situations (see Stehr, 2001: 47)

66. It is precisely the need to define and justify a goal without the "security" (of scientific) insights "among the baggage" that prompts Talcott Parsons ([1938] 1964: 27–28) in an essay about the role of ideas in social action to draw attention to the "necessity of cognitive orientation . . . an answer to the problem of justification of the ends which are in fact pursued." Such choices and justifications are what Parsons designates as "metaphysical rather than scientific propositions. This . . . is true of all *known* social systems."

67. As Joseph Schumpeter (1916/17: 15) puts it almost poetically: "The social relations of power are . . . the dye, with which the panorama of history is painted."

68. The widely shared ability to avoid knowing what the future could bring is of course also a psychological "incentive" to live with the knowledge about the limited knowledge about the outcome of events that are located in the future (cf. Gigerenzer and Garcia-Rettamero, 2017). On the other hand, political scientists who have, for example, been concerned in many ways about the lack of information among voters are now stressing that the democratic-political system works despite the ignorance of the citizens. One of the remarkable conclusions drawn by James Kuklinski (1990: 394), therefore, is that the political system "works, despite an abysmally low level of information among citizens and between citizens and representatives."

69. For a more detailed description of the concept of knowledge skills and many of its specific manifestations see Stehr, 2016: 10–12, 101–108.

70. The technical skills referred to in this context are mainly those explicated, in rather ambivalent and indirect terms, in the so-called theories of technological change (SBTC). Economists devised the theory in the 1990s to account for the comparative rise in earnings power among the more highly skilled segments of the labor force in the United States (e.g. Reich, 1992; Katz and Murphy, 1992; see the discussion of the productivity paradox, Stehr, 2000). In particular, it was argued that the information technology revolution replaced routine work tasks and enhanced the demand for conceptual or symbolic skills. These changes benefitted the more highly skilled members of the labor force. They increased income inequalities, given that those without these skills were less in demand by employers. It was, however, never shown that technology-based demands were the "cause" of the observed wage changes. In the 1990s, the story of SBTC fell apart for two reasons, as Paul Krugman (2015) observes: (1) the skill gap in terms of returns to education did not grow and (2) in relation to labor income, the share of capital earnings that had nothing to do with educational attainment grew. What accounts for this development? Paul Krugman argues that in the United States the reason is the enhanced market power of some actors and its concomitant decline for others (e.g. unions).

71. Although, as we readily conceded, this problem is at present not an immediate research and theoretical priority, it is certainly true that the knowledge skills in question may serve illegal social ends.

72. Kehrig and Vincent (2018) explore a range of correlates of the labor share at the micro-level of workers and firms.

73. Theodore Schultz (1975: 843) surmises "that the ability to deal successfully with economic disequilibria is enhanced by education and that this ability is one of the major benefits of education accruing to people privately in a modernizing economy." However, Schultz also concedes that our empirical knowledge about knowledge, the acquisition, the range and the impact of capacities is rather limited if not non-existent.

74. In his novel "The Man Without Qualities," Robert Musil emphasizes that there must be a *sense of possibility* as a complement to the *sense of reality*: "So the sense of possibility could be defined outright as the ability to conceive of everything there might be just as well, and to attach no more importance to what is than to what is not."

75. A typical overestimation of the function of information as a leverage for the development of the modern economy is, for example, Joseph Stiglitz' (2000: 1441) assessment of the historical role of information: "I would argue that perhaps the most important break with the past—one that leaves open huge areas for future work—lies in the economics of information."

76. David Autor (2014: 11) describes the limits of the automatization of occupational skills as follows: "But the scope for this kind of substitution is bounded because there are many tasks that people understand tacitly and accomplish effortlessly but for which neither computer programmers nor anyone else can enunciate the explicit "rules" or procedures. I have referred to this constraint as Polanyi's paradox, named after the economist, philosopher, and chemist who observed in 1966, 'We know more than we can tell'" (Polanyi, 1966; Autor, 2015b). Arntz, Gregory and Zierahn (2016: 25), in a cautionary estimate based on focusing on the task-content of jobs, anticipate that nine percent of all OECD jobs are potentially automatable. Skilled employment may not be immune to automation and artificial intelligence to encroaching on such jobs (cf. Autor, 2015a: 21).

77. One brief footnote concerning terminology: The now obviously well- established term "artificial intelligence" often implies as far as we can see a overgeneralized conception of what AI actually is capable of mimicking from among the many human intellectual abilities and traits. A more appropriate term would be machinal intelligence (MI). After all, AI still is dependent on human programming and numerous human capacities and traits are unlikely ever captured by machines/algorithms' (cf. Sprenger, 2019).

78. The social, economic or technical forces that are seen to drive/determine the digitalization of the world of work in particular are variously (and often alternatively) described as (1) the economic interest of the employers/owners of the means of production (cf. German Advisory Council on Global Change, page 3: www.wbgu.de/fileadmin/user_upload/wbgu.de/templates/dateien/veroeffentlichungen/weitere/digitalisierung_en.pdf), (2) massive changes of the technological regime (e.g. Iversen and Soskice, 2019) and (3) changes in the skills of the labor force (the position we favor and explain in this context).

79. The larger sovereign wealth funds in 2012 are those of UAE—Abu Dhabi (US$ 828 billion), Norway (US$ 954.1 billion); China (US$ 813.5 billion) and Saudi Arabia (US$ 515 billion). Many of the large funds have their origin in oil revenues. The only large fund that has declined in recent years is the Saudi Arabian wealth fund (SAMA Foreign Holdings). Source: Sovereign Wealth Fund Institute, 2018; www.swfinstitute.org/fund-rankings/.

80. Anthony Roberts and Roy Kwon (2017: 511), in their comparative study of the influence of financialization on social inequality of incomes in 17 OECD countries, conclude that the degree of inequality is more pronounced, especially in those countries where liberal economic policies are practiced and where the financial sector is growing disproportionately (therefore?): "the effect of finance on income inequality is greater in countries with weak collective bargaining, few labor protections and shareholder corporate governance."

81. The data on collective income distribution (labor share) support these observations: The share of labor income in industries with traditional capital endowment is stagnating, while wage income is increasing in modern industries (see Koh, Santaeulàlia-Llopis und Zheng, 2015).
82. The same trends are not observable in other countries, for example, in France. Piketty and his colleagues (2018: 604) point out that "the diverging trends in the growth of bottom 50% incomes across France and the United States—two advanced economies subject to the same forces of technological progress and globalization—suggests that domestic policies play an important role for the dynamics of income inequality."
83. See Van Loon and Aalbers (2017) who examine the financialization of real estate investment resources.
84. According to statistics on the size of global pension funds in 2015 assembled by Towers Watson, the total assets of the US pension fund reached US $ 21,779 billion. The size of the pension funds in the United States doubled in value during the decade of 2005–2015. Cf.: www.willistowerswatson.com/-/media/WTW/PDF/Insights/2016 /02/Global-Pensions-Asset-Study-2016. pdf
85. The new technology and the new forms of money enhance "the instantaneous transmission of *information* . . . in deregulated markets and the degree of *openness* to disruption that financial-market participants now face as a result of the rapid transmission of an increasingly calculable, monetizable, uncertainty" (Pryke and Allen, 2000: 270).
86. Cf. the sociological examination of new forms of money by Michel Callon (1998).
87. As Georg Simmel ([1907] 1990: 498, 500) observes, "the significance of money in determining the pace of life in a given period is first of all illustrated by the fact that a *change* in monetary circumstance brings about a *change* in the pace of life. . . [a] sudden rift and convulsions within the economic scene . . . spread to many other areas of life. . . [leading to a 'quickening' of the] pace of economic life."
88. As Charles Smith (2015: 21–22) points out with respect to the volume of transaction in the financial markets "where ten million share days was a busy day on the New York Stock Exchange in the nineteen seventies, multi billion share days on the combined equity markets is presently quite common. And this figure does not include the many millions of future and options transactions occurring on other exchanges or the numerous transactions that do not occur on a monitored exchange but rather on what are called 'black pools'."
89. In an examination of the origin of money or more generally a medium exchange, Carl Menger ([1892] 2009: 7) stresses "nothing may have been so favourable to the genesis of a medium of exchange as *the acceptance*, on the part of the most discerning and capable economic subjects, for their own economic gain, and over a considerable period of time, of eminently saleable goods in preference to all others" (our emphasis). Menger ([1892] 2009: 8) adds "When the relatively most saleable commodities have become 'money,' the great event has in the first place the effect of substantially increasing their originally high saleableness. Every economic subject bringing less saleable wares to market, to acquire goods of another sort, has thenceforth a stronger interest in converting what he has in the first instance into the wares which have become money."
90. Georg Simmel ([1907] 1989: 178) emphatically stresses that "the feeling of personal security that the possession of money gives is perhaps the most concentrated and pointed form and manifestation of confidence [trust] in the socio-political organization and order." The same linkage continues to apply under financialization.
91. Perhaps, such returns could be called "phantom wealth" (Korten, 2009: 21); however, they only represent phantom wealth if the emphasis is on the fact that such wealth is generated independently from the real economy. Otherwise, the money gained or lost is real enough.

92. The ethic of key actors in today's financial world is not easy to comprehend; however, as Arjun Appadurai (2011: 525) observes, the ethic is unlike that which motivate actors within the behavioral economics perspective, "first, they are not afraid to be pessimistic about the possibilities of certain markets, economies, and even nations. Second, they are 'contrarian' in their approach to most general opinions about investment and stock appreciation. Third, they are willing to take large bets on their pessimistic assessment of weak corporations, bad underwriting, and current credit-rating consensus. The common structural property of each of these dispositions is simple: their sense of the environment of relevant uncertainties inclines them to be more confident about their reading of downside rather than of upside risks."

93. Greta Krippner (2005: 178) estimates that the financial sector (FIRE or "finance, insurance and real estate") in the early years of the 21st century accounts at best for five to six percent of total employment in the United States (and has not grown significantly since the 1950s).

94. See David Leonhardt, "We're measuring the economy all wrong: The official statistics say that the financial crisis is behind us. It's not, *New York Times,* September 14, 2018. URL: www.nytimes.com/2018/09/14/opinion/columnists/great-recession-economy-gdp. html?action=click&module= Opinion&pgtype=Homepage. (accessed 14 July 2019).

95. "It is important to note," Krippner (2005: 193) points out with respect to her estimate of the extent of financialization, "that both of the measures developed in this paper, which rely exclusively on domestic [US] data, are vulnerable to such an objection. In the case of portfolio income, the sharp upward trend in the measure could be a reflection not of a genuine expansion of financial relative to productive sources of income, but rather the relocation of manufacturing activities (and associated income flows) outside the boundaries of the US economy."

96. The space of globalization, as is the case for other social phenomena that attain the status of *total social facts,* does not "evolve" in an even pace but knows slowdowns, stagnation or even reversals (cf. Stehr, 2001).

97. The propensity to challenge and criticize "over"-consumption is not new and therefore not unique to the age financialization. Both Aristotle and Plato endorsed such sentiments against the possible virtue of luxury, extravagance and wealth. For Adam Smith and philosophers of his generation, for example David Hume, wealth and luxury differed radically. Adam Smith in his treatise *The Theory of Moral Sentiments* supports the idea that individuals "who single-mindedly pursue 'the gratification of their own vain and insatiable desires,' they unintentionally, as if 'led by an invisible hand,' benefit society as a whole" (Westacott, 2019).

98. See the discussion by Thomas Piketty ([2013] 2014: 422) of the threats to democracy posed by the growing rentier class in modern societies: "Especially if growth slows and the return on capital increases . . . that . . . would lead to significant political upheaval."

99. For Keynes (1936: 237) successful capitalism requires the "euthanasia of the rentier," the functionless investor who extracts profits from the scarcity of capital. The rentier as a kind of parasitical economic actor is kept in chains through low interest rates. Keynes (1936: 237) expects that "the rentier aspect of capitalism as a transitional phase . . . will disappear when it has done its work."

100. The outcome of the increasing exclusion of the general work force from revenue-generating processes in the financial "industry" indicates, as Ken-Hou Lin and Donald Tomaskovic-Devey (2013: 1284) show, using cross-section industry level data that increasing dependence "on financial income, in the long run, is associated with reducing labor's share of income, increasing top executives' share of compensation, and increasing earnings dispersion among workers. . . . Our counterfactual analysis suggests that financialization could account for more than half of the decline in labor's share of income" (cf. also Koh, Santaeulàlia-Llopis and Zheng (2015); Autor et al., 2017).

101. The uneven impact of financialization is well documented in an account of the state of the divided community of Bridgeport, Connecticut (see www.businessinsider.

com/connecticut-shows-how-finance-is-ruining-America-2016-9). As the economist Thomas Philippon (2008: 2) has estimated, "historical data from the United
States shows surprisingly large variations in the economic importance of Finance. It
was high in the 1920s, but, after a continuous collapse in the 1930s and 40s, it was
down to only 2.5% of GDP in 1947. It recovered slowly until the late 1970s, and then
grew more quickly to reach almost 8% of GDP in 2006."

102. In his famous essay "Economic possibilities for our grandchildren," John Maynard
Keynes ([1930] 1963: 365–366), envisioning the future of capitalism a century later,
draws the conclusion that assuming there will be "no important wars and no important increases in population, the *economic problem* may be solved, or at least within sight
of solution, within a hundred years. This means that the economic problem is not—if
we look into the future—*the permanent problem of the human race*." Keynes' subsequent
*General Theory* offers much the same optimistic vision, "it breaks the moral calculus of
crashes as penance for excess" (Goetzmann, 2016: 466).

103. The mobility of Dahrendorf's (elite) global class across national boundaries may indeed
be without significant constraints, especially compared to past decades, however the
mobility of "skilled knowledge-based workforces in advanced economies" (Iversen and
Soskice, 2019) is perhaps much more limited. Moving an entire skilled workforce is
much more difficult if not impossible and detrimental to the bottom line.

104. There is a variety of—sometimes strongly competing—theoretical approaches in the
social sciences that attempt to identify a new ruling class, or stratum, in contemporary
society (e.g. Drucker, 1993: 175; Mason, 2016: 114–116). None of these approaches
has won a more general acceptance in the social sciences.

105. Manuel Castells asks whether the formation of a global economy may have resulted
in the emergence not only of a global class but also a *global labor force*. Castells (2000b:
255) concludes: "Thus, while there is not a unified global labor market, and therefore
not a global labor force, there is indeed global interdependence of the labor force in the
informational economy." The most important influence of the global interdependence
of the working segments of the population is, of course, the extension of global trade.

106. In her study on the emergence and the attributes of the *World Class*, Rosabeth Moss
Kanter (1995) refers to the *consciousness* of a new cosmopolitan stratum that is rich in
*immaterial* resources such as concepts, competences and contacts.

# References

Aalbers, Manuel B. (2015), "Corporate financialization," in Douglas Richardson, Noel
Castree, Michael F. Goodchild, Weidong Liu and Richard A. Marston (eds.), *The Inter-
national Encyclopedia of Geography: People, the Earth, Environment, and Technology*. Oxford:
Wiley.

Admati, Anat R. (2017), "A skeptical view of financialized corporate governance," *Journal
of Economic Perspectives* 31: 131–150.

Adolf, Marian and Nico Stehr (2017), *Knowledge*, 2nd ed. London: Routledge.

Adolf, Marian, Jason Mast and Nico Stehr (2013), "The foundations of innovation in modern societies: the displacement of concepts and knowledgeability," *Mind & Society* 12:
11–22.

Aglietta, Michel and Régis Breton (2001), "Financial systems, corporate control and capital
accumulation," *Economy and Society* 30: 433–466.

Akerlof, George A. (1970), "The market for 'lemons': Quality, uncertainty, and the market
mechanism," *The Quarterly Journal of Economics* 84: 488–500.

Alvaredo, Facundo, Lucas Chancel, Thomas Piketty, Emmanuel Saez and Gabriel Zucman
(2017), "Global inequality dynamics: New findings from WID.world," *NEWR Working
Paper* No. 23119.

Ancori, Bernard, Antoine Bureth and Patrick Cohendt (2000), "The economics of knowledge: The debate about codification and tacit knowledge," *Industrial and Corporate Change* 9: 255–287.

Appadurai, Arjun (2012), "The spirit of calculation," *The Cambridge Journal of Anthropology* 30: 3–17.

Appadurai, Arjun (2011), "The ghost in the financial machine," *Public Culture* 23: 517–539.

Arntz, Melanie, Terry Gregory and Ulrich Zierahn (2016), "The risk of automation for jobs in OECD countries: A comparative analysis," OECD Social, Employment and Migration Working Papers, No. 189, OECD Publishing, Paris.

Aron, Raymond (1962), *Dix-huit Leçons sur la Société Industrielle*. Paris: Gallimard.

Arrow, Kenneth (1994), "Methodological individualism and social knowledge," *The American Economic Review* 84: 1–9.

Arrow, Kenneth (1962), "The economic implications of learning by doing," *Review of Economic Studies* 29: 155–173.

Arvidsson, Adam (2016), "Facebook and finance: On the social logic of the derivative," *Theory, Culture & Society* 33: 3–23.

Aspers, Patrick and Jens Beckert (2011), *The Worth of Goods: Valuation and Pricing in the Economy*. Oxford: Oxford University Press.

Autor, David (2015), "Why Are There Still So Many Jobs? The History and Future of Workplace Automation," *Journal of Economic Perspectives* 29: 3–30.

Autor, David (2014), "Polanyi's paradox and the shape of employment growth," *NBER Working Paper* No. 20485.

Autor, David, David Dorn, Lawrence F. Katz, Christina Patterson and John Van Reenen (2017), "Concentrating on the fall of the labor share," *NBER Working Paper* No. 23108.

Autor, David, Frank Levy and Richard J. Murnane (2003), "The skill content of recent technological change: An empirical exploration," *Quarterly Journal of Economics* 118: 1279–1333.

Ayres, Robert U., Leslie W. Ayres and Benjamin Warr (2003), "Exergy, power and work in the US economy, 1900–1998," *Energy* 28: 219–273.

Bacon, Francis ([1620] 1902), *Novum Organum*. New York: P.F. Collier.

Barnes, Barry (1995), *The Elements of Social Theory*. Princeton, NJ: Princeton University Press.

Becker, Gary S. and Kevin M. Murphy (1992), "The division of labor, coordination costs, and knowledge," *Quarterly Journal of Economics* 107: 1137–1160.

Beckert, Jens (2006), "Trust and markets," pp. 318–331 in Reinhard Bachmann and Akbar Zaheer (eds.), *Handbook of Trust Research*. Cheltenham: Edward Elgar.

Bell, Daniel (1987), "The world and the United States in 2013," *Daedalus* 116: 1–31.

Bell, Daniel (1979), 'The social framework of the information society," pp. 163–211 in Michael L. Dertouzos and Joel Moses (eds.), *The Computer Age: A Twenty-Year View*. Cambridge, MA: MIT Press.

Bell, Daniel (1976), "Welcome to the post-industrial society," *Physics Today* 29: 46–49.

Bell, Daniel (1973), *The Coming of Post-Industrial society. A Venture in Social Forecasting*. New York: Basis Books.

Bell, Daniel (1968), "The measurement of knowledge and technology," pp. 145–246 in Eleanor B. Sheldon and Wilbert E. Moore (eds.), *Indicators of Social Change. Concepts and Measurements*. Hartford, CT: Russell Sage Foundation.

Block, Fred and Larry Hirschhorn (1979), "New productive forces and the contradictions of contemporary capitalism," *Theory and Society* 17: 363–395.

Blumenberg, Hans ([1966] 1982), *The Legitimacy of the Modern Age*. Boston, MA: MIT Press.

Boltanski, Luc and Arnaud Esquerre (2016), "The economic life of things," *New Left Review* 98: 31–54.

Bone, John (2015), "False economy: Financializaton, crisis and socio-economic polarisation," *Sociology Compass* 9: 876–886.

Borgmann, Albert (1999), *Holding on to Reality. The nature of information at the turn of the millennium.* Chicago, IL: University of Chicago Press.

Borgmann, Albert (1992), *Crossing the Postmodern Divide.* Chicago, IL: University of Chicago Press.

Bourdieu, Pierre (2015), *Sociologie générale: Cours au Collège de France 1981–1983.* Paris, France: Seuil.

Bourdieu, Pierre (2005), *The Social Structures of the Economy.* Cambridge: Polity.

Bourdieu, Pierre ([1998] 2002), *Der Einzige und sein Eigenheim.* Hamburg:VSA-Verlag.

Bourdieu, Pierre ([1979] 1982), *Die feinen Unterschiede. Kritik der gesellschaftlichen Urteilskraft.* Frankfurt am Main: Suhrkamp.

Boutang, Yann M. ([2008] 2011), *Cognitive Capitalism.* Cambridge: Polity Press.

Bozeman, Barry and Juan D. Rogers (2002), "A churn model of scientific knowledge value: Internet researchers as a knowledge value collective," *Research Policy* 31: 769–794.

Brynjolfsson, Erik, Lorin M. Hitt and Shinkyu Yang (2002), "Intangible assets: Computers and organizational capital," *MIT Business Center, Paper* 138: 1–48.

Callon, Michel (1998), "The embeddedness of economic markets in economics," pp. 1–57 in Michel Callon (ed.), *The Laws of the Markets.* Oxford: Blackwell.

Castells, Manuel ([2000] 2017), *Der Aufstieg der Netzwerkgesellschaft. Das Informationszeitalter. Wirtschaft Gesellschaft Kultur.* 2. Auflage. Wiesbaden: Springer VS.

Castells, Manuel ([2000] 2004), *Das Informationszeitalter. Wirtschaft, Gesellschaft, Kultur. 1. Der Aufstieg der Netzwerkgesellschaft.* Opladen: Leske + Budrich.

Castells, Manuel (2000a), "Material for an exploratory theory of the network society," *British Journal of Sociology* 51: 2–24.

Castells, Manuel ([1996] 2000b), *The Rise of the Network Society*, 2nd ed. Oxford: Blackwell.

Collins, Harry M. and Robert Evans (2002), "The third wave of science studies: Studies of expertise and experience," *Social Studies of Science* 32: 235–296.

Crouch, Colin (2004), *Post-Democracy.* Cambridge: Polity.

Dahrendorf, Ralf (2000a), "Die globale Klasse und die neue Ungleichheit," *Merkur* 54: 1057–1068.

Dahrendorf, Ralf (2000b), *The Global Class and the New Inequality* Jerusalem: The Israel Academy of Sciences and Humanities.

Dahrendorf, Ralf (1980), "Im Entschwinden der Arbeitsgesellschaft," *Merkur* 34: 749–760.

Darcillon, Thibault (2015), "How does finance affect labor market institutions? An empirical analysis in 16 OECD countries," *Socio-Economic Review* 13: 477–504.

David, Paul A. and Dominique Forey (2003), "Economic fundamentals of the knowledge society," *Policy Features in Education* 1: 20–49.

Davis, Leila E. (2017), "Financialization and investment: A survey of the empirical literature," *The Journal of Economic Surveys* 31: 1332–1358.

Davis, Aeron and Catherine Walsh (2017), "Distinguishing financialization from neoliberalism," *Theory, Culture & Society 34: 27–51.*

Davis, Gerald F. and Suntae Kim (2015), "Financialization of the economy," *Annual Review of Sociology* 41: 201–221.

Di Maggio, Paul and Amir Goldberg (2018), "Searching for Homo Economicus variation in Americans' construals of and attitudes toward markets," *European Journal of Sociology* 59: 151–189.

Dickson, David (1984), *The New Politics of Science.* New York: Pantheon Books.

Dore, Ronald (2008), "Financialization of the global economy," *Industrial and Corporate Change* 1: 1097–1112.

Drew, Simon, Susan Waldrona, David Gilvear, Ian Grieve, Alona Armstrong, Olivia Bragg, Francis Brewis, Mark Cooper, Tom Dargie, Colin Duncan, Lorna Harris, Lorraine Wilson, Cameron McIver, Rory Padfield and Nadeem Shah (2013), "The price of knowledge in the knowledge economy: Should development of peatland in the UK support a research levy?" *Land Use Policy* 32: 50–60.

Drucker, Peter F. (1994), *Post-Capitalist Society*. London: Routledge.

Drucker, Peter F. (1993), *Die postkapitalistische Gesellschaft*. Düsseldorf, Wien, New York, Moskau: ECON Verlag.

Drucker, Peter F. (1989), *The New Realities: In Government and Politics / In Economics and Business / In Society and World View*. New York: Harper & Row.

Drucker, Peter F. (1986), 'The changed world economy," *Foreign Affairs* 64: 768–791.

Drucker, Peter F. (1976), *The Unseen Revolution. How Pension Funds Socialism Came to America*. New York: Harper & Row.

Durkheim, Émile ([1950] 1991), *Physik der Sitten und des Rechts*. Vorlesungen zur Soziologie der Moral. Herausgegeben von Hans-Peter Müller. Frankfurt am Main: Suhrkamp.

Durkheim, Émile ([1912] 1981), *Die elementaren Formen des religiösen Lebens*. Frankfurt am Main: Suhrkamp.

Elias, Norbert ([1970] 2006), *Was ist Soziologie? Gesammelte Schriften Band. 5. Grundfragen der Soziologie*. Frankfurt am Main: Suhrkamp.

Elias, Norbert ([1984] 2005), "Knowledge and power," pp. 203–242 in Nico Stehr and Volker Meja (eds.), *Society and Knowledge. Contemporary Perspectives on the Sociology of Knowledge*, 2nd ed. New Brunswick, NJ: Transaction Books.

Elias, Norbert (1991), *The Symbol Theory*. London: Sage.

Elias, Norbert (1989), *Studien über die Deutschen. Machtkämpfe und Habitusentwicklung im 19. und 20. Jahrhundert*. Frankfurt am Main: Suhrkamp.

Epstein, Gerald A. (2005), *Financialization and the World Economy*. London: Edward Elgar.

Ezrahi, Yaron (1971), "The political resources of American science," *Science Studies* 1: 117–133.

Fligstein, Neil (2001), *The Architecture of the Markets. An Economic Sociology of the Twenty-First Century*. Princeton, NJ: Princeton University Press.

Fligstein, Neil (1990), *The Transformation of Corporate Control*. Cambridge, MA: Harvard University Press.

Forey, Dominique (2004), *Economics of Knowledge*. Cambridge, MA: MIT Press.

Foster, John B. (2007), "The financialization of capitalism," *Monthly Review* 58: 1–12.

Foucault, Michel (2007), *Security, Territory, Population. Lectures at the Collége de France*. New York: Palgrave.

Foucault, Michel ([1997] 2003), *Society Must Be Defended*. New York: Picador.

Fourcade, Marion (2009), *Economists and Societies. Discipline and Profession in the United States, Britain and France, 1890s to 1990s*. Princeton, NJ: Princeton University Press.

Fuller, Steve (1992), "Knowledge as product and property," pp. 157–190 in Nico Stehr and Richard Ericson (eds.), *The Culture and Power of knowledge. Inquiries into Contemporary Societies*. New York: Walter de Gruyter.

Funke, Manuel, Moritz Schularick and Christoph Trebesch (2015), "Going to Extremes: Politics after financial crises, 1870–2014," *Discussion Paper* No. 10884, Centre for Economic Policy Research, London.

Garicano, Luis and Esteban Rossi-Hansberg (2014), "Knowledge-based hierarchies: Using organizations to understand the economy," *NBER Working Paper* No. 20607.

Gault, Fred (2006), "Measuring knowledge and its economic effects: The role of official statistics," pp. 27–42 in Brian Kahin and Dominique Forey (eds.), *Advancing Knowledge and the Knowledge Economy*. Cambridge, MA: MIT Press.

Gehlen, Arnold (1941), *Der Mensch. Seine Natur und seine Stellung in der Welt*. 2., unveränderte Auflage. Berlin: Junker + Dünnhaupt.

Gehlen, Arnold ([1940] 1993), *Der Mensch. Seine Natur und seine Stellung in der Welt*. Berlin: Junker + Dünnhaupt.

Gehlen, Arnold ([1940] 1971), *Der Mensch*. Frankfurt am Main: Athenäum.

Giddens, Anthony (1990), "Sociology, modernity and utopia," *New Statesman & Society* 3: 20–22.

Gigerenzer, Gerd and Rocio Garcia-Rettamero (2017), "Cassandra's regret: The psychology of not wanting to know," *Psychological Review* 124: 179–196.

Goetzmann, William N. (2016), *Money Changes Everything: How Finance Made Civilization Possible*. Princeton, NJ: Princeton University Press.

Goldscheid, Rudolf (1917), *Staatssozialismus oder Staatskapitalismus? Ein finanzsoziologischer Beitrag zur Lösung des Staatsschulden*. Wien: Anzengruber.

Goldstone, Jack A. (2006), "A historical, not comparative, method: Breakthroughs and limitations in the theory and methodology of Michael Mann's analysis of power," pp. 263–282 in John A. Hall and Ralph Schroeder (eds.), *An Anatomy of Power. The Social Theory of Michael Mann*. Cambridge: Cambridge University Press.

Goodhart, David (2017), *The Road to Somewhere. The New Tribes Shaping British Politics*. London: Penguin.

Gorz, André ([2003] 2010), *The Immaterial. Knowledge, Value and Capital*. London: Seagull.

Gorz, André ([2003] 2004), *Wissen, Wert und Kapital. Zur Kritik der Wissensökonomie*. Berlin: Rotpunktverlag.

Guala, Francesco (2006), "Critical notice. A review of *Naissance de la biopolitique*: Cours au Collége de France, 1978–1979, by Michel Foucault," *Economics and Philosophy* 22: 429–439.

Guellec, Domique and Caroline Paunov (2017), "Digital innovation and the distribution of income," *NBER Working Paper* No. 23987.

Haldane, Andrew (2009), "Rethinking the financial network, speech delivered at the Financial Student Association, Amsterdam," [Online]. URL: www.bankofengland.co.uk/publications/speeches/2009/speech386.pdf (accessed 10 March 2018).

Haskel, Jonathan and Stan Westlake (2017), *Capitalism without Capital. The Rise of the Intangible Economy*. Princeton, NJ: Princeton University Press.

Hatherly, Owen (2016), "One click at a time," *London Review of Books*, 30 June. URL: www.lrb.co.uk/v38/n13/owen-hatherley/one-click-at-a-time (accessed 2 July 2016).

Hayek, Friedrich A. (1945), "The use of knowledge in society," *The American Economic Review* 35: 519–530.

Hein, Eckhard and Matthias Mundt (2011), "Financialisation and the requirements and potentials for wage-led recovery: A review focusing on the G20," Geneva: International Labour Office, Conditions of Work and Employment Branch.

Hilferding, Rudolf ([1910] 2006), *Finance Capital: A Study in the Latest Phase of Capitalist Development*. London: Routledge.

Ho, Karen (2009), *Liquidated: An Ethnography of Wall Street*. Princeton, NJ: Princeton University.

Iversen, Torben and David Soskice (2019), *Democracy and Prosperity: Reinventing Capitalism through a Turbulent Century*. Princeton, NJ: Princeton University Press.

Jacob, Margaret C. (2014), *The First Knowledge Economy. Human Capital and the European Economy, 1750–1850*. Cambridge: Cambridge University Press.

Kanter, Rosabeth M. (1995), *World Class: Thriving Locally in the Global Economy*. New York: Simon & Schuster.

Katz, Lawrence F. and Kevin M. Murphy (1992), "Changes in relative wages, 1963–1987: Supply and demand forces," *The Quarterly Journal of Economics* 107: 35–78.

Kehrig, Matthias and Nicolas Vincent (2018), "The micro-level anatomy of the labor share decline," *NBER Working Paper* No. 25275.

Keynes, John M. ([1936] 1985), "Allgemeine Theorie der Beschäftigung, des Zinses und des Geldes," in Harald Mattfeld (ed.), *Keynes—Kommentierte Werkauswahl*. Hamburg: VSA-Verlag.

Keynes, John M. ([1930] 1956), "Wirtschaftliche Möglichkeiten für unsere Enkelkinder," pp. 263–272 in John M. Keynes (ed.), *Politik und Wirtschaft. Männer und Probleme. Ausgewählte Abhandlungen*. Tübingen: J.C.B. Mohr (Paul Siebeck).

Keynes, John M. ([1923] 1924), *Ein Traktat über Währungsreform*. München and Leipzig: Duncker & Humblot.

Kindleberger, Charles (1989), *Manias, Panics, and Crashes: A History of Financial Crises*, 2nd ed. London: Macmillan.

Kitcher, Philip (1993), "Knowledge, society, and history," *Canadian Journal of Philosophy* 23: 155–177.

Kline, Ronald R. (2015), *The Cybernetics Movement. Or Why We Call Our Age the Information Age*. Baltimore, MD: John Hopkins University Press.

Knight, Frank H. ([1921] 2000), *Risk, Uncertainty and Profit*. Liberty Fund.

Knight, Frank H. (1950), "The determination of just wages," pp. 467–511 in *Twentieth Century Economic Thought*. New York: Philosophical Library.

Koh, Dongya, Raül Santaeulàlia-Llopis and Yu Zheng (2015), "Labor share decline and intellectual property products capital," *EUI Working Papers* Eco 2015/05.

Koller, Ingo (1998), "Wissenszurechnung, Kosten und Risiken," *Juristen Zeitung* 53: 75–85.

Koppl, Roger, Stuart Kauffman, Teppo Felin and Giuseppe Longo (2015), "Economics for a creative world," *Journal of Institutional Economics* 11: 1–31.

Kornberger, Martin, Dane Pflueger and Jan Mouritsen (2017), "Evaluative infrastructures: Accounting for platform organization," *Accounting, Organizations and Society* 60: 79–95.

Korten, David C. (2009), *Agenda for a New Economy. From Phantom Wealth to Real Wealth*. San Francisco, CA: Berret-Koehler.

Kreibich, Rolf (1986), *Die Wissenschaftsgesellschaft. Von Galilei zur High-Tech Revolution*. Frankfurt am Main: Suhrkamp.

Krippner, Greta R. (2005), "The financialization of the American economy," *Socio-Economic Review* 3: 173–208.

Krohn, Wolfgang (1987), *Francis Bacon*. München: Beck.

Krohn, Wolfgang (1981), "'Wissen ist Macht': Zur Soziogenese eines neuzeitlichen wissenschaftliches Geltungsanspruchs," pp. 29–57 in Kurt Bayertz (ed.), *Wissenschaftsgeschichte und wissenschaftliche Revolution*. Köln: Pahl-Rugenstein.

Krugman, Paul (2015), *International Economics: Theory and Policy with Myeconlab*. London: Pearson Education Limited.

Kuklinsli, James D. (1990), "Information and the study of politics," pp. 391–395 in John A. Ferejohn and James H. Kuklinski (eds.), *Information and the Democratic Process*. Urbana and Chicago: University of Illinois Press.

Kwon, Roy and Anthony Roberts (2015), "Financialization and income inequality in the new Economy. An exploration of finance's conditional effects," *Sociology of Development* 1: 442–462.

Lagoarde-Segot, Thomas (2017), "Financialization; Towards a new research agenda," *International Review of Financial Analysis* 51: 113–123.

Landes, David S. (1980), "The creation of knowledge and technique: Today's task and yesterday's experience," *Daedalus* 109: 111–119.

Langley, Paul (2008), *The Everyday Life of Global Finance. Saving and Borrowing in Anglo-America*. Oxford: Oxford University Press.

Leyshon, Andrew and Nigel Thrift (2007), "The capitalization of almost everything: The future of finance and capitalism," *Theory, Culture & Society* 24: 97–115.

Lin, Ken-Hou and Donald Tomaskovic-Devey (2013), "Financialization and US income inequality, 1970–2008," *American Journal of Sociology* 118: 1284–1329.

Lowe, Adolph (1971), "Is present-day higher education learning 'relevant'," *Social Research* 38: 563–580.

Luhmann, Niklas ([1991] 2005), *Risk. A Sociological Theory*. With a New Introduction by Nico Stehr and Gotthard Bechmann. New York: Routledge.

Luhmann, Niklas (2002), *Das Erziehungssystem der Gesellschaft*. Frankfurt am Main: Suhrkamp.

Luhmann, Niklas (1997), *Die Gesellschaft der Gesellschaft. Erster Teilband*. Frankfurt am Main: Suhrkamp.

Luhmann, Niklas (1990), *Die Wissenschaft der Gesellschaft*. Frankfurt am Main: Suhrkamp.

Luhmann, Niklas (1988), *Die Wirtschaft der Gesellschaft*. Frankfurt am Main: Suhrkamp.

Lui, Yujia and David B. Grusky (2013), "The Payoff to Skill in the Third Industrial Revolution," *American Journal of Sociology* 118: 1330–1374.

Lundvall, Bengt-Ake (1992), "Introduction," in Bengt-Ake Lundvall (ed.), *National Systems of Innovation*. Aalborg: Aalborg University Press.

Lyotard, Jean-François ([1979] 1994), *Das postmoderne Wissen. Ein Bericht*. Graz/Wien: Böhlau: Passagen Verlag.

Machlup, Fritz (1979), "Uses, value and benefits of knowledge," *Knowledge: Creation, Diffusion, Utilization* 1: 62–81.

Mannheim, Karl ([1938] 1953), "The age of planning," pp. 255–266 in Karl Mannheim (ed.), *Essays of Sociology and Social Psychology*. London: Routledge & Kegan Paul.

Mannheim, Karl (1929), *Ideologie und Utopie*. Bonn: Cohen.

Markham, Jerry W. (2002), *A Financial History of the United States: From the Age of Derivatives into the New Millennium (1970–2001)*. Armonk: M. E. Sharpe.

Marx, Karl ([1939–1941] 1973), *Grundrisse. Introduction to the Critique of Political Economy*. New York: Vintage Books.

Mason, Paul (2016), *Postcapitalism: A Guide to our Future*. London: Allen Lane.

Masood, Ehsan (2016), *The Great Invention. The Story of the GPD and the Making (and Unmaking) of the Modern World*. New York: Pegasus.

McClanahan, Annie (2013), "Investing in the future," *Journal of Cultural Economy* 6: 78–93.

McCulla, S., Holden, A. and Smith, S. (2013), *Improved Estimates of National Income and Product Accounts: Results of the 2013 Comprehensive Revision*. Washington, DC: Bureau of Economic Analysis.

McGinn, Colin (2017), "Does knowledge imply truth," pp. 139–141 in Colin McGinn (ed.), *Philosophical Provocations. 55 Short Essays*. Cambridge, MA: MIT Press.

McGrattan, Ellen R. (2017), "Intangible capital and measured productivity," *NBER Working Paper* No. 23233. URL: www.nber.org/papers/w23233

Menger, Carl ([1892] 2009), *On the Origins of Money*. Auburn: Ludwig von Mises Institute.

Merton, Robert K. ([1949] 1968), *Social Theory and Social Structure*. Revised and enlarged ed. New York: Free Press.

Milner Jr., Murray (2015), *Elites. A General Model*. Cambridge: Polity.

Mirowski, Philip (1990), "Why there is (as yet) no such thing as an economics of knowledge," pp. 99–158 in Harold Kincaid and Don Ross (eds.), *The Oxford Handbook of Philosophy of Economics*. Oxford: Oxford University Press.

Mises, Ludwig von (1922), *Die Gemeinwirtschaft: Untersuchungen über den Sozialismus*. Jena: Gustav Fischer.

Mounk, Yascha and Lee Drutman (2016), "When the robots rise," *The National Interest*. URL: http://nationalinterest.org/feature/when-the-robots-rise-16830 (accessed 23 June 2018).

Musil, Robert ([1930, 1932] 1978), *Der Mann ohne Eigenschaften. Robert Musil Gesammelte Werke Band 1*. Reinbek bei Hamburg: Rowohlt.

Nelkin, Dorothy (1979), "Scientific knowledge, public policy, and democracy: A review essay," *Science Communication* 1: 106–122.

Nelkin, Dorothy (1975), "The political impact of technical expertise," *Social Studies of Science* 5: 35–54.

Nelson, Richard R. (1959), "The simple economics of basic scientific research," *Journal of Political Economy* 67: 323–348.

Orhangazi, Özgür (2008), *Financialization and the U.S. Economy*. Northampton: Edward Elgar Publishing.

Ostry, Jonathan D., Prakash Loungani and Davide Furceri (2016), "Neoliberalism: Oversold?" *Finance & Development* 53: 38–41.

Parsons, Talcott ([1938] 1964), "The role of ideas in social action," pp. 19–33 in Talcott Parsons (ed.), *Essays in Sociological Theory*, Revised ed. New York: Free Press.

Phelps, Edmund S. (2013), *Mass Flourishing: How Grassroots Innovation Created Jobs, Challenge, and Change*. Princeton, NJ: Princeton University Press.

Philippon, Thomas and Ariell Reshef (2013), "An international look at the growth of modern finance," Conference Paper. URL: http://conference.darden.virginia.edu/IFC/selected_papers/10_PR_JEP_rev2_w_TABFIG_march26.pdf (accessed 19 January 2019).

Philippon, Thomas (2008), "The evolution of the US financial industry from 1860 to 2007: Theory and evidence," *NYA Stern Working Paper*. URL: http://pages.stern.nyu.edu/~tphilipp/papers/finsize_old.pdf (accessed 5 April 2018).

Phillips, Matt (2018), "Apple's $1 Trillion Milestone Reflects Rise of Powerful Megacompanies," *New York Times* August 2. https://www.nytimes.com/2018/08/02/business/apple-trillion.html?hp&%20action=click&pgtype=Homepage&clickSource=story-heading&module=first-column-region&region=top-news&WT.nav=top-news.

Piketty, Thomas ([2013] 2014), *Capital in the Twentieth-First Century*. Cambridge, MA: Harvard University Press.

Piketty, Thomas, Emmanuel Saez and Gabriel Zucman (2018), "Distributional national accounts: Methods and estimates for the United States," *Quarterly Journal of Economics* 133: 553–609.

Polanyi, Michael (1966), *The Tacit Dimension*. New York: Doubleday.

Popitz, Heinrich (1986), *Phänomene der Macht*. Autorität-Herrschaft-Gewalt-Technik. Tübingen; J.C.B. Mohr (Paul Siebeck).

Proctor, Robert N. and Londa Schiebinger (2008), *Antology. The Making and & Unmaking of Ignorance*. Stanford, CA: Stanford University Press.

Pryke, Michael and John Allen (2000), "Monetized time-space: Derivatives—Money's 'new imaginary'?" *Economy and Society* 29: 264–284.

Pryke, Michael and Paul du Gay (2007), "Take an issue: Cultural economy and finance," *Economy and Society* 36: 339–354.

Reich, Robert B. (2007), *Supercapitalism. The Transformation of Business, Democracy, and Everyday Life*. New York: Alfred A. Knopf.

Reich, Robert B. (1992), *The Work of Nations: Preparing Ourselves for the 21st-Century Capitalism*. New York: Vintage Books.

Reinhart, Carmen M. and Kenneth S. Rogoff (2009), *This Time Is Different. Eight Centuries of Financial Folly*. Princeton, NJ: Princeton University Press.

Richta, Radovan (1971), *Richta-Report, Politische Ökonomie des 20. Jahrhunderts: die Auswirkungen der technisch-wissenschaftlichen Revolution auf die Produktionsverhältnisse*. Frankfurt am Main: Makol Verlag.

Richta, Radovan (1969), *Civilization at the Crossroads: Social and Human Implications of the Scientific and Technological Revolution*. White Plains, NY: International Arts and Sciences Press.

Rimes, Hearther, Jennie Welch and Barry Bozeman (2014), "An alternative to the economic value of knowledge," pp. 154–164 in Cristiano Antonelli and Albert N. Link (eds.), *Routledge Handbook of the Economics of Knowledge*. New York: Routledge.

Rittel, Horst and Melvin M. Webber (1973), "Dilemmas in the general theory of planning," *Policy Sciences* 4: 154–159.

Roberts, Anthony and Roy Kwon (2017), "Finance, inequality and the varieties of capitalism in post-industrial democracies," *Socio-Economic Review* 15: 511–538.

Roose, Kevin (2013), "Wall street's favorite-son status is gone. It's not happy about it," *Intelligencer* December 12. http://nymag.com/intelligencer/2013/12/wall-street-unhappy-with-washington.html.

Rowley, Jennifer (2007), "The wisdom hierarchy: Representations of the DIKW hierarchy," *Journal of Information Science* 33: 163–180.

Ryle, Gilbert ([1945] 1971), "Knowing how and knowing that," pp. 222–235 in Gilbert Ryle (ed.), *Collected Papers. Volume 2: Collected Essays 1929–1968*. London: Hutchinson.

Ryle, Gilbert (1949), *The Concept of Mind*. London: Hutchinson.

Saunders, Harry (2016), "Does capitalism require endless growth? Marx and Malthus reconsidered," *Breakthrough Journal* 6: 27–40.

Schelsky, Helmut (1975), *Die Arbeit tun die anderen. Klassenkampf und Priesterherrschaft der Intellektuellen*. 2. Erweiterte Auflage. Opladen: Westdeutscher Verlag.

Schelsky, Helmut (1961), *Der Mensch in der wissenschaftlichen Zivilisation*. Köln and Opladen: Westdeutscher Verlag.

Schelsky, Helmut ([1957] 1965), "Die sozialen Folgen der Automatisierung," pp. 105–130 in Helmut Schelsky, *Auf der Suche nach der Wirklichkeit. Gesammelte Aufsätze*. Düsseldorf-Köln: Eugen Diederichs.

Schiller, Robert J. (2003), *The New Financial Order: Risk in the 21st Century*. Princeton, NJ: Princeton University Press.

Schon, Donald A. ([1963] 1967), *Invention and the Evolution of Ideas*. London: Tavistock.

Schultz, Theordore W. (1975), "The value of the ability to deal with disequilibria," *Journal of Economic Literature* 13: 827–846.

Schumpeter, Joseph A. (1954), *History of Economic Analysis*. New York: Oxford University Press.

Schumpeter, Joseph A. ([1911] 1934), *The Theory of Economic Development*. Cambridge, MA: Harvard University Press.

Schumpeter, Joseph A. ([1911] 1926), *Theorie der wirtschaftlichen Entwicklung*. München, Leipzig: Duncker & Humblot.

Schumpeter, Joseph A. (1916/1917), "Das Grundprinzip der Verteilungstheorie," *Archiv für Sozialwissenschaft und Sozialpolitik* 42: 1–88.

Schwartz, Jacob T. (1992), "America's economic-technological agenda for the 1990s," *Daedalus* 121: 139–165.

Simmel, Georg ([1900] 2004), *The Philosophy of Money*. London: Routledge and Kegan Paul.

Simmel, Georg ([1908] 1992), *Soziologie. Untersuchungen über die Formen der Vergesellschaftung. Gesamtausgabe, Band 11*. Frankfurt am Main: Suhrkamp.

Simmel, Georg ([1907] 1989), *Philosophie des Geldes. Gesamtausgabe, Band 6*. Frankfurt am Main: Suhrkamp.

Simmel, Georg ([1906] 1950), *The Sociology of Georg Simmel*. New York: The Free Press.

Simmel, Georg (1904), "Fashion," *International Quarterly* 11: 130–155.

Simmel, Georg (1890), *Über soziale Differenzierung: Sociologische und psychologische Untersuchungen*. Leipzig: Duncker & Humblot.

Sklair, Leslie (2002), "Democracy and the transnational capitalist class," *The Annals of the American Academy of Political and Social Science* 581: 144–157.

Smil, Vaclav (2017), *Energy and Civilization: A History*. Cambridge, MA: MIT Press.

Smit, J.P., Filip Buekens and Stan Du Plessis, (2016), "Cigarettes, dollars and bitcoins—An essay on the ontology of money," *Journal of Institutional Economics* 12: 327–347.

Smith, Adam ([1776] 2001), *Der Wohlstand der Nationen*. 9. Auflage, München: Deutscher Taschenbuch Verlag.

Smith, Charles (2015), *What the Markets Teach Us. Limitations of Knowing and Tactics for Doing*. Oxford: Oxford University Press.

Solow, Robert M. (1956), "A contribution to the theory of economic growth," *The Quarterly Journal of Economics* 70: 65–94.

Sprenger, Reinhard K. (2019), "Viele fürchten, wegen künstlicher Intelligenz überflüssig zu werden. Dabei hat KI ein fundamentales Problem: Sie macht keine Fehler," *Neue Zürcher Zeitung*, 26. Februar. URL: www.nzz.ch/feuilleton/ki-macht-nicht-arbeitslos-denn-sie-begeht-zu-wenige-fehler-ld.1453722 (accessed 23 April 2019).

Srnicek, Nick and Alex Williams (2016), *Inventing the Future: Postcapitalism and a World without Work*. London: Verso.

Staab, Philipp (2016), *Falsche Versprechen. Wachstum im Digitalen Kapitalismus*. Hamburg: Hamburger Edition HIS Verlagsgesellschaft.

Stehr, Nico and Alexander Ruser (2017), "Social scientists as technicians, advisors and meaning producers," *Innovation: The European Journal of Social Science* 30: 24–35.

Stehr, Nico and Marian Adolf (2018), *Ist Wissen Macht? Wissen als gesellschaftliche Tatsache*. Zweite Auflage. Weilerswist: Velbrück Wissenschaft.

Stehr, Nico and Marian Adolf (2015), *Ist Wissen Macht? Erkenntnisse über Wissen*. Weilerswist: Velbrück Wissenschaft.

Stehr, Nico (2016), *Information, Power, and Democracy. Liberty Is a Daughter of Knowledge*. Cambridge: Cambridge University Press.

Stehr, Nico (2001), *The Fragility of Modern Societies. Knowledge and Risk in the Information Age*. London: Sage.

Stehr, Nico (2000), "Deciphering information technologies: Modern societies as networks," *European Journal of Social Theory* 3: 84–93.

Stehr, Nico (1999), "The future of inequality," *Society* 36: 54–59.

Steinmüller, W. Edward (2006), "Learning in the knowledge-based economy: The future as viewed from the part," pp. 207–238 in Christian Antonelli, Dominique Foray, Bronwyn H. Hall and W. Edward Steinmüller (eds.), *New Frontiers in the Economics of Innovation and New Technology*. Cheltenham: Edward Elgar.

Stiglitz, Joseph E. (2017), "The revolution of information economics—The past and the future," *NBER Working Paper* No. 23780.

Stiglitz, Joseph E. (2000), "The contributions of the economics of information to Twentieth Century economics," *The Quarterly Journal of Economics* 115: 1441–1478.

Stiglitz, Joseph E. and Bruce G. Greenwald (2014), *Creating a Learning Society: A New Approach to Growth, Development, and Social Progress*. New York: Columbia University Press.

Swidler, Ann (1995), "Cultural power and social movements," pp. 25–40 in Hank Johnston and Bert Klandermanns (ed.), *Social Movements and Culture*. Minneapolis: University of Minnesota Press.

Tenbruck, Friedrich H. (1969), "Regulative Funktionen der Wissenschaft in der pluralistischen Gesellschaft," pp. 61–85 in Herbert Scholz (ed.), *Die Rolle der Wissenschaft in der modernen Gesellschaft*. Berlin: Duncker & Humblot.

Tobin, James (1984), "On the efficiency of the financial-system," *Lloyds Bank Annual Review* 153: 1–15.

Tomaskovic-Devey, Donald, Ken-Hou Lin and Nathan Meyers (2015), "Did financialization reduce economic growth?" *Socio-Economic Review* 13: 525–548.

Tooze, Adam (2018), *Crashed. How a Decade of Financial Crisis Changed the World*. New York: Viking.

Touraine, Alain (1998), "Culture without society," *Cultural Values* 2: 140–157.

Touraine, Alain ([1984] 1988), *Return of the Actor*. Minneapolis: University of Minnesota.

Ungar, Sheldon (2008), "Ignorance as an under-identified social problem," *British Journal of Sociology* 59: 301–326.

Urry, John (2003), *Global Complexity*. Cambridge: Polity.

Van Arnum, Bradford M. and Michelle I. Naples (2013), "Financialization and income inequality in the United States, 1967–2010," *American Journal of Economics and Sociology* 72: 1158–1182.

Van der Zwan, Natascha (2014), "Making sense of financialization," *Socio-Economic Review* 12: 99–129.

Van Eekelen, Bregie F. (2015), "Accounting for ideas: Bringing a knowledge economy into the picture," *Economy and Society* 44: 445–479.

Van Eekelen, Bergje F. (2014), "Knowledge for the West, production for the rest?" *Journal of Cultural Economy* 8: 479–500.

Van Loon, Jannes and Manuel B. Aalbers (2017), "How real estate became 'just another asset class': The financialization of the investment strategies of Dutch institutional investors," *European Planning Studies* 25: 221–240.

Vazquez, Alfredo Macias and Pablo Alonso Gonzalez (2016), "Knowledge economy and the commons: A theoretical and political approach to postneoliberal common governance," *Review of Radical Political Economy* 48: 140–157.

Veblen, Thorstein ([1908] 1919), "On the nature of capital," pp. 324–386 in Thorstein Veblen (ed.), *The Place of Science in Modern Civilization and other Essays*. New York: Viking.

Weinberger, David (2011), *Too Big to Know. Rethinking Knowledge Now That the Facts Aren't the Facts, Experts Are Everywhere, and the Smartest Person in the Room Is the Room*. New York: Basic Books.

Westacott, Emrys (2019), "What is ethical egoism?," *ThoughtCo*. URL: https://www.thoughtco.com/what-is-ethical-egoism-3573630 (accessed 14 July 2019).

Wigan, Duncan (2009), "Financialisation and derivatives: Constructing an artifice of indifference," *Competition & Change* 13: 157–172.

Zelizer, Viviana (1995), *The Social Meaning of Money*. New York: Basis Books.

Zelizer, Viviana (1989), "The social meaning of money: 'Special monies,'" *American Journal of Sociology* 95: 342–377.

Znaniecki, Florian (1940), *The Social Role of the Man of Knowledge*. New York: Columbia University Press.

Zorn, Dirk M. (2004), "Here a chief, there a chief: The rise of the role of the CFO," *American Sociological Review* 69: 345–364.

# 2

# THE PRICE OF LAND

What we call land is an element of nature inextricably interwoven with man's institutions. To isolate it and form a market for it was perhaps the weirdest of all the undertakings of our ancestors.

—*Karl Polanyi ([1944] 2001: 187)*

In *Owning the Earth*, Scottish historian Andro Linklater explores the life story of Sir Humphrey Gilbert, a scientist and adventurer sent on an expedition by Queen Elizabeth I to establish the first English colony on American soil in 1583. Linklater (2013: 2–3) describes the arrival of Gilbert in Newfoundland as follows:

On August 5, 1583, Gilbert arrived at Saint John's harbor to find almost forty fishing vessels already there, not only catching cod but drying and salting them onshore. Immediately the surveyors went to work, and, as Hayes put it, "did observe the elevation of the pole and drewe plats [plans] of the countrey exactly graded [to scale]." Before the end of the month, the first transactions had taken place, and parcels of land along the water's edge were being rented out to fishermen who until then had occupied them freely. "For which grounds" Hayes pointed out, "they did covenant to pay a certain rent and service." In return, Gilbert assured his tenants they now had the right to occupy their own particular spot from one year to the next.

On the face of it, Gilbert's behavior was absurd. For uncounted generations the granite hills overlooking the long, dog-leg inlet of Saint John's had been used by the Mi'kmaq people, who regarded it as their territory. The Basque fishermen „who had discovered the sheltered haven perhaps before Columbus sailed to America in 1492 believed that they and any others who had the audacity to cross the ocean to fish for cod had earned the right to use the landing-grounds during the summer season. But that was as far as it went.

Yet now, under English law Sir Humphrey Gilbert asserted just such a right, and on that basis proposed to charge the fishermen rent for using a part of the wilderness for activities that they had always engaged in freely. For the first time, an idea that would revolutionize the structure of society and transform the way people thought about themselves had made itself known outside its homeland.

The idea that land could achieve private economic value is a rather recent one in the history of mankind. Until the beginning of the 19th century, most of the land from Africa to Asia and to South America was still largely in communal ownership and thus considered a common good. As an existential source of all life, food, water, protection, origin and homeland, traditional societies regarded the land as a divine gift embodying an immense spiritual value. For a long time, private property claims and their transfer in trade were unimaginable. Expropriation of informal land rights by the community was common practice and generally accepted when deemed necessary for furthering a common cause (Reynolds, 2010).

But societies are subject to constant change, as are their fundamental values: "In an urban society individualism dominates and the desire and competition for individual ownership increases. In this respect land makes no exception" (Verheye, 2009: 83). With the advent of industrialization at the latest, land became a recognized commodity, and efficiency-focused value conceptions gained the upper hand over communal ideas. Linklater (2013: 5–6) writes about the emergence of private property as a profound social transformation:

> The disruption of this pattern is the great revolution of the last two hundred years. The idea of individual, exclusive ownership, not just of what can be carried or occupied, but of the immovable, near-eternal earth, has proved to be the most destructive and creative cultural force in written history. It has eliminated ancient civilizations wherever it has encountered them, and displaced entire peoples from their homelands, but it has also spread an undreamed-of degree of personal freedom and protected it with democratic institutions wherever it has taken hold.

In this chapter, our aim is to trace this powerful socio-economic revolution as the result of the invention of private property along with the inevitable societal contest about the value of land. In particular, we examine the economic, social, and ecological consequences of a transformative process that is increasingly characterized by the comprehensive financialization of land, nature, and the environment.

How has the classical agricultural notion of land been expanded by the influence of industrialization, urbanization, and resource depletion? In particular, we note that the comprehensive urge to quantify soil has shifted the focus from productive properties of land to speculative functions. It appears that neo-liberalism accomplished a hegemonic position also with regards to the discourse around the value of land to which alternative conceptions—ecological as well as spiritual—now appear entirely subordinate. Our analysis begins with classical spatial theory, which laid the foundation for economic considerations about the price of land and leads us through the industrial transformation of agrarian societies to financialization, which ultimately culminates in the all-inclusive marketization of land and nature.

## Theories of Space

In combination with human labor, land and soil constitute perhaps the oldest production factors in the history of mankind. Until the emergence of the industrial revolution in Europe during the second half of the 18th century, feudal societies were literally built on the fields. Early economists therefore dealt in depth with central questions concerning land, for instance, what form of economic activity should take place where and why; how the intensity of soil operation varied in different regions around a city; and which valuable conclusions for different location and land rents could be derived from these findings (Kurz, 2008). Like every great strand of economic theory, the ultimate goal of its contributors was to formulate a general theory of land management that was able to explain both, individual economic processes and price formation and, in particular, spatial differences (Isard, 1949: 1).

Thus, since the end of the 19th century and even more so during the mid-20th century, a rich academic literature emerged that increasingly and systematically combined geographical research with economic knowledge (cf. Launhardt, 1885; Marshall, [1890] 1920; Weber, 1909; Hotelling, 1929; Ohlin, 1933; Christaller, 1933; Palander, 1935; Kaldor, 1935; Hoover, 1936; Lösch, 1940). One of the first and arguably most important thinkers of a general theory of space, was Johann Heinrich von Thünen (Samuelson, 1983: 1468). In his work *The Isolated State* (1842), the German agricultural and economic scientist von Thünen laid the foundation for the modern economic debate about land as a means of production by providing the first comprehensive attempt at formulating a general theory of space. Many of his groundbreaking findings were of an experimental nature. Thünen himself was a landowner and farmer and thus able to derive and verify many of his intuitions from daily agricultural activities. He was decisively influenced by Adam Smith (Chisholm, 1979) and was inspired in particular by questions concerning the optimal use of agricultural land and the associated pricing of land rents.

In the first paragraph of his classical work, Thünen ([1842] 1966: 7) lays out the theoretical scenario underlying all his further considerations:

> Imagine a very large town, at the center of a fertile plain which is crossed by no navigable river or canal. Throughout the plain the soil is capable of cultivation and of the same fertility. Far from the town, the plain turns into an uncultivated wilderness which cuts off all communication between this State and the outside world.
>
> There are no other towns on the plain. The central town must therefore supply the rural areas with all manufactured products, and in return it will obtain all its provisions from the surrounding countryside.
>
> The mines that provide the State with salt and metals are near the central town which, as it is the only one, we shall in future call simply "the Town."

In the context of this particularly isolated city, Thünen develops his classical theory of land use that is considered to be the first systematic and comprehensive inquiry of the price of land. With regard to his scenario, Thünen wondered what form an optimal distribution of economic activity around the city would take. He assumed that different types of agricultural products produced different quantities of harvests and different transport costs, which in turn depended on the distance to the city's central marketplace. While transport costs are lowest in the area closest to the market, land prices are also highest due to this decisive locational advantage.

Farmers who find themselves in free competition are therefore always faced with a complicated trade-off between transport costs and land prices. This is the theoretical superstructure of Thünen's considerations. Taking into account the natural variances between different agricultural products, Thünen shows in a next step that farmers would position themselves in exact *concentric rings* around the city (see Figure 2.1).

Since vegetables, such as tomatoes, are easily perishable and difficult to transport, farmers who specialize in growing such products will settle close to the city center and accept higher land rents for lower transport costs. On the other hand, or rather on the outskirts of the district, grain farmers will be most likely to settle as their products are not only easier to transport but also relatively more durable. Higher transport costs could thus be accepted in order to save land rent. Ultimately, this static scenario amounts to an equilibrium in which farmers, depending on their type of commodity and productivity, share the agricultural land available among themselves in an economically optimal fashion.

At a certain geographical tipping point beyond the grain fields, the price of the land tends toward zero. At the same time, however, the transport costs rise to levels so high that the cultivation of even the most durable agricultural products is no longer suitable. There, civilization finds its boundaries and "uncultivated wilderness" begins (Rieter, 1995: 15). In a more sophisticated model, which Thünen developed analyzing many different agricultural products, a total of seven rings

Rent

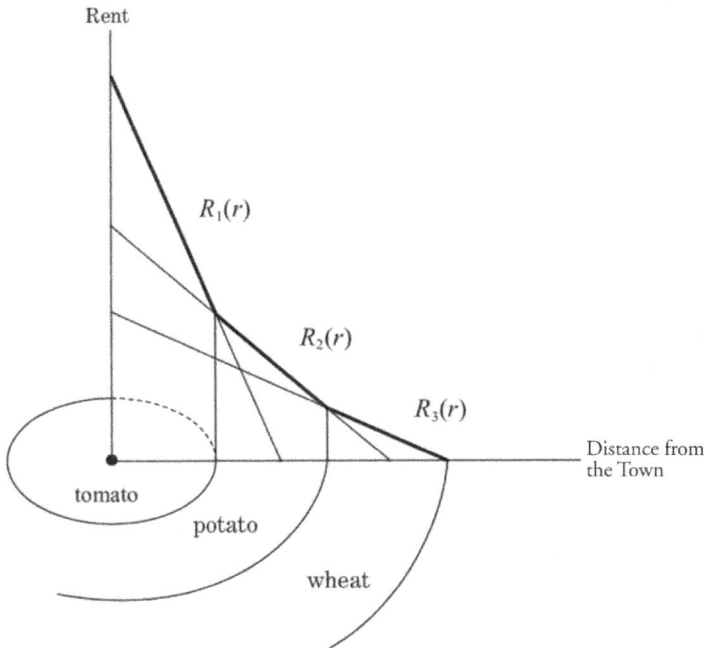

$R_1(r)$

$R_2(r)$

$R_3(r)$

Distance from
the Town

tomato

potato

wheat

**FIGURE 2.1**   Thünen's Rings With Three Products

*Source:* Fujita 2010: 6

exists. These include the free-range economy (garden plants and milk), forestry, crop rotation, paddock farming, three-field system farming, livestock breeding, and wilderness (Kurz, 2008: 149). Thünen also pointed out the advantages of growing different products in similar rings, as economies of scope and product synergies could improve farmers' cost functions.[1]

What insights does Thünen's' classical spatial theory provide with regard to the price and value of land? To him, distance from the market and resulting transport costs are obviously the most relevant variables. The lower the distance from the market, the higher the price of the land and the higher the intensity of cultivation (cf. Dunn, 1954: 6–8; Carell, 1950). However, due to the unrealistic assumption of homogeneous land surrounding the city, other important factors such as soil fertility, which plays a central role not only in David Ricardo's considerations (cf. Chisholm, 1962: 22–26), become irrelevant.

The price of land in Thünen's spatial theory derived from a combination of heterogeneous product types on homogeneous soil is thus based purely on the logistic utility value of the location (Norton, 1979). This conclusion strikingly illustrates the particular *agricultural* perspective that dominated the theoretical considerations of Thünen as a farmer in the middle of the 19th century.

With social and economic development making great strides toward the end of the 19th century, Thünen's agrarian-focused theory was quickly transformed into a modern industrial location theory and economic geography became both a comprehensive and recognized branch of the social sciences. The British economist Alfred Marshall played a major role in this development. In his *Principles of Economics* (Marshall, [1890] 1920: 225), he systematically analyzed the agglomeration of industries and was the first to recognize the importance of positive externalities in the choice of settlement that can lead to companies binding themselves to one location in the long term:

> When an industry has thus chosen a location for itself, it is likely to stay there long: so great are the advantages which people following the same skilled trade get from near neighborhood to one another. The mysteries of the trade become no mysteries; but are as it were in the air, and children learn many of them unconsciously. Good work is rightly appreciated, inventions and improvements in machinery, in processes and the general organization of the business have their merits promptly discussed: if one man starts a new idea, it is taken up by others and combined with suggestions of their own; and thus, it becomes the source of further new ideas.

This industry-centered perspective was further developed incrementally and, much later, turned into a Nobel Prize-worthy theory by Paul Krugman (1991a, 1991b).

Krugman succeeded in combining the central variables of transport costs, factor mobility, and economies of scale in order to explain differences in the spatial agglomeration of industry and agriculture. The recognition of the practical existence of transport costs, derived from Thünen's original considerations, was a decisive step for the foundation of the discipline of *New Economic Geography*. Classical economic theories long discarded the transportation factor in their limited variable models. An economic geography without transport costs, however, would surely be of little use. Furthermore, Krugman assumed complete mobility of industrial workers. In order to minimize transport costs and maximize economies of scale at the same time, profit-oriented companies always locate close to large sales markets. This is where they can recruit qualified workers, who in turn are drawn from the periphery by ample opportunities for work, high wages and strong purchasing power due to lower average prices in larger markets. As a result, companies and mobile workers are gradually agglomerating in one place. At the same time, however, there are also some workers who remain immobile. These are primarily farmers who are tied to the location of their fields in the long term. Thus, in modern industrial nations a *core-periphery model* emerges in which the manufacturing industry is concentrated in certain regions with large sales markets, while agricultural production locates mostly in the periphery.

The history of ideas in economic geography shows that modern spatial theory has evolved along the lines of and in response to profound societal transformations. The drastic transition from agricultural to industrial and, ultimately, to international trading companies has had a decisive influence on the assessment of the value of land. While initially merely the utility values of arable land were considered to be important, more complex analyses of the interactions between agriculture and industrial production became increasingly relevant. In the following section, we discuss in more detail the significance of profound social transformation processes for the historical appraisal and evolution of the price and value of land.

## The Evolution of the Value of Land

> Land is one of our most precious assets. In traditional societies it is a common good and cannot be alienated nor sold. In a modern free market system land is a commodity that is desired and can be exchanged; its value and price are commanded by offer and demand and by the underlying perception of potential benefits that can be derived from it. Land is finite in extent is in growing demand; and its value is expected to increase in the future.
>
> —*Willy Verheye (2009: 82)*

If one believes former chief economic advisor to Maggie Thatcher, Alan Walters (1983: 51), the price of land is defined as "the value of ownership of stipulated rights in perpetuity—in short, the price of the land—is equal to the estimated present value of the expected future appropriations of rents."

Such classical definitions refer to the utility value of the land, that is, not only to its material value, but to its production potential (Burt, 1986; Featherstone and Baker, 1987). For land draws its value from the potential material income that can provide for its owner; "in other words, the material value of a land depends upon the goods and services emanating from it" (Verheye, 2009: 86). Thus, in its prime characteristics land does not differ substantially from other classical forms of capital, which in the sense of Böhm-Bawerk ([1889] 1991) allow for added-value production detours. So, essentially two possibilities exist to evaluate the price of a piece of land.

On the one hand, the economic value of the land can be derived in relative terms from recent and comparable sales of other properties. This strategy is used especially in differentiated, developed markets where the production potential of different plots of land has largely stabilized. On the other hand, it is also possible to assess a piece of land solely on the basis of its production potential and independent of other business transactions. This method is used mainly in developing market environments and implies by definition a higher degree of speculation and risk potential.

However, land embodies a special characteristic that certainly makes it a unique factor of production. A piece of tradable land is finite in its extent. It can neither be reproduced nor enlarged and, most importantly perhaps, is tied to a certain location. This limits its commercial potential and directs the focus of investors from its potential price to tangible opportunity costs (Food and Agriculture Organization of the United Nations [FAO], 2003; our emphasis):

> For decision-making about land, the relevant concept is in any case not the price but the opportunity cost. Land cannot be reproduced and is spatially linked to specific location. Although land may be extra-ordinarily valuable in the center of a city, it is impossible to produce more of it, and the amount must be taken as given. At this moment, the opportunity value of the land, as perceived by the individual person (for example because of its location) is *more important than its intrinsic production value.*

This important change in the valuation of land is a direct consequence of profound societal transformation processes. In rural contexts, the production value of arable land still carries significant weight. The fertility and location, its irrigation opportunities and meteorological characteristics continue to determine the agricultural yield potential, which is ultimately reflected in the production of essential consumer goods. However, the share of agricultural land in the total amount of available space in globally trading industrial nations is steadily shrinking, while the demand for urban commercial and residential land seems to be inexorably rising.

For example, the German Federal Environment Agency (*Umweltbundesamt*, 2018) reports that the share of agricultural land shrank from 53.5 to 51.5% between 2000 and 2016. The fact that this loss took place particularly on the borders to densely populated areas suggests at least an even exchange from agricultural to urban land. At the same time, the share of company and residential building areas, roads, and airfields (settlement and traffic areas) rose by a significant 12.1% during the same period.

In an urban context, the production value of a section of land loses its relevance. In contrast to agricultural use, it does not produce immediately palpable goods that can be traded directly on the market. Rather, urban land derives its value mainly from future interest payments and returns on capital, which are generated in the process of developing residential and commercial real estate (Alonso, 1964; Muth, 1969). With the profound transition from agrarian to urban societies, the valuation of land has changed extensively. Additional determinants of land value have been added to the still relevant concept of production value (cf. Verheye, 2009: 89).

On the one hand, land is increasingly valued in terms of its financial surplus potential, which can be derived in particular from exogenous price changes. These include, for example, political decisions on the type of permissible land use, urban development potential or land and property taxation. On the other hand, the growing scarcity of available urban land reinforces speculative considerations. Against this background, urban land and scarce housing in particular are acquired by large investors on the basis of inflationary tendencies, which appear entirely decoupled from immediate production value or classic returns on capital.

This increasing influence of speculative financial interests is, however, countered by an opposing force. Worldwide, there are vast areas of land which embody neither productive nor financial value, but are nevertheless owned by federal states, municipalities or private individuals. In theory they could be traded on the market. However, these are areas whose value is not derived from economic considerations, but based rather on ecological, aesthetic, moral, and social aspects (Verheye, 2009: 87). For example, restricted nature reserves offer no direct economic benefits, but a society that fosters such protective areas through its environmental policies appears to recognize a particular kind of added value in the preservation of fauna and flora. In this essentially non-economic respect, too, far-reaching social and political transformation processes, in many cases triggered by the mounting recognition of anthropogenic climate change, lead to changing values being reflected in the price of land, sometimes even deeming it completely unsaleable.

Social and political transformation processes change the social valuation of land in fundamental fashion. Conceptually, this can be better illustrated with regard to spatial theories we have discussed above. Classical spatial theories are characterized by their particular focus on the *demand* side. There are practical reasons for this. In the middle of the 19th century, when the first comprehensive spatial theories were developed, agricultural land still was largely in the hands of powerful landowners who, following the abolition of peonage, leased productive grounds to farmers. Against this historical background, it is not entirely surprising that Ricardo and von Thünen regarded the supply of land as a given and that their theories appeared quite static in turn.

In Thünen's deliberations, for example, the supply of farmland is solely determined by the transport costs and is, apart from its distance to the marketplace, completely homogeneous. The price of land therefore manifests itself exclusively on the demand side: depending on the cultivated product and associated transport costs, a piece of land always goes to the highest bidding farmer, who in turn optimally reconciles his transport costs with the land rent.

However, the transformation of industrial societies and ongoing urbanization coupled with technological advances and a considerable reduction in transport costs make a purely demand-sided view of land prices increasingly unrealistic. Against this background, British economic geographer Alan W. Evans (1983: 121) argues for a supply-oriented theory of land prices, because "Most of the differences between the values of different pieces of land come, not from some more easily seen economic benefit, i.e. proximity to the city centre, but from the government permitting or not permitting particular kinds of development." Political regulation, which directly reflects, catalyzes and amplifies value transformation processes in democratic industrial societies thus plays a key role in the use of land and the associated assessment of its value. This becomes more obvious when von Thünen's concept of concentric rings is applied graphically to the urban context (see Figure 2.2).

Figure 2.2 illustrates that in an urban environment, the distance to the city center is still relevant, but no longer exclusively decisive. More important for assessing property prices is the political regulation of urban land use. Because in increasingly service-based knowledge economies, office space in the city center promises the greatest profit. At the same time, agglomeration effects can also lead to the development of office parks outside the center, endogenously increasing the locational value of those areas. In an urban environment, the price of land is no longer based purely on its immediate utility value, but in particular on the *political and social changeability* of its potential use. As a result, the price of land may well rise above its pure production value (Verheye, 2009: 90; Borchers, Ifft and Kuethe, 2014). This important conclusion once again emphasizes the special feature of land as a unique means of production (Evans, 1983: 123):

> [Traditional spatial] theories treat land as in principle no different from any other good. The market price is that which clears the market whether the goods in question are apples, motor cars or building sites. It seems to me, however, that it is in fact incorrect to treat land in the same manner as apples, or even cars. To do so is to ignore various features of land which are important factors in the operations of the land market. Whilst one apple

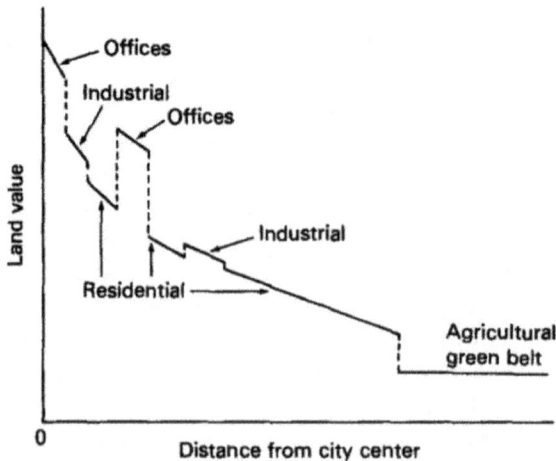

**FIGURE 2.2**   The Relationship Between Land Value and Distance to the City Center in the Urban Context

*Source:* Evans 1983: 121

may be much like another, a piece of land for the person who lives there acquires attributes which differentiate it from all other sites. These attributes may increase the value of the land to the occupier above its market value. In the terminology of welfare economics there is a "consumer surplus" attached to occupation of that land. In the terminology of Marxian economics, the use value of the land (even if it cannot be stated in money terms) exceeds its exchange value.

The empirical relevance of this finding is also increasingly observable in rural areas. Allison Borchers and her colleagues (2014: 1307) show that in large parts of the United States "the market value of farmland has been shown to exceed its use value in agricultural production" (see also Barnard, 2000; Flanders, White and Escalante, 2004; Capozza and Hesley, 1989). In the course of their investigations, they conclude that agricultural land is increasingly being evaluated with regard to its non-agricultural development potential and that nowadays, land prices depend in particular on the local proximity to relevant urban infrastructure, e.g. parks, hospitals or schools and universities.[2] As a result, in the vicinity of urban centers, average land prices can often be determined up to 50 per cent by purely speculative investments (Capozza and Hesley, 1989: 305). We can thus conclude that the transformative development of the valuation of land underlies one socio-economic trend in particular. The novel promise of growth premiums on previously unchangeable and spatially tied pieces of land, being the result of far-reaching social and industrial changes, has aroused a strong interest among the financial community. Recently, these very actors have been the main drivers of a growing financialization of land, the function, extent, and consequences of which will be subject of the following sections.

## Societal Transformations

> We might as well imagine his being born without hands and feet as carrying on his life without land. And yet to separate land from man and to organize society in such a way as to satisfy the requirements of a real-estate market was a vital part of the Utopian concept of a market economy.
> —*Karl Polanyi ([1944] 2001: 187)*

Since the Industrial Revolution, and under the increasing influence of a continuously growing and ever more differentiated market economy, contemporary societies have been subjected to fundamental transformative processes. Capitalism had the extraordinary power to remove the economy from its historical embeddedness within regulating social structures and even to reverse the direction of this effect. This constitutes, in essence, the timeless conclusion of Karl Polanyi's

*The Great Transformation.* In his groundbreaking work, land plays a particularly important role (Polanyi, [1944] 2001: 72–73; our emphasis)

> Under feudalism and the guild system land and labor formed part of the social organization itself. . . . Land, the pivotal element in the feudal order, was the basis of the military, judicial, administrative, and political system; its status and function were determined by legal and customary rules. Whether its possession was transferable or not, and if so, to whom and under what restrictions; what the rights of property entailed; to what uses some types of land might be put—all these questions *were removed from the organization of buying and selling, and subjected to an entirely different set of institutional regulations.*

Even in the heyday of European mercantilism, land remained largely a good "*extra commercium*" under the determined protection of social institutions. But "the change from regulated to self-regulating markets at the end of the eighteenth century represented a complete transformation in the structure of society" (Polanyi, [1944] 2001: 73–74). Because the introduction of our modern market economy gradually led to an erosion of the influence of formerly order-giving social institutions and to an increasing dominance of economic and financial principles.

Whereas previously, economic processes were almost naturally subordinated to social institutions and their norms, the increasing importance of economy and capital meant that all processes and values, that is "the substance of society itself," had to be subordinated to the laws of the market (ibid.: 75). A commercial society emerged, characterized by its supreme principle: the unrestricted purchasability of each and every commodity. Karl Polanyi notices, however, that few original production factors, three in number, naturally evade this principle. Among them is also land (Polanyi, [1944] 2001: 75–76; our emphasis):

> But labor, land, and money are obviously *not* commodities; the postulate that anything that is bought and sold must have been produced for sale is emphatically untrue in regard to them. In other words, according to the empirical definition of a commodity they are not commodities. Labor is only another name for a human activity which goes with life itself, which in its turn is not produced for sale but for entirely different reasons. . . *land is only another name for nature, which is not produced by man*; actual money, finally, is merely a token of purchasing power which, as a rule, is not produced at all, but comes into being through the mechanism of banking or state finance. None of them is produced for sale. The commodity description of labor, land, and money is *entirely fictitious.*

But because these important production factors had to be made purchasable as well, the *fictitious* character of these commodities became the ordering principle of the new market society. In this way, the market system has since made "nature

under the name of land . . . available for sale . . . and the use of land could be negotiated for a price called rent" (Polanyi, ([1944] 2001: 135–136).

How did this historically unique transformation of social values come about?
Polanyi ([1944] 2001: 188) identifies three historical factors that increasingly promoted the marketization of land. First, the agricultural capitalism of the Tudors
in England led to an increasingly individualistic treatment of land as commodity,
which was expressed in particular in the acceptance of rededications and enclosures and facilitated the transfer of land ownership significantly. Second, from the
beginning of the 18th century onwards, the industrialization of Great Britain and
continental Europe brought about a downright overhaul of the existing land order.
Because in the course of the transition from an agrarian to an industrial economy,
land was now required in substantial amounts for factories and workers' accom-
modations. This development culminated, third, in "the rise of industrial towns
with their need for practically unlimited food and raw material supplies," contributing to the comprehensive marketization of agriculture. As a consequence, the
traditional embeddedness of existing social structures was gradually eroded and
undermined. The most fundamental question concerning the transformation of
the value of land is, perhaps, not a historical-technical, but rather a normative one:
did market capitalism with its emphasis on individual and entrepreneurial freedom
in fact manage to abolish feudalism as the previously dominant class-structuring
element of society? Polanyi provides a clear answer (Polanyi, [1944] 2001: 188):

> Commercialization of the soil was only another name for the liquidation
> of feudalism which started in Western urban centers as well as in England
> in the fourteenth century and was concluded some five hundred years later
> in the course of the European revolutions, when the remnants of villeinage
> were abolished.

Most political economists of the 19th century agreed with Polanyi's assertion.
Classically, they regarded labor as the most important factor of production and
thus were fundamentally critical of feudal rule. David Ricardo, for example, saw
the often-aristocratic feudal lord as a parasitical beneficiary who derived his riches
neither from his own physical work nor from productive planning or coordinating activities subject to competition. He simply owned land, which was mostly
bestowed on ancestry, that continuously yielded profits that others had to earn (cf.
Heilbroner, 1989: 96; Hudson, 2012: 140).

It was precisely these rigid structures that the new mode of capitalist production was able to break open (Harvey, 1982: 343–349). The dominance of aris-
tocratic landowners was slowly but surely replaced by the increasing influence
of the urban bourgeoisie (Gunnoe, 2014). Karl Marx ([1894] 1999: 461), too,
concluded that

> The rationalising of agriculture, on the one hand, which makes it for
> the first time capable of operating on a social scale, and the reduction *ad*

*absurdum* of property in land, on the other, are the great achievements of the capitalist mode of production.

Ultimately, capitalism seemed capable of breaking up historical class structures, which were manifested in particular in the unequal ownership of land by transforming land ownership into a tradable production factor (Marx, [1894] 1999: 461):

> One of the major results of the capitalist mode of production is . . . that it divorces landed property from the relations of dominion and servitude, on the one hand, and, on the other, totally separates land as an instrument of production from landed property and landowner. . . . Landed property thus receives its purely economic form by discarding all its former political and social embellishments and associations, in brief all those traditional accessories, which are denounced . . . as useless and absurd superfluities by the industrial capitalists themselves, as well as their theoretical spokesmen, in the heat of their struggle with landed property.

The conclusion that capitalism replaced the feudal social order may well be accurate, at least in the short and medium term. But already toward the end of the 19th century it became increasingly evident that this development was by no means capable of abolishing the dominance of landowners *per se*. Rather, the feudal system was replaced by an increasingly influential finance capitalism, which driven purely by the logic of economic returns supplanted important non-economic, cultural, social and ecological functions of the land. This marked the beginning of its comprehensive financialization.

## Financialization of the Land

> Today's ultimate recipients of land rent are not the hereditary owners as was the landlord class in Ricardo's day; they are the banks.
> —*Michael Hudson (2012: 198)*

Browsing through recent company publications or investor reports, chances are that you will come across interesting metaphors for land and soil. In them, land is often described as "black gold" (Cole, 2012) or "gold with yield" (Koven, 2012). These comparisons are not accidental. Rather, they point to the profound progress of financialization, which has long discovered land as an investment object and picked up significant pace since the global economic crisis of 2008. Although the crisis has increased financial influence in land markets, financialization of land is a direct and logical consequence of societal transformation processes, which we have already described in detail.

Following the definition of American sociologist Greta Krippner (2011: 4; see also 2005), financialization describes "the tendency for profit making in the economy to occur increasingly through financial channels rather than through productive activities" (see also Epstein, 2005: 3). Applied to land and nature in particular, it can be understood as "a process of ontological reconfiguration through which different qualities of nature and resource-based production are translated into a financial value form to be traded in specialized markets" (Ouma, Johnson and Bigger, 2018: 501). The interest of international financial markets in land is growing. This is due in particular to the fact that agricultural land generally correlates strongly with the inflation rate, but less so with the prices of other investment assets. Thus, land is widely considered an attractive insurance against inflation risks and an excellent opportunity to diversify investment portfolios (HighQuest Partners, 2010: 778). In addition, land is a source of relatively secure income streams that are important for securing financial credibility and attracting additional venture capital from investors.

As discussed in detail in the previous chapter, financialization began in the 1970s, when the neo-liberal revolutions in the United States and Great Britain, triggered by a profound economic paradigm shift from Keynesianism to monetarism (Hall, 1989), led to the far-reaching repeal of the New Deal's financial market regulations (Gunnoe, 2014: 484f.; Harvey, 2005). In stark contrast, the financialization of land only began quite recently before and during the global economic crisis of 2008. Until then, investors typically refrained from investing in agricultural land as profits were incommensurable with riskier investments in more prominent sectors. With increasing market uncertainty, however, prices began to rise around 2007 and, when the crisis broke out, financial actors invested billions to insure themselves with *safe assets* against imminent losses (Fairbairn, 2014a).

It is anything but easy to quantify the real extent of global financialization of land. Even though investors' interest in farmland is still considered relatively small in absolute terms (Fairbairn, 2014a: 778), more recent estimates now place global institutional investment at US\$ 30/40 billion to US\$ 8.4 trillion (Wheaton et al., 2012). At the same time, however, growth numbers illustrate that the interest of institutional investors in agricultural land in relative terms has risen sharply over the past decade.

Against this backdrop, we want to develop a closer understanding of this pertinent development and, in doing so, begin with our inquiry at the central theme of the previous chapter. We ask about the special role that financialization of land plays in restructuring modern societies and their value systems: has it, as Marx and Polanyi expected, led to a reduction in feudal concentration of power, or perhaps simply replaced it with new, equally rigid hierarchical systems?

In order to answer this question, an important distinction must first be made. Conceptually, financial investors can be divided into two functionally differentiated groups (cf. Gunnoe, 2014: 479). On the one hand, there are traditional industrial businesses that use land immediately for the production of (manufactured) goods. In this context, land is most often acquired as a long-term production factor. On the other hand, there is an emerging group of institutional investors. They invest in land purely speculatively, not to produce a real economic product, but solely in the hope of rapid value appreciation.

Regarding the influence of the latter class of investors, academic literature offers two dominant views. American sociologist Andrew Gunnoe takes a more radical view based on recent research by Michael Hudson (2012). With a view to the sharp rise in institutional investors' interest in land, he argues "that we are witnessing an unprecedented integration between finance capital and landownership that harkens back to previous eras of rentier control," which among other things leads to a considerable increase in land prices (Gunnoe, 2014: 478). With this analysis he finds support in the camp of neo-Marxist economic geographers around David Harvey. He warns that in advanced industrial economies "land becomes a form of fictitious capital, and the land market functions simply as a particular branch—albeit with some special characteristics—of the circulation of interest-bearing capital. Under such conditions the *land is treated as a pure financial asset* which is bought and sold according to the rent it yields" (Harvey, 1982: 347; our emphasis). This blurs the functional distinction between classic landowners on the one hand, who draw their income from leasing their property, and modern investors on the other, whose profits consist of interest payments on land capital (Fairbairn, 2014a: 781). As a result, financial investors were able to use "their control over the credit system to pressure corporate owners to divest their real estate assets and bring them under control of the financial sector. In the process, financial investors have benefited greatly from an increasing stream of rental income and rising land prices" (Gunnoe, 2014: 486). From this point of view, the unfree, agrarian feudal society, in stark contrast to all hopes of the great thinkers of the 19th century, was not dissolved, but merely restructured in the form of a capitalist neo-rentier society (Hudson, 2012: 203). While ownership structures were obviously reconfigured, power hierarchies remained largely intact.

This rather radical perspective is countered by a somewhat more differentiated stance, prominently advocated by the environmental sociologist Madeleine Fairbairn. She questions the clear distinction between real (manufacturing) and financial investor groups. As already noted, the lack of transparency within the financial system makes it quite challenging to fathom the actual motivation behind investor behavior (HighQuest Partners, 2010; for an elaborate attempt see Kish and Fairbairn, 2018). But analyzing the strategic treatment of land investments, it becomes clear nevertheless that the distinct separation between financial capital on the one hand and productive capital on the other does not adequately reflect reality. Rather, agricultural land as asset category can fulfil a dual function (Fairbairn, 2014a: 782):

> Taking an Arrighian understanding of financialization as increasing accumulation through financial channels as opposed to productive ones, several

aspects of the current farmland investment boom break with the trend. Most importantly, many of the farmland investments that have been initiated since 2007 are functional agricultural projects, not just land purchases.

Instead, Fairbairn (2014a: 782–784) proposes a functionally differentiated analysis of investor strategies. The first strategy, *own-lease out*, is at the heart of neo-Marxist critique. Investors buy a piece of land and leave its financial management to an external administrator. The net income generated from rent and capital appreciation flows directly back to the owner, who does not use the property for any productive activity, but purely for speculative reasons. Applying a contrasting strategy, *own-operate*, land is seen explicitly as productive capital that can be put to real use to generate profits. New social risks such as population growth, food insecurity, energy scarcity, and climate change have given this form of investment strategy new relevance (Cotula, 2012).

The question is which of these two forms of investment strategies dominate the financial land rush of recent times. Fairbairn argues that the extent of the *own-operate* approach should not be underestimated, since under this strategy about half of the returns corresponded to classic value-added revenues from productive real investments: "Contrary to simplistic portrayals of recent large-scale farmland acquisitions as *either* productive *or* speculative, this demonstrates that they can be, and frequently are, both at the same time" (Fairbairn, 2014a: 786). But there is good reason to question this relatively optimistic analysis. As Fairbairn herself points out, increasing liquidity in land markets could very well increase *own-lease* investments. In particular, loan securitizations could offset the notorious illiquidity of land, which limited investor interest for the longest time. For example, so-called *Real Estate Investment Trusts* (REITs) are modern financial instruments that promote this process by tearing down previous investment barriers:

> Created by the US Congress in the early 1960s but taking off widely in the mid-1990s, REITs work by establishing a portfolio of individual properties owned outright, leased or held as mortgages. Individual REITs are then generally traded on stock exchanges, although they can also be structured as private (nontraded) vehicles and owned by hedge or private equity funds (McCann and Gross, 2012; Schachter, 2012). These securitized vehicles give financial actors, including more modest investors, the opportunity to invest in property shares: they benefit from increases in property value without having to bother with the complexities of profitably managing these properties. REITs can be structured to bet on increases in property value from a specific type of property like shopping malls, real estate appreciation in a specific place or other strategies. Fundamentally, REITs make urban real estate—and now certain groups of rural properties—more "liquid" as an investment. If an investment in a REIT is not working out, investors can

often simply sell out, a far smaller commitment than they would have to make to invest in property directly.

*(Knuth, 2015: 172–173)*

New financial instruments of these sorts significantly contribute to the fact that land markets are increasingly dominated by short-term-oriented, speculative investors, who strictly separate ownership from operation and hamper market access for small-scale farmers. Against this backdrop, it may very well be the case that not every form of modern land investment contributes directly to the comprehensive financialization of land. But recent developments reveal a clear and worrisome trend with significant economic, social, and environmental implications. In the following chapters, we take a functional perspective and examine these consequences in more detail in order to gain a better understanding of the underlying social transformation processes.

## Land Grabbing

Land grabbing on a great scale, such as was perpetrated in England, is the first step in creating a field for the establishment of agriculture on a great scale. Hence this subversion of agriculture puts on, at first, more the appearance of a political revolution.

—*Karl Marx ([1890] 1976: 556–557)*

Karl Marx was the first to coin the term "land grabbing." In the course of this chapter, we want to examine this particular phenomenon in more detail, since it can be considered the most distinct and socially momentous effect of the ongoing financialization of land. While in the German original of *Das Kapital*, Marx frequently speaks of "land theft," we will use the slightly more neutral and less invasive term. Land grabbing describes an economic process that takes place both, transboundary and globally (cf. White et al., 2012: 619):

"Land grab" generally refers to large-scale, cross-border land deals or transactions that are carried out by transnational corporations or initiated by foreign governments. They concern the lease (often for 30–99 years), concession or outright purchase of large areas of land in other countries for various purposes.

*(GRAIN, 2008)*

Against this definition, it is little surprising that this phenomenon has grown significantly in recent decades, especially in tandem with the globalization of the world economy. The drivers are multi-layered and often linked to each other in complex ways. The energy transition plays an important role combined with stricter climate protection measures that exert pressure on domestic energy markets in advanced industrial nations. In search of alternative and affordable energy sources, for example biofuels, investors are buying up large amounts of foreign land. The creation of new financial instruments paired with significant deregulation of international land trade have further propelled this development. In stark contrast, however, land grabs can also serve as instruments suitable for the immediate protection of land and nature.

Hence, it would be hasty to demonize land grabs *per se*. For example, private investors, NGOs, and governments increasingly buy large areas of land in order to subject them to rigorous environmental protection measures and to protect them from deforestation or detrimental commercialization. Here, too, however, it is important to differentiate investors' intentions carefully. Because on the one hand, commercial eco-tourism, which is often associated with these protective practices, can have negative consequences for ecosystems. On the other hand, the environmental protection argument is often simply used to legitimize large-scale monocultures for biofuel or food production (Fairhead, Leach and Scoones, 2012). This latter aspect points to the largest driver of contemporary land grabbing: global food scarcity.

In 2007 and 2008, the world experienced a food crisis leading to an extreme rise in food prices (see Figure 2.3). According to its calculations, the FAO (2018: 6) assumes that this crisis alone led to an increase of 75 million additional starving

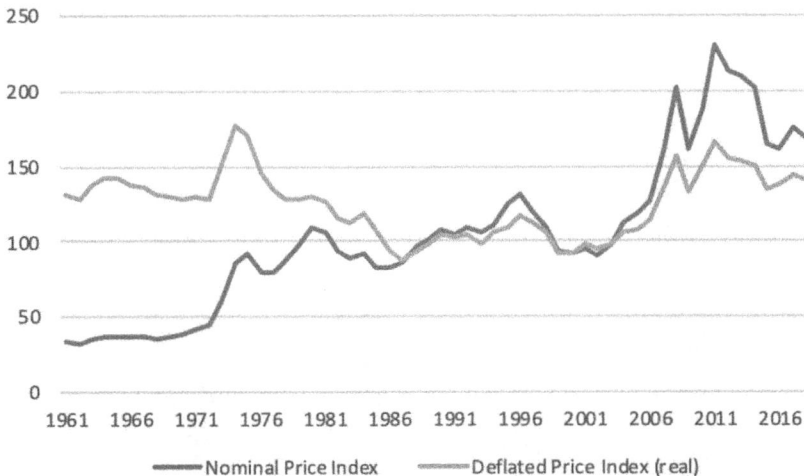

**FIGURE 2.3**    FAO Food Price Index

*Source:* FAO 2018

*Note:* 2002–2004 = 100; the real price index is deflated by the World Bank Manufactures Unit Value Index (MUV)

people worldwide, who often expressed their suffering in violent protests (see Figure 2.4).

Against this background, institutional land grabs are often justified on the grounds of improving food security and food production sites are increasingly being shifted from the global North to the South. The richer and more developed North has experienced a decline in soil productivity for years, which, on the one hand, has stirred food price inflation and, on the other hand, directed the focus of investors to untapped land in the southern hemisphere, especially in Asia and Africa (McMichael, 2012: 683). The consequences of intensified land grabbing are reflected in significant rises of foreign direct investments (FDI) in food and biofuel growing regions, which was reinforced by the American real estate and global financial crisis. Since its outbreak, investors have tried to shield risky capital investments while at the same time betting on profits from a rise in land prices (cf. Gosh, 2010; van der Ploeg, 2010; Cotula, 2012). Mapping the actual extent of these developments empirically continues to pose major challenges for researchers, especially since private land deals are largely conducted non-transparently and behind closed doors (see Anseeuw et al., 2012; von Braun and Meinzen-Dick, 2009; Cotula et al., 2009; Oakland Institute, 2011; Oxfam, 2011; World Bank, 2010). Nevertheless, it cannot be denied that the phenomenon has reached enormous proportions and continues to expand. As early as 2010, the World Bank concluded that

> the demand for land has been enormous. Compared to an average annual expansion of global agricultural land of less than 4 million hectares before

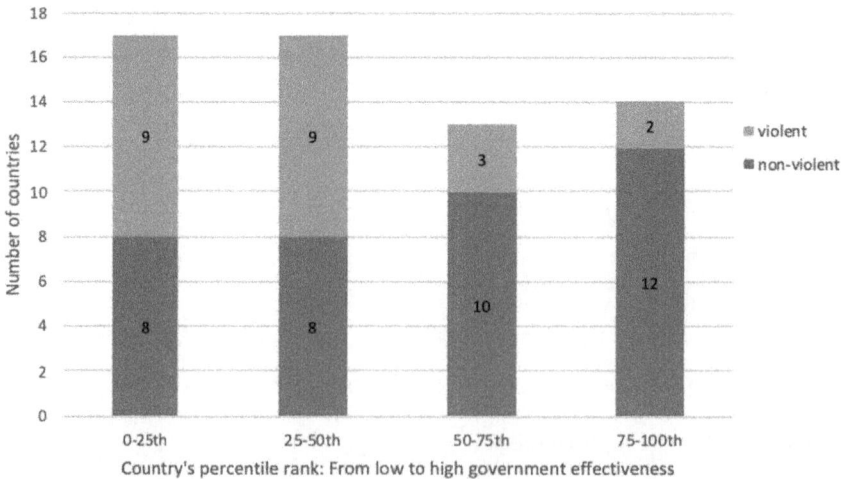

**FIGURE 2.4**  Food Protests Between 2007 and 2008

*Source:* Original figure adapted from data in von Braun (2008: 6); our figure

2008, approximately 56 million hectares worth of large-scale farmland deals were announced even before the end of 2009. More than 70 percent of such demand has been in Africa; countries such as Ethiopia, Mozambique, and Sudan have transferred millions of hectares to investors in recent years.

*(Deininger and Byerlee, 2010: xiv)*

While not every form of land grabbing should be regarded as morally reprehensible *per se*, considering rural impoverishment, exploitation and displacement, these figures pose reasonable cause for concern (Ince, 2014: 105).

Despite notable recent developments, land grabbing is by no means a novel phenomenon. One of the historically most significant cases of institutional land grabbing was introduced by the American *Homestead Act of 1862*, signed by then US President Abraham Lincoln. The Act allowed anyone over the age of 21 to claim an unpopulated piece of land of up to 160 acres and till a field on it. The land was then turned into private ownership either automatically after five years of cultivation or earlier, after six months and at a price of 1.25 US dollars per acre. This privatizing measure intended on the one hand to promote the development of unmanaged land, but on the other to service the mounting debts of the American government during the American civil war.

However, most new farmers lacked the initial capital necessary to turn fallow ground into productive farm land. As a result, most of the land acquired through the *Homestead Act* remained purely speculative, which favored liquid private investors, while disadvantaging informal occupants, above all indigenous Native American tribes (LeDuc, 1962). Little surprisingly, then as now, scientific studies examine normative questions of land grabbing, such as whether it corresponds, in essence, to an illegitimate form of land appropriation as assumed by Karl Marx (cf. Sakolski, 1932).

To answer this question for modern forms of land grabbing and in the context of an increasing financialization, one must pay close attention to the complex processes, procedures and underlying motivations and distinguish them in their form and function from earlier, colonial processes. So, what is new about modern land grabbing (Peluso and Lund, 2011: 672)?

What is so new . . . about "land grabbing"? Dutch, French, Spanish, Portuguese, and English colonizers were heavily engaged in both land grabbing and the creation of private property. . . . The ways officials implemented land controls differed from one colony to another, or differed by crop, by region of a colony, or by legal logic, and often changed over colonial times. What is new in the land grabs today are the new mechanisms of land control, their justifications and alliances for "taking back" the land, as well as the political economic context of neoliberalism that dominates this particular stage of the capitalist world system.

At the same time, Liz Alden Wily (2012: 752) notes that there is an obvious commonality between earlier and modern forms of land grabbing in legal regulations that "are designed to render untitled (but traditionally occupied and used) lands as unowned, and the state, by default, their legal owner." So, is modern financially driven land grabbing at all qualitatively distinguishable from colonialist land theft?

Here, too, Marxist and neo-Marxist literature offers valuable insights. As indicated, it is evident that Marx's hope that capitalism could break up ancient feudal power structures and deliver more justice and freedom was too optimistic. On the contrary, modern financialized processes of land trading seem to be dominated by classical hierarchical structures, too, only that the winners of this comprehensive economic reorganization process are no longer legitimized by blood and birth, but rather by their capital ownership (Knuth, 2015: 166). Today's global land grabbing—leading from the northern to the southern hemisphere—still pursues a strategy and function that corresponds to the Marxist concept of primitive accumulation in a largely unchanged way (Marx, [1890] 1976: 915):

> The discovery of gold and silver in America, the extirpation, enslavement, and entombment in mines of the indigenous population of that continent, the beginnings of the conquest and plunder of India, and the conversion of Africa into a preserve for the commercial hunting of blackskins, are all things that characterize the dawn of the era of capitalist production. These idyllic proceedings are the chief moments of primitive accumulation.

Regarding the trade with land, primitive accumulation describes a tendency inherent in capitalism to create market access for previously non-tradable goods in order to integrate them within capitalism's global sphere of influence and effect. It thus happens that vast regions in the global south that are still largely undeveloped are made accessible to satisfy ever-growing capital demand in the industrially advanced global North. Although largely nonviolent today, it is not surprising that this compulsive appropriation of southern territories awakens strong memories of the colonial past.

However, a slightly more nuanced development of Marx' classical theory reveals aspects that do distinguish modern land grabbing from colonial appropriation. Arguably, David Harvey (1982, 2003, 2005) made the most important contribution to this end with his theory of spatial fixes. He interprets modern land grabbing as a form of "accumulation by dispossession." This entails a process whereby previously public property is privatized with a few market actors benefiting from this development, while many others are now excluded from both, ownership and user right. In contrast to classic colonization that was largely state-driven, privatization and financialization play a key role in modern land grabbing. In today's capitalism, global land grabbing represents a crucial opportunity to tap new investment opportunities in times of capital shortages, thus providing a spatially fixed geographical solution to impeding crises (Harvey, 2010). In stable economic environments, capital typically prefers liquidity and the permanent possibility of withdrawing and reinvesting unprofitable investments in the short term. In times of crisis, however, this preference is abandoned, and capital seeks more inflexible but secure investment opportunities. To this end, land plays an important role during economic downturns and, consequentially, modern land grabbing is closely tied to the capitalistic growth cycle (Harvey, 2010). In this context, financialization is by no means a new, hitherto unknown process:

> Harvey does not interpret financialisation as a sign of an essentially changed economy but as a recurrent dynamic within capitalist development. . . . Harvey claims that, when assimilated, the workings of rent and interest facilitate capitalism's expanded reproduction by performing a coordinating function vis-à-vis industry and accumulation overall, pushing capital to new high-yield frontiers and facilitating its withdrawal from declining sectors and places. This process demands that land be assimilated to its "highest and best use" (Harvey, 1982: 368), the highest-yielding use available at any given moment. Harvey argues that in a fully developed capitalism, all land will be open to this rapid churning of capital and thus will function as a "financial" asset.
>
> *(Knuth, 2015: 166)*

On the capital side, land grabbing provides relief, more precisely spatial relief from the constant pressure of capital movement and offers an effective way of averting or overcoming locally limited capital crises in the short term. On the supply side, that is, on the side of public and private landowners, however, a fundamental dilemma opens up. On the one hand, they are forced to create an attractive environment for foreign investors and to provide access to capital to secure their trust and support in the future. On the other hand, public actors are also and above all obliged to safeguard the interests of their local population and to protect them from foreign appropriation (Zoomers, 2010: 443). How can this form of unequal burden sharing be integrated into the general concept of land grabbing? Derek Hall (2013: 1592) proposes a functional differentiation along the motivation of land sellers on the supply side. On the one hand, there are purely economic land grabbing processes in which suppliers willingly and voluntarily offer land for sale at a price independently set by them, for example, because its maintenance is no longer cost-efficient. This form of land grabbing would correspond to Harvey's accumulation by dispossession. On the other hand, land can also change hands through extra-economic processes. Political or legal force, or at least the threat of it, often play a role. Even if the original owners may receive compensation in the process of this form of expropriation, this transaction still does not require a willing seller. Hence, such cases correspond to a form of original accumulation that Marx identified in strikingly similar fashion in classical colonialism (cf. Akram-Lohdi, 2012: 130–131; Borras and Franco, 2012: 46).

Nevertheless, today even extra-economic land grabbing usually lacks the open, centralized, and military use of force. In the context of globalized capitalism, these processes pass more filigree and concealed. Divergent price and value conceptions of land play a decisive role in this regard, since the assessment of actual land prices can tend to deviate strongly from subjective values that specific properties may imply for formal or informal owners or occupiers. This is due in particular to the microeconomic concept of the yield gap, which is increasingly used in business communication with regard to land grabs (cf. White et al., 2012: 638; Knuth, 2015: 173). The yield gap refers to the hypothetical profit potential of allegedly undeveloped and fallow land plots. However, such underdeveloped regions are often compared with the potential of high-performance economies leading to "unrealistic" and "wildly inflated" results (White et al., 2012: 632). Even more important: this type of price determination alleges the general availability of the land, without acknowledging that it may have been used informally for a long time and might embody very high, non-economic value to its occupants. Therefore, yield gaps as economic-rhetorical instrument are "deliberately prefigurative: it implies existing economic value waiting to be unlocked and markets waiting to be tapped" (Knuth, 2015: 173) and "a euphemism for an extractive form of agriculture that caters to (inefficient, climate-threatening) overconsumption by a global minority and would further jeopardize the 'under-reproduction' of small-holding populations" (McMichael, 2012: 692). Nevertheless, the emphasis on artificially defined values seems to effectively legitimize land grabbing at the global level. For in the realm of this particular discourse, it is subject to and functions in accordance with the recognized rules of international financial capitalism, even if the underlying values are set entirely hypothetically.

Exactly here lies the crucial difference between capitalist and colonialist land grabbing. While their outcome (the extensive appropriation of foreign land) is largely similar, the function and legitimacy of the processes are entirely different. Modern, capitalist land grabbing typically refrains from open violence and, in contrast, pursues a positive discourse strategy by promising prosperity for recipients and resource security in the country of origin. This makes capitalistic land grabbing decisively less political, more durable in the long run, and ultimately, it seems, acceptable. Hence, it is precisely in the question of land that one truly recognizes the social revolution that money brought about as an impersonal, all-embodying, and socially disguising medium of exchange, whose principles capitalism adopted as its own. But at a closer look, the promises of prosperity and security appear completely empty. While land grabbing, under the pretext of economic development, does not lead to the total displacement or violent suppression of previous owners, as was common practice under colonialism, it restructures social relations between producers and consumers by actively integrating small farmers into the global processes of accumulation.[3] In stark contrast to liberal economic promises, this "conversion from independent producer to contract farmer to labourer . . . involves rapid rural proletarianization" (Hall, 2011: 206). Thus, accumulation by dispossession may not always imply actual confiscation. But it is obvious that even seemingly voluntary land sales are most often made under the pressure of international capital and its constant urge for accumulation, the influence of which remains hidden under the veil of freedom of choice and free markets. Herein lies the power of *peaceful coercion*.[4]

> Primitive accumulation in this instance operates not through the absolute dispossession of the producer and the accumulation of land as "stock," but through the capitalization of agriculture-based social reproduction by rendering it dependent on the compulsion of the market and the imperative to generate surplus for securing access to the means of subsistence.
>
> *(Ince, 2014: 125)*

Financialization of land is irresistibly driving this process, culminating in a reconfiguration of social relations that contains frightening parallels to ancient colonialism. But it is precisely the open renunciation of violence coupled with liberal promises of progress that makes this process so much more durable. And so, in our cognitive lethargy it is usually overlooked or simply ignored that (Ince, 2014: 127).

> In a dark irony of history, the extraeconomic and extralegal power inherent in primitive accumulation, which was initially wielded by colonial powers and then by postcolonial states against the former colonists, once again locks hands with global capital in the name of "development."

## The Green Value of Land

> Conservation leaders need to stop counting birds and start counting dividends that nature can pay to the people who live in it.
> —*Ger Bergkamp, Director of the World Water Council*[5]

> Trying to make nature valuable, it turns out, has had a disappointing track record.
> —*R. David Simpson (2018)*

In the previous sections, we traced a far-reaching process of societal transformation that has led us from classical spatial theory of earlier agricultural economies to changes brought about by industrialization and the modern financialization of land. All these moments are characterized by different normative conceptions of land. In the following section, we conclude our observations by examining how major societal transformations triggered by monetization, financialization, and globalization have led to a fundamental change in the social concept of land from the ground beneath our feet to a much broader understanding that also includes nature, the environment, flora and fauna. How could modern quantification assume such enormous proportions?

On February 13, 2008, the British *Guardian* published an inconspicuous article titled "The Great Green Land Grab." In it, Guardian journalist John Vidal reported a recent trend, according to which large areas of land from continental Europe to Botswana and from the Philippines to Patagonia were bought up by private investors, foundations, and billionaires with the proclaimed aim of protecting their environment and nature. He coined this development *green grabbing* that in the following years—and with the increase of classical land grabbing—gained increasing attention in social scientific and political discourse.

The term green grabbing, or more generally the financialization of nature and the environment, can be understood as the "the appropriation of land and resources for environmental ends" (Fairhead, Leach and Scoones, 2012: 237), "a process of ontological reconfiguration through which different qualities of nature and resource-based production are translated into a financial value form to be traded in specialized markets" (Ouma, Johnson and Bigger, 2018: 501). Particularly the former definition is, like classic land grabbing, normatively charged and it is not surprising that in his Guardian report John Vidal, too, expresses serious doubts that a structural privatization of land constitutes the most effective avenue for the protection of nature and the environment.

To gain a better understanding of this rather novel development, we want to retrace its historical genesis and find out how nature and the environment as quintessentially holistic concepts could be subordinated to capitalist value conceptions. Essentially, modern green grabbing is based on well-known, colonialist land grabbing processes, which are being legitimized under the pretext of environmental protection and nature conservation (cf. Peluso, 1992; Neumann, 1998). At the same time, modern financialization and monetary quantification processes bring with them new discursive elements that fundamentally influence and reshape the values of nature and the environment.

Science, and particularly the discipline of environmental economics, which slowly but successfully emerged in the 1980s, played a key role in restructuring this discourse (cf. Warford and Pearce, 1993). In 1997, Robert Costanza and his colleagues published a paper in the prominent scientific journal *Nature*, in which they claimed that, according to their calculations, the annual value of the global biosphere would lie between 16 and 54 trillion US dollars, corresponding to an average of about 33 trillion US dollars. Compared to a global gross domestic product of about 18 trillion US dollars at that time, it was not surprising that these dizzying results attracted much attention, especially in the economic and financial world. This, however, was not the initial aim of the scientists. Rather, they wanted to draw attention—analogous to the contested discussion in climate science about the price of greenhouse gas emissions—to the fact that most of the vital ecoservices and natural resources were not adequately priced, making their sustainable consumption considerably more difficult (for a differentiated critique, see Toman, 1998).

Ironically, however, their findings were "rapidly transformed into an optimistic embrace of the financial returns that might accrue if this 'value' of environmental externalities could be priced and traded" (Sullivan, 2013: 201). This profound reconfiguration of value conceptions, triggered by a scientific report, is not only promoted by the profit-oriented private sector, but also widely reproduced and institutionalized by influential public organizations such as the World Bank (McAfee, 1999; Goldman, 2001; Corson, 2010). As a result, today, the quantification of nature and the environment has become an inseparable part of mainstream economics (Fairhead, Leach and Scoones, 2012: 240):

> Whilst in the twentieth century, conservation agendas were surely implicated in the alienation of land and the regulation of land use by colonial and post-colonial regimes, this was often not with commercial intent (though it often had commercial effects). . . . Now it is explicitly so.

The immediate result of this development are new financial products akin to emission certificates that commercialize nature and the environment and make them tradable. These include new environmental investment funds and stocks, services, banking schemes, such as carbon emissions trading, and even derivatives and futures that allow betting on price fluctuations (Sullivan, 2013: 203–209).[6]

How can this profound transformation of natural values be explained? It is obvious that the environment has gradually been integrated into the natural cycle of capital by initially assigning it an economic, quantifiable value. Once integrated into this cycle, the economic assessment of the environmental production potential leads to a constant need to justify its raison d'être based on quantifiable economic advantages and services. However, this generic process of capitalist accumulation alone does not explain how the environment, nature, and earth, which throughout the history of mankind embodied explicitly non-economic, holistic and spiritual values, could so easily be integrated into the all-rationalizing capitalist system. As with our analysis of land grabbing, a study of the discourse on values provides important answers to this central question. In this case, two elements are decisive in legitimizing the increasing appropriation of the environment by the economy in general, and the financial industry, in particular.

The first discursive element is termed the *economy of repair* (Fairhead, Leach and Scoones, 2012; Leach, Fairhead and Fraser, 2012). This phenomenon describes an emergent economic sector that is based on the attempt to economize and price environmental and natural damages caused by negative externalities of the global trading system. In this sense, new products are constantly being created to remedy the negative consequences of old production (cf. Birch, Levidow and Papaioannou, 2010). The true production potential of nature and the environment, and thus their actual value, ultimately consist not in their material qualities as the basis of all life, but in the new financial possibilities of protecting, repairing and saving these qualities (Fairhead, Leach and Scoones, 2012: 242):

> The economy of repair has been smuggled in within the rubric of "sustainability," but its logic is clear: that unsustainable use 'here' can be repaired by sustainable practices "there," with one nature subordinated to the other. Once this logic of repair is grasped, so a new interplay can be discerned which is doubly valuing nature: for its use and for its repair. The damage inflicted by economic growth generating unsustainable resource thus creates the basis for the new growth economy of repair. Nature serves both— and thus acquires value; some would say its "true," full value.

In the end, the financialization of nature leads to a double-exploitation of the environment, on the one hand according to its economized benefit, on the other according to its potential repair value, but in both cases in the pursuit of maximum efficiency (ibid.).

The perversion of this value transformation process can be illustrated using an empirical example. *Ecosystem services* constitute a particularly comprehensive economic sector created in recent years as an immediate result of the developments described above (Salles, 2011; Farber et al., 2006; Armsworth et al., 2007; Barbier, 2011).

> Ecosystem services are the direct or indirect contributions that ecosystems make to the well-being of human populations. Ecosystem processes and functions contribute to the provision of ecosystem services, but they are not synonymous with ecosystem services. Ecosystem processes and functions describe biophysical relationships that exist whether or not humans benefit from them. These relationships generate ecosystem services only if they contribute to human well-being, defined broadly to include both physical well-being and psychological gratification. Thus, ecosystem services cannot be defined independently of human values.
>
> *(EPA, 2009: 12)*

Not surprisingly, social values decide which natural goods and services are ultimately worth protecting. But the financialization of the environment has led to the domination of an economic calculus representing those evaluations. Behind this lies the hope of many that the thorough economization of nature, perhaps even a moralization of the environment as wealth increases, will bring with it effective incentives for its long-term protection. Whether the incorporation of moral progress within the frame of economic utilitarianism is merely avoiding the real issue of environmental protection is a critical question (cf. Skidselsky, 2010: 141).

Under the motto "Selling Nature to Save it" (McAfee, 1999), environmentalists have for some time been forming unusual alliances with capitalists in the hope
of achieving mutual goals through common value alignment (Igoe, Neves and
Brockinton, 2010: 486)—with dubious results. For example, $CO_2$-emissions trading may well have the positive intention of limiting air pollution in general. But
with the prospect of financial gains from speculation and hoarding, this honorable
goal quickly recedes into the background. Because, according to economic logic,
what may seem worth protecting today may appear entirely irrelevant tomorrow.
In the day-to-day business of financial capitalism, values can expire just as quickly
as ultra-mobile capital can be withdrawn from investments. And there is one main
logical reason behind this fact: Economic value can only be sustained in the face
of scarcity.

On this assumption precisely, those base their hopes who see potential for
environmental protection in a comprehensive quantification and economization
of the environment. Because "if the environment is regarded as a scarce resource,
then the deterioration of the environment is also an economic problem" (Barbier, 2011: 6). Nature, however, still offers remarkable abundance, at least on a
global scale. While there are regional differences, of course, products and services
provided by the environment, such as pharmaceutical ingredients or recreational
spaces, are generally available in great diversity to profit-oriented companies
(Simpson et al. 1996).

The counterintuitive "problem" with the lack of scarcity is illustrated by
the example of ecotourism. This business model is quite simple: tourists want
to observe natural attractions and rare plants and animals which, however, must
be specially protected for this very purpose. The costs are borne by the visitors.
However, entrepreneurial rationality ensures that the income from ecotourism
is rarely invested in the sustainable protection of such sights. This is due to the
fact that these are often available in "sufficient" amounts, globally, the local protection of which would only marginally improve the consumer experience of
tourists to an extent reflected in turnover and additional income. In contrast,
investments improving the travel experience itself are much more profitable. As
a result, ecotourism providers are more likely to invest in infrastructure, airports,
luxury hotels, and culinary services—all of which exert considerable additional
pressure on ecosystems but promise significant advantages in the quality competition for customers. After all, only these investments generate income, because in a
globalized world with low transport and travel costs "The list of fascinating places
to visit remains almost limitless. As a result, like anything else that is available in
almost limitless quantities, exotic destinations in and of themselves cannot command high values" (Simpson, 2018). While infrastructure is scarce and therefore
valuable in the economic sense, the environment cannot (yet) fulfil these criteria.
This is where the economization of values constitutes a failure in every respect.

But not only that. The extraordinary focus on the financialization of nature as
the only realistic option to protect it creates a hegemonic discourse that entirely

shuts out alternative solutions and so prevents a reflective and differentiated debate on the value of the environment and nature (Igoe, Neves and Brockinton, 2010: 488):

> Given that within the tenets of capitalist principles the allocation of funds is directly related to associated potential returns on investment, conservationists who seek donor funds are increasingly under pressure to show the economic advantages of their conservation goals. Hence, the notion that the relationships between conservationist action and capitalist reality are necessarily beneficial becomes increasingly taken-for-granted. This idea becomes hegemonic when it is so systematically and extensively promoted that it acquires the appearance of being the only feasible view of how best to pursue and implement conservation goals. Alternative and critical views of this logic are consistently kept at the margins or outright silenced.

Much as in the case of classical land grabbing, capitalism thus manages to place the discursive focus on opportunities, growth, and development held ready by economization and financialization to completely suppress ecological or spiritual conceptions. Ultimately, this hegemony of values drives an unstoppable commodification and market expansion that is crucial to the continued existence of capitalism as a value in motion (Brockington, Duffy and Igoe, 2008).[7]

In addition to this seemingly positive, empowering discourse of the economy of repair, another negative discursive element has emerged in recent years, which plays an at least equally important role in quantifying the environment. Increasingly, financial interventions in nature and the environment are legitimized painting a state of crisis. The result is the discursive construction of a "disaster capitalism" (Klein, 2007; Kolbert, 2014), which quantifies food scarcity and climate impacts in monetary terms and only thus lends relevance to these extraordinary challenges.

> The underlying assumption is that the solution to such food, energy and climate 'crises' lies in capturing the potentials of so-called' marginal, empty, and available' lands across the globe. . . . While clearly deeply flawed, the justificatory discourse for urgent action and focused solution is nevertheless a powerful one, and frames a particular political economy of intervention which garners support among national governments, private sector investors and international banks and donor agencies.
>
> *(White et al., 2012: 631–632)*

The comprehensive rationalization of nature is thus presented as a system-compliant solution, which, however, can only buy a little time by kicking the can down the road. For the unruly force of capital to bogart more and more nature here to (potentially) save it there necessarily ends in an entirely unconstructive zero-sum game. Admittedly, to define the green value of land solely in monetary terms could possibly pave the way for an unlikely alliance of environmentalists and financial managers. However, this odd coalition can never truly fulfill its purpose. For their hopes lie in the economic effect of scarcity, which ultimately is the ecological aim of prevention.

## Conclusion: Determining the Price (and Value) of Land

> In each historical epoch, property has developed differently and under a set of entirely different social relations.
>
> —*Karl Marx ([1847] 1956: 173)*

In the course of our enquiry into the price of land, we have shown how conceptions of the value of land have changed along profound social, political, and economic transformations which led us from classical agricultural economies to modern industrialized nations. In particular, we observed that the price of land, which used to be derived simply from its use value as natural basis of human livelihood, in modern financial capitalism is increasingly determined by speculative motives, which even environment and nature cannot escape. More recently, this process has been given significant acceleration by a strongly increasing trend to quantify and financialize nature in order to integrate it into capitalism's efficiency-based global value system. The underlying micro-processes are multi-layered and highly complex.

We showed that the global financial crisis of 2008 was one of the main triggers for this development. To protect their investments and diversify portfolios, anxious financial investors fled into land markets that were previously considered unattractive due to their immobility and low returns. David Harvey's theory of the spatial fix can explain this change of behavior convincingly (Dodd, 2014: 243). But how can we make sense of the fact that this initially short-term solution is continued in the long term and even seems to be further intensifying? The structural transformation of the land markets is driven by collective mentality that continuously attracts new investors and thus facilitates a sustained flow of capital (Fairbairn, 2014b). Behind this curious investment endurance are societal transformation processes such as urbanization and the rise of service and knowledge economies, which are fundamentally changing land use and its value.

But really how lasting is this remarkable increase in financial interest? Above all, this question troubles investors themselves, of course. After land prices have doubled during the last ten years alone, many market observers are increasingly concerned about the sustainability of the herd-driven hunt for land, since highly distorted prices could foreshadow impending asset bubbles and overheating markets. The experience of the US agricultural recession between 1982 and 1987 is still firmly anchored in investors' memories and has fueled fears of suddenly falling yields or rising interest rates (Abbott, 2011). At the same time, land as newly discovered source of financial investment continues to promise lower but more secure revenues, which do not lose their attractiveness in unstable economic environments. Ultimately, the sustainability of the financialization of land is therefore almost impossible to predict from a purely economic point of view.

> For now it appears that institutional investors will continue to swap land among themselves in the hopes that market conditions improve and interest rates remain low. However, when interest rates do begin to rise there is reason to believe that there might be substantial losses on the capitalized value of land. At the end of the day, the ability to maintain inflated land values will depend on the banks' willingness to lend, since in reality a piece of land is only worth what a bank is willing to lend against it.
>
> *(Gunnoe, 2014: 499)*

Much greater certainty exists regarding the serious consequences of this modern development. We illustrated that global processes such as land grabbing and green grabbing resulted in a strong appropriation and expropriation of agricultural land and nature with often devastating consequences for the environment and the local population.

Karl Polanyi ([1944] 2001: 137) warned against this extreme unleashing of capitalist principles, which used to be firmly anchored within social institutions until the outbreak of the industrial age, by alerting "that leaving the fate of soil and people to the market would be tantamount to annihilating them."

But many see in the unconditional acceptance of economic values the only chance to make their particular interests heard. This is true not least for environmental organizations whose notable market faith further enables the ongoing financialization of nature. Market optimists hope that ecological scarcity could make the environment an economic problem and thus strengthen their protection (Barbier, 2011). But whether economic scarcity would really lead to the increased protection and ultimate conservation of nature remains both, historically and logically extremely questionable.

Why do people still hold on so firmly to this seemingly hopeless principle? How can rational, profit-oriented values dominate so clearly a multi-layered, profoundly contradictory, and essentially incompatible discourse about the economic, ecological, and social value of land, nature and the environment? A careful analysis of the socially and economically relevant actors involved in the discourse may help to unpack this puzzling enigma (cf. Igoe, Neves and Brockinton, 2010; Crehan, 2002). For a long time, globalized capitalism embodies a certain value system that, through its all-encompassing prevalence at all relevant levels of society, also assumes a dominant position in the discourse about the value of land and the environment (Gramsci, 1971; Cox, 1987; Gill, 1990). This value system is represented and institutionalized in all social systems by influential social coalitions, in our case by an unlike union of neoliberal financial capitalists, who act according to this efficiency-optimizing value system, and environmentalists, who in the face of the dominance of profit orientation try to integrate their particular principles and interests accordingly. To this end, they formulate their aims in the language of this dominant discourse with an explicit emphasis on economic opportunities and risks. Behind this lies the hope that protecting the ecology could become an economic problem with increased scarcity. But even if such scarcity existed locally, in this discourse, ecological values can only exist indirectly in a purely artificial, amorphous form. Through its comprehensive influence on all relevant levels of society, the all-quantifying capitalistic discourse manages to establish its value system on the basis of apparent agreement and without physical violence. As a result, "The ideas and agendas of this class thus come to permeate an entire society's understanding of the world" (Igoe, Neves and Brockinton, 2010: 489–490) and conceal actually pluralistic and often insurmountable value differences of a society.

To counteract aggressive land grabbing and the momentous rationalization of nature and the environment, this dominant discourse, which capitalism carries to even the remotest corners of the globe, must be broken. What is needed instead is an alternative, pluralistic discourse that once again transforms the social value conceptions of nature and the environment and thus reframes the "intellectual as well as policy focus": "Wresting nature from control by market logics—which compartmentalize, commoditize and privatize—must be a priority. This requires recasting the debate, asking whose values are being defined, whose services are being provided and whose goods are being sold?" (Fairhead, Leach and Scoones, 2012: 255).

The fact that historically such kinds of radical value transformation have always been possible may provide for alternative perspectives. But never before has a specific core concept been so comprehensively and firmly anchored in global discourse as capitalism is today. Therefore, the crucial question will be whether the value of land, nature, and the environment can be redefined before their actual scarcity triggers economic interest.

Ultimately, such profound change can only be promoted by institutions. Lessons from other areas of governance show that particularly the judicial system can embody powerful antitheses to capitalism's ultra-dominant value system. The European integration process provides an apt example. For many years, the EU partners argued fiercely about whether European citizens should have in principal a right to access national welfare services in other EU states, even if they were temporarily unemployed. On diplomatic levels, the international community could not agree on this fundamental issue, because wealthier core members feared systematic immigration flows into their more generous social systems. Ultimately, clarity was provided by the European Court of Justice, which ruled that based on their civil rights as EU citizens even economically inactive persons had unlimited access to social benefits (Pennings, 2012). While the legislative process was clearly dominated by specific economic values, the European Court of Justice could overrule these principles in the judicial arena.

Regarding land and the environment, there are signs that judicial power could break with entrenched value concepts in similar fashion. For example, in October 2018, a Dutch appeals court ruled that national greenhouse gas emissions ought to be reduced by 25% by 2020 against 1990 levels, amounting to eight percentage points more than originally envisioned by Mark Rutte's liberal governments. This is a highlight of many similar recent rulings. In March 2017, courts in New Zealand, Australia and India granted personal rights to rivers (O'Donnell and Talbot-Jones, 2018; Cano Pecharroman, 2018). In New Zealand, the *Te Awa Tupua Act* gave the Whanganui River and its entire ecosystem a right to health and physical integrity. At the same time in India, the Ganges and the Yamuna river received the "status of a legal person, with all corresponding rights, duties and liabilities . . . in order to preserve and conserve them" (Kothari, Margil and Bajpai, 2017). All of these groundbreaking court decisions emphasize an at least equal role of ecological, spiritual and metaphysical over economic values. The Ganges is regarded as sacred by millions of people and the Whanganui is revered by Māori native tribes as their elixir of life. The extension of such legal recognition to "a specific, identifiable, bounded natural feature (a river and its catchment)" (O'Donnell and Talbot-Jones, 2018) represents an entirely new approach. What is certain is that fundamental legal regulation on the basis of an equal and enlightened social discourse is needed to determine and enforce the *just* price of the land and nature.

But of course, legal regulation is no panacea and associated with considerable challenges regarding the implementation and compliance of judicial court rules. Institutional change triggered by legal decisions can only be sustainable in combination with an assertive executive branch. But the assertion of such alternative principles at national and international level remains highly problematic. Capitalist values that are integrated into the global legal discourse in form of personal civil rights remain very influential, and of course often so with good reason, while judicial environmental rulings rarely apply at transnational levels. In addition, although individuals are often prepared to pay a certain surcharge for climate and environmental protection, this willingness always knows limits.[8] Legitimate environmental policies must therefore deliberately and intelligently address this fundamental problem and formulate solutions in positive and empowering fashion (Prins et al., [2010] 2015). And yet, judicial regulatory measures could crucially weaken the capitalistic and largely profit-oriented discourse and provide alternative perspectives with greater attention. In any case, our enquiry has emphasized that another profound transformation of social values seems indispensable from both, an ecological and an economic perspective. For it has become increasingly undeniable that "to allow the market mechanism to be sole director of the fate of human beings and their natural environment indeed, even of the amount and use of purchasing power, would result in the demolition of society" (Polanyi, [1944] 2001: 76).

## Notes

1. For example, it made sense to cultivate animal feed in livestock breeding rings in order to optimize transport costs and production cycles.
2. This interesting development in the value of agricultural land could also present major challenges for taxation. For example, in the United States arable land is taxed according to its utility value ignoring non-agricultural utility factors, which have a considerable influence on current prices (Borchers, Ifft and Kuethe, 2014: 1317).
3. Feldman and her colleagues (2003) aptly call this process "in situ displacement": "In situ displacement captures moments of capitalist transformation in which people are not physically driven from their land or dwellings but find their livelihood increasingly precarious due to the loss or diminution of entitlements and resources. In other words, they are displaced socioeconomically but not spatially" (Ince, 2014: 126).
4. In *The Passions and the Interests*, Albert O. Hirschman (1977: 66) examines the hypothesis put forward by leading philosophers of the Enlightenment that capitalism with its rationalizing properties "would activate some benign human proclivities at the expense of some malignant ones." In this view, capitalism represents the ideal superstructure for peaceful societies, because "in this way, it would repress and perhaps atrophy the more destructive and disastrous components of human nature." Our study underlines that such a clear separation between unbridled passion and rational interests cannot be achieved in modern capitalism.
5. Quoted in Kanter (2008).
6. A practical and at the same time quite perfidious example of such forward transactions are new derivatives on the risk of species extinction. The aim is to assign monetary value to endangered species to create positive financial incentives for their conservation (Mandel, Donlan and Armstrong, 2010). Sullivan (2013: 208) aptly notes that "it seems perverse to transform the value of species survival into a price whose rise or fall is entangled with bets on their susceptibility to irreversible loss, underscored by a calculus whereby species value rises with rarity, or greater risk of extinction."
7. We expand on the concept of capital as value in motion in detail in the next chapter.
8. Roger Pielke Jr. (2011) describes this basic principle of environmental economics as the "Iron Law" of climate policy.

## References

Abbott, Charles (2011), "U.S. farmland boom may carry long-term risk: FDIC," *Reuters (online)*, 10 March. URL: www.reuters.com/article/us-fdic-farmland/u-s-farmland-boom-may-carry-long-term-risk-fdic-idUSTRE72968T20110310 (accessed 14 July 2018).

Akram-Lodhi, Haroon (2012), "Contextualising land grabbing: Contemporary land deals, the global subsistence crisis and the world food system," *Canadian Journal of Development Studies/Revue canadienne d'études du développement* 33(2): 119–142.

Alden Wily, Liz (2012), "Looking back to see forward: The legal niceties of land theft in land rushes," *Journal of Peasant Studies* 39(3–4): 751–775.

Alonso, William A. (1964), *Location and Land Use*. Cambridge, MA: Harvard University Press.

Anseeuw, Ward, Liz Alden Wily, Lorenzo Cotula and Michael Taylor (2012), *Land Rights and the Rush for Land: Findings of the Global Commercial Pressures on Land Research Project*. Rome: International Land Coalition.

Armsworth, Paul R., Kai M.A. Chan, Gretchen C. Daily, Paul R. Ehrlich, G. Kremen, Taylor H. Ricketts and M.A. Sanjayan (2007), "Ecosystem-service science and the way forward for conservation," *Conservation Biology* 21(6): 1383–1384.

Barbier, Edward (2011), *Capitalizing on Nature: Ecosystems as Natural Assets*. Cambridge: Cambridge University Press.

Barnard, C.H. (2000), "Agriculture and the rural economy: Urbanization affects a large share of farmland," *Rural Conditions and Trends* 10(2): 57–63.

Birch, Kean, Les Levidow and Theo Papaioannou (2010), "Sustainable capital? The neoliberalization of nature and knowledge in the European knowledge-based bio-economy," *Sustainability* 2(9): 2898–2918.

Böhm-Bawerk ([1889] 1991), *Positive Theorie des Kapitales*. Stuttgart: Schäffer-Poeschel Verlag.

Borchers, Allison, Jennifer Ifft and Todd Kuethe (2014), "Linking the price of agricultural land to use values and amenities," *American Journal of Agricultural Economics* 96(5): 1307–1320.

Borras Jr., Saturnino M. and Jennifer C. Franco (2012), "Global land grabbing and trajectories of agrarian change: A preliminary analysis," *Journal of Agrarian Change* 12(1): 34–59.

Brockington Dan, Rosaleen Duffy and Jim Igoe (2008), *Nature Unbound: Conservation, Capitalism, and the Future of Protected Areas*. London: Earthscan Publishers.

Burt, Oscar R. (1986), "Econometric modeling of the capitalization formula for farmland prices," *American Journal of Agricultural Economics* 68(1): 10–26.

Cano Pecharroman, Lidia (2018), "Rights of nature: Rivers that can stand in court," *Resources* 7(1). DOI:10.3390/resources7010013

Capozza, Dennis R. and Robert W. Hesley (1989), "The fundamentals of land prices and urban growth," *Journal of Urban Economics* 26: 295–306.

Carell, Erich (1950), "Johann Heinrich von Thünen und die moderne Wirtschaftstheorie," *Zeitschrift für die gesamte Staatswissenschaft* 106(4): 600–610.

Chisholm, Michael (1979), "Von Thünen anticipated," *The Royal Geographical Society (with the Institute of British Geographers)* 11(1): 37–39.

Chisholm, Michael (1962), *Rural Settlement and Land Use*. London: Hutchinson.

Christaller, Walter (1933), *Die Zentralen Orte in Süddeutschland: eine okonomisch-geographische Untersuchung über die Gesetzmassigkeit der Verbreitung und Entwicklung der Siedlungen mit städtischen Funktionen*. Jena: Gustav Fischer Verlag.

Cole, Robert (2012), "The new black gold: U.S. farmland," *The Globe and Mail*, 22 March.

Corson, Catherine (2010), "Shifting environmental governance in a neoliberal world: US aid for conservation," *Antipode* 42(3): 576–602.

Costanza Robert, Ralph d'Arge, Rudolf de Groot, Stephen Farber, Monica Grasso, Bruce Hannon, Karin Limburg, Shahid Naeem, Robert V. O'Neill, Jose Paruelo, Robert G. Raskin, Paul Sutto and Marjan van den Belt (1997), "The value of the world's ecosystem services and natural capital," *Nature* 387: 253–260.

Cotula, Lorenzo (2012), "The international political economy of the global land rush: A critical appraisal of trends, scale, geography and drivers," *Journal of Peasant Studies* 39(3–4): 649–680.

Cotula, Lorenzo, Sonja Vermeulen, Rebeca Leonard and James Keeley (2009), *Land Grab or Development Opportunity? Agricultural Investment and International Land Deals in Africa*. London & Rom: International Institute for Environment and Development, Food and Agricultural Organization of the United Nations & International Fund for Agricultural Development.

Cox, Robert W. (1987), *Production, Power, and World Order: Social Forces in the Making of History*. New York: Columbia University Press.

Crehan, Kate (2002), *Gramsci, Culture, and Anthropology*. Berkeley: University of California Press.

Deininger, Klaus and Derek Byerlee (2010), *Rising Global Interest in Farmland: Can It Yield Sustainable and Equitable Benefits?* Washington, DC: World Bank.

Dodd, Nigel (2014), *The Social Life of Money*. Princeton, NJ and Oxford: Princeton University Press.

Dunn, Edgar S. (1954), *The Location of Agricultural Production*. Gainesville: University of Florida Press.

Environmental Protection Agency (EPA) (2009), *Valuing the Protection of Ecological Systems and Services: A Report of the EPA Science Advisory Board*. Washington, DC: EPA.

Epstein, Gerald (ed.) (2005), "Introduction: Financialization and the world economy," pp. 3–16 in *Financialization and the World Economy*. Cheltenham: Edward Elgar Publishing.

Evans, Alan W. (1983), "The determination of the price of land," *Urban Studies* 20: 119–129.

Fairbairn, Madeleine (2014a), "'Like gold with yield': Evolving intersections between farmland and finance," *Journal of Peasant Studies* 41(5): 777–795.

Fairbairn, Madeleine (2014b), "'Just another asset class'? Neoliberalism, finance and the construction of farmland investment," pp. 245–262 in Alessandro Bonanno and Steven Wolf (eds.), *The Neoliberal Regime in the Agri-Food Sector: Crisis, Resilience and Restructuring*. London: Earthscan.

Fairhead, James, Melissa Leach and Ian Scoones (2012), "Green grabbing: A new appropriation of nature?" *Journal of Peasant Studies* 39(2): 237–261.

FAO (2018), *FAO Food Price Index*. URL: www.fao.org/worldfoodsituation/foodpricesindex/en/ (accessed 22 July 2018).

FAO (2003), "Overview of land value conditions," *AGL Miscellaneous Paper* No. 35/2003. Rom: Food and Agriculture Organization of the United Nations.

Farber, Stephen, Robert Costanza, Daniel L. Childers, Jon Erickson, Katherine Gross, Morgan Grove, Charles S. Hopkinson, James Kahn, Stephanie Pincetl, Austin Troy, Paige Warren and Matthew Wilson (2006), "Linking ecology and economics for ecosystem management," *Bioscience* 56(2): 121–133.

Featherstone, Allen M. and Timothy G. Baker (1987), "An examination of farm sector real asset dynamics: 1910–85," *American Journal of Agricultural Economics* 69(3): 532–546.

Feldman, Shelley, Charles Geisler and Louise Silberling (2003), "Moving targets: Displacement, impoverishment, and development," *International Social Science Journal* 55: 7–13.

Flanders, Archie, Fred C. White and Cesar L. Escalante (2004), "Equilibrium of land values from agricultural and general economic factors for cropland and pasture capitalization in Georgia," *Journal of Agribusiness* 22(1): 49–60.

Fujita, Masahisa (2010), "The evolution of spatial economics: From Thünen to the new economic geography," *Japanese Economic Review* 61(1): 1–32.

Ghosh, Jayati (2010), "The unnatural coupling: Food and global finance," *Journal of Agrarian Change* 10(1): 72–86.

Gill, Stephen (1990), *American Hegemony and the Trilateral Commission*. Cambridge: Cambridge University Press.

Goldman, Michael (2001), "Constructing an environmental state: Eco-governmentality and other transnational practices of a 'green' World Bank," *Social Problems* 48(4): 499–523.

GRAIN (2008), *Seized: The 2008 Land Grab for Food and Financial Security*. Barcelona: GRAIN.

Gramsci, Antonio (1971), *Selections from the Prison Notebooks*. Herausgegeben von Quintin Hoare and Geoffrey Nowell Smith. New York: International Publishers.

Gunnoe, Andrew (2014), "The political economy of institutional landownership: Neorentier society and the financialization of land," *Rural Sociology* 79(4): 478–504.

Hall, Derek (2013), "Primitive accumulation, accumulation by dispossession and the global land grab," *Third World Quarterly* 34(9): 1582–1604.

Hall, Peter (ed.) (1989), *The Political Power of Economic Ideas: Keynesianism Across Nations*. Princeton, NJ: Princeton University Press.

Hall, Ruth (2011), "Land grabbing in Southern Africa: The many faces of the investor rush," *Review of African Political Economy* 38: 193–214.

Harvey, David (2010), *The Enigma of Capital*. New York: Oxford University Press.

Harvey, David (2005), *A Brief History of Neoliberalism*. Oxford: Oxford University Press.

Harvey, David (2003), *The New Imperialism*. New York: Oxford University Press.

Harvey, David (1982), *The Limits to Capital*. Oxford: Basil Blackwell.

Heilbroner, Robert L. (1989), *The Worldly Philosophers: The Lives, Times and Ideas of the Great Economic Thinkers*. New York: Simon & Schuster.

HighQuest Partners (2010), "Private financial sector investment in farmland and agricultural infrastructure," *OECD Food, Agriculture and Fisheries Papers* No. 33. Paris: OECD Publishing.

Hirschman, Albert O. (1977), *The Passions and the Interests: Political Arguments for Capitalism before Its Triumph*. Princeton, NJ: Princeton University Press.

Hoover, Edgar M. (1936), *Location Theory and the Shoe and Leather Industries*. Cambridge, MA: Harvard University Press.

Hotelling, Harold (1929), "Stability in competition," *Economic Journal* 39(153): 41–57.

Hudson, Michael (2012), *The Bubble and Beyond: Fictitious Capital, Debt Deflation and the Global Crisis*. Dresden: ISLET Verlag.

Igoe, Jim, Katja Neves and Dan Brockinton (2010), "A spectacular eco-tour around the Historic Bloc: Theorising the convergence of biodiversity conservation and capitalist expansion," *Antipode* 42(3): 486–512.

Ince, Onur Ulas (2014), "Primitive accumulation, new enclosures, and global land grabs: A theoretical intervention," *Rural Sociology* 79(1): 104–131.

Isard, Walter (1949), "The general theory of location and space-economy," *Quarterly Journal of Economics* 63(4): 476–506.

Kaldor, Nicholas (1935), "Market imperfection and excess capacity," *Economica* 2(5): 35–50.

Kanter, James (2008), "The failing business of conservation," *Financial Times (online)*, 8. October. URL: https://green.blogs.nytimes.com/2008/10/08/the-failing-business-of-conservation/ (accessed 1 August 2018).

Kish, Zenia and Madeleine Fairbairn (2018), "Investing for profit, investing for impact: Moral performances in agricultural investment projects," *Environment and Planning A: Economy and Space* 50(3): 569–588.

Klein, Naomi (2007), *The Shock Doctrine: The Rise of Disaster Capitalism*. London: Penguin.

Knuth, Sarah Elisabeth (2015), "Global finance and the land grab: Mapping twenty-first century strategies," *Canadian Journal of Development Studies/Revue canadienne d'études du développement* 36(2): 163–178.

Kolbert, Elizabeth (2014), *The Sixth Extinction: An Unnatural History*. New York: Henry Holt.

Kothari, Ashish, Mari Margil and Shrishtee Bajpai (2017), "Now rivers have the same legal status as people, we must uphold their rights," *The Guardian (online)*, 21 April. URL:

www.theguardian.com/global-development-professionals-network/2017/apr/21/riv
ers-legal-human-rights-ganges-whanganui (accessed 23 June 2018).

Koven, Peter (2012), "ETF may stand for exchange-traded farmland," *Financial Post (online)*, 19 January. URL: https://business.financialpost.com/investing/etf-may-stand-for-exchange-traded-farmland (accessed 15 July 2018).

Krippner, Greta (2011), *Capitalizing on Crisis: The Political Origins of the Rise of Finance*. Cambridge, MA: Harvard University Press.

Krippner, Greta (2005), "The financialization of the American economy," *Socio-Economic Review* 3(2): 173–208.

Krugman, Paul (1991a), "Increasing returns and economic geography," *Journal of Political Economy* 99: 483–499.

Krugman, Paul (1991b), *Geography and Trade*. Cambridge, MA: MIT Press.

Kurz, Heinz-Dieter (ed.) (2008), "Johann Heinrich von Thünen," pp. 140–158 in *Klassiker des ökonomischen Denkens. Band 1*. München: Verlag C.H. Beck.

Launhardt, Wilhelm (1885), *Mathematische Begründung der Volkswirtschaftslehre*. Leipzig: B.G. Teubner.

Leach, Melissa, James Fairhead and James Fraser (2012), "Green grabs and biochar: Revaluing African soils and farming in the new carbon economy," *Journal of Peasant Studies* 39(2): 285–307.

LeDuc, Thomas (1962), "History and appraisal of U.S. Land Policy to 1862," *Agricultural History* 36(4): 222–224.

Linklater, Andro (2013), *Owning the Earth: The Transforming History of Land Ownership*. London: Bloomsbury.

Lösch, August (1940), *Die Räumliche Ordnung der Wirtschaft*. Jena: Gustav Fischer.

Mandel James T., C. Josh Donlan and Jonathan Armstrong (2010), "A derivative approach to endangered species conservation," *Frontiers in Ecology and the Environment* 8(1): 44–49.

Marshall, Alfred ([1890] 1920), *Principles of Economics*, 8th ed. London: Macmillan.

Marx, Karl ([1894] 1999), *Capital: A Critique of Political Economy. Volume III: The Process of Capitalist Production as a Whole*. New York.: International Publishers.

Marx, Karl ([1890] 1976), *Capital: A Critique of Political Economy. Volume 1*. London: Penguin Books.

Marx, Karl ([1847] 1956), *The Poverty of Philosophy*. Moscow: Foreign Languages Publishing House.

McAfee, Kathleen (1999), "Selling nature to save it? Biodiversity and the rise of green developmentalism," *Environment and Planning D: Society and Space* 17(2): 133–154.

McCann, James D. and Philip S. Gross (2012), "Potential tax benefits of private REITs for hedge funds and private equity funds," *Private Investment Forum*, Spring 2012, Marcum Accountants and Advisors. URL: http://www.marcumllp.com/publications-1/poten tial-tax-benefits-of-private-reits-for-hedge-funds-and-private-equity-funds (accessed 14 July 2019).

McMichael, Philip (2012), "The land grab and corporate food regime restructuring," *The Journal of Peasant Studies* 39(3–4): 681–701.

Muth, Richard F. (1969), *Cities and Housing*. Chicago, IL: University of Chicago Press.

Neumann, Rodrick P. (1998), *Imposing Wilderness: Struggles over Livelihood and Nature Preservation in Africa*. Berkeley: University of California Press.

Norton, William (1979), "The relevance of von Thünen theory to historical and evolutionary analysis of agricultural land use," *Journal of Agricultural Economics* 30(1): 39–47.

Oakland Institute (2011), *Understanding Land Investment Deals in Africa*. URL: www.oaklan dinstitute.org/land-deals-africa-publications (accessed 25 July 2018).

O'Donnell, Erin L. and Julia Talbot-Jones (2018), "Creating legal rights for rivers: Lessons from Australia, New Zealand, and India," *Ecology and Society* 23(1). DOI:10.5751/ ES-09854-230107

Ohlin, Bertil (1933), *Interregional and International Trade*. Cambridge, MA: Harvard University Press.

Ouma, Stefan, Leigh Johnson and Patrick Bigger (2018), "Rethinking the financialization of 'nature'," *Environment and Planning A: Economy and Space* 50(3): 500–511.

Oxfam (2011), "Land and power: The growing scandal surrounding the new wave of investments in land," *Briefing Paper* No. 51. Oxford: Oxfam International.

Palander, Tord (1935), *Beiträge Zur Standortstheorie*. Uppsala: Almqvist & Wiksells Boktryckeri AB.

Peluso, Nancy Lee (1992), "The political ecology of extraction and extractive reserves in East Kalimantan, Indonesia," *Development and Change* 23(4): 49–74.

Peluso, Nancy Lee and Christian Lund (2011), "New frontiers of land control: Introduction," *Journal of Peasant Studies* 38(4): 667–681.

Pennings, Frans (2012), "EU citizenship: Access to social benefits in other EU member states," *The International Journal of Comparative Labour Law and Industrial Relations* 28(3): 307–334.

Pielke Jr., Roger (2011), *The Climate Fix: What Scientists and Politicians Won't Tell You about Global Warming*. New York: Basic Books.

Polanyi, Karl ([1944] 2001), *The Great Transformation*, 2nd ed. Boston, MA: Beacon Press.

Prins, Gwythian, Isabel Galiana, Christopher Green, Reiner Grundmann, Mike Hulme, Atte Korhola, Frank Laird, Ted Nordhaus, Roger Pielke Jr., Steve Rayner, Daniel Sarewitz, Michael Shellenberger, Nico Stehr and Hiroyuki Tezuka (2010), *The Hartwell-Paper. A New Direction for Climate Policy after the Crash of 2009*. URL: https://eprints.lse. ac.uk/27939/1/HartwellPaper_English_version.pdf (accessed 2 January 2019).

Reynolds, Susan (2010), *Before Eminent Domain: Toward a History of Expropriation of Land for the Common Good*. Chapel Hill: University of North Carolina Press.

Rieter, Heinz (ed.) (1995), *Johann Heinrich von Thünen als Wirtschaftstheoretiker: Studien zur Entwicklung der ökonomischen Theorie. Band XIV*. Berlin: Duncker & Humblot.

Sakolski, Aaron M. (1932), *The Great American Land Bubble: The Amazing Story of Land-Grabbing, Speculation and Boom from Colonial Times to the Present Time*. London and New York: Harper & Bros.

Salles, Jean-Michel (2011), "Valuing biodiversity and ecosystem services: Why put economic values on nature?" *Comptes Rendus Biologies* 334(5–6): 469–482.

Samuelson, Paul (1983), "Thünen at two hundred," *American Economic Association* 21(4): 1468–1488.

Schachter, Robert (2012), "Rebounding of the real estate investment trust (REIT) – Tax considerations and potential legislation," *Private Investment Forum*, Spring 2012, Marcum Accountants and Advisors. URL: http://www.marcumllp.com/publications-1/ rebounding-of-the-real-estate-investment-trust-reit-tax-consi derations-and-poten tial-legislation (accessed 14 July 2019).

Simpson, R. David (2018), "The trouble with ecosystem services: When pricing everything means valuing nothing," *The Breakthrough Journal* 9 (Summer 2018). URL: https://the-breakthrough.org/index.php/journal/no.-9-summer-2018 (accessed 1 August 2018).

Simpson, R. David, Roger A. Sedjo and John W. Reid (1996), "Valuing biodiversity for use in pharmaceutical research," *Journal of Political Economy* 104(1): 163–185.

Skidelsky, Robert (2010), *Keynes: The Return of the Master*. New York: Public Affairs.

Sullivan, Sian (2013), "Banking nature? The spectacular financialisation of environmental conservation," *Antipode* 45(1): 198–217.

Thünen, Johann Heinrich von ([1842] 1966), *The Isolated State*. Edited with an introduction by Peter Hall. Oxford: Pergamon Press.

Toman, Michael (1998), "Why not to calculate the value of the world's ecosystem services and natural capital," *Ecological Economics* 25: 57–60.

Umweltbundesamt (2018), *Struktur der Flächennutzung*. URL: www.umweltbundesamt.de/daten/flaeche-boden-land-oekosysteme/flaeche/struktur-der-flaechennutzung#textpart-1 (accessed 20 July 2018).

van der Ploeg, Jan Douwe (2010), "The food crisis, industrialized farming and the imperial regime," *Journal of Agrarian Change* 10(1): 98–106.

Verheye, Willy H. (ed.) (2009), "The value and price of land," pp. 82–110 in *Land Use, Land Cover and Soil Sciences: Land Use Planning. Band III*, Oxford: Eolss Publishers Co. Ltd./ UNESCO.

Vidal, John (2008), "The great green land grab," *The Guardian (online)*, 13 February. URL: www.theguardian.com/environment/2008/feb/13/conservation (accessed 1 August 2018).

von Braun, Joachim (2008), *Food and Financial Crises: Implications for Agriculture and the Poor*. Washington, DC: International Food Policy Research Institute.

von Braun, Joachim and Ruth Meinzen-Dick (2009), "'Land grabbing' by foreign investors in developing countries: Risks and opportunities," *Policy Brief 13*. Washington, DC: International Food Policy Research Institute.

Walters, Alan A. (1983), "The value of land," pp. 40–62 in Harold B. Dunkerley and Christine M. E. Whitehead (eds.), *Urban Land Policy: Issues and Opportunities*. Oxford: Oxford University Press for the World Bank.

Warford, Jeremy J. and David W. Pearce (1993), *World without End: Economics, Environment, and Sustainable Development*. New York: Oxford University Press.

Weber, Alfred (1909), *Über Den Standort der Industrien*. Tübingen: J.C.B. Mohr.

Wheaton, Bradley, William J. Kiernan, Samuel Morris and Andrew Sliper (2012), "Farmland: An untapped asset class?" *Food for Thought*, December. Sydney: Macquarie Agricultural Funds Management. URL: www.macquarie.com/dafiles/Internet/mgl/com/agriculture/docs/food-for-thought/food-for-thought-dec2012-anz.pdf (accessed 18 July 2018).

White, Ben, Saturnino M. Borras Jr., Ruth Hall, Ian Scoones and Wendy Wolford (2012), "The new enclosures: Critical perspectives on corporate land deals," *Journal of Peasant Studies* 39(3–4): 619–647.

World Bank (2010), *Rising Global Interest in Farmland: Can It Yield Sustainable and Equitable Results?* Washington, DC: World Bank.

Zoomers, Annelies (2010), "Globalisation and the foreignisation of space: Seven processes driving the current global land grab," *Journal of Peasant Studies* 37(2): 429–447.

# 3

# THE PRICE OF CAPITAL

> Money always has the potential to become a moral imperative unto itself.
> Allow it to expand, and it can quickly become a morality so imperative that all
> others seem frivolous in comparison.
>
> —*David Graeber ([2011] 2014: 319)*

In the spring of 1519, Spanish explorer Hernán Cortés and his crew landed at
the beaches of Mexico where they were received by the native Aztecs. Hoping
to appease the alien sailors and to motivate a prompt departure, Moctezuma, the
king of the Aztecs, gifted the Spaniards with gold, diamonds and valuable fabrics.
He soon had to realized, however, that this generous gesture had an opposite
effect. Much to the Aztecs surprise, the Spanish had an unexpectedly strong interest in gold. For the indigenous peoples of Mexico, the precious metal had only
an aesthetic value, was used for the manufacture of jewelry and only rarely as a
means of exchange in the form of gold dust. Active trade was primarily conducted
with cocoa beans (Harari, [2011] 2014: 173). In response to Moctezuma's question as to why the Spanish were so fond of gold, Cortés replied: "Because I and
my companions suffer from a disease of the heart which can be cured only with
gold" (López de Gómara, 1943: 106).

The history of colonization by the European trading powers offers essential
insights into the technical functionalities and the social value of capital. Contrary
to conventional wisdom, many of the expeditions, almost all of which ended in
the violent subjugation or complete annihilation of indigenous populations, were
not organized by central governments but rather driven by profit-oriented private
initiatives.[1] Thus, the historical conquistador can also be regarded as an archetypal
entrepreneur (Graeber, [2011] 2014: 316ff.). Capital and debt played a central role

in the arduous expeditions. Most of the explorers had borrowed large amounts of money and were heavily indebted. Their daring ventures were a risky bet that the new territories including all their treasures and trading opportunities could be turned into high profits. Cortès's relationship with his creditors, who expected an estimated five to seven percent annual return on their loans, resembled the basic principle of modern capitalist monetary systems as early as the 16th century. Credit and debt require investment and profit—a compulsive system that has, in the history of mankind, often culminated in conquest and decline. Mexico was no exception.

Moctezuma welcomed the Spanish conquistadores to his town of Tenochtitlán and offered them a spacious quarter in one of his palaces. But soon considerable tensions arose, not least as the result of religious differences, which eventually led to bloody conflicts in which some Spaniards lost their lives. During the riots, the conquistadores captured King Moctezuma and Cortés took *de facto* control of Tenochtitlán. In another rebellion and with the loss of numerous more men, the Spanish were intermediately driven out of the capital but eventually secured a final victory over the Aztecs after a long and relentless siege and with the help of allied Mexican native tribes as well as an adventive smallpox and flu epidemic. From their new organizational center in Tenochtitlán, the Spanish conquerors led numerous military operations over the following years, subduing many indigenous peoples and gaining extensive control over Mesoamerica.

In addition to the plundering and destructive dynamics that the capitalist system of credit and debt can unleash, the conquest of the Aztec empire provides a second important insight. While indigenous peoples from Central America and Central Africa to Southeast Asia traded with a colorful variety of exchange media, gold and silver coins became a globally accepted means of payment as a result of the European conquests. The foundation for the global appropriation of finance capital was thus laid as early as the 16th century.

> The appearance of a single transnational and transcultural monetary zone laid the foundation for the unification of Afro-Asia, and eventually of the entire globe, into a single economic and political sphere. People continued to speak mutually incomprehensible languages, obey different rulers and worship distinct gods, but all believed in gold and silver and in gold and silver coins. Without this shared belief, global trading networks would have been virtually impossible. The gold and silver that sixteenth-century conquistadors found in America enabled European merchants to buy silk, porcelain and spices in East Asia, thereby moving the wheels of economic growth in both Europe and East Asia.
>
> *(Harari, [2011] 2014: 184)*

In this chapter, we examine the underlying social dynamics of capital and financialization and ask which societal value transformations and associated lines of conflict manifest themselves particularly in its price. First, we explore the meaning of capital and its price, the rate of interest. Then, we turn to the modern social relationship between capital and debt, examine deeper-lying institutional conditions that lead to capital inequality, and discuss regulatory approaches to ease the social tensions that arise from these processes. But first some theoretical reflections on the price of capital.

## Interest Rates: Managing Non-Simultaneity

> It is assumed that we do not discount later enjoyments in comparison with earlier ones, a practice which is ethically indefensible and arises merely from the weakness of the imagination.
>
> —*Frank P. Ramsey (1928: 543)*

Trading capital confronts participants with difficult decisions. On the demand side, there is an obligation to make continuous interest payments that must be carefully weighed against uncertain return on investment. On the supply side, capital lenders must ask themselves what the renunciation of current consumption and its shift to the future really is worth to them. In contrast to classical synchronous trading processes, this social constellation involves different time horizons between which the price of capital acts as a mediating force. Economists call the principle underlying this decision-making situation the "time preference," that is, the relative value of a good received at an earlier versus a later date. The subjective time preference translates into an interest rate that depends on individual and collective tastes and behavior and constitutes the price necessary to convince a person to sacrifice today's consumption and making her capital available to others instead. It follows logically: the larger the (personal) renunciation, the higher the price to be paid to impel postponed consumption.

From a purely economic perspective, this problem seems quite trivial and can be represented fairly simply in form of a mathematical formula (Beck, 2014: 197ff.). If someone agrees to lend a certain amount of money for, say, a year, the price of this service may be determined as follows:

$$V_{t+1} = V_0 \cdot (1+i) \tag{1}$$

where $V_{t+1}$ represents the total value reimbursed after one year, $V_0$ represents the initial amount lent, and i indicates the individual time preference rate, that is, the corresponding compensation value depending on the severity of foregone consumption. If the sum is to be lent and paid back over several, say two, years, the formula can be extended accordingly:

$$V_{t+2} = V_0 \cdot (1+i) + V_0 \cdot (1+i) \tag{2}$$

In a simplified form:

$$V_{t+2} = V_0 \cdot \left(1 + i\right)^2 \tag{3}$$

Thus, it follows that in a generalized form the price of capital $V_t$ lent over $n$ years at a time preference rate of $i$ can be determined as follows:

$$V_{t+n} = V_0 \cdot \left(1 + i\right)^n \tag{4}$$

To economists, this simple formalization could already serve as an answer to our question of the price of capital. In the end, as with any other form of commodity, its price depends on one's willingness to pay (demand side) and a counterpart's s (supply side). But this simple discounting formula embodies much more than a purely rational decision-making process would initially suggest. For the question of the price of capital deals at the core with the highly intriguing question of the economic and social management of time. Relative to two different points in time, the formula embodies a concept of justice, values which are socially determined. The inconspicuous letter $i$ in our trivial mathematical formula accentuates that interest is a concept of tremendous moral and philosophical depth and as such embodies considerable social poignancy. Prices may seem to embody objective, entirely mathematical entities. However, values manifested in them are essentially contentious social constructs or, as Marcel Mauss argues, a total social fact (*fait social total*). Capital in its various manifestations makes no exception.

## What Is Capital?

> *Capital is always immaterial by nature,* since it is not matter which makes capital, but the *value* of that matter, value which has nothing corporeal about it.
> —Jean-Babtiste Say (cited in Marx,
> [1857–61] 1986: 235)

In order to arrive at an improved understanding of the difficult question regarding the price of capital, we must first establish a better conception of what is actually meant by that term. Finance capital (hereafter simply 'Capital'), just like the other concepts discussed in this book, represents a production factor which helps economically active individuals to perform activities and achieve certain goals. In this economic understanding, capital is needed to generate added value from a certain amount of input by combining it with other means of production. Conversely, the value of capital is therefore "defined as the discounted future income stream to be derived from it" (Barna, 1961: 78). Capital can take many different forms, the design of which has important implications for its value and pricing (Bourdieu, 1983, 1986).[2] And while in all its forms, capital embodies a classical economic production factor, it appears to be far more controversial regarding the question of its price. Monetary profits derived from capital investments usually differ from the standard value-added type of production in that neither active (additional) work has to be invested, nor is a tangibly measurable product created under all circumstances. Rather, money "works." This important peculiarity is at the center of frequently formulated critiques of capital and interest. Thus, in order to arrive at a better understanding of the concept of capital that allows exploring the question of its price and value, we must first turn to one of political economy's most astute critics and his seminal definition.

Karl Marx carried out his influential considerations on the nature of capital, its role for the modern economic system, and its manifold implications for the structure of industrial societies in his intellectual centerpiece *Das Kapital*. Of course, his conception of capital and critical conclusions are of central importance for the question of the price and value of this very production factor in classical economics. Discussing his works will reveal that his original theses and theoretical underpinnings are an often-recurring theme in the discussions about the appropriate or "just" price of capital which have been pertinent ever since the introduction of a coin-based economic system several thousand years ago.

In the first volume of *Capital*, Karl Marx derives his definition and formulates his critique in several plausible steps, leading from the nature of the commodity via the monetary exchange process finally to his conception of capital. According to Marx, the commodity is the elementary form of any capitalist society. Each product embodies a *use value* that enables satisfying specific needs depending on individual preferences. However, as different commodities do not exhibit any sort of measurable equivalent that would make them comparable to each other, it is impossible to distinguish their use values, both in qualitative and quantitative terms. They have but one characteristic in common: they are all the product of human labor. Hence, the commercial value of different commodities can only be compared in terms working hours invested in their production and embedded within them. This conclusion constitutes the central theme of Marx' capital theory.

Of course, the fact that different commodities can in principle only be made comparable in terms of the amount of human labor manifested within them represents a considerable problem in the context of daily barter. Because when trading, the utility of very different commodities must be made comparable in order to arrive at an accepted rate of exchange. For example, cloth, which keeps warm, can be traded for a certain quantity of wheat that nourishes, that is to say, the use values and labor embodied in these commodities are equated, even though the goods do not share any natural quality of the other. Hence, the comparability of commodities and their relative values and prices are solely a product of social exchange:

> The fact that the products of labour—such useful things as coat, linen, wheat, iron, etc.—are *values, definite magnitudes of value* and in general

*commodities*, are properties which naturally pertain to them only *in our practical interrelations* and not by nature like, for example, the property of being heavy or being warming or nourishing.

*(Marx, 1867: 773)*

During barter, commodities are assigned relative characteristics that they do not embody in their natural form. However, since—in the context of a differentiated economy—it is logistically impossible to define a specific exchange ratio between each and every two commodities (C–C), a universal item must be determined that has the power to make any product (and the labor embodied within) objectively comparable, that is, represent the use value of one commodity in terms of the quantity of another. Karl Marx (1887: 60–61) calls this means of exchange the "universal equivalent." In principle, any commodity could assume this role, however, it must be generally accepted as such by a trading society in order to enable multilateral exchange processes:

> To the owner of a commodity, every other commodity is, in regard to his own, a particular equivalent, and consequently his own commodity is the universal equivalent for all the others. But since this applies to every owner, there is, in fact, no commodity acting as universal equivalent, and the relative value of commodities possesses no general form under which they can be equated as values and have the magnitude of their values compared. So far, therefore, they do not confront each other as commodities, but only as products or use-values. . . . [Owners] cannot bring their commodities into relation as values, and therefore as commodities, except by comparing them with some one other commodity as the universal equivalent. . . . The social action therefore of all other commodities, sets apart the particular commodity in which they all represent their values. Thereby the bodily form of this commodity becomes the form of the socially recognised universal equivalent. To be the universal equivalent, becomes, by this social process, the specific function of the commodity thus excluded by the rest. Thus it becomes—money.

Money assumes a mediating role and reduces the complexity in economic exchange processes. It becomes the universal equivalent and obtains value without embodying natural utility. As such, it can position itself between two traded commodities and make them comparable (C–M–C). It assumes its objective function solely and exclusively in the context of exchange. At the same time, this classic exchange process with money as a mediating entity does not generate any form of added value. Like is simply traded with like.

Capital changes this situation fundamentally. When utilized in barter, it creates *surplus value* by inverting the causal chain of the classic exchange process. Trade with capital can thus be represented as M−C−M, whereby the final result of this process is an increase in monetary value:

> The exact form of this process is therefore M−C−M′, where M′ = M + ΔM = the original sum advanced, plus an increment. This increment or excess over the original value I call "surplus-value." The value originally advanced, therefore, not only remains intact while in circulation, but adds to itself a surplus-value or expands itself. *It is this movement that converts it into capital.*
>
> *(Marx, 1887: 106; our emphasis)*

Money becomes capital by combining labor with other means of production in a production process. To achieve this, it must be constantly in motion, be shifted, relocated, and reinvested.

Therefore, Karl Marx defines capital as *value in motion*. In this understanding, capital is not a haptic object that can be determined or described in its form, but rather a dynamic process. If money is moved, that is, added to the cycle of value-added production, it becomes capital. Inversely, if the constant process of investing and reinvesting is interrupted or entirely put to halt, money is no longer capital. This logic implies that in order to function as such, capital must always be in motion and must, by nature, always evolve, grow, expand, and multiply. The incessant strive for constant value production (*utilization*) thus becomes the central theme of capital and the primary objective of the capitalist.

Based on this understanding, Marx formulated his capital critique, which is of particular importance for the question of the price and value of capital and its social implications. Since the scope and depth of Marx' critique already fills entire volumes, for the purpose of precision and conciseness only two central aspects will be addressed here. First, the capitalistic exchange relationship of M−C−M′ shifts the power structure in the market in particular and, consequentially, in society in general. While in the context of the classical exchange of commodities, two equitable trading partners were involved in exchanging goods of identical use value without putting one in a less favorable position, the introduction of capital constitutes the origin of the dependent relationship between capitalist and worker:

> On leaving this sphere of simple circulation or of exchange of commodities, which furnishes the "Free-trader Vulgaris" with his views and ideas, and with the standard by which he judges a society based on capital and wages, we think we can perceive a change in the physiognomy of our dramatis personae. He, who before was the money-owner, now strides in front as capitalist; the possessor of labour-power follows as his labourer. The one with an air of importance, smirking, intent on business; the other, timid

and holding back, like one who is bringing his own hide to market and has nothing to expect but—a hiding.

*(Marx, 1887: 123)*

As argued in the further course of this chapter, the principle of social inequality and the inherent systemic redistribution from the poorer to the richer social strata that results in the continued accumulation of capital on the part of the owner of the means of production and the simultaneous abandonment of the ownership of the means of production by the workers, is an important argument for many critics of interest rates. Because after all, it is the price of capital that enables the surplus value derived from it and hence determines indirectly the imbalance in barter relations.

The particular ability to generate *eo ispo* surplus value, according to Karl Marx, is a property that is artificially attributed to capital in the context of economic exchange, which it does not embody in reality. This peculiarity illustrates the inherent "fetish character of capital," which reaches its most unnatural state in the interest-bearing form. Money, a commodity which by definition as universal equivalent does not embody natural value is capable of producing a surplus increment solely from itself (M–M′):

> In interest-bearing capital, therefore, this automatic fetish, self-expanding value, money generating money, are brought out in their pure state and in this form it no longer bears the birth-marks of its origin. The social relation is consummated in the relation of a thing, of money, to itself. Instead of the actual transformation of money into capital, we see here only form without content. As in the case of labour-power, the use-value of money here is its capacity of creating value—a value greater than it contains. Money as money is potentially self-expanding value and is loaned out as such—which is the form of sale for this singular commodity. It becomes a property of money to generate value and yield interest, much as it is an attribute of pear-trees to bear pears. And the money- lender sells his money as just such an interest-bearing thing. But that is not all. The actually functioning capital, as we have seen, presents itself in such a light, that it seems to yield interest not as a functioning capital, but as capital in itself, as money–capital. This, too, becomes distorted. While interest is only a portion of the profit, i.e., of the surplus- value, which the functioning capitalist squeezes out of the labourer, it appears now, on the contrary, as though interest were the typical product of capital, the primary matter, and profit, in the shape of profit of enterprise, were a mere accessory and by-product of the process of reproduction. *Thus we get the fetish form of capital and the conception of fetish capital.* In M—M' we have the meaningless form of capital, the perversion and objectification of production relations in their highest degree, the interest-bearing form, the simple form of capital, in which it antecedes its

own process of reproduction. It is the capacity of money, or of a commodity, to expand its own value independently of reproduction—which is a mystification of capital in its most flagrant form.

*(Marx, [1894] 1959: 266–267; our emphasis)*

This seemingly unnatural ability of money to create surplus value from itself constitutes the second central theme in frequent critiques of interest rates. At the same time, Karl Marx recognized that credit is an indispensable ingredient in repealing or preventing interruptions and stagnations in the capital cycle. This conclusion results directly from the definition of capital as value in motion.

If the movement of capital is interrupted or prevented, the value embodied within it disappears. Economic crises can arise when the free circulation of capital is impaired. Such stagnations can occur, for example, when diverse production strategies have different turnover times. While some production processes and investment strategies realize new surplus value relatively quickly, others may require longer amortization times, for example the production of highly complex machines. Various liquidity problems that can arise from different time horizons of individual investments must constantly be balanced or eliminated in order to guarantee the long-term stability of the economic system. In theory, this could be achieved by individual saving. Producers could constantly withdraw portions of active capital during the production process to secure sufficient supply of liquidity at all times. For example, a certain proportion of the value of a machine could be saved and reinvested in a new machine if need be.

However, this system of careful provision would only be possible in a world with full information about the risk of wear and tear and future prices for equivalent equipment. Even more importantly, this procedure would lead to an enormous accumulation of reserves, that is of immovable and ergo worthless capital. This wicked timing represents one of the most convincing arguments for the inevitability of loans and interest rates. If different liquidity periods were not bridged by pricing and trading capital, increasing amounts of immovable reserves would lose its value and the capitalist system would sooner or later collapse (Harvey, 2017). Against this background and despite all valid objections raised by Marx and other critics, a functioning, price-based credit system is the fundamental ingredient of any modern socio-economic system, balancing different turnover times and reinvestment cycles and avoiding the immobilization of productive capital.

With his landmark definition of capital as "money begetting money" and as value in motion, Karl Marx outlined the basic philosophical problem of capitalism, its systemic dilemma if you will. Because on the one hand, capital and its price have profound implications for inequalities and the social structure of an industrialized society, but on the other hand, they play an indispensable role for its sustained functionality. This wicked quandary gives rise to the moral philosophical problem of interest dealing with the difficult question of whether capital should in principle have a price, and if so, how it should be configured.

## Interest Rates and Their Critics

> And this is the explanation of the name interest, which means the breeding of money. For as offspring resemble their parents, so usury is money bred of money. Whence of all forms of money-making it is most against nature.
> —*Aristotle (1912, Chapter 10)*

Let us recall briefly the mathematical manifestation of the interest rate derived at the beginning of this chapter. The discounting formula provides formally the classic definition of the price of capital: "Interest constitutes a reward for the provision of capital for a certain period of time; it is calculated according to the duration of the provision as a certain fraction of the capital" (Weber, 2002: 1537; our translation). Hence, interest is not a remuneration for actual (physical) work or immediate production. Rather, it embodies a price merely for temporally providing the value of commodities in monetary form. Therefore, Karl Marx emphasized that the interest rate, that is the direct return from money lending activities, represents the decisive factor that defines capital and distinguishes it from a classic loan:

> The lender expends his money as capital; the amount of value, which he relinquishes to another, is capital, and consequently returns to him. But the mere return of it would not be the reflux of the loaned sum of value as *capital*, but merely the return of a loaned sum of value. To return as capital, the advanced sum of value must not only be preserved in the movement but must also expand, must increase in value, i.e., must return with a surplus-value, as, $M + \Delta M$, the latter being interest or a portion of the average profit, which does not remain in the hands of the operating capitalist, but falls to the share of the money-capitalist.
>
> *(Marx, [1894] 1959: 237)*

The explicit distinction between "operating capitalist" and "money-capitalist" is of central normative importance for Marx's oeuvre as a whole. Because in his conception the sole and exclusive use value of capital is the realization of profit: "The value of money or of commodities employed as capital does not depend on their value as money or as commodities, but on the quantity of surplus-value they produce for their owner. The product of capital is profit" (Marx, [1894] 1959: 240). While the operating capitalist adds labor and other production factors to capital to create real surplus value, the monetary capitalist benefits—often to a much greater extent—merely from the temporal provision of liquidity. Put simply, he lets money (and therefore others) "work" for him. Naturally, this critical conception of profit-generating money opens space for vehement moral objections that critics of interest payments expressed perpetually ever since the ancient origin of coinage.

One of the most vehement critics of interest rates in antiquity was Aristotle. In his chrematistics, the art of acquiring wealth, the Greek philosopher defined coin money as a pure and immutable means of exchange, and thus explicitly not as an immediate source of value. Since interest could not actually increase the existing money supply, no profit should be expected from providing loans:

> for usury is most reasonably detested, as it is increasing our fortune by money itself, and not employing it for the purpose it was originally intended, namely exchange. And this is the explanation of the name (Tokos), which means the breeding of money. For as offspring resemble their parents, so usury is money bred of money. Whence of all forms of money-making it is most against nature.
>
> *(Aristotle, 1912, Chapter 10)*

The concept of the "infertility of money" was later taken up by the clerical philosopher Thomas Aquinas during the Middle Ages, who along with Albertus Magnus is regarded as one of the original thinkers of the "just price" (De Roover, 1958; Wilson, 1975; Vance, 2008). In line with Aristotle, for him the sole objective of money lies in measuring the relative value of different kinds of goods. As an objective, universally transferable unit of measurement, money's value must remain immutable. It would therefore deeply contradict the very nature of money to sell it at a higher price and so to increase its original value in the context of trade over a certain period of time. Because, "[t]he use of money is nothing more than its substance. It is a consumable commodity. Who s interest for money sells substance and use of money separately, hence sells the same thing twice, which obviously contradicts the basic concept of justice." (Weiß, 2005: 128, our translation; cf. Noonan, 1957).

Furthermore, and above all, the founders and scholars of today's world religions recognized and emphasized the equity principles accentuated by interest's earliest critics. As a consequence, economic imperatives and behavioral norms as well as interest prohibitions play an important role in religious ethics (Noonan, 1957, 1966). Judaism, Christianity, and Islam all have in common that the protection of the needy and the prevention of economic inequality were always at the center of economic dogmatism (Hanke, 2005: 158). For example, in the New Testament,[3] Luke insists to issue interest-free loans exclusively to enable the poor and needy to improve their lives. In practical terms, the Christian church tried to address usury and exploitation with strict interest caps. But with the rise of international trade in the 11th century and much later with the sustained dominance of mercantilism, the economic and social environment changed fundamentally and initial interpretations of interest restrictions and prohibitions had to be reconsidered. In Judaism, for example, the often-recited ban on interest only applied to members of the own religious community.[4] Thus, instead of being considered an absolute norm of divine origin, the Jewish prohibition of interest was rather a positive law in its explicit relation to non-Jews (Hanke, 2005: 159). Ultimately, this understanding of interest restriction facilitated its practical economic implementation in the context of increasingly comprehensive and long-term trading relationships.

Modern economic criticism of interest rates was expressed in particular during the 20th century. Arguably, the most influential theory of an interest-free economy was formulated by self-educated Austrian economist Silvio Gesell ([1916] 1958) in his widely acclaimed work *The Natural Economic Order*. In it, he resolutely rejected the storage function of money and pleaded for the abolition of the gold standard combined with negative gross interest rates in order to freeze the average net interest rate at zero. This non-interest-bearing *Freigeld* ("free money") was intended to prevent hoarding and to make its circulation velocity controllable. Behind this was the idea that, in contrast to real economic goods, the absence of storage costs in combination with interest payments made money-hoarding virtually free of charge and allowed for effortless income and speculation. In addition, exponentially rising compound interest catalyzed debt dynamics that resulted in extreme growth pressure. But since perpetual growth on which this system is based can impossibly be achieved at all times, economic crises, social unrest, and violent conflicts are necessary consequences of this economic order. Silvio Gesell's *Freigeld* was introduced in a local experiment during the recession in 1932 by Michael Unterguggenberger, mayor of the Austrian village Wörgl. The results were extremely surprising as unemployment could be reduced quickly by an immediate strengthening of local consumption. Wörgl's *Freigeld* was soon again banned by the Austrian Administrative Court, which ruled that the alternative currency violated the central bank's currency monopoly. But this could not distract from the perceived success of the experiment and during the latest financial crisis the concept of *Freigeld* once again gained attention. However, irrespective of insurmountable problems with the comprehensive introduction of a *Freigeld* economy, its advocates must acknowledge that "corroding" money would only be suitable as local currency. That is because the risk-free margin of the interest rate, which they criticize so vehemently, accounts for only a small share of the total interest rate. The risk premium, which is intended to insure lenders against default, is much more relevant. In local, little anonymous contexts, the risk of default may well be manageable. In modern societies with differentiated economic systems and global capital flows, however, a risk premium is absolutely indispensable (Binswanger, 2010).

The unstoppable growth of the world economy also proved a severe challenge for theological critics and with secularization introduced by the Reformation movement, the influence of occidental religious interest bans diminished. This, however, is not true for Islam, where even today a rigorous ban on interest is still in practice. Since both, theoretical justifications as well as the practical implementation provide important lessons about the transforming nature of the price of capital, the special features of the Islamic economy are subsequently explored in more detail.

## Interest in the Islamic Economy

More than any other faith in our world, Islam is considered to be the religion of trade. For thousands of years, Mecca, the religious center of Islam and its most important pilgrimage city, served as the largest commercial center of the Arabian Peninsula. Prophet Muhammad was a merchant. It is therefore unsurprising that large sections of the Qur'an deal with trade and the overall regulation of market activity. Indeed, for many Islamic scholars, the importance of economic life in the Qur'an proves that "the history of Islam in many areas can only be grasped by understanding its social and economic order" (Hanke, 2005: 157; our translation). Against this background, however, it is all the more surprising that the practice of Islamic economics and Islamic banking in particular has so far only played a very minor role in scientific discourse. It seems that particularly with regard to the question of the price of capital and the practical implementation of state or religiously imposed interest prohibitions, the Islamic economic system has been largely overlooked. Although the Islamic banking sector now already comprises a total of around two trillion US dollars, only rather recently it has received increased (Western) scholarly attention (see Siddiqi, 2004; Pfannkuch, 2009).

In the Holy Qur'an, the prohibition of interest (Arabic: "*riba*") finds frequent mentioning, but is particularly referred to in the Surah of the Cow (2: 275):

> Those who consume interest cannot stand [on the Day of Resurrection] except as one stands who is being beaten by Satan into insanity. That is because they say, "Trade is [just] like interest." But Allah has permitted trade and has forbidden interest. So whoever has received an admonition from his Lord and desists may have what is past, and his affair rests with Allah. But whoever returns to [dealing in interest or usury]—those are the companions of the Fire; they will abide eternally therein.

However, comparing different translations of the Qur'an, a serious interpretation problem with these economically so highly important passages arises. In fact, some scholars came to conclude that "any attempt to translate the Qur'anic term, 'riba'" in any language, is not only futile, but is also the source of much confused thinking on the subject" (Rahman, 1964: 1). While some versions translate riba in very general terms as "interest," others interpret it as "usury." In addition, there are many more lexical meanings including "to grow," "to increase," "to prosper," "to rise," and "to nurture." Little surprisingly, the important normative difference of varying interpretations and translations provides the basis for ongoing discussions on what is actually to be understood by the term riba (cf. Nienhaus, 1982: 206; Reissner, 1984: 155). In the original verses from the early Meccan period, riba was only condemned morally. However, when Islam achieved sustained political dominance riba as an economic practice was explicitly forbidden. Since then, the understanding of the conservative Sunni faith of riba as a general prohibition of interest has prevailed and is widely applied as such in practice (Lohlker, 1996: 138). In this understanding, riba is derived from the Arabic term "raba" (English: "growth") interpreted as any form of surplus value without an equivalent counter value (IBP, 2015: 23); a concept that can end in exploitation and must therefore be prohibited.[5] This ethical imperative can also be derived from Islam's economic belief system, in which Allah is considered to be the creator and sole owner of all existing goods. This justifies social and ethical obligations, above all to prevent self-enrichment (Herden, 2000).

The Qur'an distinguishes two types of riba (cf. Hanke, 2005: 164). *Riba al-Nasiah* concerns the interest rate on a classic loan, which is also subject of the scenario described above. Here, a reimbursement of the borrowed sum plus an interest premium is due after a period specified in advance. This additional surcharge represents an unethical enrichment and is therefore prohibited as riba by the Qur'an.[6] *Riba al-Nasiah* is complemented by *Riba al-Fadl*. This concept extends the interpretation of riba beyond the classic monetary interest on a loan to any form of trade in which an exchange of two identical goods at different quantities takes place. In principle, this can apply to any type of product, but is particularly relevant with regards to the practice of currency exchange. For example, according to Sharia law, if two different currencies are to be exchanged at the same price, no commission may be charged. Here again, different time horizons play an important conceptual role. Due to its immediate relevance in trade, *Riba al-Fadl* is characterized by the simultaneity of trade relations, while *Riba al-Nasiah* is relevant with regards to asynchronous exchanges that happen between two points in time.

In addition to Allah being the creator and rightful owner of all things, in Islamic theology there are essentially two justifications for the prohibition of riba depending on the specific nature of a loan (cf. Noorzoy, 1982: 6–7). In this sense, a loan can either be made available for direct consumption or as a capital base for corporate investments. Strictly speaking, both of these forms of credit provision are prohibited as riba, however on the basis of different ethical objections. In the Sharia's understanding, consumer loans are only taken out by debtors, if they have difficulties financing a minimum standard of living due to a lack of sufficient income. In this conception, being contentious as it is, it would be immoral for a high-earning individual to gain additional wealth from the neediness of a poorer person. Thus, the prohibition of riba in this case should be interpreted as an incentive to make a charitable donation rather than unjust profit. While consumer loans with an interest payment are forbidden, donations are expressly desired by the Qur'an.[7] Thus, Islam places the protection of the underprivileged and the fight against economic inequalities through the unjust redistribution from poor to rich at the center of its economic philosophy promoting co-operation and social justice (Rahman, 1964; Samiullah, 1982; Qureshi, [1970] 1974: 45–48; Ali, 1964: 173–175).[8]

The situation is different with regard to corporate loans for capital investment. Here, similar to many other interest critiques, the idea of "working money" is fiercely rejected. Corporate bonds and other types of financial assets are seen as sources of profit and enrichment that neither require the lender to invest physical labor nor to be actively involved in the weal and woe of the company. Hence, this form of riba aims to nudge direct investments in physical (and thus rightfully productive) capital rather than simply in speculative financial assets and company shares. Again, this understanding clearly indicates the predominant idea in Islam that money has no intrinsic productivity. Of course, the validity of this rather controversial but nevertheless crucial assumption will have to be examined in more detail in the course of this chapter.

At this point it becomes clear: if one considers the different justifications of an actively practiced prohibition of interest, very similar arguments emerge that were formulated in antiquity by Aristotle, translated by world religions into ethical codes of conduct, and substantiated theoretically by Karl Marx and others. Both the protection of the poor from exploitation by an elitist financial class of capital owners and the "unnatural" concept of "money begetting money" occur in one form or another, although an active exchange of ideas between critics of interest who were geographically, temporally and conceptually very far separated never took place. Rather, the striking similarity of arguments against the dominance of interest seem to stem from concepts of justice deeply anchored within us, which manifest themselves independent of social, cultural or religious influences. However, Islam is the only world religion that even today continues the challenging task to integrate money into its behavioral ethics against its nature as an essentially disguising and anonymous medium of exchange. Practiced rigorously, these critical concepts should entirely prevent the development of a successful banking and financial system. This raises the question of how Islam could nevertheless establish a billion-dollar banking business and which lessons can be drawn for the price of capital and the effectiveness of money as a moral medium.

## Can an Interest-Free Economy Exist?

Is an interest-free economy feasible? Different trials exemplified the practical problems that a rigorous prohibition of interest can entail. Neoclassical economics offer a theoretical explanation for these practical challenges. Here, the interest rate is derived from the net productivity of capital. Only on the basis of positive net productivity can capital generate surplus value and provide the ground for savings or additional capital generation. A prohibition of interest would require the long-term interest rate, and thus the net productivity of capital to remain at zero at all times while net savings could not be achieved. This purely hypothetical thought experiment would only be possible in a world in which both, the supply of production factors and technical development remained at a constant (Noorzoy, 1982: 7; Hicks, 1965). Although the exact nature of the relationship between interest rates and savings remains empirically untapped, these economic deliberations illustrate nevertheless the fundamental relevance of interest rates for a productive and constantly growing economy. On these economic grounds, it is not entirely surprising that even where interest is traditionally considered immoral, different models have been developed to circumvent interest prohibition.

In addition, on a practical note, "the abolition of interest presupposes the highest degree imaginable of co-operative spirit" (Rahman, 1964: 39). This means that in a society lacking mutual cooperation and trust, market mechanisms in general and price systems in particular organize economic coordination. Social trading systems surpassing classical tribal communities in size lack the practical preconditions for the abolishment of an interest rate. And so, Islam allows four different trading practices in particular that enable a functional banking system despite the strict prohibition of riba (cf. Hanke, 2005: 169ff.; Herden, 2000).

The *Mudaraba* is considered to be the most Sharia-compliant form of investment as it can be directly derived from the Qur'an. It can be understood as a practice of profit sharing. When an investor provides a certain amount of capital to a company, he receives a predetermined share of the subsequent profit in return. The profit mark-up on the originally invested amount of capital functions as a substitute for interest payments. However, in this system, in the event of a corporate loss the investor also bears the entire risk of his deposits, while the entrepreneur is largely protected financially. Unsurprisingly, this counterintuitive regulation often leads to serious practical problems as an investor obtains no significant control or supervisory rights while bearing the entire financial risk. Since this construct is based only on mutual trust (which is ultimately to be rewarded through profit sharing), it is quite unproblematic for the entrepreneur to disguise profits or to cover up important challenges or mismanagement of the company. Although the Mudaraba is closest to the original trading commandment in the Qur'an conceptually, this form of interest evasion fails to comprehensively establish itself as general trade practice due to its severe restrictions. Although Islamic financial institutions have been able to develop and improve the classic Mudaraba by acting as risk mediators between investors and entrepreneurs, "these problems have led to a massive loss of capital for Islamic banks in the past. As a consequence of these difficulties, only about five percent of Islamic banks' capital transactions are currently conducted through Mudaraba" (Hanke, 2005: 170; own translation). A second instrument for avoiding riba is the *Ijara Thumma al Bai*. This construct is comparable to a classic leasing transaction compiled of a rent (Ijara) and a purchase (Bai). In a first step, physical capital is leased to be used in the production process. At the end of a previously specified rental period, the debtor purchases the leased capital at a price that had also been agreed upon in advance. Ultimately, the rent from the leasing contract replaces a generic interest rate and is nevertheless conform with riba law. Thirdly, Islamic banks can practice the *Bai al-Inah* as part of their lending business. To grant loans, banks complete a double purchase transaction. In a first step, the bank sells a loan in the form of assets to a customer, who repays it in later instalments. The loan, however, is immediately bought back by the bank at a lower price and in the form of a cash payment. At the end of this double transaction of purchase and repurchase, the actual loan consists in the cash payment of the bank and the interest (and thus the bank's profit from the loan transaction) in the mark-up of the final total instalments to be paid on the original price of the loan. Thus, strictly speaking, in this case two identical goods (money) are traded at different prices—a practice strictly forbidden as riba by the Qur'an. It is therefore little surprising that this form of credit loan is by far the most controversial in Islamic banking, because it represents a rather unsophisticated circumvention of the riba prohibition (Hanke, 2005: 172). Finally, the fourth and most commonly used strategy of bypassing the riba is the *Murabaha*. Here, the bank acts as an intermediary in a classic commercial relationship between customer and seller in order to facilitate credit-based consumption that is nevertheless conform with Sharia law. If a customer wishes to purchase a product with the help of a loan, the bank steps in and buys the product from the dealer at the original price. In a second step, the bank sells the product to the customer at a higher cost without imposing additional interest on an instalment. However, foregone interest is priced into the difference between the original and the later price. And yet, this bargain is nevertheless conforming with the Qur'an and no incident of riba.

Which conclusions can be drawn from the Islamic prohibition of interest and its practical implementation for our enquiry of the price of capital? Analyzing the various objections to interest reveals an inherent conflict between ethical concepts of justice on the one hand and economic rationality and practicability on the other. In the debate about interest prohibition, the protection of debtors usually stands against basic principles of economic efficiency, for example the simple fact that scarce goods—such as money and capital—must necessarily fetch a price in order to be mobilized in a barter transaction. In particular, two distinct fronts emerge. Firstly, the ethical argument of protecting the poor and combating inequality is usually countered by the need of a rightful compensation of capitalist lenders for their foregone consumption. Secondly, productivity and incentive arguments embodied in interest and essential for the functioning of the economic investment cycle contrast with conceptions about the unnatural capacity of "working" money and unearned income.

In practice, the Islamic prohibition of interest and its natural circumvention show that neither of these two fronts can easily be neglected or dismissed. Neither is a functional economy without interest or interest-like constructs really imaginable, nor should the economic and social consequences of interest-based capitalism be ignored. Rather, these opposing views must be reconciled in one form or another. Thus, rest of this chapter fathoms why, and against all morally valid objections discussed so far, a price of capital could be justifiable and how it should be designed in order to reconcile the opposing and yet equally relevant concerns as optimally as possible.

## Why Does Capital Have a Price?

Interest fulfils a great variety of important economic functions. This at least is a fundamental truth that economists could always agree on. And so, there are many verifiable reasons why the provision of capital should have a price (Beck, 2014: 206–207). These are supported both by theoretical and practical considerations and contribute to the healthy functioning of the economic system in particular and the social system in general. For instance, interest rates can serve to internalize uncertainty and risks. A creditor (Italian: *creditore, credere;* English: *to believe*) at all times *believes* in the full reimbursement of the original loan. If belief in the solvency of the debtor vanishes, the interest rate resembles a risk premium depending on the probability of default. Since the future is naturally uncertain, without the possibility of internalizing such basic risks a functioning economic system would be unimaginable. Closely linked to this concept, an interest rate can also serve to internalize compensation for damages. If a debtor cannot repay a loan by a specific due date, an interest on arrears may apply.

Independent from the individual debtor's ability to repay a loan, the logic of a healthy, steadily growing economy also requires an interest rate mechanism to compensate for inflation risks. If losses of purchasing power on the part of the creditor were not adequately compensated, issuing a loan would be economically unreasonable. Only an interest rate corresponding to the level of inflation could prevent the lender from being disadvantaged and thus enable the long-term sustainability of the economic cycle of borrowing and investing. As mentioned briefly, this function of interest plays an important role in the interpretation of the Qur'an and the regulation of the Islamic economy. More moderate clerics argue that interest rates up to the level of inflation do not represent a case of riba as no immoral profit and enrichment result from this.

In addition to these relevant objections to an interest-free economy, from both an economic and ethical perspective the argument of opportunity costs weighs the heaviest. A creditor forfeits more than just a current sum of money during the period of a loan. She also loses the opportunity to consume or invest herself. Now, of course, the economic and social context, the borrower's immediate needs, the lender's total capital wealth, and the marginal utility of the imparted sum are all important determinants of this argument. In their dogmas, the world religions commonly emphasize debtor protection and thus that opportunity costs be internalized as charitable alms or donations. Hence, an unanimous principle of justice, universally embedded in social codes of conduct, seems to legitimize a compensation of opportunity costs through an interest premium. In Islamic banking, too, compensating mark-ups of this kind are calculated, albeit in more disguised forms. The effects of this principle of social order can further be underpinned by insights from behavioral economics. Regardless of culture, society, or faith, people seem to assume a rather short-term self-reflective perspective when assessing their own life situation. And assessing her own condition, an individual distinguishes cognitively between a present and a future ego. Whether rational or not, the well-being of the future ego is usually less important to man than that of the present. There is therefore a tendency to prefer short-term consumption to long-term investments, especially since unknown risks could lead to losses that would put the future self relatively worse than the present. In this way, interest not only has the power to mediate between creditor and debtor, but also between diverging self-imageries of a single individual at different points in time (Beck, 2014: 207).

Despite all tenable criticism, these important functional justifications of interest are embodied both in normative and theoretical arguments for a price of capital. A historical analysis of the long-term development of interest rates proves the fundamental importance of interest in impressive fashion. In *A History of Interest Rates*, the American economic historians Sidney Homer and Richard Sylla ([1963] 2005: 57–64; 135ff.) show that the average long-term trend of interest rates in antiquity and the Middle Ages describes a U-shaped inverted parabola (see Figure 3.1). This indicates that interest rates in all important ancient and medieval civilizations started initially at a high level, then declined steadily with the development and associated security and stability of an empire, before escalating again shortly before the altogether fall of a civilization. Accordingly, "interest rates accurately reflect the well-being and functionality of a society. The development of interest rates over a certain period of time represents the "fever curve" of a nation" (Bernstein, 2005: 49; own translation). The interest rate functions as important socio-economic variable by internalizing uncertainty and risk ever since the origin of coinage.

Thus, the price of capital crucially serves as an indispensable source of information with regards to the overall economic and social condition of a civilization.

This essential function was also emphasized by Friedrich Hayek, in his resolute opposition to the prohibition of interest. Building on a state skepticism that he adopted from Locke and Hume, in *The Road to Serfdom* Hayek outlined the dangers of an autonomous, monopolistic, and interventional state. He was particularly concerned that state intervention would lead to a tampered, dysfunctional price system, which then would lose its socially most important function as an information system:

> Fundamentally, in a system where the knowledge of the relevant facts is dispersed among many people, prices can act to coordinate the separate actions of different people in the same way as subjective values help the individual to coordinate the parts of his plan
>
> *(Hayek, 1945: 526).*[9]

In *The Road to Serfdom*, Hayek argues that prices can only function as information transmitters if they can be determined freely and unimpeded by state activity in liberal and unregulated markets:

> The important point here is that the price system will fulfil this function only if competition prevails, that is, if the individual producer has to adapt

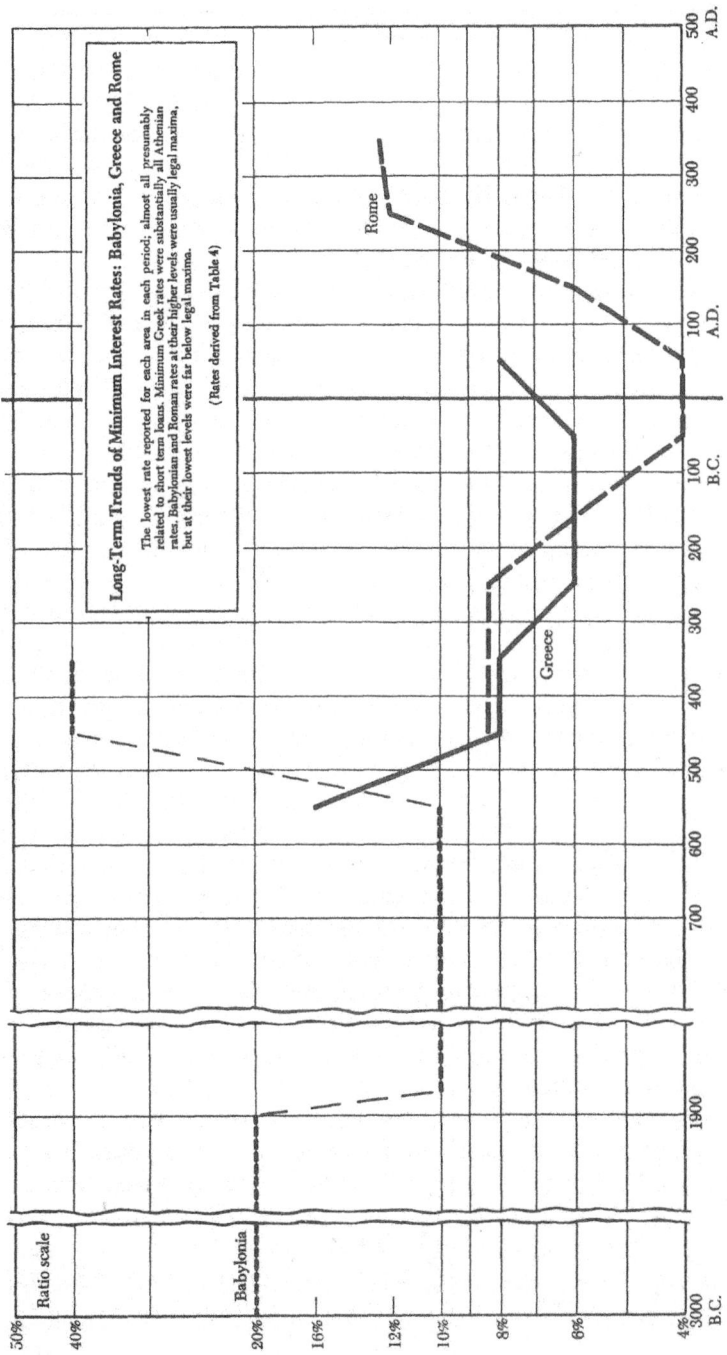

**Long-Term Trends of Minimum Interest Rates: Babylonia, Greece and Rome**

The lowest rate reported for each area in each period; almost all presumably related to short term loans. Minimum Greek rates were substantially all Athenian rates. Babylonian and Roman rates at their higher levels were usually legal maxima, but at their lowest levels were far below legal maxima.

(Rates derived from Table 4)

**FIGURE 3.1** Long–Term Interest Trends in Antiquity

*Source Homer and Sylla (1963) 2005: 63*

himself to price changes and cannot control them. The more complicated the whole, the more dependent we become on that division of knowledge between individuals whose separate efforts are co-ordinated by the impersonal mechanism for transmitting the relevant information known by us as the price system.

*(Hayek, [1944] 2001: 52)*

Accordingly, state manipulation or let alone a complete prohibition of interest would prevent the functioning of capital prices as information systems. As a result, individuals would make (market) decisions on the basis of incomplete information and could even (unknowingly) be forced into involuntary behavior. In an absolute state, as the Austrian Hayek could observe it directly from England in 1944, this would ultimately lead to the (unconscious) subjugation of individuals and complete restriction of their civil rights.

If all the sources of current information are effectively under one single control, it is no longer a question of merely persuading the people of this or that. The skillful propagandist then has power to mould their minds in any direction he chooses and even the most intelligent and independent people cannot entirely escape that influence if they are long isolated from all other sources of information.

*(Hayek, [1944] 2001: 158)*

Even though the devastating economic and social consequences of non-regulated capital markets have become obvious at the latest since the recent global financial crisis, Hayek's liberalism nevertheless stresses the fundamental importance of free money and capital trade. Interest, like any other form of price, is a medium for conveying information that serves as an allocation mechanism enabling rational and thus economically optimal decisions. For example, the yield levels of investments provide information on the scarcity of goods in a market. In Hayek's neoclassical understanding, without a price for capital it would be impossible to identify shortages or overcapacities and to balance them in an economically optimal way. At the same time, this argument emphasizes that a capitalist economy based purely on altruism, as imagined in theological ideal conceptions, would fail inevitably since it would lack important information about neediness and scarcity.

Against this background and with the manifold economic and ethical reasons for the importance of interest rates in mind, many scholars recognize an economic error of fact, particularly in religiously motivated prohibitions of interest (Weiß, 2005: 142ff.). For as mentioned above, a frequently-stressed argument against interest supported by Aristotle and many religious thinkers is derived from the alleged unnatural character of value-begetting money. This view implies that money has no productivity per se and therefore should not be the source of effortless income. Its only legitimate functions lie in the exchange and preservation of value, as well as in its nature as a universal unit of account. From an economic point of view, however, this perspective seems too short-sighted. Religious economics are frequently accused to suffer from a narrow or incomplete understanding capital as production factor:

> The philosophical argument was based on the lack of a capital theory: prohibiting interest payments (in contrast to the legal unemployed pension income on land) it remained unrecognized that money can in fact be quite fruitful if invested as capital. This capacity is comprehensively obtainable only in the modern economy, as it was explicitly prevented by the prohibition of interest rates in the Middle Ages.
>
> *(Kerber, 1993: 1341ff.; our translation)*

Nonetheless, it would be fallacious to claim that theology lacked economic understanding and know-how. Rather, it must be assumed that a deeply ethical understanding of the problem always opposed economic efficiency-based arguments and thus prevented a revision or questioning of interest prohibition for a very long time. Debtor protection and the emphasis of economic fairness always took precedence. At the same time, however, the natural circumvention of interest prohibition—especially where it is applied most rigorously—illustrates the conceptual and practical problems inherent in theological economics and is at the same time a harbinger of extensive societal financialization, which interest-bearing capital implies in the last instance.

Against this background, the price of capital on the one hand seems inevitable because of its essential importance for the modern economic system. But on the other hand, it may also be subject to and source of considerable problems. However, before discussing these difficulties and possible takeaways in more detail, we first need to outline the most important interest theories below. Because their history of ideas has always dealt with the central question of determining the "right" (or "just") interest rate while pointing to important empirical problems in measuring the price and value of capital and resembling many of the philosophical arguments discussed up until this point.

## Measuring Capital and Its "Just" Price

The question of how an optimal interest rate could be determined in theory has been occupying economists for decades (cf. Shoven and Topper, 1992; Böhm-Bawerk, [1889] 1991; Wicksell, 1893; Åkerman, 1923; Walras, [1954] 2003; Fisher, 1930; Hayek, [1941] 2009; Keynes, 1936; Knight, [1921] 1964). The central problem lies in the function of interest as a mediating medium between the present and the future and the associated uncertainty regarding a wide range of unknown factors. Against this background and since the mid-19th century in particular, economic theories have been developed and constantly enhanced by including increasingly complex assumptions and influencing factors. In his work *Interest Theory* (1967), German economist Friedrich A. Lutz was the first to systematically summarize the history of ideas of the most important thinkers. Since there are countless contributions to this specific issue with many different angles, for the sake of brevity, we want to refer to the classical theoretical models of Irving Fischer and John Maynard Keynes in particular. In order to reenact adequately the history of ideas, however, a few remarks are in order about the works of the allegedly first systematic thinker of interest theory.

Austrian economist Eugen von Böhm-Bawerk ([1889] 1991) is widely considered to be one of the first theorists to systematically address the challenge of an economic theory of interest. He justified an interest rate by observing that people seemed to have a "preference for the present" (*Gegenwartspräferenz*), that is a tendency to prefer assured consumption in the present over uncertain investments in the future. Only with the promise of interest could capital owners be motivated to lend their money. The crucial difference that distinguishes Böhm-Bawerk's theory from previously dominant religious and moral considerations lies in the dissimilarity of assumption. He rejected the prevailing idea of money being naturally unproductive and thus the conclusion that it should and could not be *eo ipso* a source of surplus value. Rather, he realized that money, invested in a meaningful way, could indeed be directed into a so-called "production detour" (*Produktionsumweg*). This way, money can be invested in physical capital such as a machine, which in turn contributes to increased productivity and efficiency rates of a company. Thus, by building this machine, workers can indirectly contribute significantly more productivity to the actual production process of a commodity than it would be possible at the same expense without the machine. Ultimately, this increase of productivity is only possible with the contribution of capital and a temporal shift of alternative consumption. According to Böhm-Bawerk, it would therefore only be appropriate to share the additional surplus value generated from an increase of productivity with the capital investor, not least to create incentives for future investments. Herein lies the practical justification of interest. No less relevant is the theoretical justification for a price of capital. In this sense, interest "allows the entrepreneur to choose production detours of such length that the overall budget ("subsistence fund"; *Subsistenzfonds*) suffices to maintain the original amounts of production factors during this period" (Lutz, 1967: 17; our translation). In Böhm-Bawerk's theory, as in many subsequent economic conceptions, interest serves as an incentive and informational system to achieve the most efficient and economically optimal allocation of capital resources. With his original analysis, Böhm-Bawerk laid the groundwork for more complex approaches to follow, which dealt in in more detail with the question of how an optimal interest level could actually be determined.

In his *Theory of Interest* (1930), American economist Irving Fisher modeled geographically the original principle of interest, that is to compensate opportunity costs, in the form of indifference curves. As argued above, the answer to the question of the "just" price of capital depends on many individual and social factors influencing the perceived severity of consumption cutting or rather, impatience of consumption. According to classical indifference theory, a capital owner is essentially indifferent with regards to holding a certain amount of capital today and an unequal amount of capital in the future for as long as both values lie on the same individual indifference curve. The slope of a tangent along the indifference curve describes in its inclination the *time preference* (see Lutz, 1967: 79), that is, how much more future capital an individual is prepared renounce in order to realize current consumption (see Figure 3.2). In the opposite sense, time preference describes the minimum rate of interest that would be required to incentivize a loan. Fisher's indifference curves thus reflect individual and collective preferences from which (as for any other form of classic commodity) the price of capital can be derived.

Following these considerations, British economist John Maynard Keynes, too, regarded interest as the "reward for parting with liquidity" (Lutz, 1967: 121; our translation). Interest "is the 'price' which equilibrates the desire to hold wealth in

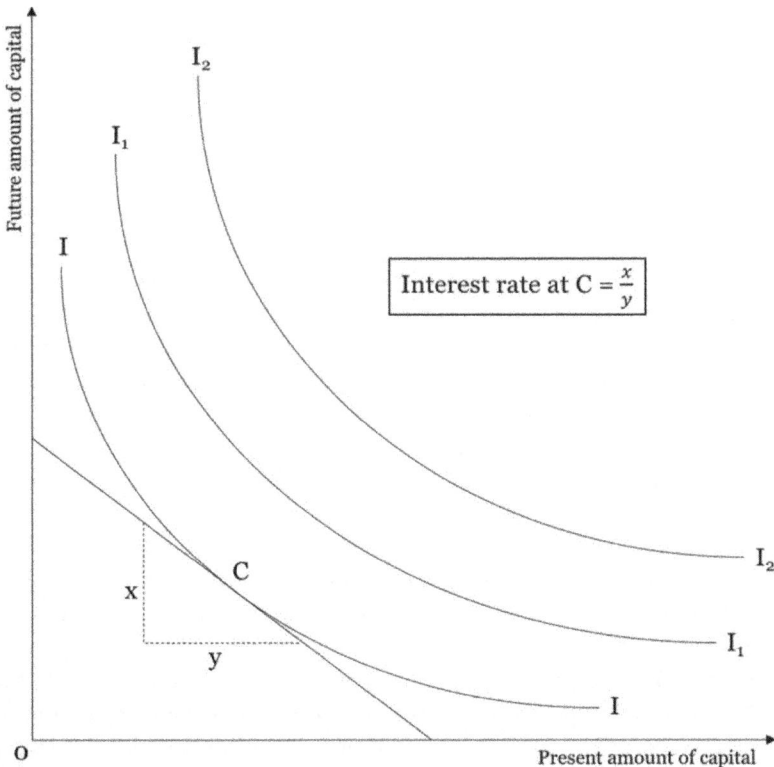

**FIGURE 3.2**  Fisher's Model of Indifference Curves

the form of cash with the available quantity of cash" (Keynes, 1936: 166–167). Consumers have a natural preference for holding cash (*liquidity preference*) in order to be able to realize important spending at all times. This function allowed Keynes to integrate the concept of interest in his general monetary theory. The individual desire to hold money can be expressed by a curve that reflects the specific liquidity preference for various hypothetical interest rate levels (Lutz, 1967: 121). From this, one can derive a liquidity preference curve that represents the amount of money held depending on the interest rate. Ultimately, this model allows to estimate the price of capital in relation to an individual's liquidity preference.

This rather superficial overview of pertinent interest rate theories accentuates two important problems in determining the "just" price of capital. Firstly, an attempt to economize or theorize the price of capital emphasizes the crucial role of individual and collective, hence, deeply *social* influencing factors. Like any form of commodity, be it a second-hand car, a mansion in Central London, a financial certificate, or a professional footballer playing for FC Barcelona, capital is worth only as much as a buyer is prepared to pay for it or as a seller is prepared to give up. This willingness depends on cultural and social factors that determine the price and value of capital under the constant influence of profound societal transformation processes. In this sense, interest rates can certainly be represented mathematically or geometrically in relative terms, but it is almost impossible to make a conclusive statement about its absolute let alone "just" value, at least from a solely economic angle.

Furthermore, and directly linked to this, a second considerable challenge lies in the difficulties of measuring capital. Ultimately, an exact quantification of a certain amount of capital at a specific point in time can only be achieved in a stationary economy (Lutz, 1961). Because a capital stock can only accurately be measured if external influencing factors such as technological development or productivity rates are kept constant. However, such assumptions contradict the nature of any real economy. For as Karl Marx noted correctly, capital constitutes value in motion. This very nature makes a stationary measurement of capital and interest in a highly dynamic and ever-changing environment, embedded in complex social processes, practically impossible. Thus, we can only ever have a very "vague notion of what is meant by "more" or "less" capital (Lutz, 1961: 16):

> So long as the economy is undergoing any sort of change, and capital goods are altering their form, we cannot know exactly to what extent capital is increasing or decreasing. . . . In our theoretical models, we are obliged none the less to proceed as if capital were precisely measurable. . . . Perhaps, then, we shall have to give up the search for the 'true' measure of capital, just as we had to abandon the search for the "ideal" index number, and the "correct" depreciation formula. The hopelessness of this search is a penalty of the very existence of economic change.

Both of these objections illustrate the difficulty connected to the search for the "just" price and value of capital. Unsurprisingly, there are as many economically justified propositions for fair or efficient levels of interest rates as well as ethical or religious rejections of a price of money. On the one hand, the interest rate appears to embody genuinely individual and collective parameters. On the other hand, however, the prohibition of interest and its evasion in practice also make clear that the basic normative principle of compensating people for renouncing consumption is generally accepted beyond social and cultural borders. Even in the conservative Islamic economy, interest bans are intuitively circumvented to provide future incentives for capital investment. Against this background, the central difficulty in pricing capital lies in the fact that

> while the valuation of income goods is characteristically a market valuation, the values of the goods which enter into the capital stock are characteristically imputed values. We cannot take over a market valuation for them; we have to set values upon them ourselves.
>
> *(Hicks, 1961: 19)*

Values, and particularly that of capital, are ultimately man-made and thus socially determined—in the words of Marcel Mauss a total social fact (*fait social total*).

Against this background, it becomes sufficiently evident that purely economic considerations about the "right" price of capital soon reach their limits, for this important question must explicitly include society as a whole. Paradoxically, however, the economic perspective is becoming even more and more relevant by introducing complex time- and focus-consuming technicalities into public discourse (Romer, 2016). This development constitutes the central difference to earlier considerations about the "just" price of capital:

> [The medievals'] amalgamated discussion of price from an economic and ethical perspective was much deeper than the modern one, in the sense that it rendered contemplation of economic technicalities, which are dear to modem economists, of secondary importance, and reflected on the moral and ethical aspects of market exchange as well as the notion of 'value', issues whose serious discussion today are simply dismissed on economic grounds alone.
>
> *(Hamouda and Price, 1997: 208)*

Insofar, rather than the exact economic determination of its price, the social implications reflected in the constant change of capital's unknown parameters influencing economic, political and social institutions might be of much greater relevance. Therefore, the remaining course of this chapter explores the manifold consequences that an increasing social appropriation of capital could imply in the context of more recent financialization. How should the price of capital be structured in order to reconcile the competing objections for and against interest and in particular the fragile relationship between economic incentives and social inequality? From these empirical considerations, important conclusions can be drawn about the ("just") value of capital and the evolution of its social relevance.

## The Relationship of Capital, Debt and Guilt in Modern Societies

> None are more hopelessly enslaved than those who falsely believe they are free.
> —*Johann Wolfgang von Goethe ([1809] 1982: 397)*

During the last decade since the outbreak of the global financial crisis, it has repeatedly become clear how ambivalent and unstable the relationship between society and capital is. Since mid-September 2011, *Zucotti Park* in the heart of Manhattan's financial district served as home to the *Occupy Wall Street* movement, which quickly found numerous sister movements and supporters in many other countries. The central s of this soon-to-be global movement were based on a stricter control of the financial sector, the fight against social inequality and the reduction of influence of politics by powerful economic interests. Against this background, it seemed only fitting to rename Zucotti Park for the time of occupation to its original name: *Freedom Park*. With its demands, the movement expressed a determined protest against the increasing social appropriation of capital, the constant compulsion to sustained growth and escalating inequality concerning its ownership, control, and freedom the of choice. But what are the reason for the prolonged dominance of capital by in all social strata?

The seemingly inexorable motor of the steady social appropriation of capital is growth or, put more precisely, its inseparable counterpart, debt. The highest goal of capital as an economy-structuring element is the prevention of its immobilization, a threat that looms constantly and especially in times of overall economic contraction. For as has already been stated, capital value is in motion. Debt therefore plays a central role in the maintenance of capital, because in classical, equilibrium-oriented economics every unit of (capital) value is matched by a unit of debt. Hence, "the financial assets of one person . . . are always the debt of another" (Leinweber, 2015: 1; our translation). Figure 3.3 illustrates this relationship empirically. According to the calculations of the German Bundesbank, instead of a gross debt of 2.4 trillion euros in 2014, Germany owns net assets of just over 400 billion euros, and amount which, incidentally, has been quite stable since the turn of the millennium.[11]

Taking this thought to its logical end, one comes to the conclusion that debt in the modern economic system is not only a logical consequence of wealth, but also indispensable in the process of saving. In social discourse, saving is often starkly contrasted

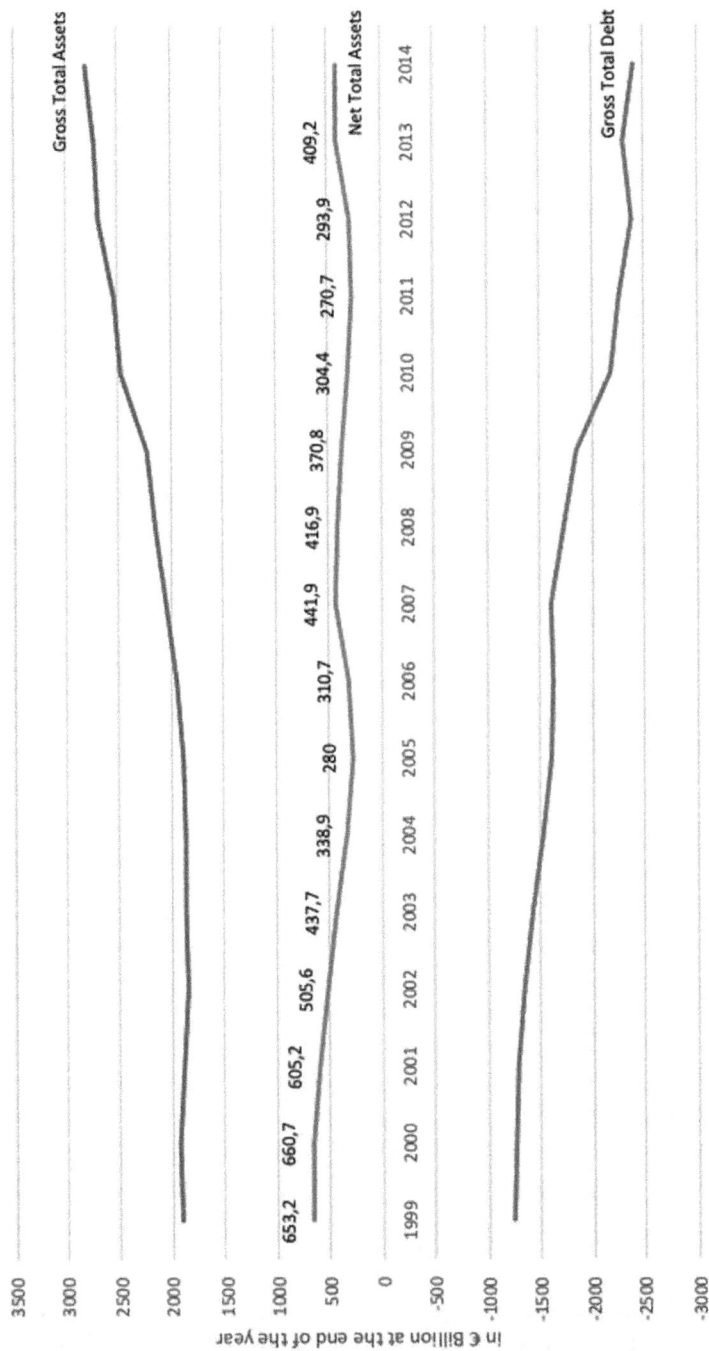

**FIGURE 3.3** Debt and Assets in Germany Between 1999 and 2014

*Source:* Original figure adapted from Statistisches Bundesamt and Deutsche Bundesbank (2015: 8–9); our figure[10]

Gross Total Assets

Net Total Assets

Gross Total Debt

in € Billion at the end of the year

3500
3000
2500
2000
1500
1000
500
0
-500
-1000
-1500
-2000
-2500
-3000

1999 2000 2001 2002 2003 2004 2005 2006 2007 2008 2009 2010 2011 2012 2013 2014

653,2 660,7 605,2 505,6 437,7 338,9 280 310,7 441,9 416,9 370,8 304,4 270,7 293,9 409,2

with debt as a virtuous and entirely opposite activity. But actually, they are two sides of the same medal. After all, saving (i.e. an income surplus) is the accounting underbelly of investment (i.e. an expenditure surplus) (Ehnts, 2018). One might argue that this principle only applies in a closed economy without foreign trade. But such practical objections do not change the logical fact that debt and savings must in principle not be regarded as opposites but rather as complementary prerequisites. Excessive savers are necessarily promoting current account deficits elsewhere; an uncomfortable truth that the euro partners had to learn in the aftermath of the debt crisis.

Even if debt and wealth always cancel each other out in macroeconomic terms, their relationship plays a decisive role in the socio-economic context. For debt embodies *anti-value* and thus constitutes the basis of the counterpart to the owning class and of inequality and social division. With regards to this two-sided construct, modern economies are always the scene of structural power struggles, of ascent and descent, of responsibility and sin. For the debtor, in relation to the creditor, has a morally justified duty to preserve and reimburse capital:

> Debts as anti-value represent a claim to future value production, which can only be redeemed through value production. The anti-value of debt thus becomes one of the most important incentives and levers for securing further production of value and added value.
>
> *(Harvey, 2017; our translation)*

Debt embodies a deeply moral concept that can be used in any form as an instrument of social power by legitimizing and confirming existing hierarchical structures (cf. Graeber, [2011] 2014: 69). The American anthropologist and co-founder of the Occupy Wall Street movement David Graeber ([2011] 2014: 14) sees in the unstoppable indebtedness of private individuals and nation states the consequence of impersonal, mathematized relationships in the eye of threatening violence and the cause of the "moral confusion" that is quite obviously underlying this concept.[12] In particular, the market-based social system of modern states illustrates the contradiction that arises from a sinful understanding of monetary indebtedness. On the one hand, debt is considered an immoral obligation, "a matter of self-indulgence, a sin against one's loved ones." At the same time, however, this immoral obligation must also be entered into by virtually everyone, because in the modern, capitalist system of growth and progress "one must go into debt to achieve a life that goes in any way beyond sheer survival" (Graeber, [2011] 2014: 379).

As a consequence of these structural preconditions, market societies are becoming more and more assumed by debt, which creates incentives to be productive, to generate added value and to keep capital in motion:

> Overburdening weak and marginalized social groups with debt is a way of disciplining debtors and turning them into productive workers. Or using

a more obvious example: Highly indebted students and homeowners in the US are extremely restricted in their future degrees of freedom. It is no coincidence that these methods of securing value production have come to the fore, because it is becoming increasingly difficult for capital to organize value production in a conventional way. The tentacles of indebtedness continue to penetrate society and eventually capture everyone with a single credit card in their wallet. Even more frightening is the indebtedness of the states. In the same way that individuals are disciplined by their debt, states are exposed to the threat of anti-value that bondholders exert. There is a danger that the economic system and social welfare states could collapse under the dead weight of anti-value.

*(Harvey, 2017; our translation)*

Similar coercive processes are taking place at the macrosocial level between markets and societies and their respective governments. The financialization of the international capital system plays a crucial role, laying the ground for "disciplining neoliberalism" since the early 1980s (Rommerskirchen, 2015). This concept describes a system "in which the actions of governments, as well as firms and workers, are internally and externally disciplined by market forces, or put differently, by the power of capital" (Gill, 1998: 8). This process works through interest rates. Should investors get the feeling that states could take on excessive debt burdens in order to achieve their political agendas, they can punish them immediately by raising long-term interest rates, notwithstanding democratic legitimacy of such fiscal efforts. For even minimal increases in interest rates in the context of mounting government deficits can lead to noticeably rising costs for taxpayers and an outflow of international capital (Gros, 2012). The fact that even international organizations such as the International Monetary Fund or the European Commission often approve of this fiscal straitjacket strategy by the markets illustrates the extent to which the contradictions of "democratic capitalism" have already materialized in everyday politics (Streeck, 2011).

The consequence of the international debt system, which commits itself primarily to inexorable capital movement and sustained economic growth is ever-growing socio-economic inequality between the owning and the indebted classes. For even if this system promises opportunities for social ascent at the individual level, which it continues to proof, undoubtedly a structural accumulation of capital can be observed at the macro level. Like a magnetic force, money always strives toward capital. But this system is not infinitely durable. With excessive inequality, the fragile relationship between these classes threatens to tip-over and thus the legitimation of the entire system under capitalism's most important imperative proclaimed by Marx ([1890] 1976: 742): "Accumulate, accumulate! That is Moses and the prophets!"

## Inequality of Capital

> This boundless drive for enrichment, this passionate chase after value, is common to the capitalist and the miser; but while the miser is merely a capitalist gone mad, the capitalist is a rational miser.
>
> —*Karl Marx ([1890] 1976: 254)*

Inequality[13] is a deeply ambiguous concept and of worth only in relative terms. The question of how a modern society is structured under the constant influence of the debt and capital system is a highly complicated one. Between the members of the Organisation for Economic Co-operation and Development (OECD) inequality is growing steadily. However, if we look at global developments, the picture is less clear as the so-called "elephant graph" illustrates (see Figures 3.4 and 3.5; cf. Milanovic, 2016; Lakner and Milanovic, 2015).

Comparing growth within different percentiles of the global income distribution shows that since the early 1990s there has been a remarkable increase in middle class income in poorer countries (point A) and in the income of the extremely rich 1 percent in developed countries (point C). China and India in particular are responsible for the growth of the middle classes in the lower percentiles, where progressive market integration and sustained economic growth provide increased wealth, while inequality at national and regional levels remains largely unchanged.

The richest segment includes mostly Americans, who alone account for about 50 percent of the world's top 1 percent (Milanovic, 2016). On the other side of the spectrum, the losers of recent developments are situated in the middle classes of the "old," richer OECD countries between the 65th and 85th percentile (point B). Within this stratum the most striking social development of the last three decades has taken place. Here, people experienced tangible economic decline and social regression, that is, the palpable shrinking of a formerly anchored, economically successful, and largely carefree middle class (Nachtwey, 2016). The perceived relative change in the financial and social position of many members of this class, whether triggered by globalization, urbanization, or migration, produces feelings of alienation and political abandonment and revitalizes class struggles, which nowadays are increasingly structured by more complex social conditions and differences than purely income inequality (cf. Beramendi et al., 2015). As observable in most of the European Union, the United Kingdom and the United States, the result is often political instability that radical protest parties can turn into electoral support (Voss, 2018; Vlandas and Halikiopoulou, 2015, 2016).

What are the reasons for increasing relative capital inequality in advanced industrial economies and the shrinking of their middle classes? In 2013, Thomas Piketty offered a comprehensive and much debated answer to this question in his influential work *Capital in the 21st Century*. In it, he formally and empirically argued how the capitalist relationship between debtor and creditor leads to

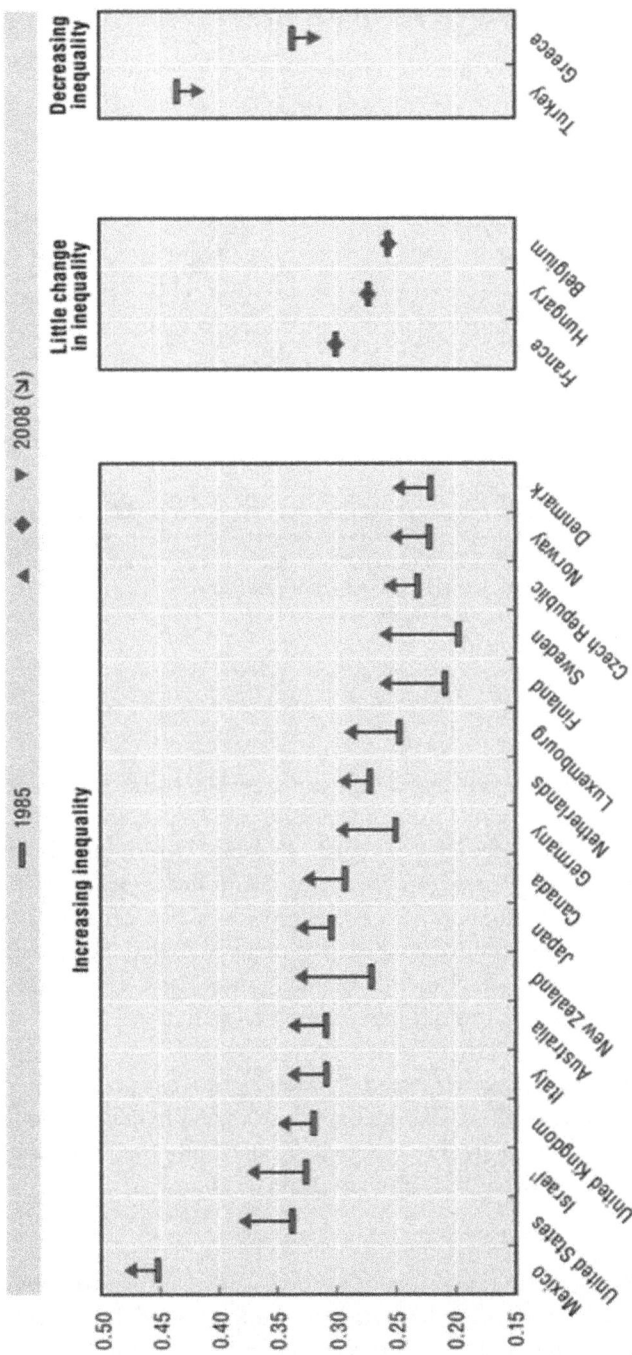

**FIGURE 3.4** Inequality in the OECD

*Source:* OECD, 2011:24

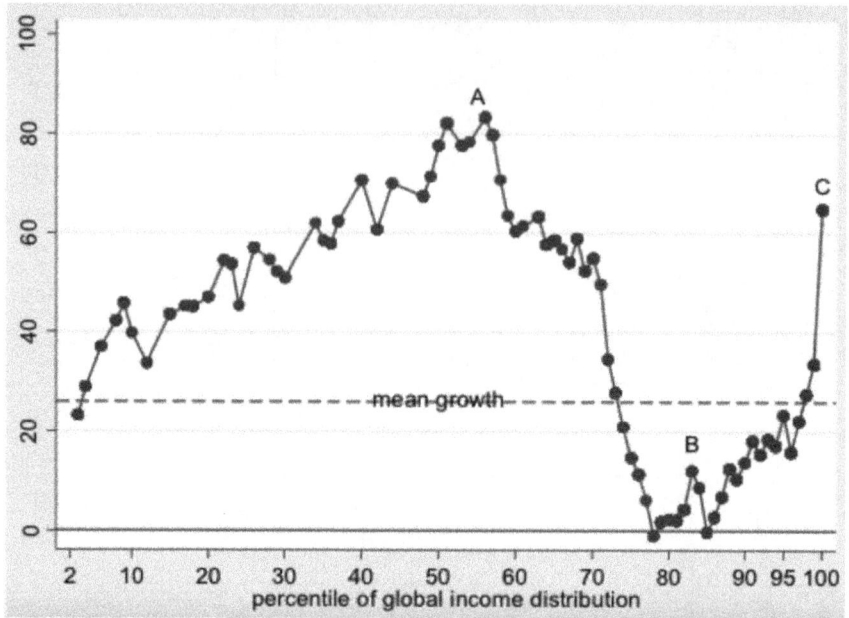

**FIGURE 3.5** The Elephant-Graph

*Source:* Milanovic, 2016

structural and perpetual inequality of capital ownership. In his theory, the ratio of return on capital to economic growth is paramount. Depending on the overall ratio of capital to income, the level of return on capital determines the share of capital in national income. The higher this share, the greater capital inequality. For if the return on capital surmounts the general growth rate of the economy, capital assets grow faster in value than wages or average economic income (Piketty, [2013] 2014: 39ff.; Piketty and Saez, 2014). Piketty provides a simple example to highlight the importance of this ratio for wealth concentration:

> For example, if [the growth rate] $g = 1\%$ and [the rate of return on capital] $r = 5\%$, saving one-fifth of the income from capital (while consuming the other four-fifths) is enough to ensure that capital inherited from the previous generation grows at the same rate as the economy.
>
> *(Piketty, [2013] 2014: 351)*

Of course, Piketty's ambitious attempt to formulate a universal theory of inequality in the 21st century is not left without critics. Most of the critical voices, however, focus on his methodology and data collection and are sometimes highly politically charged (cf. Delsol, Lecaussin and Martin, 2017). Rarely are structural concerns expressed. In the latter fashion, Peter Turchin (2018) notes that Piketty's theory fails to explain why inequality decreased significantly during the middle of the 20th century (see Figure 3.6a).

Piketty explains the temporary reduction in inequality during this time with exogenous shocks, especially the world wars of the 20th century, which caused expropriation, mass mobilization, capital destruction, and, after all, wide-ranging redistribution. With this focus, however, he overlooks much more important endogenous factors that have always prevented exorbitant inequality and full capital accumulation in the highest percentiles. Less than exogenous, often coincidental events, firmly institutionalized political-economic structures such as extensive welfare states and tax systems ensure that an infinite increase in inequality can be largely prevented (cf. Piketty, 2015: 524–527.). At the same time, recent developments since the 1980s with another sharp rise in capital inequality illustrate how relevant Piketty's argument remains for explaining long-term socio-economic trends over decades and even centuries.

Piketty's theory is of significant importance when determining the (just) value of capital, since the return on capital measures the potential of concentrated wealth accumulation. Interestingly, historically the average rate of return on capital has remained relatively stable at 4 to 5% during the past 2000 years and has never fallen well below 2 to 3 percent. This remarkable stability can be explained in part by the short-term self-reflective perspective and the "preference for the present" described above, which economic individuals and communities seem to apply in strikingly similar fashion across national and cultural borders. For as already discussed, the rate of return results from the willingness to forego current consumption in the eye of economic and social risk. A time preference rate of about 4 to 5% seems to have been a historic norm. At the same time, however, it is clear that "savings behavior and attitudes toward the future cannot be encapsulated in a single parameter" (Piketty, [2013] 2014: 360). Because it is a highly complex combination of cultural, social, economic, psychological, technological, and demographic parameters, which ultimately constitutes the long-term rate of return on capital. And nonetheless, the discrepancy between a historically stable return on capital and fluctuating world growth is considerable (see Fig. 3.6d).

The problem of the widening of this gap is exacerbated by recent political and economic developments. In a policy brief by the *Centre for European Policy*, economist John Springfield (2018) points to a remarkable shift in the wage Phillips curve, which describes the negative correlation between wage growth and the unemployment rate. In principle, classical economy assumes that low unemployment rates lead to rising wages as employers have to invest more money to persuade employees in secure employment and without significant labor market competition to change jobs. However, this effect has been weakened considerably since 2015. In Germany, for example, in the eighth year after the outbreak of the European financial crisis, the employment rate has reached record levels, while wages have remained stagnant. The income Phillips curve has shifted to

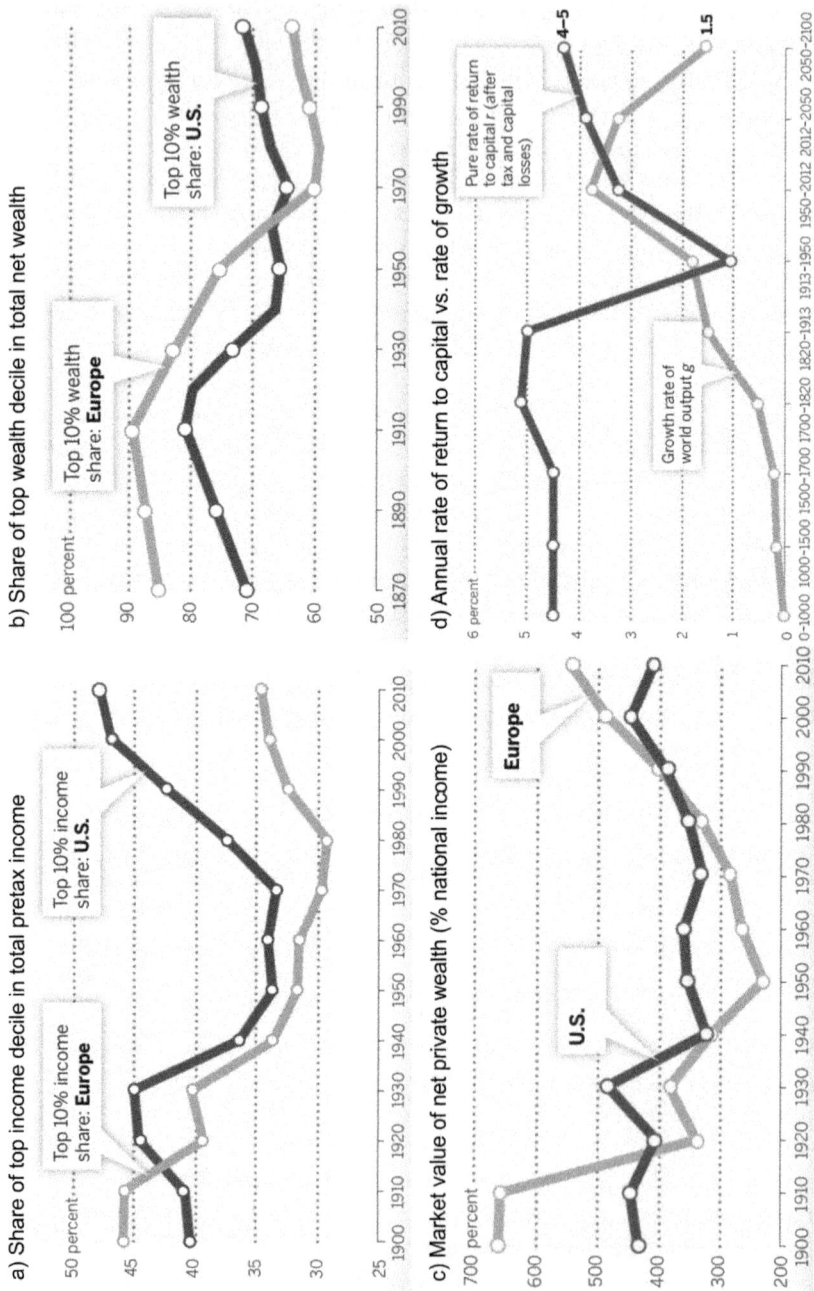

**a) Share of top income decile in total pretax income**

Top 10% income share: **Europe**

Top 10% income share: **U.S.**

**b) Share of top wealth decile in total net wealth**

Top 10% wealth share: **Europe**

Top 10% wealth share: **U.S.**

**c) Market value of net private wealth (% national income)**

Europe

U.S.

**d) Annual rate of return to capital vs. rate of growth**

Pure rate of return to capital r (after tax and capital losses)

Growth rate of world output g

**FIGURE 3.6**   Selected Figures on the Evolution of Inequality in Europe and the United States

source: Piketty and Saez, 2014: 838–841

the left: a considerably lower unemployment rate is now needed to achieve an additional unit of wage inflation. While a decade ago, an unemployment rate of 8 per cent was sufficient to achieve wage growth of 3%, today an unemployment rate of 3 to 4% is required. The reasons for this significant shift of the wage Phillips curve lie in particular in dualising and flexibilizing labor market reforms, the rise of precarious employment, a decline in trade union coverage, and an increasing individualization of employment relationships (Voss, 2018; Taylor, 2017; Solow, 2015; Weil, 2014). The consequence of this development, which can also be observed in many European countries, is a reduction in the share of labor income and thus a further disimprovement of the imbalance between labor and capital income. While returns on capital remain stable at the rise, wage incomes have been stagnating or falling for some time. Immediately linked to this development, American labor and industrial scientist Thomas Kochan identifies a historic social contract between employees and employers "to describe the expectation that wages for average workers will grow in rough tandem with aggregate productivity growth" (Kochan, 2013: 293). Since the mid-1970s, however, this social contract has been broken constantly both in the USA and in Germany. While labor incomes stagnate, economic productivity continues to rise (cf. also Graeber, [2011] 2014: 375f.; Streeck, 2013: 7).

What conclusions can be drawn from these findings? The most important is the following: The value of capital and its social appropriation still structure a class society in the long run. For capital strives toward capital and accumulates continuously. The most important and controversial question, however, is how this modern class society is stratified and how social fallout can be best managed. Class is still key, but the antagonisms between workers and capital owners, which Karl Marx emphasized so famously, have become much more complicated (Fessler and Schürz, 2017). To shed light on this, a differentiated approach to conceptualizing modern wealth distribution is needed. Unfortunately, statistical studies of inequality too often focus only on differences between deciles, percentiles and top shares (Alvaredo, Atkinson and Morelli, 2017, 2013; Piketty, [2013] 2014, 2011). Without an accurate micro-understanding of power relations between different socioeconomic groups, which would provide valuable insights into the relative relations of inequality, such enquiries are of little analytical value (Piketty, 2017: 548).

The Austrian economists Pirmin Fessler and Martin Schürz (2017) have responded to this problem with a new analytical approach. In a first step, they define different functions of assets (see Figure 3.7), from access to which three clearly distinguishable social classes can be derived. Renters are at the bottom of the social hierarchy. They do not own real estate and pay rent for housing. Savings are held in particular as precautionary measure. Owners stand above them. They possess real estate and save rent, which can be regarded as non-cash capital income. Finally, the capitalists are at the top of the capital distribution. They live in their own property, draw capital income from business investments or company ownership and generate additional income from real estate that they provide to

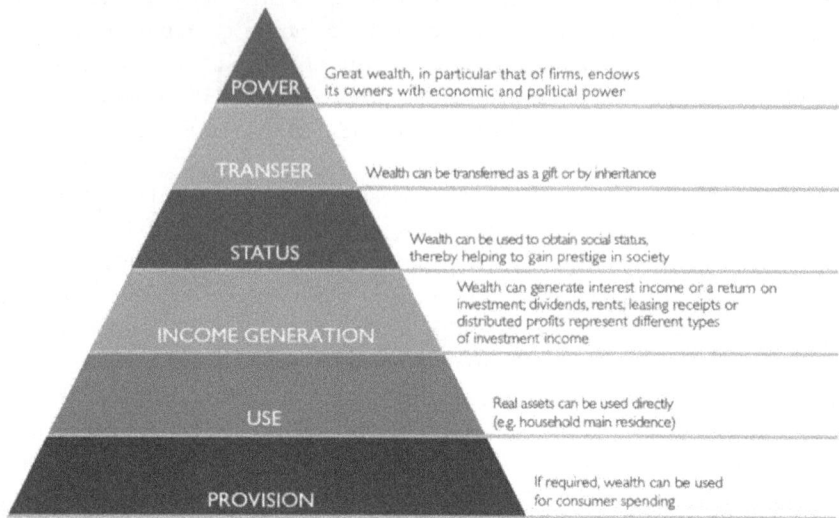

**FIGURE 3.7** The Functions of Wealth

*Source:* Fessler and Schürz, 2017: 7

the renting class. As employers they also hire renters and owners and derive further income streams from both their labor and consumption (Fessler and Schürz, 2017: 8). Access to and use of assets differ significantly for each class. On this basis, this model allows to calculate country-specific structures of capital distribution (see Figure 3.8). As expected, across Europe, and regardless of the country-specific distribution of total wealth, renters are located at the bottom, owners in the middle, and capitalists at the upper end of the wealth distribution. An important finding from this differentiated, relational view of capital distribution and social classes is that Piketty's general theory of the divergence of capital and labor income can be confirmed in principle:

> Regardless of large country differences in the share of renters, renters' median yearly gross income is (mostly substantially) larger than their median net wealth. In most cases, yearly income is about 2–5 times larger than net wealth, which translates to capital/income ratios of 0.2 to 0.5. For owners, that relationship is turned around. Capital-to-income ratios based on medians for owners are well above 5—and they go up to 13 for capitalists.
> *(Fessler und Schürz, 2018)*

However, there is also considerable national variation with regards to the points of class intersection, that is, the transition from one class to the above. This is particularly due to differences in welfare state institutions. In countries with

a) Renters, owners and capitalists

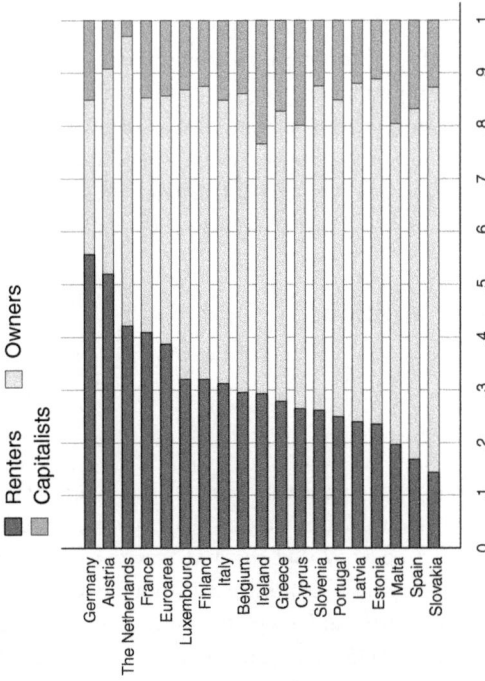

■ Renters  □ Owners
▨ Capitalists

b) Each group's share of total net wealth

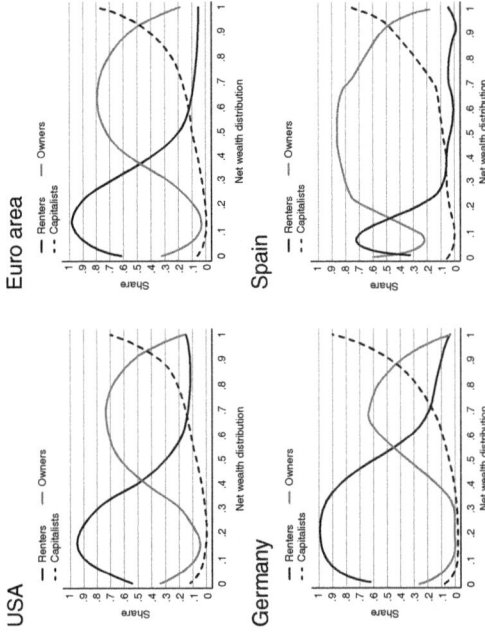

**FIGURE 3.8**  Structural Differences of Socio–Economic Groups in Selected OECD-Countries

*Source:* Fessler and Schürz, 2017: 14; 2018

higher social spending and greater ownership of collective assets, such as large pension funds, the renter class more prosperous after taxation. Here, tax codes and levy schemes provide for more effective redistribution. This constitutes the second fundamental conclusion from this differentiated type of analysis. Political economic institutions can provide very powerful instruments to contain capital inequality and to reorganize class structures. Thus, the value of capital for individual classes ultimately depends on its particular regulation and relationship to other types of income. In terms of specific instruments, the interest rate does represent a potential adjusting screw. Not only theological advocates of capped interest rates believed in this, but also the great John Maynard Keynes (1936: 317), who was convinced that a constantly low interest rate level would spell "the euthanasia of the cumulative oppressive power of the capitalist to exploit the scarcity-value of capital"; a hope he derived from Silvio Gesell's ([1916] 1958) *Freigeld* theory.

However, compared to other forms of financial income, such as profits from shares and warrants, interest income remains relatively low and bans or artificial price fixing both radical and risky measures. Above all, in their function they do not fundamentally question excessive returns on capital *per se* (Piketty, [2013] 2014: 722). Unlike interest rates, there are less radical and more effective ways of exerting influence. At the center of scientific and political attention has long been a capital or wealth tax with a very changing history of implementation and abolition. In the concluding section of this chapter, we examine in more detail such specific policy measures for regulating the value of capital. While it can certainly provide an answer to profound problems of ever-growing inequality, at the same time it is also a telling signpost of the ongoing political and social struggle over the sovereign definition of the value of capital. For ultimately "Capital is not an immutable concept: it reflects the state of development and prevailing social relations of each society" (Piketty, [2013] 2014: 47). After all, capital acts as the mirror of a society including all its social norms, values and social relations.

## Capital and Wealth Taxation

> The great art of wealth taxation is doing it without doing it.
> —*Stefan Bach (2016: 216)*[14]

Taxation is the most important regulatory instrument of a welfare state. It allows to correct the inequitable results of a liberal market order depending on social conceptions of justice and equality (Scheve and Stasavage, 2016; see Figure 3.9). Inherently, taxation expresses a distributional dispute between owners and the dispossessed, between minority and majority, and an ever-changing consensus on the appropriate extent of state intervention and civil and economic freedom. Yet again, we are facing with a complicated trade-off. On the one hand, historical experiments with markets controlled entirely by states have demonstrated in

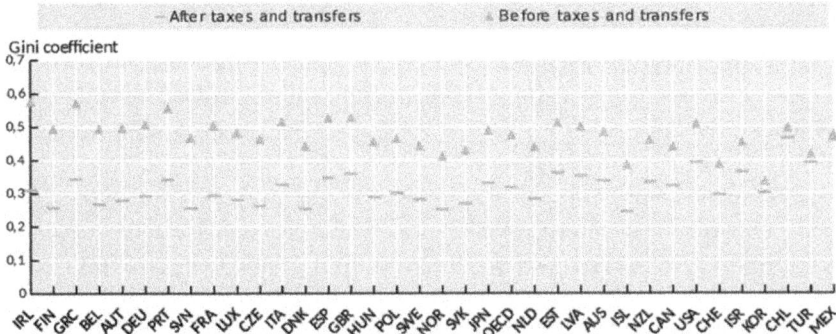

**FIGURE 3.9**  Difference in Economic Inequality Pre- and Post-Tax and Transfer Payments in 2013

*Source:* OECD, 2017

impressive fashion that artificial price fixing is logistically impossible and leads to highly inefficient results (cf. De Roover, 1958). On the other hand, the negative consequences of unregulated capital accumulation and deregulated markets have already been discussed in detail. What is needed, therefore, is to find a golden mean that reconciles the justified objections of both sides in the best way possible.

In general, there are two targets for capital taxation. On the one hand, a tax can be levied on dynamic income flows, that is a tax on capital gains or dividends. From both a politically and technical perspective, this type of taxation is relatively unproblematic, as its logic is essentially similar to other existing taxes such as the classic income tax. However, due to the theoretical similarity of these two types of income, the level of a tax on capital gains in relation to income remains highly controversial. For instance, while in the United States capital and labor income are considered equal and taxes at the same rates, in Germany, considerable discrepancy exists between taxed forms of income. While the income tax is imposed progressively, capital gains are taxed only at a flat rate of 25 percent. Above a certain income threshold, each additional euro is subject to a top tax rate of 42%, while only 25% of the same euro flow back to the state if earned from capital gains. In other words, a German worker pays an average tax rate of around 25% (IAQ, 2016) on a yearly salary of 50,000 euros, while a capital investor is guaranteed to pay the same tax regardless of the total amount of his capital earnings. As a result, the individual average tax burden of Germany's super rich is falling with rising income within the highest percentile despite a progressive income tax (Bach, Corneo and Steiner, 2012).

A second target for capital taxation is private wealth. In contrast to the dynamic nature of capital gains, this tax poses greater technical problems and is significantly more controversial. For while a tax on capital gains is levied on current income flows, a wealth tax targets stationary property. Its successful collection depends heavily on individual definitions of assets to be taxed as well as on their elicitation and accessibility. Nevertheless, and despite these fundamental concerns, advocates of a wealth tax emphasize its ability to manage the difficult balancing act between efficiency and equity:

> A progressive levy on individual wealth would reassert control over capitalism in the name of the general interest while relying on the forces of private property and competition. Each type of capital would be taxed in the same way, with no discrimination a priori, in keeping with the principle that investors are generally in a better position than the government to decide what to invest in.
>
> *(Piketty, [2013] 2014: 532)*

A progressive wealth tax reconciles state regulation and the protection of market efficiency via two logics. On the one hand, the "contributive logic" requires high capital income earners to compensate for relatively lower tax burdens and thus to fulfil their social obligations in a more equitable way. A wealth tax can thus contribute to a fairer treatment of different types of income by addressing the obvious discrepancy between income and capital tax rates. On the other hand, a capital tax pursues a "logic of incentives" that takes into account the protection of efficient market mechanisms by representing a deduction on gross returns. It can thus put pressure on wealthy investors to manage their capital more efficiently in order to achieve a positive net return. Failing to do so triggers an incentive to sell and surrender capital to more competent investors (Piketty, [2013] 2014: 525–527). This increases the total economic welfare of capital. Hence, a wealth tax can be seen as the most likely means of reconciling both equitable distributive justice and efficient market incentives.

But what would an optimal taxation of capital look like? This is a complex and highly controversial question, at the core of which lies the best possible balance between redistribution and overall economic welfare (cf. Bach, 2016; Diamond and Saez, 2011; Kopczuk, 2013; Farhi and Werning, 2010; Straub and Werning, 2014; Piketty, [2013] 2014; Saez and Stantcheva, 2018). Regarding the latter factor, the potential of capital flight is a particular cause for concern. Opponents of the wealth tax argue that with a sufficient level of capital mobility enhanced by globalization and intensified tax competition, capital could evade domestic tax collection by relocating to other jurisdictions. Economists define this risk as the elasticity of capital supply. The more elastic capital supply, the more sensitive it will be to an increase in capital taxation. Recent studies have proven that the long-term elasticity of capital is a sufficient variable, at least in mathematical terms, to determine an optimal level of capital taxation (Saez and Stantcheva, 2018).

Against this backdrop, two academic contributions have proven to be fundamental, both arguing against a capital tax. The studies by Christophe Chamley

(1986) and Kenneth Judd (1985), assembled in the Chamley-Judd theorem, showed that in the long run capital is infinitely elastic. Thus, in the eye of a capital tax rational entrepreneurs would lose incentives to save capital, to use it optimally, or reinvest it. Total capital gains would therefore decrease. Tony Atkinson and Joseph Stiglitz (1976) arrive at a similar result, albeit applying a different focus. They argue that an income tax alone is sufficient to compensate for given inequalities, since consumption preferences are largely homogeneous and the only source of income inequality in the long run are differences in the abilities and skills of workers. In this line of thinking, a positive tax on capital would be unequitable, since individual's saving behavior is not the primary cause of social inequality. Therefore, in the Chamley-Judd model, a capital tax is undesirable from an efficiency point of view, while in Stiglitz-Atkinson model questions its effectiveness for redistribution. Combining these influential studies, the question of capital taxation is redundant, as both sides of the trade-off are conflicted.

But of course, the generalizing assumptions at the heart of these two theories allow for justified criticism. It is often argued, for example, that in reality consumer preferences not as homogeneous as suggested in the Stiglitz-Atkinson model (Saez, 2002; Mirrlees, 1976). Empirical studies show a positive correlation between individual income and the propensity to save (Banks and Diamond, 2008). Furthermore, the opportunities of tax avoidance are distributed very unevenly within societies and are heavily dependent on national circumstances. As Alstadsæter and her colleagues (2017) show, the tax avoidance rate is relatively higher among the richest income groups. While workers in standard employment typically have their income tax deducted from their paychecks directly, self-employed entrepreneurs have in general greater opportunities to avoid taxes. National tax elasticity therefore depends on the number of self-employed and their respective socio-economic backgrounds and varies significantly across country (Fessler and Schürz, 2017: 29). With these objections in mind, a capital tax could certainly represent an effective instrument to counter social inequality in a resolute fashion.

However, the most pressing problem of all these deliberations, whether for or against capital taxation, remains its purely hypothetical character. Regrettably, to date very few empirical studies exist that could provide real data-based insights into the issue of capital taxation and without excessively relying on economic axioms and assumptions. One of the few valuable case studies of this kind was conducted rather recently by a Danish-American team of economists (see Jakobsen et al., 2018). In a case study, they analyzed the effect of a wealth tax in Denmark and during and after its implementation. Until 1997, Denmark levied one of the highest capital tax rates in the world. Initially, the tax rate was 2.2% and, thanks to very high tax allowances, only affected households above the 97th percentile of the wealth distribution. The flat rate tax was charged on the total net assets, i.e. total asset wealth minus private debt. However, between 1989 and 1991 the tax rate was first reduced to 1% and eventually abolished altogether at the end of 1996.

Nonetheless, the fiscal consequences of the institutional changes provide valuable conclusions for the general effectiveness of capital taxation. According to their calculations, Jakobsen and his colleagues (2018: 3) conclude that the abolition of the tax led to a 20% increase in wealth of over 20 years for families between the 98th and 99th percentile. Families in the highest percentile could even increase their wealth by 70% over 30 years compared to estimated worth at unchanged tax levels. These findings provide impressive evidence of the actual effectiveness of taxes as a political instrument for redistribution put the trade-off between efficiency and equity back into the spotlight. For such convincing empirical evidence raises the question of why capital taxation has lost political popularity since the 1990s, not only in Denmark, where it was gradually abolished.

The discourse about the societal treatment of capital seems to be heavily dominated by economic efficiency concerns. There are various reasons for this, the comprehensive discussion of which would go beyond the scope of our considerations.[15] The concern of tax evasion and capital flight plays an important role; however, it is often greatly overestimated, especially in political discourse. That is, because certain institutional conditions that companies find in their countries of origin and which they have largely helped to shape themselves (e.g. logistical networks, sales markets, political stability) offer strong incentives against simple relocation. Against this background, frequently-expressed warning of the super-rich to relocate their companies and possessions to other countries in case of capital taxation is often nothing more than an empty threat. Also, if a tax reform were introduced at European level, a fiscal *race-to-the-bottom* could effectively be counteracted. The specific way of how a capital tax could be levied offers ground for more understandable concerns. Because taxing stationary wealth usually requires the sale of assets or property to service the tax burden. This is problematic specifically with regards to businesses funds on which in jobs depend. It is further argued that capital investments are generally more productivity-enhancing than consumption expenditure besides having been taxed already (cf. Bach, 2016: 214ff.). However, such objections are usually formulated with a broad brush without providing convincing empirical evidence and could certainly be considered in the legal design of tax regulations. The immediate consequence of such categorical objections, however, is that economic efficiency concerns are systematically overestimated, rendering the implementation of a capital tax practically impossible, even if it affected only a marginal fraction of the richest percentile of the population.

This becomes all the clearer when considering the few existing political feasibility studies. Recently, an American team of researchers led by Raymond Fisman et al. (2017) conducted a representative survey of American voters' individual tax preferences. They found that on average respondents preferred a positive taxation of capital at 0.8 per cent (inheritances should even be taxed at 3 percent). Even more insightful were the findings drawn from the respondents' decision-making process:

> We complement our analysis of subjects' chosen tax rates with an examination of respondents' open-ended explanations of how they made their

decisions. In general, *subjects do not mention efficiency concern*s (e.g., that higher taxes on wealth would reduce savings or induce capital flight or that higher labor income taxes would discourage work). Simplicity of the tax schedule (e.g., a flat tax) is attractive to many. Also, "double taxation" is often noted as an objection to taxing wealth, with respondents saying it was "already taxed" at the time it was earned. *These considerations are quite removed from the trade-offs that economists weigh in the classic optimal tax framework.*

*(Fisman et al., 2017: 2; our emphasis)*

Quite obviously, and in stark contrast to public debate, efficiency issues seem to play only a subordinate role in voters' personal assessments. At the same time, the survey highlights the remarkable effectiveness that a capital tax could have even at a low rate targeting only the highest wealth percentiles. Fisman's (2017: 25) calculations show that the preferred tax rate would generate additional government revenues of 1.1 trillion US dollars regardless of potential capital flight; a sum that would correspond to more than a quarter of the current US household budget. Thus, an analysis of individual preferences illustrates that capital tends to be over-protected regarding the democratic will of voters. The likelihood of introducing a capital tax to combat escalating inequality should not be easily discarded. In the end, we are left with the important realization that capital taxation should not be overly judged on the grounds of economic efficiency and potential welfare losses. Rather, in more normative terms, it could convey the majoritarian opinion that highly unequitable distribution of assets is socially undesirable. This important point is picked up in more detail in the concluding section of this chapter, as well as the pertinent question of the social consequences of political inaction in the face of escalating capital inequality. To this end, it seems that the value of capital, in terms of both its societal appropriation and legal protection, is generally appraised higher than it might be conducive to sustainable social cohesion.

## Conclusion: Determining the Price (and Value) of Capital

> One cannot have a just society . . . if the main purpose of economic activity is the manufacture of money.
>
> —*Robert Skidelsky (2010: 146)*

Capital is a driving force. It creates new value and is the most important ingredient of all prosperity in advanced economies. But at the same time, it structures social relations and produces different classes, hierarchies, dependencies and oppression. We have shown that the price of capital is socially determined and manifests itself in an ongoing dispute between concerns over efficiency and equity. Ultimately, efficiency prevails. With increased financialization, capital assumes ever more parts of society, forcing social individualization and the optimization of each individual through its persistent urge to be constantly productive. The *Great Transformation*, of which Karl Polanyi first spoke in 1944, continues to take place largely unchecked and live before our very eyes.[16] While, historically, economic action was always embedded in social institutions and their respective norms and values, today, ever larger sections of society serve exclusively economic purposes in the name of capital. As Polanyi noted quite aptly, today's profound financialization took its inexorable course when labor, land, and money were turned into tradable commodities during the outbreak of the Industrial Revolution. Here began the creeping triumph of capital and the particular norms and values embodied within. The concept of debt plays a pivotal role in this regard. Under the guise of a free market and the economic empowerment of each individual, it creates social dependencies and justifies relationships of coercion (Graeber, [2011] 2014). Economic relations in more and more anonymous social environments increasingly determine how we behave, communicate, and define our habitus.

The internet has long since become the most important social arena in this regard. People increasingly meet each other online, often organized on the basis of optimizing calculations by profit-oriented dating services. So-called *influencers*— rarely was a job title more accurate—earn millions of dollars on social platforms such as YouTube, Facebook and Instagram advertising physical perfectionism and matching products, and find countless disciples and devotees in Millennials and the Generation Z. The constant strive for the ideal, physical and material envy, and the omnipresent fear of imperfection and blemish determine social relationships, not only within the "Generation Facebook" (Leistert and Röhle, 2011; Jang et al., 2015).[17] The growing addiction to social reassurance is being exploited in a targeted manner by large tech companies:

> Sean Parker, ex-president of Facebook, recently admitted that the world-bestriding social media platform was designed to hook users with spurts of dopamine, a complicated neurotransmitter released when the brain expects a reward or accrues fresh knowledge. "You're exploiting a vulnerability in human psychology," he said. "[The inventors] understood this, consciously, and we did it anyway." Peddling this addiction made Mr. Parker and his tech-world colleagues absurdly rich. Facebook is now valued at a little more than half a trillion dollars. Global revenue from smartphone sales reached $435-billion (US). Now, some of the early executives of these tech firms look on their success as tainted. "I feel tremendous guilt," said Chamath Palihapitiya, former vice-president of user growth at Facebook, in a public talk in November. "I think we all knew in the back of our minds . . . something bad could happen. The short-term, dopamine-driven feedback loops that we have created are destroying how society works," he went on gravely, before a hushed audience at Stanford business school. "It is eroding the core foundations of how people behave."

*(Andrew-Gee, 2018)*

Digital consumption assumes an ever-larger share of our lifetime (Center for the Digital Future, 2017). Since almost all social platforms are financed through extensive data collection and personalized advertising, the most important aim of tech companies is to keep the attention of users at the highest possible level. Likes and notifications (information about new messages and activities on one's timeline) delivered day and night by apps to smartphone screens, play a key role in this:

> The makers of smartphone apps rightly believe that part of the reason we're so curious about those notifications is that people are desperately insecure and crave positive feedback with a kneejerk desperation. Matt Mayberry, who works at a California startup called Dopamine Labs, says it's common knowledge in the industry that Instagram exploits this craving by strategically withholding "likes" from certain users. If the photo-sharing app decides you need to use the service more often, it'll show only a fraction of the likes you've received on a given post at first, hoping you'll be disappointed with your haul and check back again in a minute or two. "They're tying in to your greatest insecurities," Mr. Mayberry said.
>
> *(Andrew-Gee, 2018)*

It is certainly too early to make a final judgement about this very recent social development and the micro- and macrosocial effects of the digitization of our everyday lives. However, our observations emphasize that particular economic values embodied in capital are continuously penetrating society and increasingly determine our social relationships and behavior. Social platforms and constant access to smartphones are the media that transport these values disguised in commercial advertising and formulated by professional *influencers*. More importantly, in the constant strive for digital reassurance and social conformity, users themselves become the industry's most important ambassadors, voluntarily and unpaid, by constantly sharing content and personal data. The result of all these social technological innovations is an entirely new, billion-dollar industry, the *Like-Economy*, in which information and data serve as the currency and the *timeline* functions as a marketplace. In this digital universe "the social is of particular economic value" (Gerlitz and Helmond, 2013: 1349).

Acknowledging all positive aspects of technologization of our daily lives—increased comfort, barrier-free communication, constant access to information—the public must be aware of the dimensions of this social construct and take a clear stand. For the value of capital must never be defined exclusively and unbridled in the market, but must always be the subject to social regulation. In this chapter, we have shown that the taxation of extreme wealth can be a decisive step in the right direction. But even if it were a powerful political expression of the normative relevance of socio-economic equality and justice to which a society collectively commits itself, the complexity of the social dominance of capital also illustrates that such tax alone would not be a universal panacea (Taylor, Ömer and Rezai, 2015). Rather, sustainable solutions must effectively counteract social relations of dependency that a purely efficient conception of the value of capital constantly and purposefully produces (cf. Atkinson, 2014).

> What is required are policies that go beyond the tax code to shift the very balance of power between workers and employers. Doing so would allow real wages to catch up to productivity and capital gains to be more equitably shared among the population. It would shrink inequality for years to come.
>
> *(Taylor, 2017)*

But to abolish the unequal balance of power between capitalists and workers remains the unachievable dream of every progressive thinker. Instead, some observers put increased hope in new social roles that workers could assume in modern economies. For instance, the Japanese literary scholar Kojin Karatani (2003) expresses the hope that workers could exercise power as consumers rather than in their natural, producing role, because as such they are clearly more relevant to the continuation of added value and growth (cf. Dodd, 2014: 79ff.; Stehr, 2007). But this position must also be met with justified skepticism.[18] At least in the context of an export-oriented growth model, the extent of consumers' political power thus remains rather modest to put it mildly.

All these developments illustrate that when economic freedom proclaimed as the highest good in the name of a hyper-efficient democratic capitalism, political freedom and social self-determination inevitably fall by the wayside. For

> democratic capitalism as a political economy [is] ruled by two conflicting principles, or regimes, of resource allocation: one operating according to marginal productivity, or what is revealed as *merit* by a "free play of market forces," and the other following social need, or *entitlement*, as certified by the collective choices of democratic politics.
>
> *(Streeck, 2011: 3)*

Democratic capitalism thus posits a challenging dilemma for political decision-makers, the outcome of which is ultimately determined by the value of capital the appreciation of efficiency over equity embodied within. Recent political developments in Europe and the United States illustrate the serious consequences of excessive capital inequality and social financialization where political trust is increasingly undermined and social capital destroyed. Joseph Stiglitz warned of these particular consequences as early as 2012 (p. 125):

> When the social contract gets broken, social cohesion quickly erodes. Governments and societies make decisions—expressed through policies, laws, and budgetary choices—that either strengthen that contract or weaken it. By allowing inequality to metastasize unchecked, America is choosing a path of destruction of social capital, if not social conflict.

Karl Marx saw in escalating capital inequality nothing less than an unavoidable end of the system brought about by a revolution of the proletariat. But if Marx made one fundamental mistake in his bold predictions, it was this. For the past decade has shown that while economic crisis paired with staggering levels of inequality may bring about temporary uprisings and street battles, as observed on Athens's Syntagma Square, but a genuine change of system remains highly unlikely. Capitalism draws its enormous resilience from its ability, to use Marx' own terminology, to plant in all proletarians the deep desire to belong to the bourgeoisie themselves in some distant future. Capitalism thus exerts tremendous social attraction and legitimizes itself by the ultimately empty promise of making prosperity possible for everyone. The result is a dispersion of classical class consciousness. The few successful celebrate their individual ascent and are presented as role models, while many others remain only with a subtle feeling of loss of social connection and lack of identification, eventually culminating in political and social irrelevance (Nachtwey, 2016). Since capitalism undermines class coordination capacities necessary for commonly organized protest so successfully the most likely consequence of a system whose incentives are defined purely by scarcity is exclusion, hatred and internal competition for resources within the poorest social strata, as long as a politically relevant majority of voters benefit from the system and supports its continuous existence (Iversen and Soskice, 2019).

To counteract these worrisome developments, the value of capital and its "just" price must always be subject to constant social assessment. Perhaps the motto should sound *Back to the Middle Ages!* For "the medieval notion of the just price . . . was an outcome of neither an exclusively economic analysis nor a completely ethical argument, but an amalgam of some features of each" (Hamouda and Price, 1997: 192). To rebalance the discourse about the just price of capital must be the explicit goal of free societies, only that today, in contrast to the regulating influence of the church, an enlightened civil society should be at the heart of these ambitious efforts. The question which conditions a society recognizes as fair can never be left solely and permanently to a cryptic social entity such as "the markets." Quite to the contrary: To adequately counter the social dominance of capital and the societal appropriation of financial values, in the last instance, can mean nothing less than "re-establishing the ideological primacy of the collective over the individual, and of the public over the private" (Lapavitsas, 2013: 803; our translation).

## Notes

1. The *British East India Company* is arguably the most popular example of such private initiative.
2. In our analysis of the price of labor in Chapter 4 we present critically and in detail the different forms of capital, specifically human capital.
3. "But love your enemies, and do good, and lend, expecting nothing in return, and your reward will be great, and you will be sons of the Most High" (Luke, 6:35).

4. "Thou shalt not lend upon interest to thy brother; interest of money, interest of victuals, interest of anything that is lent upon interest: unto a foreigner thou mayest lend upon interest; but unto thy brother thou shalt not lend upon interest" (5th Book of Moses, 23, 19–20).

5. More moderate scholars disagree with this rather fundamentalist view. In their perspective, "Riba is an exorbitant increment whereby the capital sum is doubled severalfold, against a fixed extension of the term of payment of the debt" (Rahman, 1964: 40). Here, economic interest is not problematic by default, but rather its unjustified magnitudes.

6. Here again, the definition and extent of unlawful enrichment are subject to fierce debate. Some Islamic scholars argue with good reason that only an interest rate exceeding the rate of inflation could be interpreted as unjust enrichment and thus as forbidden riba. In contrast, an interest rate up to the rate of inflation should be interpreted as Sharia-compliant, as no increase in real purchasing power is achieved. (IBP, 2015: 23).

7. Specifically, it says in the Surah of the Cow (The Holy Qur'an, 2:280): "And if someone is in hardship, then [let there be] postponement until [a time of] ease. But if you give [from your right as] charity, then it is better for you, if you only knew."

8. Against this highest maxim, it is hardly surprising that the Qur'an promotes rigorous interest prohibition: "The Meccan verses of the Qur'an are replete with the denunciation of the economic injustice of contemporary Meccan society, the profiteering and stinginess of the rich, and their unethical commercial practices such as cheating in the weight and measurements, etc., how is it possible then that the Qur'an would have failed to condemn an economic evil such as riba?" (Rahman, 1964: 3).

9. In *The Road to Serfdom,* Hayek ([1944] 2001: 51f.) outlines this argument in more detail: "As decentralisation has become necessary because nobody can consciously balance all the considerations bearing on the decisions of so many individuals, the coordination can clearly not be effected by 'conscious control,' but only by arrangements which convey to each agent the information he must possess in order effectively to adjust his decisions to those of others. And because all the details of the changes constantly affecting the conditions of demand and supply of the different commodities can never be fully known, or quickly enough be collected and disseminated, by any one center, what is required is some apparatus of registration which automatically records all the relevant effects of individual actions, and whose indications are at the same time the resultant of, and the guide for, all the individual decisions. This is precisely what the price system does under competition, and which no other system even promises to accomplish."

10. According to Deutsche Bundesbank's economic balance sheet, government's gross assets are calculated adding all fixed assets, the value of land (including cultivated land) and all financial assets. Since it is almost impossible to determine the exact value (in particular of non-material assets and non-mobile capital such as buildings, land and nature), it is usually significantly underestimated. Gross debt is calculated as the total amount of capital borrowed. The government's net assets describe the difference between these two figures.

11. This value amounts to about 14 percent of Germany's GDP at current values (our calculations on the basis of Statista, 2016).

12. In a similar fashion, proponents of *primordial debt theory* argue that individuals are indebted by virtue of their existence simply by being born into a society. British sociologist Geoffrey Ingham (quoted in Graeber, [2011] 2014: 59) refers in this context to the close etymological connection between debt and sin: "In all Indo-European languages, words for 'debt' are synonymous with those for 'sin' or 'guilt,' illustrating the links between religion, payment and the mediation of the sacred and profane realms by 'money.' For example, there is a connection between money (Geman Geld), indemnity or sacrifice (Old English Geild), tax (Gothic Gild) and, of course, guilt." Same is true

for the German language, where the word "Schuld" (debt) describes both an economic obligation and a moral sin (cf. Rasch, 2013; for a more detailed reference to debt and religion see Rasch, 2003). Against this backdrop, it is hardly surprising that the first ever documented word for freedom, the Sumerian word *amargi*, literally translates to "the return to mother," used to describe children who had been sold to creditors by their indebted parents and had successfully worked off their debt (cf. Kramer, 1963: 79; Graeber, [2011] 2014: 65).

13. We are aware, of course, that this term is both multifarious and vague. It can refer to any relative comparison and is not negatively charged in principle. Certain forms of inequality can and must be morally justifiable (Stehr and Machin, 2016; Wilkinson and Pickett, 2009; Atkinson, 2015). However, when we speak of inequality in our context, we specifically mean inequality of capital ownership. And as we show, this often deeply contradicts normative notions of distributive and competitive justice with negative implications for political stability and social cohesion as well as the growth of political polarization that is now observable in countries with rising income inequality.

14. Our translation.

15. We deal with this question in more detail in our chapter on the price of land.

16. In our analysis of the price of land (Chapter 2) we discuss the works of Karl Polanyi and the implications for an analysis of modern financialization critically and in great detail.

17. Various studies have investigated the effect of the use of social media on physical and mental well-being and self-esteem. It was found that young people in particular internalize certain physical ideals, such as slimness, the more time they spend using social media (Tiggemann and Slater, 2013; Valkenburg, Peter, & Schouten, 2006). Pronounced narcissism among adolescents, physical insecurity and so-called "Fear of Missing Out" are direct consequences of these developments (Moon et al., 2016; Marwick, 2015). However, a thorough analysis of existing literature on this problem also reveals a considerable need for further research. In particular, future research should focus on the effects on personal optimization pressure and the underlying role of the profit-oriented social media industry.

18. This is emphasized by recent political-economic developments in Germany, to which we also refer in our studies on the price of labor (Chapter 4). Since the turn of the millennium and in particular since the introduction of the so-called Agenda 2010, an increasing flexibilization of labor can be observed, which expresses itself in stagnating wages and precarious employment. Of course, these developments impede individual purchasing power of German consumers. But instead of keeping wages at an appropriate level to secure stable domestic demand, international competitiveness and falling unit labor costs require substituting weakened domestic consumption with record-level export surpluses (cf. Hassel, 2011; Thelen, 2014: 151; Odendahl, 2017).

# References

Åkerman, Gustaf (1923), *Realkapital und Kapitalzins*. Stockholm: Stockholm University.

Ali, S.A. (1964), *Economic Foundations of Islam*. Calcutta: Orient Longmans.

Alstadsæter, Annette, Niels Johannesen and Gabriel Zucman (2017), "Tax evasion and inequality," *Preliminary Draft*. URL: http://gabriel-zucman.eu/files/AJZ2017.pdf (accessed 30 May 2018).

Alvaredo, Facundo, Anthony B. Atkinson and Salvatore Morelli (2017), "Top wealth shares in the UK over more than a century," *Department of Economics Research Paper Series* No. 01/WP/2017, University Ca' Foscari of Venice.

Alvaredo, Facundo, Anthony B. Atkinson, Thomas Piketty and Emmanuel Saez (2013), "The top 1 percent in international and historical perspective," *Journal of Economic Perspectives* 27(3): 3–20.

Andrew-Gee, Eric (2018), "Digital distraction: Your smartphone is making you stupid, antisocial and unhealthy. So why can't you put it down?" *The Globe and Mail (online)*. URL: www.theglobeandmail.com/technology/ your-smartphone-is-making-you-stupid/ article37511900/ (accessed 8 June 2018).

Aristoteles (1912), *Politics: A Treatise on Government*. London & Toronto: J.M Dent & Sons Ltd.

Ashraf, Nava and Oriana Bandiera (2017), "Altruistic capital," *American Economic Review: Papers & Proceedings* 107: 70–75.

Atkinson, Anthony B. (2015), *Inequality: What Can Be Done?* Boston, MA: Harvard University Press.

Atkinson, Anthony B. (2014), "After Piketty?" *The British Journal of Sociology* 65(4): 619–638.

Atkinson, Anthony B. and Joseph E. Stiglitz (1976), "The design of tax structure: Direct versus indirect taxation," *Journal of Public Economics* 6(1–2): 55–75.

Bach, Stefan (2016), *Unsere Steuern: Wer Zahlt? Wie Viel? Wofür?* Frankfurt am Main: Westend Verlag.

Bach, Stefan, Giacomo Corneo and Viktor Steiner (2012), "Effective taxation of top incomes in Germany," *German Economic Review* 14(2): 115–137.

Banks, James and Peter Diamond (2008), *The Base for Direct Taxation: Mirrlees Review*. Institute for Fiscal Studies. URL: www.ifs.org.uk/mirrleesreview (accessed 30 May 2018).

Barna, Tibor (1961), "On measuring capital," pp. 75–94 in Douglas C. Hagu (ed.), *The Theory of Capital: Proceedings of a Conference held by the International Economic Association*. New York: Stockton Press.

Beck, Hanno (2014), *Behavioral Economics: Eine Einführung*. Wiesbaden: Springer.

Beramendi, Pablo, Silja Häusermann, Herbert Kitschelt and Hanspeter Kriesi (eds.), (2015), *The Politics of Advanced Capitalism*. Cambridge: CUP.

Bernstein, William J. (2005), *Die Geburt des Wohlstands: Wie der Wohlstand der modernen Welt entstand*. München: FinanzBuch Verlag.

Binswanger, Mathias (2010), "Der Zins ist kein Übel," *ZEIT Online*, 13 Januar. URL: www. zeit.de/online/2007/46/besser-wirtschaften-mathias-binswanger/komplettansicht (accessed 3 September 2018).

Böhm-Bawerk, Eugen von ([1889] 1991), *Positive Theorie des Kapitals*. Stuttgart: Schäffer-Poeschel Verlag.

Bourdieu, Pierre (1992), *Die Verborgenen Mechanismen der Macht. Schriften zu Politik und Kultur, Band 1*. Hamburg: VSA-Verlag.

Bourdieu, Pierre (1986), "The forms of capital," pp. 241–58 in John Richardson (ed.), *Handbook of Theory and Research for the Sociology of Education*. Westport, CT: Greenwood.

Bourdieu, Pierre (1983), "Ökonomisches Kapital, kulturelles Kapital, soziales Kapital," pp. 183–198 in Reinhard Kreckel (ed.), *Soziale Ungleichheiten*. Göttingen: Schwartz Verlag.

Center for Digital Future (2017), *The World Internet Project International Report*, 8th ed. Los Angeles, CA: USC Annenberg School for Communication and Journalism.

Chamley, Christophe (1986), "Optimal taxation of capital income in general equilibrium with infinite lives," *Econometrica* 54(3): 607–622.

De Roover, Raymond (1958), "The concept of the just price: Theory and economic policy," *The Journal of Economic History* 18(4): 418–434.

Delsol, Jean-Philippe, Nicolas Lecaussin and Emmanuel Martin (eds.), (2017), *Anti-Piketty: Capital for the 21st Century*. Washington, DC: Cato Institute.

Diamond, Peter and Emmanuel Saez (2011), "The case for a progressive tax: From basic research to policy recommendations," *The Journal of Economic Perspectives* 25(4): 165–190.

Dodd, Nigel (2014), *The Social Life of Money*. Princeton, NJ: Princeton University Press.

Ehnts, Dirk (2018), "Von Schulden und Ersparnis," *Makroskop (online)*, 13. März. URL: https://makroskop.eu/2018/03/von-schulden-und-ersparnis/ (accessed 30 August 2018).

Farhi, Emmanuel and Iván Werning (2010), "Progressive estate taxation," *The Quarterly Journal of Economics* 125(2): 635–673.

Fessler, Pirmin and Martin Schürz (2018), "Analysing wealth inequality: A conceptual reflection," *Institute for New Economic Thinking (online)*, 24 April. URL: www.ineteconomics.org/perspectives/blog/ analysing-wealth-inequality-a-conceptual-reflection (accessed 30 May 2018).

Fessler, Pirmin and Martin Schürz (2017), "The functions of wealth: Renters, owners and capitalists across Europe," *Draft prepared for the First WID.world Conference*. Paris School of Economics, 14.-15. Dezember.

Fisher, Irving (1930), *The Theory of Interest*. New York: Macmillan Co.

Fisman, Raymond, Keith Gladstone, Ilyana Kuziemko and Suresh Naidu (2017), "Do Americans want to tax capital? Evidence from online surveys," *NBER Working Paper* No. 23907. Cambridge, MA: National Bureau of Economic Research.

Flassbeck, Heiner and Friederike Spiecker (2015), "Unser Geldsystem XXXI: Schulden, Schulden ohne Grenzen?" Flassbeck-Economics: Kritische Analyse und Kommentare zu Wirtschaft und Politik, 21. Januar. URL: www.flassbeck-economics.de/abo-preview-unser-geldsystem-xxxi-schulden-schulden-ohne-grenzen/ (accessed 27 March 2016).

Gerlitz, Carolin and Anne Helmond (2013), "The like economy: Social buttons and the data intensive web," *New Media & Society* 15(8): 1348–1365.

Gesell, Silvio ([1916] 1958), *The Natural Economic Order*. London: Owen.

Gill, Stephen (1998), "European governance and new constitutionalism: Economic and monetary union and alternatives to disciplinary neoliberalism in Europe," *New Political Economy* 3(1): 5–26.

Goethe, Johann Wolfgang von ([1809] 1982), *Die Wahlverwandtschaften. Hamburger Ausgabe, Bd. 6 (Romane und Novellen I)*. München: dtv Verlag.

Graeber, David ([2011] 2014), *Debt. The First 5000 Years*. New York and London: Melville House.

Gros, Daniel (2012), "On the stability of public debt in a monetary union," *Journal of Common Market Studies* 50(2): 36–48.

Hamouda, Omar F. and Betsy B. Price (1997), "The justice of the just price," *Journal of the History of Economic Thought* 4(2): 191–216.

Hanke, Marcus (2005), "Zinsverbot und islamische Bank. Von Datteln und Kreditkarten," pp. 157–176 in *Geld- und Kreditwesen im Spiegel der Wissenschaft*. Wien: Springer.

Harari, Yuval Noah ([2011] 2014), *Sapiens. A Brief History of Humankind*. Toronto, ON: McClelland & Stewart.

Harvey, David (2017), "Wert und Anti-Wert: Krisen sind immer überall möglich," *Deutschlandfunk (online)*, 26. März. URL: www.deutschlandfunk.de/re-das-kapital-8-9-wert-und-anti-wert-krisen-sind-immer.1184.de.html?dram:article_id=381929 (accessed 19 March 2017).

Hassel, Anke (2011), "The paradox of liberalization: Understanding dualism and the recovery of the German political economy," *LSE 'Europe in Question' Discussion Paper Series, Paper* No. 42/2011.

Hayek, Friedrich A. ([1941] 2009), *The Pure Theory of Capital.* Auburn, AL: The Ludwig von Mises Institute.

Hayek, Friedrich A. ([1944] 2001), *The Road to Serfdom.* London and New York: Routledge Classics.

Hayek, Friedrich A. (1945), "The use of knowledge in society," *The American Economic Review* 35: 519–530.

Heckman, James J. (2018), "The race between demand and supply: Tinbergen's pioneering studies of earnings inequality," *NBER Working Paper* No. 25415.

Herden, Lutz (2000), "Kreativer Umgang mit dem Zinsverbot," *Der Freitag,* 5. Mai. URL: www.freitag.de/autoren/der-freitag/kreativer-umgang-mit-dem-zinsverbot (accessed 8 April 2018).

Hicks, John R. (1965), *Capital and Growth.* New York: Oxford University Press.

Hicks, John R. (1961), "The measurement of capital in relation to the measurement of other economic aggregates," pp. 18–31 in Douglas C. Hague (ed.), *The Theory of Capital: Proceedings of a Conference held by the International Economic Association.* New York: Stockton Press.

Homer, Sidney and Richard Sylla ([1963] 2005), *A History of Interest Rates,* 4th ed. Hoboken, NJ: John Wiley & Sons.

IAQ (2016), *Einkommensteuertarif 2016: Grenz- und Durchschnittssteuersätze.* Institut für Arbeit und Qualifikation der Universität Duisburg-Essen. URL: www.sozialpolitik-aktuell.de/tl_files/sozialpolitikaktuell/_Politikfelder/Finanzierung/Datensammlung/PDF-Dateien/abbIII21a.pdf (accessed 5 June 2018).

IBP (2015), *Islam: Investment Laws in Muslim Countries Handbook, Volume 1.* Washington, DC: International Business Publications.

Iversen, Torben and David Soskice (2019), *Democracy and Prosperity: Reinventing Capitalism through a Turbulent Century.* Princeton, NJ: Princeton University Press.

Jakobsen, Katrine, Kristian Jakobsen, Henrik Kleven and Gabriel Zucman (2018), "Wealth taxation and wealth accumulation: Theory and evidence from Denmark," *Paper Draft.* URL: www.henrikkleven.com/ uploads/3/7/3/1/37310663/jjkz_wealthtax_feb2018.pdf (accessed 30 May 2018).

Jang, Jin Yea, Kyungsik Han, Patrick C. Shih and Dongwon Lee (2015), "Generation like: Comparative characteristics in Instagram," *Understanding & Protecting Kids Tech Use.* DOI: 10.1145/2702123.2702555

Judd, Kenneth L. (1985), "Redistributive taxation in a simple perfect foresight model," *Journal of Public Economics* 28(1): 59–83.

Karatani, Kojin (2003), *Transcritique: On Kant and Marx.* Cambridge, MA: MIT Press.

Kerber, Walter (1993), "Zins," pp. 1339–1343 in Georges Enderle (ed.), *Lexikon der Wirtschaftsethik.* Freiburg, Basel & Wien: Herder.

Keynes, John Maynard (1936), *Allgemeine Theorie der Beschäftigung, des Zinses und des Geldes.* München & Leipzig: Duncker & Humblot.

Knight, Frank H. ([1921] 1964), *Risk, Uncertainty and Profit.* New York: Sentry Press.

Kochan, Thomas A. (2013), "The American jobs crisis and its implication for the future of employment policy: A call for a new jobs compact," *ILR Review* 66(2): 291–314.

Kopczuk, Wojciech (2013), "Incentive effects of inheritances and optimal estate taxation," *The American Economic Review* 103(3): 472–477.

Kramer, Samuel Noah (1963), *The Sumerians: Their History, Culture and Charakter*. Chicago, IL and London: Chicago University Press.

Lakner, Christoph and Branko Milanovic (2015), "Global income distribution: From the fall of the Berlin Wall to the Great Recession," *World Bank Economic Review* 30(2): 203–232.

Lapavitsas, Costas (2013), "The financialization of capitalism: 'Profiting without producing'," *City* 17(6): 792–805.

Leinweber, Hartmut (2015), "Eurozone am Wendepunkt oder am Abgrund?" Marktreport 2015, Finanzsozietät Marburg, 9. Juli. URL: www.fsmr.de/fileadmin/downloads/marktberichte/2015/Eurozone_am_Wendepunkt_o der_am_Abgrund_.pdf (accessed 13 July 2015).

Leistert, Oliver and Theo Röhle (eds.), (2011), *Generation Facebook: Über das Leben im Social Net*. Bielefeld: Transcript Verlag.

Lohlker, Rüdiger (1996), *Schari'a und Moderne. Diskussionen zum Schwangerschaftsabbruch, zur Versicherung und zum Zinswesen*. Stuttgart: Harrassowitz.

López de Gómara, Francisco (1943), *Historia de la Conquista de Mexico*. Mexico City: Editorial Pedro Robredo.

Lutz, Friedrich A. (1967), *Zinstheorie*. Tübingen: Siebeck.

Lutz, Friedrich A. (1961), "The essentials of capital theory," pp. 3–17 in Douglas C. Hague (ed.), *The Theory of Capital: Proceedings of a Conference held by the International Economic Association*. New York: Stockton Press.

Marwick, Alice E. (2015), "Instafame: Luxury selfies in the attention economy," *Public Culture* 27(1): 137–160.

Marx, Karl ([1857–61] 1986), *Collected Works, Volume 28*. New York: International Publishers.

Marx, Karl ([1890] 1976), *Capital: A Critique of Political Economy, Volume 1*. London: Penguin Books.

Marx, Karl ([1894] 1959), *The Capital: A Critique of Political Economy, Volume 3*. Moscow: Institute of Marxism-Leninism.

Marx, Karl (1887), *The Capital: A Critique of Political Economy, Volume 1*. Moscow: Progress Publishers.

Marx, Karl (1867), *Das Kapital. Band 1 (Urfassung)*. Hamburg: Verlag von Otto Meissner.

Milanovic, Branko (2016), "The greatest reshuffle of individual incomes since the Industrial Revolution," *Vox EU: CEPR's Policy Portal (online)*. URL: https://voxeu.org/article/greatest-reshuffle-individual-incomes-industrial-revolution (accessed 25 May 2018).

Mirrlees, James (1976), "Optimal tax theory: A synthesis," *Journal of Public Economics* 6(4): 327–358.

Moon, Jang Ho, Eunji Lee, Jung-Ah Lee, Tae Rang Choi and Yongjun Sung (2016), "The role of narcissism in self-promotion on Instagram," *Personality and Individual Differences* 101: 22–25.

Nachtwey, Oliver (2016), *Die Abstiegsgesellschaft: Über das Aufbegehren in der regressiven Moderne*. Frankfurt am Main: Suhrkamp.

Nienhaus, Volker (1982), *Islam und Moderne Wirtschaft. Einführung in Positionen, Probleme und Perspektiven*. Graz: Verlag Styria.

Noonan Jr., John T. (1966), "Die Autoritätsbeweise in Fragen des Wuchers und der Empfangnisverhütung," *Diakonia* 1: 79–106.

Noonan Jr., John T. (1957), *The Scholastic Analysis of Usury*. Cambridge, MA: Harvard University Press.

Noorzoy, M. Siddieq (1982), "Islamic laws on Riba (interest) and their economic implications," *International Journal of Middle East Studies* 14: 3–17.

Odendahl, Christian (2017), "The Hartz myth: A closer look at Germany's labour market reforms," *Centre for European Reform*, July, London.

OECD (2017), *Core Government Results*. Paris: OECD Publishing. URL: http://dx.doi.org/10.1787/gov_glance-2017-graph156-en (accessed 31 May 2018).

OECD (2011), "An overview of growing income inequalities in OECD countries: Main findings," pp. 21–45 in *Divided We Stand: Why Inequality Keeps Rising*. URL: www.oecd.org/els/soc/49499779.pdf (accessed 25 May 2018).

Pfannkuch, Katharina (2009), *Das Zinsverbot in der Praxis des Islamic Banking*. Hamburg: Igel Verlag.

Piketty, Thomas (2017), "Toward a reconciliation between economics and the social sciences," Chapter 5 in Heather Boushey, J. Bradford DeLong and Marshall Steinbaum (eds.), *After Piketty—The Agenda for Economics and Inequality*. Cambridge, MA: Harvard University Press.

Piketty, Thomas (2015), "Capital, inequality, and power," *HAU: Journal of Ethnographic Theory* 5(1): 517–527.

Piketty, Thomas ([2013] 2014), *Capital in the 21st Century*. Cambridge, MA: Harvard University Press.

Piketty, Thomas (2011), "On the long-run evolution of inheritance: France 1820–2050," *The Quarterly Journal of Economics* 126(3): 1071–1131.

Piketty, Thomas and Emmanuel Saez (2014), "Inequality in the long run," *Science* 344(6186): 838–843.

Polanyi, Karl ([1944] 2001), *The Great Transformation: The Political and Economic Origins of Our Time*. Boston, MA: Beacon Press.

Qureshi, Anwar Iqbal ([1970] 1974), *Islam and the Theory of Interest*, 2nd ed. Lahore: Sh. Muhammad Ashraf.

Rahman, Fazlur (1964), "Riba and interest," *Islamic Studies* 3(1): 1–43.

Ramsey, Frank P. (1928), "A mathematical theory of saving," *The Economic Journal* 38(152): 543–559.

Rasch, William (2013), "Vom Gläubiger abfallen," *The European*. URL: www.theeuropean.de/william-rasch/5983-schulden-in-der-sprache (accessed 15 February 2016).

Rasch, William (2003), "Schuld als Religion," pp. 249–264 in Dirk Baecker (ed.), *Kapitalismus als Religion*. Berlin: Kulturverlag Kadmos.

Reissner, Johannes (1984), "Die innerislamische Diskussion zur modernen Wirtschafts- und Sozialordnung," pp. 155–169 in Werner Ende and Udo Steinbach (eds.), *Der Islam in der Gegenwart*. München: C.H. Beck.

Romer, Paul D. (2016), "The trouble with macroeconomics," *Commons Memorial Lecture of the Omicron Delta Epsilon Society*. Stern School of Business, New York University.

Rommerskirchen, Charlotte (2015), "Debt and Punishment: Market Discipline in the Eurozone," *New Political Economy* 20(5): 752–782.

Saez, Emmanuel (2002), "The desirability of commodity taxation under non-linear income taxation and heterogeneous tastes," *Journal of Public Economics* 83: 217–230.

Saez, Emmanuel and Stefanie Stancheva (2018), "A simpler theory of optimal capital taxation," *Journal of Public Economics* 126: 120–142.

Samiullah, Muhammad (1982), "Prohibition of Riba (interest) & insurance in the light of Islam," *Islamic Studies* 21(2): 53–76.

Scheve, Kenneth and David Stasavage (2016), *Taxing the Rich: A History of Fiscal Fairness in the United States and Europe*. Princeton, NJ: Princeton University Press.

Shoven, John B. and Michael Topper (1992), "The cost of capital in Canada, the United States, and Japan," pp. 217–236 in John B. Shoven and John Whalley (eds.), *Canada-US Tax Comparisons*. Chicago, IL: University of Chicago Press.

Siddiqi, Mohammad Nejatullah (2004), *Riba, bank interest and the rationale of its prohibition*. *Visiting Scholars' Research Series* No. 2. Dschidda: Islamic Development Bank.

Skidelsky, Robert (2010), *Keynes: The Return of the Master*. New York: Public Affairs.

Solow, Robert M. (2015), "The future of work: Why wages aren't keeping up," *Pacific Standard (online)*, 11 August. URL: https://psmag.com/economics/the-future-of-work-why-wages-arent-keeping-up (accessed 25 May 2018).

Springfield, John (2018), "The German wage puzzle," *Centre for European Reform: Insight*, 1 March. URL: www.cer.eu/sites/default/ files/insight_JS_1.5.18.pdf (accessed 25 May 2018).

Statista (2016), "Bruttoinlandsprodukt (BIP) in Deutschland von 1991 bis 2015 (in Milliarden Euro)," URL: http://de.statista.com/statistik/daten/studie/ 1251/umfrage/entwicklung-des-bruttoinlandsprodukts-seit-dem-jahr-1991/ (accessed 27 March 2016).

Stehr, Nico (2007), *Die Moralisierung der Märkte: Eine Gesellschaftstheorie*. Frankfurt am Main: Suhrkamp.

Stehr, Nico and Amanda Machin (2016), "Introduction: Inequality in modern societies. Causes, consequences and challenges," pp. 1–36 in Amanda Machin and Nico Stehr (eds.), *Understanding Inequality: Social Costs and Benefits*. Friedrichshafen: zu | schriften der Zeppelin Universität.

Stiglitz, Joseph E. (2012), *The Price of Inequality*. New York: W.W. Norton & Company.

Straub, Ludwig and Iván Werning (2014), "Positive long run capital taxation: Chamley-Judd revisited," *MIT Working Paper*. URL: https://economics.mit.edu/files/14044 (accessed 30 May 2018).

Streeck, Wolfgang (2013), "The politics of public debt: Neoliberalism, capitalist development, and the restructuring of the state," *Max-Planck-Institut für Gesellschaftsforschung, MPIfG Discussion Paper* No. 13/7, Colone.

Streeck, Wolfgang (2011), "The crisis in context: Democratic capitalism and its contradictions," *MPIfG Discussion Paper* No. 11/15. URL: www.mpifg.de/pu/mpifg_dp/dp11-15.pdf (accessed 4 June 2018).

Taylor, Lance (2017), "Why stopping tax 'reform' won't stop inequality," *Institute for New Economic Thinking (online)*, 15. Dezember. URL: www.ineteconomics.org/perspectives/blog/why-stopping-tax-reform-wont-stop-inequality (accessed 25 May 2018).

Taylor, Lance, Özlem Ömer and Armon Rezai (2015), "Wealth concentration, Income distribution, and alternatives for the USA," *Institute for New Economic Thinking Working Paper* No. 17. URL: www.ineteconomics.org/uploads/papers/WP17-Lance-Taylor-Income-dist-wealth-concentration-0915.pdf (accessed 4 June 2018).

Thelen, Kathleen (2014), *Varieties of Liberalization and the New Politics of Social Solidarity*. New York: Cambridge University Press.

Tiggemann, Marika and Amy Slater (2013), "NetGirls: The Internet, Facebook, and body image concern in adolescent girls," *International Journal of Eating Disorders* 46(6): 630–633.

Turchin, Peter (2018), "Economics can't explain why inequality decreases," *Evonomics: The Next Evolution of Economics (online)*. URL: http://evonomics.com/economics-cant-explain-why-inequality-decreases/ (accessed 23 May 2018).

Valkenburg, Patti M., Jochen Peter and Alexander P. Schouten (2006), "Friend networking sites and their relationship to adolescents' well-being and social self-esteem," *CyberPsychology & Behavior* 9(5): 507–513.

Vance, Laurence M. (2008), "The myth of the just price," *Mises Institute (online)*, 31 März. URL: https://mises.org/library/myth-just-price (accessed 8 April 2018).

Vlandas, Tim and Daphne Halikiopoulou (2016), "Why far right parties do well at times of crisis: The role of labour market institutions," *European Trade Union Institute, Working Paper* No. 2016.07, Brussels.

Vlandas, Tim and Daphne Halikiopoulou (2015), "Risks, costs and labour markets: Explaining cross-national patterns of far-right party success in European parliament elections," *Journal of Common Market Studies* 54(3): 636–655.

Voss, Dustin (2018), "The political economy of European populism: Labour market dualisation and protest voting in Germany and Spain," *LEQS Discussion Paper* No. 132. London: London School of Economics. DOI: https://dx.doi.org/10.2139/ssrn.3144649

Walras, Léon ([1954] 2003), *Elements of Pure Economics*. London: Routledge.

Weber, Klaus (2002), "Zinsschuld," pp. 1536–1537 in Klaus Weber (ed.) *Creifelds Rechtswörterbuch*, 17th ed. München: C.H. Beck.

Weil, David (2014), *The Fissured Workplace*. Cambridge, MA: Harvard University Press.

Weiß, Andreas Michael (2005), "Zinsen und Wucher: Das kirchliche Zinsverbot und die Hindernisse auf dem Weg zu seiner Korrektur," pp. 123–156 in Ulrike Aichhorn (ed.) *Geld- und Kreditwesen im Spiegel der Wissenschaft*. Wien: Springer.

Wicksell, Knut (1893), *Über Wert, Kapital und Rente nach den neueren nationalökonomischen Theorien*. Madison: G. Fischer.

Wilkinson, Richard and Kate Pickett (2009), *The Spirit Level: Why Equality Is Better for Everyone*. London: Penguin Books.

Wilson, George W. (1975), "The economics of the just price," *History of Political Economy* 7(1): 56–74.

# 4

# THE PRICE OF LABOR

To expect payment for labor is not "natural" to man.
—*Karl Polanyi ([1944] 2001: 277)*[1]

The meaning we associate today with the terms of "labor" or "work" (in the sense of manual and mental labor)[2] is a product of industrial society.[3] What constitutes work in industrial society is much more narrowly defined than work in pre-industrial society or is even absent as an activity and motive force. Work activities based on *remuneration* in industrial society became more clearly separated from non-work activities in a number of ways. This distinction between work and non-work activities is reflected by the emergent boundaries between the economic sphere and other social spheres: the spatial division between the place of work and the places of other contexts of social conduct is among the most important differentiations in industrial society. This separation of unacknowledged women's work from labor is directly related to the invisibility of women's work.

What is equally self-evident in addition to the differentiation between work time and leisure is the essential fact that a market-generated income (and the livelihood ultimately based on this income, especially at a later stage in the biography of individuals) is the most important source of welfare for the overwhelming majority of the population. The bulk of people are not owners of capital. And if we take a longer-term perspective what is also evident is that work is not what it used to be, and in the future, it will even less likely be what it was in the past. Societal transformations, demographic changes, political circumstances, migration patterns, assembly line-based labor, mechanization, electrification, computerization, digitalization, and now emerging, robotization and artificial intelligence have produced constant change and upheaval.

Among the four means of production, the degree of *control and regulation* that typically applies to labor—issuing both within the world of work and from the decrees originating from outside of the world of work but applicable to labor—exceeds the regulation to which knowledge, real estate or capital are subjected in modern societies (cf. Baecker, 2007). Finally, the usage of the term "work" today is most often restricted to work associated with employment or self-employment and steady patterns of working life and careers.[4]

## Perspectives

Europe and North America are both at the core of most social-scientific narratives about work—may the focus lie on the past, the present or the future. Today, from a global perspective different forms of labor characteristic of distinct historical times can be identified in societies on different paths and levels of industrialization. Such comparable forms of work that occur simultaneously across the global include enslaved, waged, coerced, child, and invisible labor.

In our search for the price of labor, we consider a range of perspectives that claim to provide an answer to questions of how valuable labor is. Importantly, we distinguish specifically between the supply of and demand for labor. Our suggestion is that attributes of the supply rather than the demand side are important for understanding the past, present and future evolution of the world of work.

Specifically, we examine how the price of labor is computed in classical economic discourse (for example by Adam Smith) and how modern economic theories differ from their classical predecessors. In the contemporary world of work, developments such as financialization, automation and artificial intelligence acquire significant importance which are, as we argue, developments that concern essentially the supply-side of modern labor markets.

Finally, we distinguish between material and moral elements of remuneration, analyze the theory and legitimacy of minimum wages, the idea of just wages and consider empirical evidence that has accumulated about the price of labor. Rather than conducting small-scale comparative case-study research, most of the evidence consulted by us concerns macro-level data conducted in North America and Europe.

Our presentation of different positions that examine the value or the price of work in its dual role as costs of production and a source of aggregate demand—both in practice and in the social sciences—cannot be separated from a number of other themes including the idea of the moral force of labor that are more generally concerned with the changes in the working and employment structures in modern society. Among these eminent economic but also political and ethical issues is the question of the future of paid labor. that is the question of human worth in the world of work that has been asked again and again since the industrial revolution, most prominently of course by economists in light of technical changes. In other words, economists tend to describe changes in the *demand* for certain skills as a close function of technical change (cf. Stokey, 2018: 344), less often, linked to macroeconomic policies that also impact job creation through the management of aggregate demand (cf. Alarcon, 2018: 4) or even less frequently to overall societal changes, for example, to changes in the educational achievements of the population, changes in gendered labor or ideas that become powerful social facts. In economics, the impact of technology tends to be overstated while behavioral changes are occluded.

## Supply and Demand

The fear of societies against a massive loss in the socially necessary scope of work (aggregate labor demand in a society), and finally even a society without work, is at the center of this discussion, just as, for example, the technical transformations of the world of work, most recently through the evolution of robotics and artificial intelligence. These developments are supposed to cause major changes not only regarding needed skills, the attractiveness, the organization, and the general nature of labor but also massive future social disruptions. In instance of some observations, the very future of humanity is seen at stake (Reese, 2018).

The paradox explored in past and present investigations of the impact of technological change on the world of work is the extent to which "technological change threatens social welfare not because it intensifies scarcity but because it augments abundance" (Autor, 2015b: 1) and thereby often sustains as well as enhances social inequality. But the contradictions do not end there.

There are significant examples of productivity-enhancing technologies that increase employment rather than reduce the volume of work. Automation or information technologies increase employment for some groups without reducing net employment (see Bessen, 2017). They point to the fact that in the past many of the fears associated with automation turned out to be false. As George Borjas and Richard Freeman (2019: 2) surmise "today we see robots taking job from humans in the media but not in real world labor markets."

However, in contrast, the *new* canonical narrative concerning the use of computers, robots and artificial intelligence has given new impetus to the fear that machines will replace human beings and create considerable unemployment and with it the prospect of "idleness without work [that] is a torment" (Benjamin, [1938] 2006: 127). Optimistic economists say no. Other economists warn that the new technological developments that at times are labeled part of the fourth industrial revolution (cf. Soete, 2018: 29)[5] will replace not only human muscles but also human skills and minds and enhance polarization and wage inequality (cf. Frey and Osborne, 2013).

There are also bold predictions about the future of work, in which work is completely eliminated. Forecasts about the future of work vary widely and at first sight only confirm that the future is uncertain. Observations about the probable future *volume* of work are based mainly on pure speculation, visions and wishful thinking. On the other hand, the question of the future distribution and change in the skill structure of work is arguably more interesting than the question of the total volume of the remaining or growing work. The problem of shifts in the specific skills is more consequential and should have a lasting influence on the price of the work.

One of the main theoretical correctives in contrast to the ruling *demand-side perspectives* we intend to stress in our discussion of the price of labor, the transformation of the world of work, and the nature of the modern work society is the *supply-side* point of view.[6] Briefly, the supply-side perspective of the transformation of many attributes of the world of labor does not subscribe to the plain idea that the driver of these changes has to be attributes of massive changes of the technological regime (e.g. Iversen and Soskice, 2019: 194).[7] The technology-centered demand perspective is currently associated with the frequent expectation of further, possibly even more comprehensive technical transformations of the world of work, for example through the "digitization" of work processes and artificial intelligence.

Max Weber describes a typically demand-side perspective, though in his case for the sphere of *industrial* production. Weber ([1921] 1972: 199) notes that "under the pressure of competition profitability depends on a much human labour as possible being eliminated by labour-saving machines, and especially the highest-paid variety who cost the business most. Hence skilled workers must be replaced by unskilled workers or workers trained directly at the machine. The process is inevitable and is continually occurring." The cause of the profound transformation in the type of skills needed is systemic and governed in its details by the corporation as the employer.

The supply-side perspective comes into sharp focus also at a time when concern about a massive loss of jobs meets the sober observation that there is in many countries a massive shortage of individuals ready to fill the many job vacancies. It therefore appears to be much more realistic and meaningful to ask, as David Autor (2015a) does, "why are there still so many jobs?"

The supply-side perspective of the resource of labor stresses the characteristics that are attributes of the collective and individuals who make up the working age population of a society and the skills people bring to the market. For example, the driver for the push toward the adoption of new technologies, even the generation of new technologies, in service and production industries may be significantly linked to characteristics of the composition of the labor force in a country.

Specifically, as Daron Acemoglu and Pascual Restrepo (2018b) have shown, changing demographics (the supply side) is a most significant factor enhancing or slowing the adoption of new technologies by firms.[8] An aging work force is linked to automation, particularly through robotics in response to a scarcity of middle-age workers (between the ages of 26 and 55).[9] Large country-to-country variation on the adoption of new automation and robotic technologies therefore is to a significant extent explained by demographic country differences.

An emphasis on the demand-side perspective that is the dominant approach not only in the social sciences but in the typical pronouncements of employer organization and the management of corporations about the future demand for certain skills,[10] is on the other hand linked to the conviction that the nature of the workplace, especially the technology found there, the entrepreneur, for example, her overwhelming one-sided power or the state of the economy are the governing and decisive factors that make for the uniqueness of the modern work society.

This may have been the case in the past, at least for much of the early history of industrial society and may well have captured the salient realities of the working society in the last century. Friedrich Engels classical description of the conditions of the working class in England is driven by a world of work in which demand-side attributes dominated. Engels' working class no longer exists in the developed world except in unusual niches unaffected by societal changes that signal the transformation to a world of work that is more dependent on demand-side attributes of labor.

Observations of the modern world of work, which are convinced that it is demand that determines typical changes in the modern arbitrary world, are based on the widespread *fallacy* that companies for example are indeed capable not only of naming precisely these cognitive and non-cognitive abilities that will be necessary in the future, but also of describing the processes within the framework of which these abilities are acquired in the first place. Since there is likely to be a significant delay between the identification and implementation of the learning of such skills in schools, universities and at work, it is unlikely that there will be a simple congruence between the skills anticipated and the skills actually lived in the working world decades later.

In the context of an examination of the growth of knowledge workers later in this chapter, we refer to Peter Drucker as one of the early proponents of the supply-side thesis.[11] Drucker stresses the historically unique increase in the educational attainment of the labor force in the Unites States looking for work in the years after the end of World War II when most of the jobs created during the war where no longer required and in later decades as a main societal force that triggers significant changes in the world of work.

On the other hand, the so-called "rising human capital hypothesis" refers to a change in the *demand* for specialized skills prompted by technological developments.[12] The rising human capital hypothesis stipulates that the share of labor cost as a proportion of the total cost of production increases. Whether the rising human capital thesis in fact is related to a change in the demand rather than the *supply* of employees with higher skills is a contentious matter. In any event, the "progress of technological rationality is supposed to lead automatically to the triumph of human capital over financial capital and real estate, capable managers over fat cat stockholders. and skill over nepotism" (Piketty, [2013] 2014: 21). The human capital hypothesis implies as well that overall social inequality should recede. The evidence for such a trend is rather weak, however.[13]

The uncertainties surrounding the developments of the future world of work listed are significant and cannot be eliminated easily.[14] Uncertainty about future economic and societal development itself can have an influence on the price of labor. Past efforts to anticipate for example the impact of *technological changes* on labor, whether technical advances substitute for, complement or enhance the aggregate of demand for labor, often have been unable to forecast the future. What is evident, however, is that technology on its own does not determine employment effects of technical innovations including of course in our age computerization, digitalization and artificial intelligence. Similarly, efforts by economists to foretell occupational skills that will be displaced or human skills likely to persist have failed to turn out to be accurate only a few years later. For example, in a study of "How computerized work and globalization shape human skill demand," Frank Levy and Richard Murnane (2005: 8) use the example of the truck driver as a job that is unlikely to undergo automation in the foreseeable future. We know now, of course, that self-driving trucks or taxis will be developed and work succeeding on making such trucks and taxis safe on busy roads is no futuristic pipe dream anymore. And, it can be expected that further automation or digitalization of work will have an impact on the price of labor.

One has to recognize, of course, that in many public (perhaps also social scientific) discussions and prognoses of the future of the world of work a strong ideological element is present. For example, reference to the job killing forces of automation as "evidence" of a future of human obsolescence is mobilized as an ideological weapon in the struggle between capital and labor.

## Monetarizing Labor

In now turning to how labor is monetarized, we recognize of course that wages do not constitute the full compensation that individuals obtain from employment. The additional compensation to the nominal wages' individuals may receive, we designate the moral compensation of labor; work does not have to be merely drudgery; and as has been shown, workers may indeed sacrifice monetary rewards for higher moral "pay" (e.g. Kniesner et al., 2012). If a tradeoff between different rewards is possible and even encouraged, differences in monetary wages among similar occupations could easily emerge (see Mas and Pallats, 2017).[15] If one substitutes the notion of "working conditions" for moral pay, we can expect that working conditions vary substantially across workers, occupations, corporations and demographic characteristics of the working population. But that working conditions play a major role in job choice decisions and job satisfaction likely holds across all segments of the labor force.

A discussion of the price of labor can easily be reduced to a narrow, that is, isolated analysis of the monetarized economic nature and payoff of work, ignoring a host of other attributes of the employee, his perception of the worth of labor, and the membership in certain collectivities (workers' bargaining power; cf. Kramarza,

2017) that co-determine her wages or income; for example, a narrow formula of this type asserts that an employee's income is equal to his marginal productivity, i.e. his contribution to the output of the place of employment. Wage growth tends to slow or is halted, all else equal, as productivity growth slows or stops (and *vice versa*). This is, in essence, the classical conception of the value of labor. However, there are many other socially constructed attributes that feed into wages. One should, therefore, add other attributes to a (classical) canonical discussion of the price of labor and its "value."

The most widely researched and discussed attributes involve quantitative empirical information about (average) wages and income of employees plus fringe benefits actually paid, and, to trends in real wages for example. The so-called non-wage items of the employment "income include employers' contributions to pension, medical and dental plans and unemployment insurance; and premiums for life insurance and workers' compensation. The non-wage component of labor income has risen dramatically over the years as a consequence of pension reforms, changes in unemployment insurance regulations, and the increasing portion of medical and dental plan premiums paid by employers" (Pold and Wong, 1990: 1).

Empirical information about the evolution in income and wages gives rise to studies about short- or long-term trends in remuneration, inequalities in wage levels, the premium paid for (quantity and/or quality of) education[16] or various skill levels[17] and the amount of downward price rigidity of labor (e.g. due to minimum wages, labor union influence). The canonical data employed in studies of the price of labor and its changes over time, however, do not allow for any reliable inferences about the *value* of work among the many social groups who are directly or indirectly part of the world of work.

Labor always comes with other relevant personal attributes and significant societal consequences. As Ralf Dahrendorf (2000: 12) stresses with particular emphasis, and as it is indeed widely understood, under the present social circumstances of a working society (*Arbeitsgesellschaft*), "[e]mployment not only provides a living for people; it is also the key to their entitlements and thus to the welfare state; moreover, it gives people self-esteem, even meaning for their lives." The meaning employment provides importantly offers social recognition both to its incumbents and dependents. The notion of work as a central life interest (cf. Dubin, 1956) therefore signal unmistakably that work is not only a burden but can be of significant value for human beings.[18] Labor is more than a disutility, a fact that is strengthened in modern economies where physical toil and repetitive tasks decline progressively.

Importantly, the price of labor (as well as the wage structure) is connected to a wide range of additional (and puzzling) individual and collective attributes of the working population. It is convenient to distinguish between purely *economic* properties (that is, market organized/driven factors such as the unemployment rate, cf. Phillips, 1958), *mixed or hybrid qualities*[19] (combination of market and non-market phenomena,[20] for example, fiscal policies'; cf. Mulligan, 2015, or the segmentation of consumers; cf. Wilmers, 2017, international trade relations and outcomes for wages; cf. Autor et al., 2014, the power of the buyer; cf. Wilmers, 2018)[21] and strictly *non-economic properties* (i.e. socio-structural dimensions such as gender; cf. Blau and Kahn, 2017; Mortensen, 2005, or ethnic membership; see Bonacich, 1976); further non-economic characteristics may include the sector of the economy, technical progress (e.g. computerization), the organizational or relational context of work (cf. Avent-Holt and Tomaskovic-Devey, 2010; Tomaskovic-Devey, 2014), proportion of highly qualified employees (Barth et al., 2017), knowledge and skills,[22] employment location,[23] price of the other resources of production, demographical processes such as the supply of labor (e.g. demand elasticity),[24] the age structure of the working population[25] as well as to norms and regulations pertaining, for example, to health and safety at work and last but not least that wages are political prescribed (i.e. minimum wage).

We would also count the process of digitalization among the hybrid processes that affect the price of labor and the distribution of income among the working population. Digitalization should impact the price of labor unless we consider the process of digitalization as a strictly technical process and not as a development that gives rise to the demand for complimentary skills[26] and hence is not neutral with respect to income differentials. Dominique Guellec and Caroline Paunow (2017: 1) in their analyses of the impact of digital innovation on the *distribution* of income make the case that "the increasing importance of digital innovation . . . is magnifying rents that that contribute to increasing the income share of the top income groups . . . specifically . . . to top executives, key employees, and shareholders, but little to the average worker."

Among the additional significant hybrid factors affecting the price of labor in general include competition (globalization) between workers in developing and developed economies. The simultaneity of differently developed economies (as the result of demographic factors, different histories, location) leads to the fact that the price of work in developed societies is pushed down.[27] However, not only economic considerations determine the difference in wages between countries. Political, legal, and cultural differences are important as well assuming that we are confronted with hybrid effects on the price of labor.

The non-economic factors we will designate later in this chapter as the *moral dimensions* of the value of labor.[28] The strictly non-economic (mainly no-wage) factors of the price of labor (for example, within a good-faith economy) are historically prior to the emergence of the "economical" elements of the benefits of laboring. An often neglected but not necessarily unimportant attribute of a job is its (felt) altruistic impact and therefore moral payoff.[29] Another dimension (and empirical indicator) of the moral compensation of work may for example be linked to the "perceived" quality of the job (see Handel, 2005) and hence the satisfaction a job offers to their incumbents. Also, the status of the employing organization has its influence on the price of the work, for example whether a company is in a restructuring phase (see Dencker and Fang, 2016). The age (cf. Ben-Porath, 1967) or the health of the employee (Stephens Jr. and Toohey, 2018), but also the security and the stability of the employment are additional factors that determine the price of the work, as does the intrinsic satisfaction with the work carried out. The moral component of the price of labor constitutes and hence demonstrates the close convergence rather than the distinctiveness of culture and the economy.[30] The assessment of the value of the work has at least a double component. The often-conflicting evaluations do not necessarily meet. On the one hand there is the self-assessment of one's own work and on the other hand there is the external assessment. One expects to be respected.

It is not surprising therefore, as a study by the London School of Economics (De Neve and Ward, 2017: 19) shows that "well-paying jobs are conducive to happiness," but that all of the other factors linked to employment we have listed "were found to be strongly predictive of varied measures of happiness; some of the most important job factors that were shown to be driving subjective wellbeing included work-life balance, autonomy, variety, job security, social capital, and health and safety risks."[31] Happiness is hardly a core economic objective but a cultural icon.

In short, the concept of being "employed" hides a massive variety and differences among jobs as well as the motives and preferences of the employees[32] and ways of assessing their worth. In addition, present-day changes in employment patterns include a great diversity of arrangements under which economic work takes places. Full-time regular employment compared to the past becomes much less prevalent In the United States over a fifth of all workers have less than full-time jobs. Given the great range of employment patterns, we have very little systematic information about alternative employment arrangements (cf. Cappelli and Keller, 2013).

If one combines the price of capital and the price of land as well as the other relevant attributes impacting on the price of labor, it quickly becomes evident that any precise determination of *the* price of labor is impossible to achieve or, rather, that *the price of labor is a political price* determined both by demand as well as supply-based attributes of labor power. Put in more conventional and narrower terms (IMF, 2017: 75), demand and supply of labor respond to the business cycle and slower moving secular forces. In other words, the price of labor is normatively institutionalized. Perhaps the most evident example of a price of labor that is politically determined would be the minimum wage.

As we will demonstrate, the price of labor is in general terms the outcome of a combination of two elements: a *material* part and a *moral* (or political) part. The material component refers to labor for a living, and moral components of wages, that is, living for work. Both components should not be seen as strictly separate attributes. There are subtle and at times explicit interrelations between moral and material forms of compensation. Material needs are not constant. Material needs and their evaluation based on our moral conceptions change. By the same token, our moral lives are of course affected by our existential conditions.

The difficulties of determining the value of each component of the price of labor vary. It is possible, or so it would seem, to establish the overall or general value of the material-existential component of the price of labor, for example, the changing value of the goods and services needed at any given time to ensure the mere survival of a typical household (material necessities).

In contrast, it is virtually impossible to come to any precise let alone general determination of the moral component, because any such understanding is an essentially contested matter. The inability to obtain anything close to a general, let alone natural or just definition of the price of labor turns any such analysis not only into a complex undertaking, but also into a fascinating exercise in social and economic theory.

One of the general remarks possible about the existential (material) and the moral value of labor are to observe that the former varies much less than the moral ingredient of the price of labor. It follows that the proportion of the price of labor that makes up its moral component may differ significantly from occupation to occupation or from country to country and the overall developmental stage of the economy. The moral component of the price of labor is a hybrid "price" composed of pecuniary (strictly economic) and a non-pecuniary element (for example the appreciation offered for a job well-done). How happy or dissatisfied one may be with one's work can manifest itself in very different ways in monetary and/or non-monetary values. From the traditional economics point of view, the monetary part of the price of work is the most important aspect of any career or job. As Greg Kaplan and Sam Schulhofer-Wohl (2018: 1) therefore stress on the basis of economic analysis, "the disutility of supplying one hour of labor is assumed to be the same whether that hour is spent building cars on an assembly line, waiting tables at a restaurant, teaching a class, or pitching for the White Sox. In consequence, in conventional models, the tradeoffs workers make between consumption and leisure can be assessed solely by looking at hours worked and [pecuniary] wages." A working hour is simply a working hour. This analysis obstructs, for example, the view of the psychological rewards of different occupations. From the employees' point of view, there are quite simply "good" and "bad" jobs (including worthy or lowly employers; Kalleberg, 2011).

## Work Is More than a Paycheck

> The material and intellectual aspects of human beings, their intellect and their will gain a unity in work that remains inaccessible to these potentialities so long as one views them, as it were, in peaceful co-existence. Work is the unified stream in which they mix like river sources, extinguishing the diversity of their nature in the similarity of the product.
>
> —*Georg Simmel ([1900] 2004: 413)*

The value of (free) labor in the sense of manual and mental labor cannot be separated from the person of the owner of the capacity to work, nor the context in which work is carried out or the history and the traditions of particular tasks that enhance the value of work performed under given circumstances.

Like interest and rent, wages tend to have a contractual basis. Despite the heading of our chapter—the price of labor—we intend to also refer to many additional and often highly contested dimensions of labor that serve as criteria for establishing wage differentials, such as those between male and female employees or, as we noted, the willingness to sacrifice monetary income for preferred working conditions.

Work has always had pleasurable, ethical or otherwise satisfactory properties that point far beyond monetary income. Dignity, justice, sustainability and satisfaction, to name but a few of these "pleasant" job characteristics, belong to such a list of significant outcomes or even central attributes of work. But *desirable* features of a non-monetary kind are often not the only ones closely associated with wage differentials.

Thus, one must keep in mind that in the eyes of many, work directly or indirectly has often multiple non-monetary *negative* effects (cf. Graeber, 2018) such as displeasure, painfulness, boredom, embarrassment, avoidance, burden, exhaustion, meaninglessness, oppression, uselessness and alienation. In any case, these non-monetary attributes of work are in no way derivatives of individual attributes, they are *socially* constructed dispositions and represent secular changes that individuals associate with working for a living (cf. Kaplan, and Schulhofer-Wohl, 2018).

Among the societal changes relevant to our analysis are the individualization of work (cf. Castells, [1996] 2000: 216, 282), the decline in the share of labor as a percentage of the GDP of nations (Autor et al., 2017), impactful demographic transformations in societies (i.e. a sudden surge of immigration; see Clemens and Hunt, 2017), the legal regime and the social security system pertaining to labor, as well as the secular retrenchment of the collective organization of workers (Goldfield, 1989; Pinto and Backfield, 2011), the decline of the amount of physical work or the globalization process in its impact on the price of work (Krugman and Venables, 1995; Bourguignon, 2015). All of these changes in attributes of jobs are mediated by changing levels of educational attainment of the work force in advanced societies.

Aside from the great variance and variety of attributes that are associated with labor, employment, and unemployment, there is the equally varied set of prices of labor. One factor that certainly makes a difference in the price of labor in more than one respect is the social status of the occupation and the time and place of work. There are major wage differences within and among societies, for example, depending on the social origins of the individuals (cf. Laurison and Friedman, 2016) or between female and male workers, individuals with different health conditions, rural and urban areas, young and old, manual and knowledge workers, organized or non-organized labor, different generations, large and small firms, rich and poor countries, non-skilled and skilled workers, social skills (cf. Deming,

2017), private and public employment, provision of state wage subsidies, sectors of employment, whether work takes place in a firm that experiences shocks to company revenues[33] and, last but not least, the social power or lack of social power commanded by wage earners.

Until the opening of cross-border markets, internationally mobile senior executives and managers, for example, were paid "on a scale according to their qualifications ... the opening of markets [in the 1970s and onwards] and the merging of businesses led to the performance ... being judged on an international scale" (Touraine, [2010] 2014: 23). The same cannot be said for the price of the labor of "ordinary" workers. As a matter of fact, the discrepancies between these two classes of labor have escalated over the last decades.

Many of the criteria we have enumerated impacting the price of labor reflect attributes that can be more or less directly and often unequivocally ascribed to individuals. On the other hand, our list also includes criteria that affect the value of a person's work but are actually collective facts, that is, represent attributes the individual is largely unable to control. Attributes that cannot be directly ascribed to individuals should not be expected to be of direct benefit to her; for example, in the sense that one can expect to call on a legally enforceable right. In some instances, a collective characteristic may even have a negative effect, for example, if one is assigned to the collective of migrants. Moreover, the different attributes of labor we have enumerated are sanctioned in the labor market in the sense that they are typically associated with distinctive wage levels that cannot be easily erased. The substitution of one type of labor for another type of labor, for example, in the proportion female over male, requires a considerable amount of time, if not changes in the legal context of employment. The competition in the labor market between individuals with personal attributes such as young or older is imperfect, contentious and often highly politicized.

Similarly, there are significant distinctions in how work and the price of labor are apprehended. Wages may be conceived of as unit costs or income, as payments to maintain the human resources of production or as earnings to secure the future livelihood, social standing and self-respect of members of a household, as assets or costs, as an inducement or a disincentive.[34]

In other words, wages may be considered to consist of two main parts: material compensation and moral compensation. Moral compensation would generally refer to earnings that acknowledge and reward the social status of the worker. Similarly, major societal conditions, for example, technological changes, population dynamics, major economic crises such as the Great Depression, or wage determination under conditions of social and political upheaval as compared to wages negotiated in contexts of relative societal and political calm are relevant factors explaining the price of labor. Typically, all these factors that constitute elements of the price of labor are co-determinants of the value of labor.[35] It is evident therefore that a determination of the precise value of labor is very difficult if not highly complicated. In any event, our discussion of the price of labor as a factor of production will start with a presentation of some of the most influential theories surrounding the issue, many of which continue to be relevant to this day for a discussion of the price and value of labor. We will first turn to Adam Smith's theory of wages. Smith's central economic interest is in production and the costs associated with manufacturing goods.

## The Wages of Labor

Adam Smith ([1776] 2012: 69) advances his basic thesis regarding the value of work in the chapter entitled "Of the Wages of Labour" in his classical treatise *An Inquiry into the Nature and Causes of the Wealth of Nations*. It reads: "The produce of labour constitutes the natural recompence or wages of labour." In other terms, the wages or the price of labor is determined by the price received for the product produced by the laborer.

A "natural" remuneration for work presupposes a society and, thus, an economic life that is still in something close to a state of nature. The only factor of production that counts in such a society is labor. The price of a commodity, therefore, must be exchanged in proportion to the cost of labor (Smith, [1776] 2012: book one, Chapter 6). There is neither private land ownership nor what must be described as the accumulation of capital; the worker can fully appropriate the wages of work; there is (as yet) no landowner or provider of capital with whom the worker has to share the fruit of his or her labor.

It was, of course, the French Enlightenment Philosopher Jean Jacques Rousseau who, perhaps more than any other thinker, provided the crucial point of departure for understanding the origin of the distinction between natural and social differences (see also Dahrendorf, 1968; Hirschman, 1982; Gissis, 2002; Berger, 2004) and, hence, between the natural and the "social" value of labor. In his essay on "The Origin of Inequality Among Men and Whether it is Legitimated by Natural Law," published prior to Adam Smith's *Wealth of Nations*, Rousseau ([1794] 1984: 207) made the fundamental point that it does not make much sense

> to investigate whether there might not be an essential connection between the two inequalities (the natural and the social). For it would mean that we must ask whether the rulers are necessarily worth more than the ruled, and whether strength of body and mind, wisdom, and virtue are always found in the same individuals, and found, moreover, in direct relations to their power or wealth; an equation that slaves who think they are being overheard by their masters may find useful to discuss, but that has no meaning for reasonable and free men in search of the truth.

Since social inequality is not a function of or determined by natural inequality, differences in the price of labor cannot be deduced from natural inequality. Jean-Jacques Rousseau proposes that social inequality arose as the result of the emergence of private property. There is a natural state of human affairs in which social inequality corresponds to natural differences. Rousseau explains the process that accounts for the origin of social inequality and legitimizes social inequality at the same time, in one modest sentence: "The first man who, having enclosed a piece of ground, bethought himself of saying *This is mine*, and found people simple enough to believe him, was the real founder of civil society."[36]

Entirely in line with Rousseau's observations about the order in which natural and social inequality rule in human affairs, therefore, Adam Smith ([1776] 2012: 69–70) notes: "In that original state of things which precedes both the appropriation of land and the accumulation of stock, the whole produce of labour belongs to the laborer. [...] But this original state of things, in which the labourer enjoyed the whole produce of his own labour, could not last beyond the first introduction of the appropriation land and the accumulation of stock."

Jean-Jacques Rousseau's emphasis on the role of property relations in conditioning the societal relations has been reaffirmed, as is well known, by various prominent thinkers including David Hume, Georg Wilhelm Friedrich Hegel and, of course, Karl Marx. The impact of reflections of the determining role of property on the price of labor has been significant. We will designate their position the *capital theory of social inequality and labor*.

As the evolution of societal associations proceeds, superseding the state of nature of human life, the price of labor becomes divisible in many, but not necessarily all instances. Adam Smith ([1776] 2012: 69) emphasizes that the price of work would not have remained constant even in the state of nature. On the contrary, wages would have increased with every improvement of the productive forces of work "to which the division of labour gives occasion." From a historical perspective, however, the privatization of land and the accumulation of capital started long before the massive increase in labor productivity in the modern economy since the onset of the industrial revolution.

The rent demanded by the landowner, for instance in the form of part of the produce, for the use of the land represents the first deduction from the product of labor. The profit skimmed off by the provider of capital in exchange for the means needed for gathering in the harvest or fabricating a product constitutes the second deduction.[37]

Conceivably, an "independent workman" may have enough capital of his own to allow him to exclude a provider of capital from the proceeds of his work. In this case, the revenue consists of two different parts, the wages and the profits from capital. Adam Smith ([1776] 2012: 71) adds that in his time, cases like these were "not very frequent; and in every part of Europe twenty workmen serve under a master for one that is independent."

More generally, however, Adam Smith ([1776] 2012: 70) emphasizes:

> The produce of almost all other labour is liable to the like deduction and other arts and manufactures of profit. In all arts and manufactures the greater

part of the workmen stand in need of a master to advance them the materials of their work, and their wages and maintenance till it be completed. He shares in the produce of their labour, or in the value which it adds to the materials upon which it is bestowed; and in this share consists his profit.

In sum, these first reflections by Adam Smith about wages are not getting us much further in our endeavor to more exactly determine, let alone quantify, the price of work.

Adam Smith's ([1776] 2012: 72) reference to something akin to the minimum wage, however, may offer a helpful clue: "A man must always live by his work, and his wages must at least be sufficient to maintain him." In many cases, however, the wage must actually be higher to allow a worker to strive and provide for a family. Another considerable influence on the price of labor is the *demand* for and *supply* of workers (cf. Lewis, 1954). The demand for workers is a function of the prosperity and productivity characteristic of a society.

Adam Smith ([1776] 2012: 74) points out that "[i]t is not the actual greatness of national wealth, but its continual increase, which occasions a rise in the wages of labour." Interestingly, he goes on to observe that it is therefore not "in the richest countries, but in the most thriving, or in those which are growing rich the fastest, that the wages of labour are highest." Smith refers to wages in the North American colonies of his time, noting that real wages, too, were much higher there than in London. But, Smith ([1776] 2012: 75–77) adds: "Though the wealth of a country should be very great, yet if it has been long stationary, we must not expect to find the wages of labour very high in it. . . . But it would be otherwise in a country where the funds destined to the maintenance of labour were sensibly decaying. Every year the demand for servants and labourers would, in all the different classes of employments, be less than it had been the year before."

Adam Smith ([1776] 2012: 105) realizes that actually there is such a thing as substantial wage differentials. These differentials he argues are due to five factors: "First, the agreeableness or disagreeableness of the employments themselves; secondly, the easiness and cheapness, or the difficulty and expense of learning them; thirdly, the constancy or inconstancy of employment in them; fourthly, the small or great trust which must be deposed in those who exercise them;[38] and, fifthly, the probability or improbability of success in them." Smith's list covers a wide range of factors that even today account for fluctuations in the price of work. Moreover, Smith ([1776] 2012: 111) notes, wage levels are influenced by social prestige: "The public admiration which attends upon such distinguished abilities makes always a part of their reward; a greater or smaller, in proportion as it is higher or lower in degree."

In the classical economic theory of Adam Smith, David Ricardo, and James Mill, the production factor "labor" is quite clearly a commodity whose price is not least a function of power relations in the market. The price of work obtained in the market, however, gravitates toward the *natural price of work*. David Ricardo

([1817] 1911: 93) offers a precise definition of the natural price of labor, and therefore the prospect faced by the largest segment of the population: "The natural price of labour is that price which is necessary to enable labourers, one with another, to subsist and perpetuate their race, without either increase or diminution." The subsistence wage is close to as matter of fact converges with our concept of material or existential compensation for work. However, we do not assert that there is a "natural" tendency for wages to fulfill an "iron law of wages." In an affluent society, the existential component of wages becomes the smallest constituent of the total wage. The considerations about the existence an iron law of wages, then, readily lead to the conclusion that high levels of unemployment are a function of excessive wage costs.[39]

Arthur Pigou (1933: 252) offers a particularly clear formulation of this relation: "With perfectly free competition . . . there will always be at work a strong tendency for wage rates to be so related to demand that everybody is employed." But since the price of labor is not completely flexible, there are phases of unemployment. It is this classical relation of earnings from work and employment that is challenged by John Maynard Keynes.

From the perspective of classical wages theory, the owners of the production factor "labor" have next to no share in growing market proceeds brought about by increased capital mobilization, or in higher productivity resulting from technological developments. For Karl Marx, this constellation is the reason why the factor "labor" is open to exploitation by the owners of capital.

## The Value of Work

John Maynard Keynes' reflections about the economic role and value of labor must be seen as a response to the dramatic events known as the Great Depression between 1929 and 1933, when unemployment rates in many countries in Europe and North America rose dramatically, putting more than a quarter of the workforce out of work and making output fall by one-third. In the United States, for example, the production of the Model A, the main car manufactured by Ford at the time, fell by half between 1930 and 1931. Economic ideas in the 20th century took decisive turns in response to the economic and political crisis of the Great Depression. Much of the reflections about the value of work must, therefore, be seen in connection with the pressing societal problem of employment rates and their political repercussions.

The dominant view among economists at the eve of the Great Depression was that wages that were too high and lacked flexibility would result in unemployment. This approach to the value of work, for example by Arthur Pigou (1933), deliberately neglects a range of other economic "variables" such as consumption, interest rates, technological development, and international trade. The view that high wages contribute to unemployment had considerable appeal also beyond the discussions among the professional economists about the causes of unemployment. But the opposite view that high wages cause prosperity and low wages cause underconsumption also took hold and did so not only in John Maynard Keynes' general theory and its implications for economic policies.

Keynes ([1936] 1961), too, refers to but a limited number of components he considers relevant to his theory of economic development. Of these components, two are non-physical and one is physical. The non-physical components are money and time. The only physical unit is labor. Keynes ([1936] 1961: 136) accepts—or, as he formulates it, sympathizes with—the pre-classical doctrine that "everything is *produced* by labour together . . . with what used to be called *art* and is now called *technique*, aided by natural resources which are free or costing a rent according to their scarcity or abundance."

John Maynard Keynes ([1936] 1961: 215) further notes that there is no constant or uniform value of labor. The value of labor varies. Various kinds of services and facilities are scarce for a mixture of reasons, and "therefore expensive relatively to the quantity of labour involved . . . smelly processes command a higher reward, because people will not undertake them otherwise." Frank Knight (1950: 507), however, adds in opposition: "some work is pleasant but highly paid, other work onerous and the pay is miserable."

In general, Keynes was convinced that adjustments of the price paid for labor could not be the key to avoiding unemployment. Higher incomes resulting from wage raises boost consumption and the improved effective demand impacts on employment. However, Keynes ([1936] 1961: 17) also accepts the classical notion that unemployment is a function of excessively high wages: "I am not disputing this vital fact which the classical economists have (rightly) asserted as indefeasible."[40]

At the same time, Keynes ([1936] 1961: 262) is convinced that a "reduction in money-wages will have no lasting tendency to increase employment except by virtue of its repercussion either on the propensity to consume for the community as a whole, or on the schedule of marginal efficiencies of capital, or on the rate of interest." He insists that any examination of the impact of wage reductions needs to consider the propensity to consume as well as the marginal efficiency of capital and the rate of interest. What is more, "the reduction in wages disturbs political confidence by causing popular discontent" (Keynes, [1936] 1961: 264). Ultimately, Keynes ([1936] 1961: 303) concludes: "We have full employment when output has risen to a level at which the marginal return from a representative unit of the factors of production has fallen to the minimum figure at which a quantity of the factors sufficient to produce this output is available."

John Maynard Keynes ([1936] 1961: 10) assertion in his *General Theory is* that money and real wages move in opposite directions. At least in the short run, falling money wages (or nominal wages) and rising real wages are likely to accompany falling employment rates. This is the case because labor is prepared to accept lower wages under conditions of a decline in the demand for labor while real wages "inevitably' can be expected to increase because of the increased marginal return to capital when output declines. Keynes' (1939: 34) critics pointed out, however, that in the United States and in England statistically a rise in money wages is accompanied by a rise in real wages, while a drop in money real wages does not trigger an increase in real wages. Keynes accepts these corrections to this theory. As far as policy consequences were concerned, Keynes attempted to find a way of attaining employment equilibrium without using wage rates as leverage (cf. Gallaway and Vedder, 1987: 36–37). What did economists have to say about wages after Keynes seminal contribution?

## The Modern Price of Labor

> The most valuable asset of a 21st-century institution (whether business or non-business) will be its knowledge workers and their productivity.
>
> —*Peter Drucker (1999: 79)*

Although we call it the modern view of the price of labor, more recent inquiries into the price and the value of work do not abandon classical concepts entirely. Rather, modern conceptions *transcend* classical theories. In contrast to the classical theories of the price of labor, the modern view seeks to capture the full empirical complexity of the attributes, dimensions, and processes that affect the value of labor (cf. Stehr, 1992). In the classical conception and its various amendments and corrections, labor is for the most part conceived of in an undifferentiated fashion. Labor is labor and often so "productivist" labor.

Peter Drucker's stress on the decisive influence of knowledge and information as the most valuable assets that employees' control and that presumably determine differential wages is still part of the classical conception of the value of labor. Drucker, of course, wants to emphasize what is new about labor in the modern economy. But by limiting himself to knowledge or information, Drucker fails to take into account much of what we call the *moral* components wages in the immaterial economy.

We are now taking it for granted that wages in modern economies are reimbursed in money. But in much of the 16th century and later, for example in Naples in 1751, "the peasant population and all those who received wages in kind (bacon, salt, salt meat, wine or oil) were outside the money economy" (Braudel, [1979] 1992: 468). Monetary wages are, indeed, a modern invention (cf. Person, 1932). A discussion of the transition undergone by the world of work in the knowledge-based economy should simulate, or so one would assume, research and debate on what these changes might imply for the value of labor, for wage disparities and social inequality.

## Manual Workers and Knowledge Workers

Prior to World War I, the largest single stratum of the working population in virtually every country of the world was employed in agriculture. Farmworkers still represent the majority of workers in many parts of the world. But this is clearly past and passing history of the world of work. Today, in the so-called developed world, often less than five percent of the working population is employed in agriculture. In many ways, the enormous rise in the productivity of agriculture reflects and is based on the same technologies that account for the rise in the productivity in industrial manufacturing. Blue-collar workers who had become the largest single group within the working population by 1950 displaced agricultural farmers and workers beginning after the end of World War I. Only 40 years later, the strata of the industrial workers and their societal influence were in decline. For example, the number of American workers employed in apparel manufacturing plunged from 900.000 in 1990 to fewer than 120.000 today. On a global scale, these jobs are not necessarily lost but have shifted spatially through global trade rules to countries such as India, China, Mexico or Bangladesh.

After the turn of the century, in the developed world, industrial workers accounted for less than one eight of the workforces. Both retreating strata of the working population will not disappear entirely nor will the large group of service workers. But the world of work is radically transformed. As Peter Drucker (1994: 8) notes, "the rise of the class succeeding industrial workers is not an opportunity for industrial workers. It is a challenge. The newly emerging dominant group is 'knowledge workers'." Knowledge workers (immaterial labor) have of course been part of past economic life. How large the group of knowledge workers within immaterial economies is today can only be answered with a clear conception of what knowledge work actually entails. Toward the end of the last century, Peter Drucker (1994: 8) anticipates that knowledge workers could make up a third or more of the workforce. For the most part, these knowledge workers are better paid than the industrial workers.

Access to the knowledge work force is gained through education, that is, the command of human capital. Knowledge workers make a living by thinking; "Knowledge workers have high degrees of expertise, education, or experience, and the primary purpose of their jobs involves the creation, distribution, or application of knowledge" (Davenport, 2005 10). The conception of knowledge work advanced by Davenport and the conception of access to the knowledge workforce also favored by Peter Drucker supports a narrow idea of the nature of knowledge work.

For it is important to note that the distinction between manual work and knowledge work does not refer to mutually exclusive tasks. The differentiation is never absolute. However, information on the exact relationship between the two forms of work is scarce, if not unknown, and the possible trends in the development of their relationship are also undiscovered.

The distinct groups of knowledge workers in modern (capitalist) societies are not confined to a social class in terms of classical political economy.[41] There are knowledge workers engaged in manual work and there is manual work that incorporates knowledge work. Knowledge work may require highly developed manual skills and as well as significant intellectual capacities. Thomas Davenport (2005: 3) offers a narrower definition of the knowledge work, when he describes the work of knowledge workers as "responsible for sparking innovation and growth in . . . organization[s]. They invent . . . new products and services, design . . . marketing programs, and create . . . strategies."

Both classes of knowledge workers are in immediate control of significant elements of labor as means of production, for example, knowledge workers, who are physicians performing operations in close "alliance with machines." As Peter Drucker (1999: 87) states:

> Employees who do manual work do not own the means of production. They may, and often do, have a lot of valuable experience, but that experience is valuable only at the place where they work. It is not portable. Knowledge workers, however, own the means of production. That knowledge between their ears is a totally portable and enormous capital asset. Because knowledge workers own their means of production, they are mobile.

Investments of corporations are increasingly shifting toward knowledge, skills, and programs and away from investment in machines and tools. Productivity gains are a function of the application of knowledge gains realized in the knowledge society. Knowledge work is less structured and more difficult to structure and standardize than production work or administrative tasks. The variety of tasks typical of knowledge work is greater than that of manual work. It follows that knowledge work lends itself less to observation; in many ways, knowledge work is not completely invisible but less visible than other types of work activity. It is widely assumed that knowledge workers, given the nature of their work and perhaps the conditions for their productivity enjoy a greater degree of autonomy within their employing organizations. Hierarchies and processes of social control in organizations do not disappear in the wake of the increase in knowledge workers, but they are flattened. Social exclusion does not vanish as knowledge work evolves to become the prevailing form of work (cf. Kleinman and Vallas, 2001).

As Karl Marx ([1939–1941] 1973: 705) outlines in his *Grundrisse* (Foundations of the Critique of Political Economy, Marx's manuscripts of 1857–1858), with the advance and application of technology and science,[42] the worker is no longer the principal agent of production, and what appears to be

> the mainstay of production and wealth is neither the immediate labor performed by the worker, nor the time that he works—but the appropriation

by man of his own general productive force, his understanding of nature
and the mastery of it; in a word, the development of the social individual.

In contrast to Marx's conception of "knowledge work," the productive forces
of *industrial* society are for the most part based "on the direct labor of workers, measured and exploited in terms of labor time"; while the productive forces
of advanced society are "based on the capacity of people to learn" (Block and
Hirschhorn, 1979: 367). What now becomes crucial, rather than the quantity of
labor and the social organization of work, is the quality or, as Karl Marx formulates it, the "power of the agencies."[43] For Marx, this transformation already signals
the end of bourgeois society and the demise of an exploitation-based economy
and the exchange value as the measure of the use-value of commodities.

The definition of knowledge workers as the "dominant occupations group
with high levels of education, professional development and autonomy" that will
be affiliated with an "evolving global community" (Lindley, 2002: 95) therefore
fails to grasp the full transformation of the emerging work throughout the labor
market. This transformation of the world of work also implies that knowledge
workers may in all likelihood be replaced by the robotization of work processes.

In a study on the future demand of "highly skilled" workers in the United
States, Paul Beaudry and his colleagues (2013) estimate that the peak demand
for such workers (in particular, the demand for workers with cognitive skills)
occurred in the year 2000 and has since declined. The authors suggest that the
employment rate in the US economy started to contract around 2000 and that
the contraction mainly affected "high skilled workers," but has "indirectly affected
lower skill workers by pushing them out of jobs that have been taken up by higher
skilled workers displaced from cognitive occupations. This has resulted in high
growth in employment in low skilled manual jobs with declining wages in those
occupations and has pushed many low skill individuals out of the labor market"
(Beaudry, Green and Sand, 2013: 33). The "de-skilling" process impacts workers
in all segments of the labor force.

## The Revolution of Knowledge Workers[44]

It is, of course, a widely shared assumption that the growth of the number of
knowledge workers in the modern economy occurs in response to the changing
demands or requirements in the world of work that especially its modern technological regime imposes. Peter Drucker presents a much more surprising and
perhaps plausible hypothesis about the reasons for the growth of the number of
knowledge workers in modern society.

He suggests that the stimulus for the increasing demand for knowledge-based
work has to do less with more difficult and complex job skills, changing technological regimes, the growing complexity and specialization of the economy or
enhanced functional steering and coordination needs. The growth of knowledge
workers has more to do with the substantial extension in the working life span

of individuals and the enhanced knowledge with which individuals come to the labor market in the first place. The observed shift toward knowledge-based jobs should be seen to result from changing occupational preferences and choices of new entrants to the labor market, although changes in the job content and ways of achieving job satisfaction certainly are part of the transformation.

In the United States for example full scale labor force entry of adult college trained baby boomers coupled with steady retirements of less-educated persons who reached working age during the 1930s and 1940s resulted in quantum increases in the average educational endowment of the labor force. Prime working age participants with four years or more of college training rose by 64 percent to 25.5 million during the 1980s and those with one to three years rose by 58 percent to 20.8 million (Wetzel, 1995: 60).

If we follow Peter Drucker, it is not so much the *demand* for labor and particular skills as the result of more complex and exacting jobs, but the *supply* of highly skilled labor that underlies the transformation of the world of work. More specifically the "direct cause of the upgrading of the jobs is . . . the upgrading of the educational level of the entrant into the labor force" (Drucker, [1968] 1992: 279).[45] It would follow, for example, as Goldin and Katz (2008: 119) note that "as the workforce becomes more skilled, technologies that use greater skill are adopted."[46] It is possible but difficult to foretell that once the world of work has been thoroughly transformed that "demand" attributes will become more prominent attributes influencing the texture of the labor market.[47]

The much more common perspective is that rapid diffusion of information and communication technologies has altered the production process and the delivery of services and that the employment structure has changed as a result. The new technologies increase the demand for highly skilled workers. Put more technically, most observations "model changes in workforce skill as a function of changes in industry capital intensity and industry-level investment in computer equipment" (Doms, Dunne and Troske, 1997: 254).

To the best of our knowledge, there are no empirical studies that explicitly examine the relationships stipulated by Drucker. However, two recent intensively discussed and researched economic issues that arrive at largely unanticipated results may offer at least an indirect measure of confirmation of his thesis. First, a large volume of empirical studies of the US labor market triggered by the observation that income inequalities between well-paid and more poorly paid jobs have risen considerably in recent years, prompted economist to ask what developments may be responsible for these pertinent income trends. In particular, the relations between technological change, skill level and income have been studied. The primary assumption examined in these studies is that the increasing polarization of the labor market may be linked to technical changes that in turn cause firms to hire more highly skilled labor (Gottschalk, 1997). Second, there are research designs directed toward analyses of the causes of the "productivity puzzle" that could be relevant.

For the researchers concerned with the growing polarization of income levels, two explanations are of particular interest. First of all, the growing differentiation of pay for skilled and lesser skilled labor may be caused by technological change. More precisely, the increase in *demand* for skilled labor and a growing proportion of skilled workers in the labor force is seen as induced by technical developments (Johnson, 1997). The second explanation has a family resemblance to the first account: the *demand* for technologically more sophisticated products and services has triggered a growing need for a highly skilled work force (cf. Bernard and Jensen, 1997: 5). In other words, changes that can be attributed in one way or the other to demand induced forces provoke a change in the balance of skilled to lesser skilled workers. And, as a result, these transformations in the nature of demand activate and accelerate a growing inequality in incomes by skill levels.

In a broadly based cross-sectional empirical study at the level of individual manufacturing firms and using individual rather than aggregate data for the American economy, Doms, Dunne and Troske (1997) have examined the relationship between technology use,[48] education, occupation and wages of the employees in the manufacturing sector. One is able to conclude that there is a growing covariance between the degree of technology use in firms, that is to say, the progress made in automating both the development and the production process, and the educational level of the employees. The conclusion therefore not only is that "skilled workers and advanced manufacturing technologies are complements" but also that the proportion of employees "in skilled occupations rises significantly with the number of technologies employed" (Doms, Dunne and Troske, 1997: 261, 263; see also Berman, Bound and Geliches, 1994) *as well as* the proportion of employees not directly active in the production process.[49] A variety of controls confirms these findings. In addition, the authors report that employees in firms with extensive technology deployment earn higher wages and salaries.

The cross-sectional data however cannot offer an answer to questions about the timing of the observed marked substitution in favor of skilled labor in the manufacturing firms that are technology intensive. As a result, Doms, Dunne and Troske attempt to extend their analysis by relating the utilization or adoption of different technologies over time in these firms to changes in the different variables such as the wage levels, the proportion of employees not directly involved in the production process, etc. Aside from methodological problems caused by a lack of valid longitudinal data, the overall result of their efforts to operationalize "technology adoption" is that "technology adoption is relatively uncorrelated with the changes in the nonproduction labor share, workers' wages, or labor productivity" (Doms, Dunne and Troske, 1997: 277).

One possible "explanation" for the "negative" finding would be that the firms the authors considered in their study already employed or hired a large number of highly skilled employees prior to the adoption of new technological means. Thus, "if plants that adopt technologies have more skilled workforces prior to adoption, then we would expect that the pre-adoption wages and labor productivity should be correlated with future technology use" (Doms, Dunne and Troske, 1997: 277). The results of their study once more are far from transparent. The authors sum up the relation they are able to document as follows: "Plants that adopt a large number of new technologies have more skilled workers both pre- and postadoption" (Doms, Dunne and Troske, 1997: 279). As Drucker assumes, one cannot preclude the possibility that highly skilled employees force the modernization of their work places in the first instance. It is likely therefore that the supply rather than the demand of skilled workers constitutes the motor of the rapid and radical transformation of the world of work.

Additional support of Drucker's thesis of a supply induced transformation of the world of work is provided by aggregate data about the growing "skill level" of the population in most OECD countries. According to Johnson (1997: 42), the relative skill supply measured as a ratio in the population of high school to college equivalency in the US has risen from 0.105 in 1940 to 0.496 in 1993. In five decades, the proportion of the population with a college education has increased fivefold. The increase of college educated labor was particularly strong in the 1970s, reflecting a growing proportion of college students in the latter half of the sixties. It would be far too simple to suggest that the tremendous increase in the collective skill level of the work force simply occurred in direct response to market forces. Although individuals will respond to perceived market opportunities, the fit not only in terms of time between perceived market opportunities and education could hardly be expected to be exceptionally close. Too many other factors and forces impinge upon those choices and after many years of education perhaps result in "higher skill levels."

In the modern economy, as we have noted, knowledge is a most important resource. As a result, the production of knowledge *and* learning are among the most significant processes in the knowledge society.[50] Knowledge societies are changing with rapid speed. For this reason alone, it is not sensible to adopt a strict demand or storage model of the kinds of skills and competencies that schools, universities and other educational institutions ought to deliver. Future occupational requirements of the world of work and their obsolescence are difficult if not impossible to anticipate or predict. A decisive feature of the labor market in knowledge societies is its absolute unpredictability. The storage model—schools and universities supply those skills and competencies that can be immediately utilized at work—has to be replaced by a model that couples work and education and wages under conditions of uncertainty and agency.

## Financialization and Labor

In our introductory discussion of the properties of the immaterial economy we have highlighted a characteristic trend of the last three decades, that is, the growing financialization of economic transactions. The decoupling of the real economy, i.e. production, trade and consumption, and the shift toward the financial sector has, of course, repercussions on the price of labor as well as major elements of modern labor institutions. For example, the financialization process impacts the bargaining power and the employment protection of employees in finance (cf. Darcillon, 2015).[51] The repercussions of changes in labor market institutions should, in turn, affect the price of labor in financial businesses although the data on such links wait to be constituted.

To begin with, the financial sector's capacity to create jobs is low. In contrast to the discourse around the development of post-industrial societies, in which the shift of employment from industry to service sectors constitutes the central theme, this type of analysis regarding the immaterial financial sector remains largely irrelevant. The observation that the finance sector of the economy is not a job machine confirms the more general finding by Beaudry, Green and Sand (2013: 2–3) that the demand for skilled workers to fill more cognitive intensive occupations has actually declined since 2000 in the United States. Moreover, in the years of the growing dominance of financialization, increases in general incomes and wages have been notably low for the great majority of the employed population.

One key statistics-based assumption concerning the remuneration of all employees is that there is a causal relation between the growing financialization of the economy and the earning capacity. What can be observed is a stagnation or even contraction of wages in contrast to a rise in the incomes of the higher earners' groups. The reduction in the share of surplus generated that goes to the general workforce is a function of where revenues are generated in the immaterial economy. The generation of surplus decoupled as we saw from production in the immaterial economy is increasingly gained in the financial sector. Lin and Tomaskovic-Devey's (2013: 1284) data for the United States indicate that far more than half of the decline in labor's share of income (see also Figure 4.1) is due to the financialization sector. During the period between 1980 and 2007, the share of the finance sector's profits tripled in the United State from a postwar average of 15 percent to a peak 45 percent of all profits. The OECD data reproduced in Figure 4.1 arrive at a percentage of labor's share of GDP rather profits that is also in a significant and persisting decline. The OECD figure at least intuitively seems to mirror the assumption that lower levels of labor's share of income can be attributed (at least partially) to finacialization, as the most financialized economies (UK, USA) show lower and relatively stable levels since the mid-80s.

What the impressive data about both the share of profits of the workforce and the allocation of labor' share in relation to the GDP in the modern economy fail to consider entirely is the question of the ways in which individuals come to be member of the labor force or beneficiaries of the surplus-generating world of finance, in the first instance. Other dimensions also play a role and tend to be mobilized in more conventional accounts of the growing disparity in income levels. More conventional phenomena to which reference is made would be declining union membership among workers, technological change, globalization, and more and more investments drawn into the financial sector. But what the data we

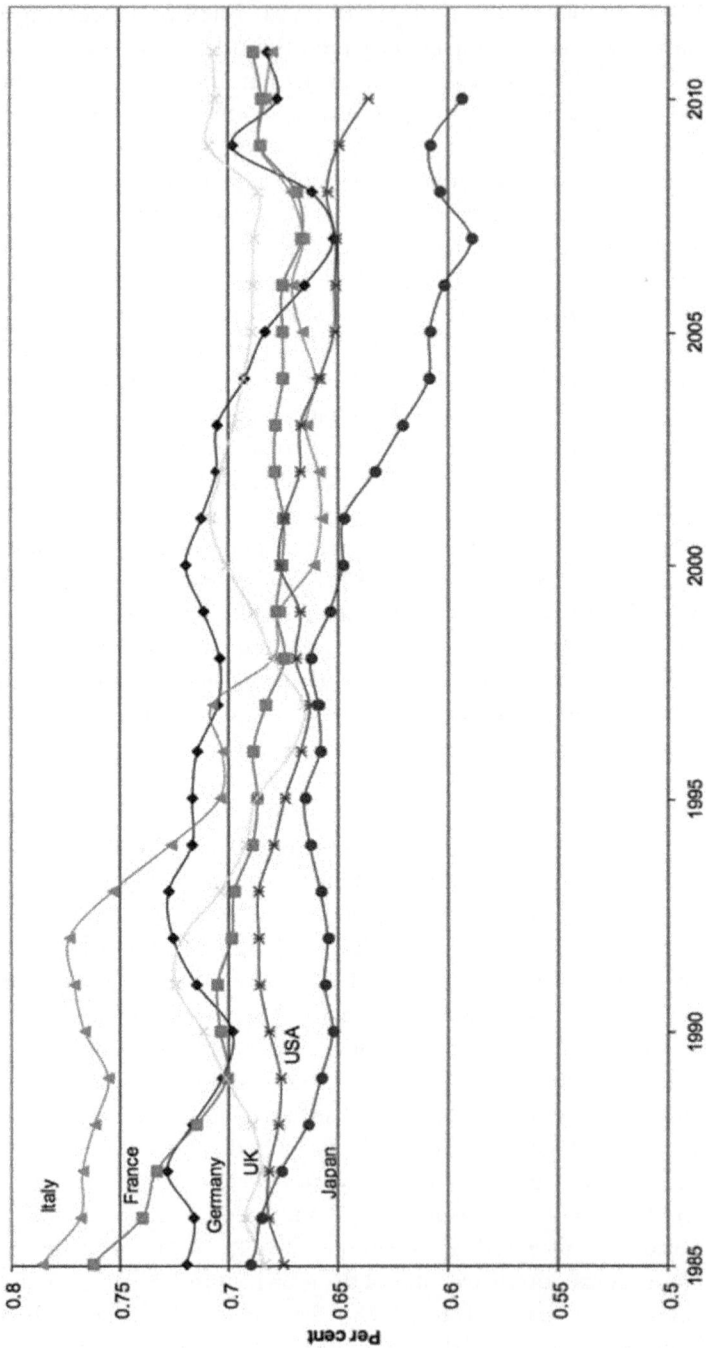

**FIGURE 4.1** Share of Labor in GDP in Selected Countries, 1985–2011

*Source:* Bourguignon (2014)

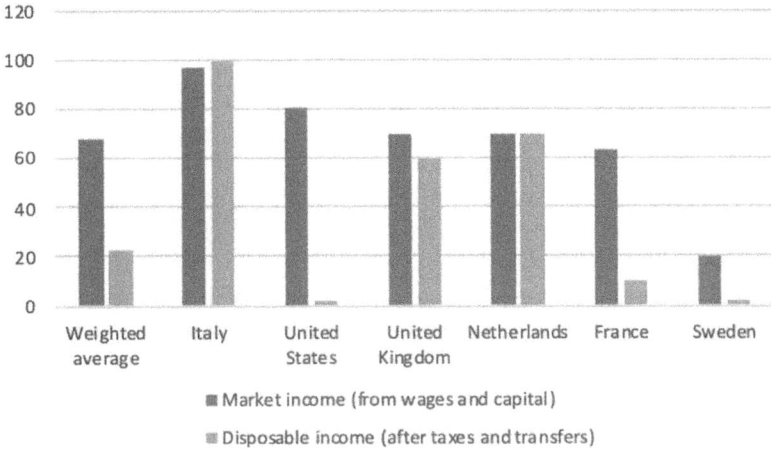

FIGURE 4.2   Percent of Households in Segments With Flat or Falling Income, 2005–2014

*Source:* Dobbs et al. (2016)

have reproduced unequivocally demonstrate is that socio-economic inequality soared.

In the post-war decades, household *incomes* in the world's 25 developed economies steadily rose.[52] But as a McKinsey study (Dobbs et al., 2016) shows, between 2005 and 2014 the great majority of households saw their household incomes stagnate or decline, with 60 and 70 percent of all households affected. In the previous 12 years between 1993 and 2003, only an extremely small minority of 2 percent of all households was affected. The number has risen explosively from 10 million to a stunning 540 to 560 million.[53]

These differences already clearly show that there is a number of other factors besides financialization and the 2007–2009 financial crisis that are involved in this development. In many countries at the present time, the economy booms. But not all who are employed benefit.[54]

We have little systematic information about the incomes of employees in the firms of the financial word. A small number of empirical, mostly qualitative studies offer initial information about the working conditions in the financial industry. The results tend to indicate that the working conditions are anything but pleasant. Jean Cushen (2013: 329) reports on the result of a case study of a subsidiary of a knowledge-intensive, high technology, and multinational corporation. He sums up his findings by reporting that financialization

in addition to creating employment insecurity, financial insecurity and work intensification, can also prompt role insecurity, suppression of voice and enactment of falsely optimistic behaviors. The continuous stream of performative interventions caused employees to feel anything could happen to their role at a moment's notice; the cumulative effect of which was insecurity and distress.

Jean Cushen's observations about the impact of financialization on the working environment and the social relations in organizations in the financial world are a useful reminder that what is called automation or digitalization of labor also is it technology-based (that is, the representation of information in bits) but that technological change is driven by humans with specific intentions and interests; for example, automation is a competitive necessity. Companies producing cars have no choice but to deploy the latest technologies such as robots in production. By the same token, wage increases enhance the likelihood of substituting machines. For example, a study of minimum wage earners in the United States between 1980–2015 finds that this group is quite vulnerable to employment changes and job loss because of automation following a minimum wage increase (Lordan and Neumark, 2017).

This observation, in turn, leads us directly into the heart of a controversial discussion in social science and society, which has been contested for decades, and is often filled with expressions of anxiety about the consequences of technical change on the amount of socially necessary work (aggregate labor demand). As a rule, economists are opposed to the thesis, which is simplistic in their view, that an increase in technical induced labor productivity must be associated with a collective loss of work. However, the consensus of economists is by no means without its own critics (for example, Heilbroner, 1965: 34–36, Sachs and Kotlikoff, 2012).

We have of course witnessed many changes in the development of technology over the last two centuries. The multitude of technological changes should caution the observer to treat technology as a kind of black box: technology of technology. Depending on the nature of specific technologies, the impact on the volume of work and the prices of labor should not be homogeneous. Some technical inventions might enhance employment and wages; other developments were detrimental to employment and wages. Still other changes benefit some groups in the work force and their wages while other groups may suffer from lower or stagnating wages and even by losing their jobs. In other terms, the unequal impact of different technologies on the world of work only enhances the uncertainty about its economic consequences.

The uncertainties associated with a glance into the future of work and its price are obvious: the nature and pace of relevant technology changes, which parallel or complementary skills are required, how is productivity affected, what will be the future course of the economy and the national and international political environment, social values, etc. Decades ago, Robert Solow (1965: 18) therefore issued a stern warning: "It would be a fantastically . . . complicated job to discover the net effect of *all* technological progress in any single year on employment. No one

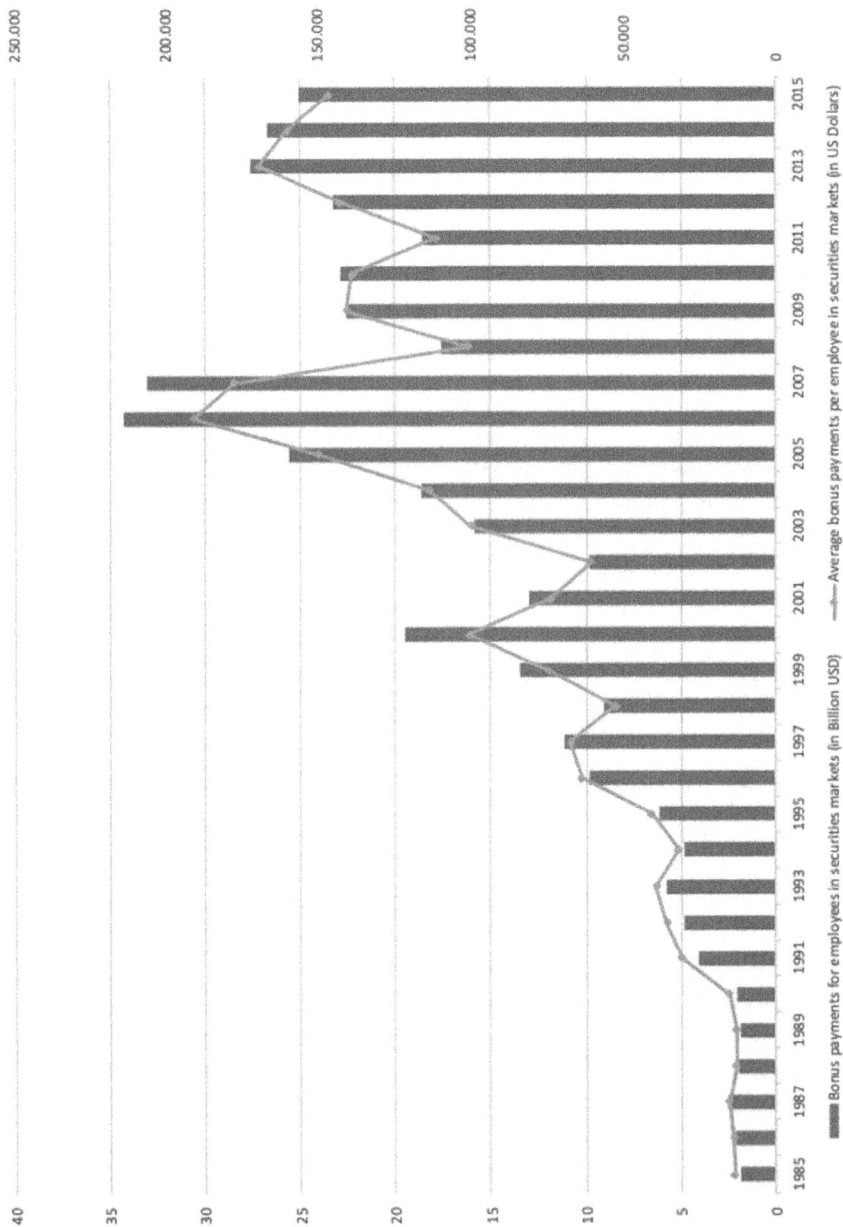

**FIGURE 4.3** Bonus Payments at Wall Street

*Source:* Statista, 2017 (https://de.statista.com/statistik/daten/studie/151182/umfrage/wall-street-bonuszahlungen-seit-1985/)

can possibly know; so, no one has the right to speak confidently." Moreover, how decisive is technological development on its own for the aggregate volume of employment in a country and how important are the many other factors such as the *demand* (see Bessen, 2018: 14)[55] or outlay for good and services that influence both the number of jobs and the price paid for labor? Will a useless class emerge in the not too distant future?

The forecasts for the future of work in view of new technological developments spread over the entire range of possible scenarios: From the end of the work society, hardly discernible differences compared to the present or the past in the scope of socially necessary work, to robots that become the colleagues of the worker, to work for only a few highly qualified and manually active persons. In any case, these forecasts are often politically inspired predictions, which on the other hand bear witness to our dilemma of anticipating the future adequately, let alone shaping it.

It is the case, paradoxically perhaps, that the questions we have just enumerated dominate the discussion about the future of work. It is a paradoxically state of the dialogue among professional social scientists and many segments of the public, for example, labor unions, employee organizations and politicians with a rather limited capacity to foretell the future. It is paradoxical because the controversial debates occur at a time when in many countries for example Germany but also the United States the supply of workers fall way short of the demand. This occurs at a time, when many observers are certain that the greatest threat to the present economic well-being is the shortage of individuals able and willing to meet the demand of employers for workers.

## When the Robots Rise[56]

Will robots steal our jobs?[57] In 1930, John Maynard Keynes ([1930] 1963: 364), in his thoughtful essay "Economic Possibilities for our Grandchildren," draws attention to the dangers of an upcoming "technical unemployment":

> We are being afflicted with a new disease of which some readers may not yet have heard the name, but of which they will hear a great deal in the years to come—namely, *technological unemployment*. This means unemployment due to our discovery of means of economizing the use of labour outrunning the pace at which we can find new uses for labour.

However, in line with the spirit of many subsequent discussions about the impact of technical innovation on the volume of employment, Keynes offers the irrepressively optimistic view that the technological unemployment he anticipates "is only a temporary phase of maladjustment"; moreover in a hundred years from the time Keynes ([1930] 1963: 364–365) penned his predictions (which we are about to reach), all this means is that "in the long run. . . *mankind is solving its economic problem"* and that the standard of living "in progressive countries . . . will be between four to eight times as high as it is to-day." Moreover, in his essay, Keynes distinguishes between absolute and relative needs suggesting that many individuals will devote their time and energies to non-economic activities once their absolute needs have been met. This distinction between absolute and existential needs resonates to a degree with our dichotomy between material and moral compensation. After an expected period of displacement and adjustment, Keynes anticipates a fifteen-hour workweek in support of a high standard of living. Keynes cautiously adds that his prediction assumes "no important wars and no important increase in population."

The framework that dominates social scientific and political discussion about the impact of technological change on employment, at least since David Ricardo's ([1821] 1973: 388) suspicion that the substitution of machinery for human labor may cause unemployment, is for the most part two-dimensional or dichotomous. On the one hand, one encounters the view as proposed by Ricardo (also Lederer, 1938) that the future of work is under threat and that automation for example will spell the end of work for humans and, on the other hand, that technological change invariably will increase the demand for labor (e.g. Kaldor, 1932: 185–189), as has indeed been in evidence in the past. What does the strict opposition leave out between the loss of socially necessary labor and the optimistic view that technology itself in the end will solve the problem it creates by generating new demand for labor? As we will indicate, the picture is in all likelihood more complicated. Both economic responses and political reactions determine whether the aggregate demand for labor may not change at all (cf. Acemoglu and Restrepo, 2018b). But this does not mean that adjustment processes are prompt or fully compensate the loss of jobs.[58] The lesson that many draw from past experiences of the interplay between the volume of work and technological changes is that the economic and social change can be most difficult for some individuals and lead to lasting maladjustments for communities, regions, and entire societies but that the changes are beneficial to society in the long-run creating more wealth and better jobs.

For decades after John Maynard Keynes' apprehension about technological unemployment, concerns about a drastic decline of the volume of socially necessary or paid work in the near future have been voiced many times and discussed in contentious debates.[59] The worries or optimism about the consequences of technological change in industry, however, are much older, as a speech from a debate in the House of Lords from 1812 shows: "The Earl of Lauderdale sharpened [Lord] Byron's thesis [debating the renewed protest of the Luddites in England] that the misled workers were acting against their own interests: "Nothing could be more certain than the fact that every improvement in machinery contributed to the improvement in the condition of persons manufacturing the machines, there being in a very short time after such improvements were introduced a greater demand for labour than ever before" (cited in Leontief, 1982: 188).

Most of the time these predictions were wrong. One can only speculate at this point why each and every one of the predictions turned out to be false and whether a social mechanism akin to the self-defeating hypothesis might have been at work. Nevertheless, despite these disappointments, expectations about the future of work remain a central element of macroeconomic thinking, economic activity and political action. And, as is worth repeating, most of the scholarly work pertains to developments in Europe and North America.[60]

In the decade of the 1950s, 1960s and later, and despite historically unprecedented low levels of unemployment and rapidly rising standards of living, discussions about the future of work were by no means muted.[61] The overall headline of the intense debate among economists, politicians, employers and labor unions in a number of industrialized countries was "automation," the "automation revolution" and technological advances such as solid-state electronics.[62]

The consensus at the time was that "automation's most important impact will not be on employment but on the qualifications and functions of employees ...Automation will upgrade the semi-skilled machine operator of today into a highly skilled and knowledgeable technician—multiplying his income" (Drucker, 1955a: 44).

Peter Drucker's optimistic outlook issued in United States is shared at about the same time by Helmut Schelsky in Germany. Schelsky offers the following observation: "automation will actually create more jobs, both in the same factories and companies and above all because of the increasing needs and consumption opportunities in other industries and professions" or "at least with the current slow and continuous introduction of automation the current labor shortages that exist in all highly developed industrial societies, automation could alleviate this concern" (Schelsky, [1957] 1995: 109). If we limit out analysis to that of the professional observers, the points of view offered by their optimistic outlook over many decades has only changed insignificantly to this day.

The changes in the world of work underway or pending especially in term of the loss of work can also be an occasion to offer an upbeat assessment of the changes: Ulrich Beck's ([1999] 2000: 178–179) conviction at the turn of the century, for instance that the "work society is drawing to a close, as people are more and more replaced by smart technology" does not deserve to be called a catastrophe. His answer is a definite no. For "only when all passive toil at machines has been successfully done away with, will human creativity be free to answer in detail the great questions of the second modernity (such as: "how will democracy be possible after the full-employment society" (Beck, [1999] 2000: 5) Rising unemployment can no longer be explained as the result of cyclical economic crises but is due "rather to the successes of technologically advanced capitalism" (Beck, [1999] 2000: 2). Beck's counter-model to the decline of the work society is based not upon additional leisure but upon political freedom. The counter-model is a "multi-activity society in which housework, family work, club work and voluntary work are prized alongside paid work and returned to the centre of public and political life" (Beck, [1999] 2000: 125). The outcome of the vanishing work society Beck hopes of a new political society that rests on civil labor. Will robots indeed lead us into a better economic and political future?

## Will Robots Set Us Free?

But we need to turn our attention in response to this set of questions to the views of the workers also and hence those directly effected in the future by robots and automation.[63] Are robots bringing prosperity to everyone? Can we even expect that robots will set us free? Karl Marx expected as much. In his *Grundrisse* (Marx, [1939–1941] 1973) 1858), he sketched a future in which technology liberates the worker from the drudgery of work. The idleness full automation would allow enabled the worker to pursue and perfect self-development in her or his chosen activities in science, sport, and arts. In his *Eros and Civilization*, Herbert Marcuse (1955) joins Marx a century later in taken up the promise that robots may set us free. Marcuse (1955: 129) concludes: "The very progress of civilization under the performance principle has attained a level of productivity at which the social demands upon instinctual energy to be spent in alienated labor could be considerably reduced." None of the credible contemporary observers of the transformation of work from economics to any of the other social sciences has seconded Marcuse's hopes that robots will emancipate the worker from labor, change the relations of production or at least save us time. The central concern of professional observers continues to be much more conventional, namely how scary might automation be? Corporate leaders are less inclined to be concerned about the loss of jobs. Some managers and heads of large corporations find the idea of robots displacing humans attractive, after all robots can be expected to be less contentious and demanding about work conditions and pay. For example, President Donald Trump's brief pick for Secretary of Labor, Andy Puzder who withdrew his nomination for the position has said that, in some ways, robots made better employees than people: "They're always polite, they always upsell, they never take a vacation, they never show up late, there's never a slip-and-fall, or an age, sex, or race discrimination case."[64]

We cannot expect that the perceptions and expectation of the workers converge with those of the professional observers or managers of possible changes in the world of work. One of the few recent studies that attempt to do just that is based on an analysis of the findings of a Eurobarometer poll "*Public Attitudes toward Robots*" covering more than 11,000 respondents in 20 European countries (Dekker, Salomons and van der Waal, 2017). The authors assume that the preeminent perception to robots and automation in the work place is fear, among possibly other motives, especially among workers who anticipate that the technological changes will affect their economic standing, that is, that workers display fear based on attitudes of self-interest. It is of course not unknown that self-interests deceive.

Dekker, Salomons and van der Waal (2017: 539) attempt to discover which members of the labor force are most fearful. Not surprisingly, the purely descriptive data of the study show that "those (a) in economic positions that are more likely to be negatively affected by robotics are more likely to be fearful of robots at work, along with, to some extent, those living in countries (b) with adverse economic conditions and (c) where employees are less protected from market forces." More concretely, the authors report that concern about robots among "managers, professionals and the highly educated—who hold positions in the labor market that are unlikely to be affected negatively by the introduction of robotics—fear robots at work less than manual and white-collar workers and the less well educated" (Dekker, Salomons and van der Waal, 2017: 555).

Frequently the conclusion about the influence of so-called technical progress on the world of work remains upbeat: „The basic fact is that technology eliminates jobs, not work" (Bowen, 1966: 9).[65] What definitely will change is therefore the nature of work and the associated earnings. It is important therefore to focus on tasks and skills not on jobs or occupational titles. As the widely discussed 2014 study, *The Second Machine Age* by Erik Brynjolfsson and Andrew McAfee (2014: 11) maintains, arguing along the same lines, "there's never been a worse time to be a worker with only 'ordinary' skills and abilities to offer, because computers, robots, and other digital technologies are acquiring these skills and abilities at an extraordinary rate." It follows of course that "technological progress is going to leave behind some people, perhaps even a lot of people, as it races ahead" (Brynjolfsson and McAfee, 2014: 11). Over a longer period, as David Autor (2014: 4) maintains, "the past two centuries of automation and technological progress have not made human labor obsolete: the employment-to-population ratio rose during the 20th century even as women moved from home to market; and although the unemployment rate fluctuates cyclically, there is no apparent long-run increase."

As far as we can see, the main reason for David Autor's (2015a: 5) upbeat conclusion that automation though in the past it substituted for labor and was expected to do so, still does not eliminate the majority of jobs is because automation "*complements* labor, raises output in ways that lead to higher demand for labor and interacts with adjustments in labor supply (our emphasis)." However, manual task-intensive occupational activities are not complemented by technological change or knowledge capacities. Summing up his position, David Autor (2015: 5) emphasizes, "even expert commentators tend to overstate the extent of machine substitution for human labor and ignore the strong complementarities between automation and labor that increase productivity, raise earnings, and augment demand for labor."

Past trends cannot necessarily represent a robust guide to future developments. The anticipated triumph of automatization and digitalization of work processes stir growing concerns regarding the scope of work needed in society. Yuval Noah Harari (2016: 370) summarizes the perils of an uncertain future of the working environment as follows: "The most important question in twenty-first century economics may well be what to do with all the superfluous people. What will conscious human do one we have highly intelligent non-conscious algorithms that can do almost everything better?"

In 1982, Wassily Leontief predicted that man's role in production would change just as dramatically as the role horses did who had lost their importance for agriculture when they were replaced by tractors. With the advent of solid-state electronics, according to Leontief's (1982: 188) expectation, "machines . . . take over the functions of the human nervous system not only on production but in the service industries as well. . . . The relation between man and machine is being radically transformed."

But what impact will the radical transformation brought about by contemporary technological change have on employment and perhaps wages? Why did employment numbers not sink despite uncountable work-saving discoveries and the rapid advancement of the automatization of work? Will there be *involuntary technological unemployment* in the future?[66] Employment and unemployment are not merely a function of technological change. The demand for work, population growth, the volume of investments, interest rates, regulations, trade unions, the financial sector, foreign trade and so on all have their separate or relational impact on employment. It is very difficult to factor out the contribution of any one of the multiple factors that influence employment rates.

The role of labor "from time immemorial" has been the principle factor in the production process. However, "there are reasons to believe human labor will not retain this status in the future" (Leontief, 1982: 190). The massive reduction in the average annual hours of work between the mid-19th century and today[67] must be considered to represent a huge displacement of workers without any workers necessarily losing their job. During the same time period, the real wages discounted by inflation increased by a large margin.

Leontief is prepared to cautiously appraise the effect of technological change on employment. In the past, workers have been able to absorb potential technological unemployment by voluntarily reducing the average number of hours worked. Because of the "greatly expanded opportunities [in the eighties] to replace labor by increasingly sophisticated technology it *appears* that the impersonal forces of the market no longer favor that possibility" (Leontief, 1982: 192; our emphasis).[68] History in different societies shows, however, that different responses by governments, businesses and union to technological change have resulted in distinct outcomes for their employment regimes (also Leontief, 1952: 150). The circumstances that happen to be at work decide about the fate of labor.

Some 40 years later we still encounter a rather similar as well as optimistic and yet cautious conclusion about the technological transformations of the world of work and the consequences for the volume of employment. A European report on robotics entitled "Robotics 2020"[69] offers such an upbeat perspective on the deployment of robots in the world of work. In the executive summary of the report we encounter the following observation:

> Robotics Technology will become dominant in the coming decade. It will influence every aspect of work and home. Robotics has the potential to

Average Annual Hours Actually Worked (total emloyment)

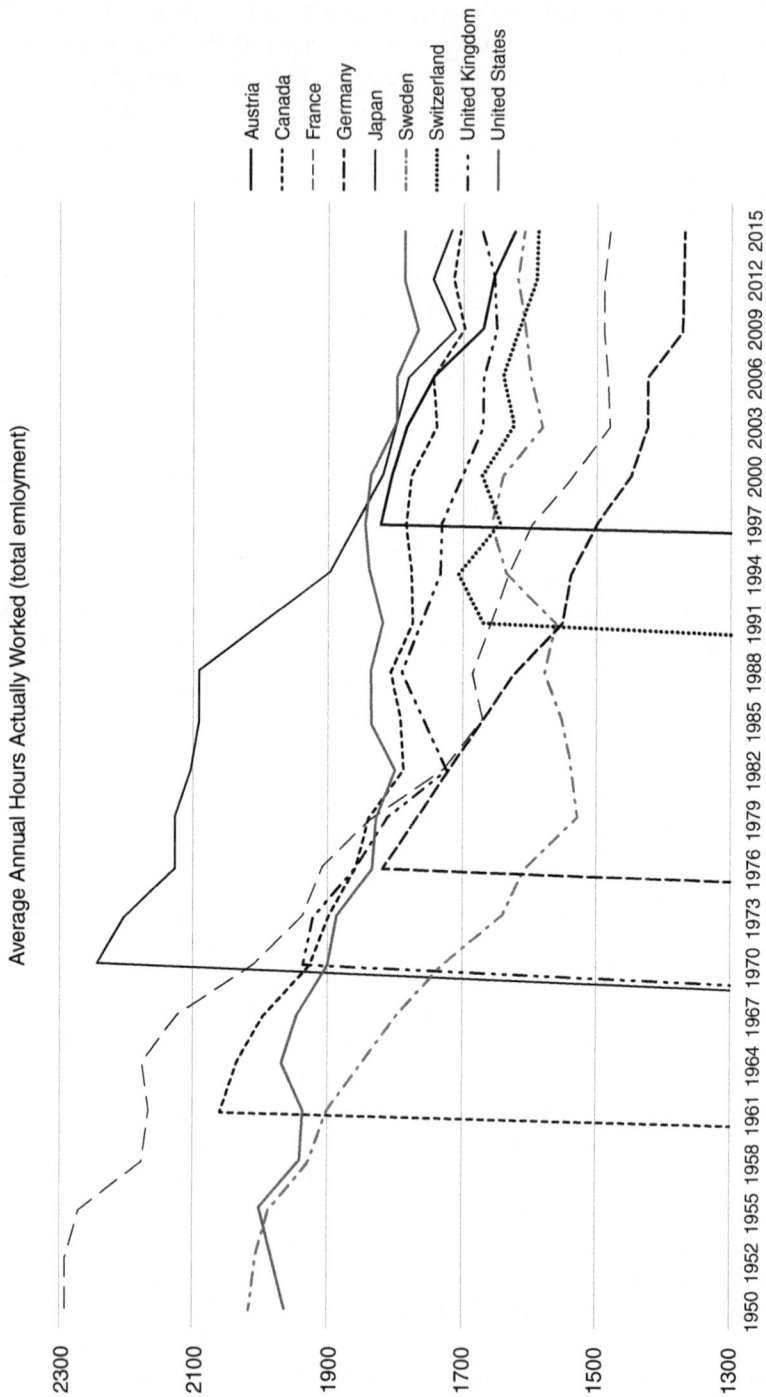

Austria
Canada
France
Germany
Japan
Sweden
Switzerland
United Kingdom
United States

2300

2100

1900

1700

1500

1300

1950 1952 1955 1958 1961 1964 1967 1970 1973 1976 1979 1982 1985 1988 1991 1994 1997 2000 2003 2006 2009 2012 2015

**FIGURE 4.4**   Average Annual Hours Worked

*Source:* OECD, 2017, "Hours Worked: Average annual hours actually worked," OECD Employment and Labour Market Statistics (database)

transform lives and work practices, raise efficiency and safety levels, provide enhanced levels of service and *create jobs*. Its impact will grow over time as will the interaction between robots and people.

*(emphasis added)*

Manuel Castells ([1996] 2000: 281–282) concludes in his assessment of labor related social developments that "institutions and social organizations of work seem to play a greater role than technology in inducing job creation or destruction." If technology as such does not play a causal role in the reduction of existing or in formation of new work, it nonetheless "profoundly transforms the nature of work and the organization of production" and enhances for instance the individualization of the work process.

While the terminology has somewhat shifted since the last part of the 20th century, no noticeable change has occurred in the nature of the concerns and contested predictions about the future of work (see for example the dystopia written by Jeremy Rifkin (1995) as "The End of Work"). Today the changes in the world of work are evoked and analyzed primarily in terms of the "uprising of robots" (for example, Drutman and Mounk, 2016). In an interview with the German weekly *Der Spiegel*, the American economist Andrew McAfee says there is evidence "that we will yet live to see a science fiction world come true where the economy is largely automatized and many jobs have been taken over by a host of robots."[70]

What exactly is meant by the reference to robots in the working world? In general what is referred to are physical devices, for example, a machine run by a computer and/or intangible programs (including the collaboration between humans and robots) that are used to carry out the activities, to take over work processes, or to achieve goals which were formerly directly, or indirectly the activities of the working person.[71] These include self-propelled trucks or locomotives, trades without salespersons, diagnoses without specialists, security services without security forces, school lessons and lectures without teachers or professors, care without nurses and hospital rooms without nurses, supplies without delivery personnel, therapy without therapists, etc.[72] In other words, a robot does not necessarily, as many seem to imagine, come with the likeness of a human being.

The common conclusion of the earlier debates and predictions revolving around the idea of automation was still optimistic. There are now more frequently, as we have indicated, forecasts of an overall decline in the volume of socially necessary labor brought about by productivity gains. Although in February 0f 2017, the *New York Times* for example published an editorial titled "No, robots aren't killing the American dream,"[73] this upbeat prediction is in the end anything but optimistic about the future of work. The apparent conclusion of the newspaper is not supported by much more direct and pessimistic predictions. For instance, the head of the International Monetary Fund, Christine Lagarde, maintains that the economic pains experienced in some countries are not due to globalization, but instead to the rise of robots eliminating jobs. Former President Barack Obama warned at about the same time that the "next wave of economic dislocations won't come from overseas. It will come from the relentless pace of automation that makes a lot of good middle-class jobs obsolete."[74]

What makes the *New York Times* editorial a part of the pessimistic assessment of the impact of robots in the workplace is their conclusion that—as yet unanticipated technological breakthroughs may come at any time—"the problem with automation isn't robots; it's politicians, who have failed for decades to support policies that the workers share the wealth from technology-let growth." In recent decades, gains from productivity improvements and improving technology have not benefitted those remaining in the work force, let alone those who became unemployed.

One of the most important unresolved problems is therefore that neither collective bargaining nor statutory compensation of individual persons who lose their jobs and thus suffer significant economic disturbances is on the policy agenda in most countries. Nor are reflections about the political impact of a sustained loss of jobs. Generous compensation may allow an occupational reboot although past experiences in this regard does not give rise to optimism. But who pays for the transition costs and the shortfall of tax revenue? One idea to compensate for the loss of tax revenue as the result of the displacement of workers by robots is floated by a member of the European Parliament in 2016, endorsed by Bill Gates and supported by Robert Shiller (2017),[75] who suggest to tax robots. When robots replace workers, the company should incur taxes equivalent to that worker's income taxes. Right now, Gates notes, "the human worker who does, say, $50,000 worth of work in a factory, that income is taxed and you get income tax, social security tax, all those things. If a robot comes in to do the same thing, you'd think that we'd tax the robot at a similar level."[76] But even if there might be widespread political agreement about the desirability of a tax on robots in the future, the implementation of a *new* tax would face enormous formal (e.g. constitutional) and political push back let alone the systemic issues (given the nature of tax systems in different countries) and the attendant socio-economic consequences (for instance, the impact of societal inequality, see Guerreiro, Rebolo, and Teles, 2017). More generally, as David Autor (2015a: 8, 28) cautiously emphasizes, "rapid automation may create distributional challenges that invite a broad policy response. . . . If machines were in fact to make human labor superfluous, we would have vast aggregate wealth but a serious challenge in determining who owns it and how to share it."

A recurrent claim in the discussions conducted in the last decades about the effects of automation or the increasing number of robots in production plants and offices is that such a transformation of the means of production cannot leave the price of labor unaffected. In short: once the demand for work largely exceeds the supply, the price of work will fall massively. The society will be rigidly divided into two parts: on the one hand those who are employed, on the other the presumably larger group of the unemployed. This, then, might also result in a number of drastic political consequences due to increasing class antagonisms in the world of work[77] as well as in higher and more widespread social inequality (see also Machin and Stehr, 2016). The polarization of incomes in the wake of technological change is being documented in a number of studies. Slow wage growth can be observed for those in low-skill jobs while the incomes for abstract task-intensive labor such a managerial, professional and technical positions are rising (cf. Autor, 2015a: 15–19).

The polarization of society in relation to the labor market can, however, also be described as a division of the skills and competencies demanded by the labor market, in particular as a shift in the relation of the importance of different qualifications. A large number of empirical studies confirm the polarizing transformation of the labor markets on the basis of occupational skills (cf. Autor, Dorn and Hansen, 2015; Goos, Manning and Salomons, 2014; Goos and Manning, 2007).

The digitalization and automation of work processes strengthens the demand for competences, which are complementary to the growing technologization of the working world. The standard definitions of these complementary abilities are so-called "higher skills," as opposed to routine abilities which means "amplifying the comparative advantage of workers in supplying problem-solving skills, adaptability, and creativity" (Autor, 2015a: 5) or as we have defined it as knowledge skills. The result of this shift in demand is of course that the price of complementary competencies for digitization and automation is increasing.

Automation is described as *technological* progress, while technological progress manifests itself in the form of automation. The terms are obviously equivalent. But this also implies that discussions and debates about the future of work rarely distinguish between scientific and technical advances and their practical implementation, or between innovation and diffusion (as in the case of Joseph Schumpeter).

The choice of this ambivalent designation for the problem at hand reflects the current and increasingly widespread resignation among observers concerning the fact that it is exceedingly difficult to delimit and classify, by whatever criteria, the specific effects technological changes will have on the economy. On the other hand, observers used to be generally optimistic that release and compensation would balance each other out.[78]

If technological changes have the effect of decreasing the volume of available work it becomes fairly easy, the authors argue, to calculate the requisite rate of growth of the domestic product (or other compensatory measures such as a reduction of the hours worked) in order to determine exactly when the gain in jobs would equal the loss of work.[79] At least in this respect, trust in the self-healing capacity of the economic order is undiminished. The typical conclusion of most of these studies is that while automation and other technological changes are bound to generate a decline in the amount of work—with declines and gains in productivity varying considerably throughout the industrial sector of the economy—, the decisive factors for estimating their overall impact on the amount of available work are the volume of production and, to a lesser extent, the hours worked.[80]

In short, discussions about the consequences of automation go along with the firm conviction that growth and employment move in a strictly parallel manner. Economic expansion coincides with a shortage in the supply of labor, while a slump has exactly the opposite impact and results in a growing surplus of individuals unable to find work.

The conviction that employment levels are dependent on economic cycles is not a figment of the imagination of economic observers but is also reflected in the macro-economic data of the time. The widespread optimism about the employment effects of technological changes in the sixties and well into the eighties was based on the observation that overall employment was not growing despite considerable productivity gains particularly in industry: "During the 1980s most technology employment analyses focused on the complexity of the many interactions linking the introduction of new technologies, changes in work organisation, skill mismatches and sectoral unemployment" (Soete, 1996: 384 cited in Stehr 2002: 107).

Ultimately, technological changes were supposed to result in higher incomes, more employment opportunities and lower numbers of hours worked, despite the pains of structural adjustments. After all, as history shows, all technological advances will displace workers but ultimately lead to new and better employment. In light of new technological changes, the decisive question is of course: will these dynamics of the labor market recur (cf. Mokyr, Vickers and Ziebarth, 2015)? What would appear to be obvious is that the kind of work that may be displaced in the future is not the kind or work that was displaced in the past.

In the last few years, however, a novel discussion about labor-supplanting technologies in the context of the ongoing globalization of economic transactions has emerged. The recent discussion about the growing deployment of different types of *robots* as well as the *digitalization* of tasks performed in work settings not only in production but also in the services sector, for instance in medicine, police work, finance[81] or the legal system, sectors that up to now were supposed to be impervious to labor-saving technological developments, presents a different picture of what this might mean for labor and for the workforce needed if there is to be no overall loss in turnovers.

It is also conceivable that automation will put an end to many low-skilled jobs with repetitive work processes and/or frugal pay such as those, for instance, in the fast-food industry. The impact of robots, for example, industrial robots on total employment or the share of low-skilled workers' employment remains a highly contentious field of research. Based on a broad panel study of robot adaptation across 17 developed countries from 1993–2007, Georg Graetz and Guy Michaels (2015) estimate that robots do not significantly reduce total employment but did reduce the share of low-skilled workers as a part of the aggregate employment. In other terms, Graetz and Michaels find no evidence that the rising exposure to robots becomes a major work killer. Wolfgang Dauth and his colleagues (2017) referring to the deployment of robots in the German manufacturing sector between 1994–2014 discover similar trends and note that robots do not raise wages. The use of robots has a heterogeneous effect for different workers. High-skilled employees gain income while medium-skilled workers experience a negative impact on their wages. The overall share of labor income declines as a result.

Some even speak of the end of work in this context. Would that be the ultimate future paradise, or the belated collapse of capitalism predicted by Karl Marx? And will it also mean an end of the value of work?[82] What kind of society would be a society without paid work for the vast majority of the adult population aspiring to work for the purpose of not only to gain an income but for self-fulfillment for example?

Carl Frey and Michael Osborne (2013: 44–45) propose a model of the future world of work focusing on the job characteristics of 702 *occupations* rather than single job-tasks that are likely to be non-sustainable. About 47 percent of all occupations in the United States are at high risk. The main concern of this model, however, is still with the effects that computerization and the first use of robots have on work activities:

> Our model predicts that most workers in transportation and logistics occupations, together with the bulk of office and administrative support workers, and labour in production occupations, are at risk. These findings are consistent with recent technological developments documented in the literature. More surprisingly, we find that a substantial share of employment in service occupations [low-skill and low-wage], where most US job growth has occurred over the past decades, are highly susceptible to computerization.

One of the most widely cited and discussed studies on the impact of robots on the world of work is Erik Brynjolfsson and Andrew McAfee (2014: 39) approach. Erik Brynjolfsson and Andrew McAfee (2014: 39) postulate that the risk of unemployment induced by technological developments is real, and propose a list of winners vs. losers with respect to technological changes: "(1) high-skilled vs. low skilled workers, (2) superstars vs. everyone else, and (3) capital vs. labor." Brynjolfsson and McAfee's categories partially overlap. Nor are they new. The incomes of employees with better education and training have been improving for decades. This is true also for the stratum of the most privileged (superstars) or for individuals and families whose income is derived from capital gains. Whether a different approach stressing the possibility of automating or digitalizing *specific job-tasks and abilities* rather than occupations might lead to different estimates of the shrinkage of the socially necessary labor still have to be examined in detail (cf. Autor, 2015a; Arntz, Gregory and Zierahn, 2016).

The critique of the anticipated developments of the world of work by Erik Brynjolfsson and Andrew McAfee for example is based on the observation that the authors not only have failed to learn from the failures of previous prognoses about technological unemployment but misinterpret the history of technology. At

| 2016 | 2026 | 2036 | 2046 | 2056 | 2066 | 2076 |
|------|------|------|------|------|------|------|

- Beat humans in new levels of Angry Birds
- Master poker enough to win World Series of Poker
- Fold laundry
- Transcribe speech
- Assemble any LEGO
- Outperform Atari game testers on all games
- Read text aloud
- Write a high school essay
- Drive a truck
- Generate a Top 40 pop song
- Beat the fastest human in a 5K race
- Translate a new language with Rosetta Stone
- Retail salesperson
- Write a NYTimes Best Seller
- Perform surgery
- Research math
- All human tasks

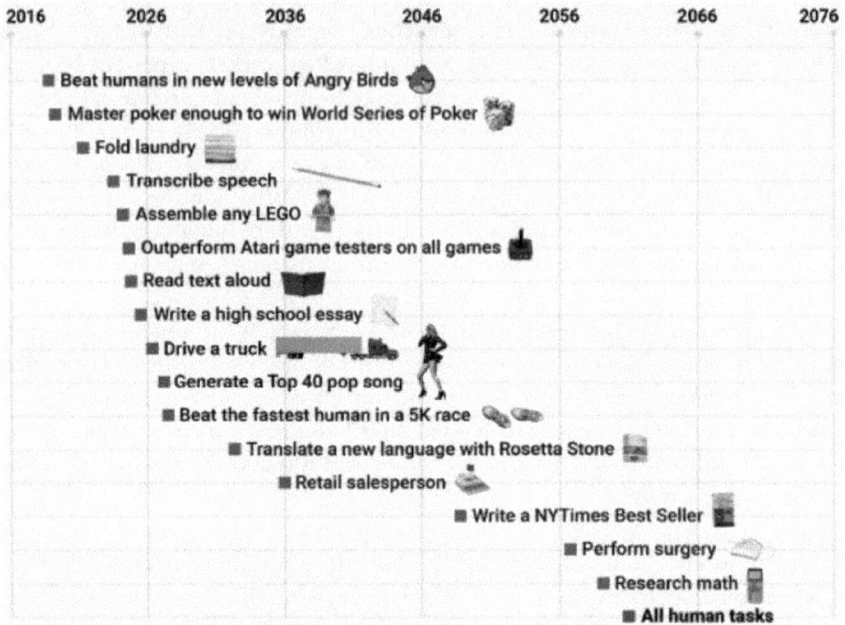

**FIGURE 4.5**  When Jobs/Tasks Will Be Taken Over by Machines

*Source:* Grace et al. (2017)

the turn of the 19th to the 20th century, significant technical innovations, incomparable to the present age, were made and commercialized. These inventions did not lead to massive unemployment and hence, why should less dramatic changes such as digitalization today produce significant technological unemployment? The opposite assertion simply amounts to unnecessary fatalism (cf. Hirschi, 2017).

In any case, one can only soberly conclude with Frey and Osborne (2013: 45): "for workers to win the race, they will have to acquire *creative and social skills*" (our emphasis; see also Davenport and Kirby, 2016: 225–251). The jobs that are and will be displaced, for example in the mining industry, are irreversibly lost. Political efforts to reverse the trend are unlikely to succeed. As a recent survey of the *New York Times* concludes: "the coal industry has been replacing workers with machines and explosives . . . no one—including Mr. Trump—can bring them all back."[83] The much more likely scenario will be that the trend of a loss of jobs in the mining industry will persist in the next decade or more.

A report issued by McKinsey takes a different approach to anticipating the range of jobs that will be affected by the introduction of "automation technologies." The point of departure for the McKinsey Report (Chui, Manyika and Miremadi, 2016) is not an estimate of the jobs that will or will not be replaced. Instead, the report focuses on the *work activities* of jobs and emphasizes that very few occupations will be eliminated *entirely* by robots in the next decade: "it will affect portions of almost all jobs to a greater or lesser degree, depending on the type of work they entail."

A useful example illustrating that robots or artificial intelligence will not displace entire job categories, for example the job of the translator, would recognize that the shift brought about by robotization, artificial intelligence and technological progress will indeed displace many of occupational task heretofore typical of the labor of a translator but will or cannot not eliminate the work of translation carried out by humans entirely. The tasks typical of the work of a translator in the future will shift toward vetting of translations carried out by translation software. We will likely need fewer conventional translators but more translators with supplemental skills that cannot be substituted by automation. The net result could well be a significant reduction in the numbers of translators and a shift of the task translators performed toward "authors" with the assistance of translation software. The economic value of the translators of the tasks (the translation of translations) that remain the purview of the translators will necessarily increase.[84]

An additional analysis looking toward the future and focusing on workplace sectors in the world of employment published in March of 2017 by PwC UK[85] concludes that the "analysis suggests that around 30% of UK jobs could potentially be at high risk of automation by the early 2030s, lower than the US (38%) or Germany (35%), but higher than Japan (21%). The risks appear highest in sectors such as transportation and storage (56%), manufacturing (46%) and wholesale and retail (44%), but lower in sectors like health and social work (17%)." However, the

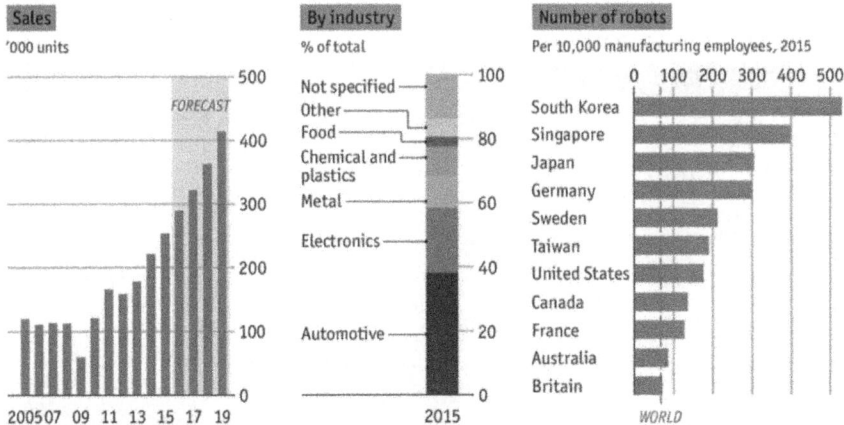

**FIGURE 4.6**   The Growth of Industrial Robots

*Source: The Economist,* March 27, 2017

same report repeats the optimistic idea that actual job losses through automation may eventually be negligible:

> new automation technologies will both create some totally new jobs in the digital technology area and, through productivity gains, generate additional wealth and spending that will support additional jobs of existing kinds, primarily in services sectors that are less easy to automate. The net long-term impact of automation on total UK employment could therefore be either positive or negative. Average pre-tax incomes should rise due to the productivity gains, but these benefits may not be evenly spread across income groups.

For its examination of the impact of automation, the report by McKinsey attempts to ascertain more meaningfully whether specific work activities can be carried out by "demonstrated technologies" and, hence, whether automation is

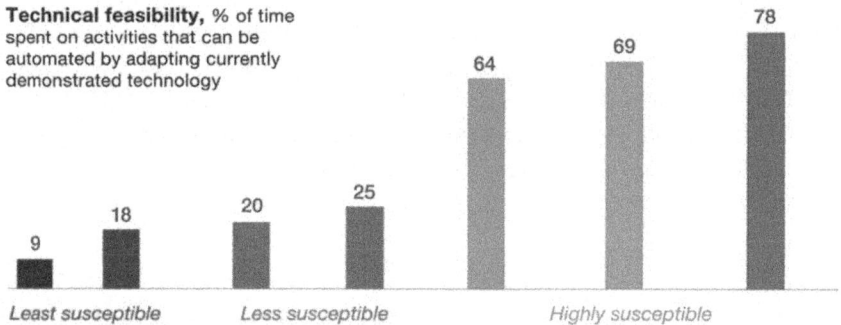

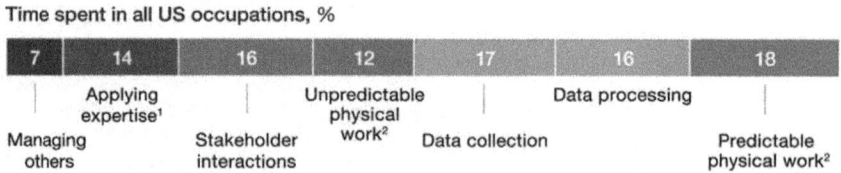

**Technical feasibility,** % of time spent on activities that can be automated by adapting currently demonstrated technology

*Least susceptible*     *Less susceptible*     *Highly susceptible*

**Time spent in all US occupations, %**

| 7 | 14 | 16 | 12 | 17 | 16 | 18 |
|---|----|----|----|----|----|----|

Managing others | Applying expertise[1] | Stakeholder interactions | Unpredictable physical work[2] | Data collection | Data processing | Predictable physical work[2]

In practice, automation will depend on more than just technical feasibility. Five factors are involved: technical feasibility; costs to automate; the relative scarcity, skills, and cost of workers who might otherwise do the activity; benefits (eg, superior performance) of automation beyond labor-cost substitution; and regulatory and social-acceptance considerations.

[1]Applying expertise to decision making, planning, and creative tasks.
[2]Unpredictable physical work (physical activities and the operation of machinery) is performed in unpredictable environments, while in predictable physical work, the environments are predictable.

**FIGURE 4.7**   Technical Feasibility, % of Time Spent on Activities That Can Be Automated by Adapting Currently Demonstrated Technology

*Source:* Chui, Manyika and Miremadi (2016)

technically feasible. Every job involves multiple activities, some of which are more likely to be displaced by technology. The degree to which occupations are likely to be affected varies by the extent to which their work activities involve routinized activities such as collecting or processing data or, on the other hand, interacting with customers.[86] On this basis, the report arrives at an overall estimate of the work hours that are likely to be replaced in the sector examined.

But the degree to which work activities can be replaced by technology is but one aspect:

> A second factor to consider is the cost of developing and deploying both the hardware and the software for automation. The cost of labor and related supply-and-demand dynamics represent a third factor: if workers are in abundant supply and significantly less expensive than automation, this could be a decisive argument against it. A fourth factor to consider is the benefits beyond labor substitution, including higher levels of output, better quality, and fewer errors. These are often larger than those of reducing labor costs. Regulatory and social-acceptance issues, such as the degree to which machines are acceptable in any particular setting, must also be weighed.
>
> *(Chui, Manyika and Miremadi, 2016)*

In other words, whether or not robots will displace jobs and work activities, on the one hand, and create new ones, on the other, will depend on the interplay between these factors. But the conclusion that the evolution of robotics and other forms of automation (especially digitalization, artificial intelligence, biology, nanotechnology) could lead to the creation of a new class, the class of the "useless" is none the less a speculative idea that is gaining traction.[87] In any event, the relation between automation and the labor market remains far from straightforward. The development of technology is both impossible to grasp, let alone predict with any reliability and at times occurs of course in leaps and bounds, that is, with tipping points. Exponential advances in technology could well make even the most cautious predictions look trivial (cf. Autor, 2015a; Pratt, 2015). For now, the task for example still remains to make machine learning more robust and more intelligent.

However, studies continue to be produced that attempt to shed light onto this difficult and essentially contested issue of the impact of robots and other technical changes on the nature of work and the volume of necessary work. A recent publication of the National Bureau of Economic Research (Acemoglu and Restrepo, 2017) estimates, for example, for every additional robot deployed by American industry 5.6 jobs are lost. An Austrian (Nagl, Titelbach and Valkova, 2017) study predicts that "digitalization" of the world of work will affect about nine percent of the work force. But what one can say with certainty is that the future impact of automation on employment remains uncertain.

What impact future technical developments will have on the price of labor remains controversial as well. This statement also applies to the consequences of past technical developments on the price of labor. Who can benefit from the technical developments and which work forms are more likely to be part of the losers? How exactly is the price of labor affected by technical changes (see Acemoglu, 2002, Acemoglu and Autor, 2011)? Any evidence-based assertion in response to these questions is virtually impossible to arrive at present. However, were technical developments produce particular challenges and require scare skills for certain occupations, that is knowledge skills in particular, are likely to benefit the most financially (see Stockey, 2016: 34).[88]

The identical statement may be formulated concerning the impact of globalization on the price of labor. A meta-analysis of the relevant literature on this issue compiled by Elhanan Helpman (2016: 39) concludes that the impact of globalization on the price of labor is quite low:

> A major conclusion from my review of the literature is that the prevalent view that globalization is primarily responsible for the large increase in the inequality of labor compensation has no basis in the evidence. Yes, globalization impacted the wages of different types of workers to different degrees, and yes, it contributed to an increase in the wages of skilled relative to unskilled worker through multiple channels. Yet, in sum, all these effects explain only a fraction of the rise in wage inequality in rich and poor countries alike.

The rise of the robots has at the present time not led to an overall employment displacement in the economies of the developed world given its context of increasing labor shortage (cf. Soete, 2018: 41). Even if robots lead to job displacement the frequent upbeat assumption is that it will be short term. Over longer periods of time, as the report on *The Future of Work, Good Jobs for All* (Eichhorst et al., 2018) paradigmatically suggests "new technologies lead to the creation of new sectors, new products and new jobs. Policies to accelerate this process will reduce the impact of automation and globalization on the life of workers and their families" (as noted by Alarcon, [2018: 2] in a comment on the Report).

Our attention now turns more specifically to the question of material and moral components of wages and income. The assumption would be that moral compensation or non-wage attributes of the price of labor varies substantially throughout the work force, demographic groups such a gender, race or education as well as historical times. Moreover, the moral attributes of wages should have a significant impact in aspiring to choose a particular job and the degree of satisfaction with a particular job.

## Material and Moral Compensation

> [For the worker:] his so-called necessary requirements, as also the manner in which they are satisfied are themselves products of history, and depend

therefore to a great extent on the level of civilization attained by a country; in particular they depend on the conditions in which, and consequently on the habits and expectations with which the class of free workers has been formed. In contrast, therefore, with the case of other commodities, the determination of the value of labour-power contains a historical and moral element

—*Karl Marx ([1890] 1976: 185*

If one assumes with David Ricardo's "iron law of wages" ([1817] 1911: 57) that—given a rigid volume of work necessary to be carried out in a society—the price of labor is controlled by the supply of labor, then the price of labor will in the long run fall to the subsistence minimum: "In the natural advance of society, the wages of labour will have a tendency to fall, as far as they are regulated by supply." Reaching Ricardo's floor price of labor—called the iron law of wages by Ferdinand Lassalle—is, moreover, a desirable outcome; thus, "like all other contracts wages should be left to the fair and free competition of the market, and should never be controlled by the interference of the legislature."

Thomas Hobbes ([1651] 1985: 183), in contrast to David Ricardo, offers another, not purely economic justification for a largely *identical* wage level for all employees. In his *Leviathan*, he draws attention to the essential equality and equal worth of all humans:

> Nature hath made men so equal, in the faculties of the body, and mind; as that though there be found one man sometimes manifestly stronger in body, or of quicker mind than another; yet when all is reckoned together, the difference between man, and man, is not so considerable, as that one man can thereupon claim to himself any benefit, to which another may not pretend as well as he.

Although the renowned slogan "from each according to his ability, to each according to his needs" did not originate with Karl Marx, it has become a popular catchphrase with its usage by Marx in his *Critique of the Gotha Program* (1875). In the context of Marxian political economics, it was a promise associated with the future conditions of "higher communism": since the supply of goods and services would be plentiful and satisfy the needs of the working person while work itself would no longer be onerous but enable the individual to carry out the kinds of tasks that fit his or her abilities the pledge from each according to his ability, to each according to his needs could be realized.[89]

To complete and conclude at this point our brief digression into the history of classical conceptions of the value of labor, a quote from Adam Smith (1776] 2012: 106) points us to another basic dimension of compensation: "A man educated at the expense of much labor and time to any of those employments which require extraordinary dexterity and skill, may be compared to one of those expensive machines."

The conception of the classical political economists about the price of labor suggests that we are dealing with two basic components of the value of work: (1) the subsistence minimum (necessities) or the *material* income and (2) the compensation that recognizes *moral* achievements including of attributes of the group(s) to which the individual belongs. How closely the two components of the price of labor are related is an empirical question. There are trade-offs between material-existential and moral wages. The material component of wages is due to the worker "irrespective of the person concerned." The moral component of wages may extend to wages that are actually *withheld* from the worker or wages that are paid in return for certain skills, attributes, social prestige, accomplishments and the memberships in certain demographic groups. Moral pay that may be withheld may come in the form of a symbolic return for the security and stability of work, its health, the societal utility of the work carried out by the employee or the opportunity to engage regularly in additional qualification.[90]

The quote from *Das Kapital* at the beginning of our section on the material and moral determination of wages indicates that Karl Marx' views transcends the standard definition of wages often attributed him. Our distinction between a moral and a material-existential component of the price of labor resonates partially at least with the conception advanced by Marx and a distinction John Maynard Keynes ([1930] 1963: 365) offers about unique classes of human needs. Keynes, in the context of speculating about the future of the economy suggests that in the long run, say in one hundred years from 1930 (when he offered his prognosis), the standard of life will have progressed immensely. It might even be possible to speak of the ability that mankind "is solving its economic problem."

One obvious objection would be to counter that human needs are really insatiable hence such a forecast cannot but be false or wishful thinking. Keynes response to such skepticism he himself identifies is to differentiate between human needs that can indeed be satisfied completely and that do not tend to increase, therefore. The two classes of needs are those that are absolute in "the sense that we feel them whatever the situation of our fellow human beings may be" and needs that are relative "in the sense that we feel them only if their satisfaction lifted us above, makes us feel superior to, our fellows." The second class of needs may well be insatiable. There may come the time when the absolute needs are satisfied and that we "prefer to devote our further energies to non-economic purposes."

It is evident that there are commonalities between our conception of the moral and the material component of wages and absolute and relative needs as defined by Keynes. The likelihood that the material component of earnings may reach a plateau (may be satiated) cannot be rejected out of hand. However, the material component of wages is not absolute or a-historical but evolves, is socially constructed and differs from period to period and for different social strata. In general, however, the proportion of the total income spent on material-existential necessities in relation to the total income declines with rising incomes. This relation is known as Engel's (1857) law: consumers spend a smaller share of their budget on material necessities as their wages improve. Engel's law leaves open the question what could be responsible for the rise in the wages of workers? Is it for example technological change?

John Maynard Keynes description of relative needs also has an affinity to our notion of moral earnings. But contractual and noncontractual moral income is not merely driven by the desire to enhance one's (that is, individual) social standing. Moral compensation has strong collective attributes, for example, compensation that pertains to gender, education, social class or migratory status and leads to collective or even legal efforts that employers should recognize such claims. Moral compensation embodies noneconomic as well as economic characteristics and is a function of the institutional context of employment.

Moreover, the concern with and interest in moral income is not only confined to employment conditions but extends well beyond the boundaries of work into many regions of society. The moral-political component of wages has both performance-focused and equitable distribution-focused properties. The material component of wages can never compensate for the moral component. The moral part of wages has strong emotional properties that a purely economic perspective on the value of work is unable to account for. Individuals and collectivities of workers—assuming there is a choice -are to varying degrees prepared to sacrifice higher wages for better working conditions.

Karl Marx's notion that labor produces all the wealth but that a portion of this worker produced wealth is withheld from him leads to the conclusion that actual wages lack a significant component, namely the wealth-creating part that becomes profit for the owner of capital.[91] In short, Marx's theory of the exploitation of the worker provides a perspective on the unequal redistribution of income. Probably, it would be fair to suggest what is within the Marxian perspective withheld is what we call the moral component of compensation of the worker.

In so far as wages and income in modern societies always come with both a moral and a material component—the former being often larger than the latter—the price of labor in the end is a political price. The principle of determining the value of wages by limiting them to their natural function as classical economists including of course Marx still held, does not apply to the modern economy. Unlike what André Gorz ([2003] 2010: 39) still advocates that the value of the commodity of labor is equivalent to the value of the commodities a worker may get in exchange for it, that is, equivalent to the "purchasing power" of the wages he needs to ensure the reproduction of his capability to work, simply does not apply in advanced economic systems.

The distinction between the material and the moral components of the value of labor resonates, if in a limited fashion, with attempts to identify two classes of producers in modern society, but they are not intended to reconstitute the classical concept of social classes and its original social context. Helmut Schelsky's (1975: 179) differentiation between "productive" and "non-productive labor" is a case in point. One could suggest that the so- called class of productive laborers is responsible for the provision of material goods and services in a society while the non-productive class provides for the foundation of the moral concepts and meaning that, in turn, is mobilized to generate and justify systems of moral compensation.

In the tradition of both Karl Marx and Thorstein Veblen, the productive class is concerned with the fabrication of material goods for the sustainment and enhancement of life, including services and other facilities designed to make life easier at the material level, whereas the "opposite class" can in a first step only be defined in purely negative terms. The opposite class is not concerned with the fabrication of material goods for the sustainment and enhancement of life.

More precisely, the opposite class according to Helmut Schelsky (1975: 180) is primarily concerned with the *production of meaning*: "The producers of meaning represent the unproductive class that, for their part, exploits the producers of goods." Schelsky (1975: 180) qualifies his argument by saying that "information, knowledge, acquired during education and training, and even moral and intellectual beliefs constitute a very important component of the modern form of sustaining and enhancing life and should, thus, be conceived of as 'goods'." The meaning producers seek "to use their functional contributions [to the production of material goods] to gain supremacy over the classes of the producers of goods" (see also Bell, 1973: 148–154).

Helmut Schelsky's differentiation between the social classes is open to criticism on a number of reasons. For instance, the modern production of material goods invariably includes work that requires intellectual skills, making a distinction between "classes" that relies on the skills of their members is more or less artificial. Modern labor has always also relied on special cognitive skills. The purely non-material work that the producers of meaning are supposed to perform requires material resources and means of production, part of which are even constructed and produced by the class of material producers, computers or robots being cases in point. The work-based functions of the production of goods and "meaning" increasingly tend to converge; which, in turn, affects the workers' self-concept and constrains the opportunities to exercise power. Helmut Schelsky does refer to the Marxian conception of class in his definition of the productive class but fails to specify the extent to which this class develops class-consciousness as a result of the conditions of their work.

But how is one to specify concretely the value of the existential component of the price of labor in the sense of a minimum living wage? Multiple approaches to quantify the value of the existential component have been developed over time. We mean to refer prominently to the concept of a minimum wage, the idea of the universal basis income[92] and perhaps the amount of money that is exempt from seizure (in German "*unpfändbares Ezxistenzminimum*").[93] We will concentrate on the idea of the minimum wage that has been instituted in many countries in contrast for example to the universal basic income.

## Minimum Wages

One of the concrete references for the volume of the material compensation of labor may be found in the notion of a minimum wage. A minimum wage refers to the lowest wage that employers may *legally* be forced to pay workers. The common definition of the minimum wage already indicates that the wage in question is a *political price* set by legislation or collective agreement. That minimum wages are a political price is well documented in Figure 4.8. It shows the large differences in the minimum wage not only within countries with dissimilar GDP but also across countries with similar levels of economic well-being. Minimum wages are importantly linked to non-cash compensation such as health insurance that has a significant relevance for the welfare of the individual worker.

The overall impact of the minimum wage in a country on its overall wage structure "is dependent on its level in relation to the existing national wage structure" (Lübker and Schulten, WSI Report, 2018: 5). As a result, we are able to note that "in many countries, the minimum wage is below 50% of the median, a level normally seen as a poverty wage that is not sufficient to allow for a decent standard of life. This includes Germany (46.7%), currently in 18th place in the ranking. When set against the national wage distribution, the German minimum wage continues to represent a very low pay standard" (Lübker and Schulten, 2018: 5). Changes in the minimum wage structure impact the value of the non-cash component of the minimum wage. For example, as Jeffrey Clemens, Kahn and Meer

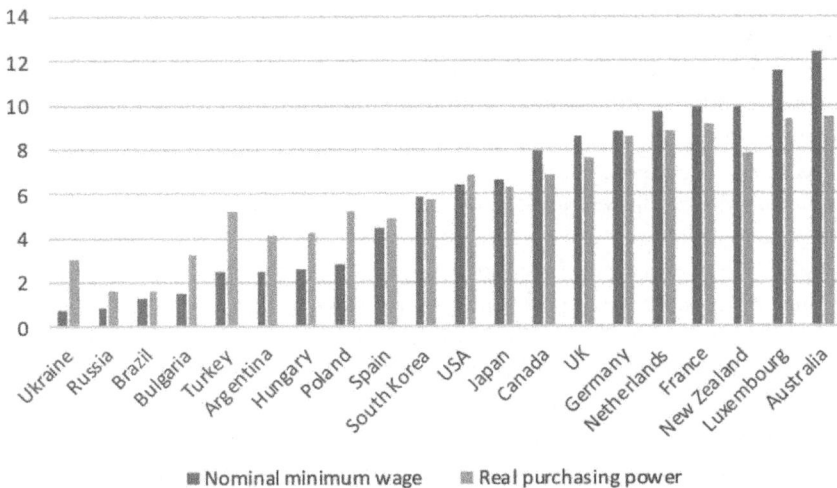

**FIGURE 4.8**  Nominal Minimum Wage and Real Purchasing Power in Selected Countries (in €)

*Source:* WSI Minimum Wage Database, 2018 (www.boeckler.de/pdf/p_wsi_report_39e_2018.pdf)

(2018: 36) show for the United States, "state minimum wage increases resulted in declines in employer-sponsored health insurance for minimum wage earners."

On exactly what basis lawmakers or organizations that represent workers set the minimum wage is not only an open but, in most instances, a highly contested issue. Whether the lawmakers or others empowered to set the minimum wage in a state, a region, an industrial field or the nation in fact orients their deliberations and decision with reference to what we have call the material wage is by no means assured. The same incertitude across the board applies to the ways in which minimum wages are changed.

The first minimum wage *law* was enacted in 1894 in New Zealand. In the United States, the first minimum wage law can be traced to the *The Fair Labor Standards Act Of 1938*.[94] In its initial formulation the minimum wage was set at 0.25 Dollar per hour for covered workers. The Act has been amended multiple times since 1938. "In 1938, the act applied to industries whose combined employment represented about 20 percent of the labor force. Coverage has been expanded over time, and the wage now covers approximately 130 million workers or 84 percent of the labor force" (Center for Poverty Research, University of California, Davis).[95] It is trivial but noteworthy nonetheless that the "gold" standard on which minimum wage are calibrated are hours worked; perhaps the least contentious quantitative standard on which minimum wages are calculated. The minimum wage could also be linked to other criteria be they work-related such as productivity or extraneous to work performed such as the number of individuals who are supported by the wage paid.

Most recently, the hourly federal minimum in the United States stagnates at US$ 7.25 (effective July 24, 2009 from US$ 6.55) or US$ 15,080.00 a year. Many US States and localities apply their own minimum wage. In 18 states and D.C., the hourly minimum wage is indexed to inflation of prices. Increases in the minimum wage occur automatically. Only in these seven US States the Federal minimum wages applies: Alabama, Georgia, Louisiana, Mississippi, South Carolina, Tennessee, and Wyoming.

As our conception of the existential price of labor implies what counts from the perspective of the employee is not the nominal value of the minimum wage but what the minimum wage will buy. Figure 4.8 therefore also contains information for each country about the purchasing power of the minimum wage. Taking account of the purchasing power reduces but does not eliminate the differences in the minimum wages across the European Union. Outside of Europe, high cost of living, for example, in Australia, New Zealand and Canada lower the value of their high nominal minimum wage levels. The same applies to a certain degree to the minimum wage in the United States.

As we have observed, one of the statistical standards against which the *value* of the minimum wage can be calibrated is its relation to the median of the national wage structure. In the United States, given its Federal minimum wage the relation is very weak. The Federal minimum wage in 2016 represents only 34.9 percent of the median wage level of full-time workers; in Turkey the figure is 75.8 percent.

## Just Wages[96]

The answer to the question of what are just wages invariably points to a moral foundation or to socio-political considerations of what constitutes a fair compensation for work. The consensus, if any, about inequities extends at best to the extremes of a distribution of phenomena that is valued. This of course leaves the bulk of income earners out in the cold when it comes to the determination of a just return for their labor. But there is a much bigger hurdle. In an age of growing economic inequality in many societies, of manager remunerations that may exceed the income of the average employee by an incredible multiple, or of incomes stagnating over a significant period of time, the issue of just wages has indeed gained special relevance.

Many social scientists strongly maintain that the just-wage issue is altogether alien to economic discourse. Unlike classical economics, neoclassical economics is not political economics. For example, when Niklas Luhmann (1993) was asked to contribute to a volume devoted to economic ethics, he was extremely puzzled and did not really know what to write about: the ethics of economic conduct in modern society, in his eyes, is not a meaningful subject matter. In short, whenever possible, and Luhmann obviously agreed, one should refrain from moralizing economic processes (cf. Wolf, 1996: 258). Within the confines of the neoclassical conception of the marketplace, *individuals* are supposed to refrain from considering and checking each other's moral beliefs (Luhmann, [1970] 1982: 200).[97] Among economic actors, a switch from normative to cognitive attitudes occurs. Ideally, communication is strictly limited to economic matters. One might sum up this attitude by saying people simply want more for less.[98]

Max Weber ([1922] 1978: 636), too, aptly describes the sober, distanced, and indirect personal relations that characterize the social climate of the ideal-typical modern marketplace with its strong interest in or utility-based orientation to market exchanges:

> The market community as such is the most impersonal form of practical life into which humans can enter with one another . . . The reason for the impersonality of the market is its matter-of-factness, its orientation to the commodity and only to that. When the market is allowed to follow its own autonomous tendencies, its participants do not look toward the persons of each other but only toward the commodity, there are no obligations of brotherliness or reverence, and none of these spontaneous human relations that are sustained by personal unions.[99]

Based on these considerations of the system specific foundations of social conduct with the economic system, any consideration of moral rewards as part of the wages of employees is really out of bounds. However, almost any really practiced discussion of and struggle about the price of labor involves *moral* considerations.

Wages have, in other words, an economic and a normative dimension. Whether the economic and the moral dimension can be clearly separated at all is of course a contested matter.

In an ideal-typical entrepreneurial, free-market (first-best) economy, the *economic* value of wages or profit, that is, "every personal income . . . will exactly measure the value-product contributed . . . by whatever resources that person actually furnishes to production . . . every individual member of the economy will receive the consequences of his own activity" (Knight, 1950: 500). In an ideal-typical economy, in a *Gedankenexperiment* (thought experiment) of pure economic relations, wages do not incorporate a moral dimension: yet "free competition is all right in theory, but it doesn't work in practice" (Knight, 1950: 502).[100]

Since free competition only operates in theory, any expectation of an "objective" answer to the question of what constitutes fair wages—that is, an answer resting on the assumption that an unencumbered market provides an objective outcome—must be abandoned. The discourse about what constitutes a just wage is a contested, value-laden discourse affected by many additional social institutions that obviously fail to obey the rule not to cross into economic territory.

As a rule, the question of the *"subjective"* features of just wages is not at the forefront of the analysis of fair wages in economics or sociology (cf. Schumpeter, 1916). An exception is the work of Wilhelm Baldamus. Therefore, Baldamus' (1960)[101] theoretical approach to an industrial sociology of just wages deserves our special attention. A central aspect of his industrial sociology analysis of the just-wage issue is that the *"motivation, i.e.* the conscious aims and attitudes of those involved in the industrial production process" should gain center stage (Baldamus, 1960: 15). This type of an analysis of just wages is "never just about the *actual* shape of industrial production methods, market forms, remuneration, organizational practices, etc. It is primarily about how these things are subjectively *interpreted* by those individuals and groups who are exposed to them" (Baldamus, 1960: 16). The motivational structure or the individual assessment of the work or the workload, or the comparison with fellow workers (cf. Breza, Kaur and Shamdasani, 2016; also Festinger, 1954), in turn, very much depends on a society's ideas about what, for example, is appropriate, fair and just.

Just wages, in particular the equitable sharing of the results of industrial work, that is, of wages and entrepreneurial profits, between employees and employers are a soci0-cultural product: "the workplace is a social organism where the relational aspects of pay cannot be divorced from its economic value" (Breza, Kaur and Shandasani, 2016: 26). But what exactly makes statements regarding the equitable distribution possible and useful, even at times when "the outward manifestation merely appears to be a function of ethically neutral market processes" (Baldamus, 1960: 18)?

Drawing on qualitative empirical findings, Wilhelm Baldamus (1960: 32) concludes that "regardless of the wage system, evaluative comparisons between work arduousness (*Arbeitsmühe*) and wages play a central role especially among industrial workers. At the same time [. . .] such evaluations are subject to specific constraints due the awareness of the obligation to work as well as the desire for a reasonable standard of living [material remuneration] and a socially appropriate (*standesgemässe*) occupation."

The notion of work arduousness must be differentiated or seen in relative terms. Work arduousness differs depending on the work setting but also on the type of corporation or the economic sector. Work arduousness refers to the "totality of a worker's mental and physical efforts [. . .] that are needed to obtain a certain result in the form of wages" (Baldamus, 1960: 46–47). The concept of relative labor effort thus has a close proximity to our concept of moral compensation.

The neglect of subjective factors makes it impossible for the theory of wages in terms of neoclassical productivity theory to determine just wages in their dependence not only on age, gender or skills differentials (see Katz and Murphy, 1992) but also on differences in the work effort and on factors such as self (= training) costs and "psychological income" (professional interests, job satisfaction, social-professional status).

The just-wage issue is thus a question of the relationship between *burdens* and *wages*. All conceptions of occupations and occupational lives are dependent on societal beliefs; moreover, they are subject to historical change: "The level of work arduousness that is still considered tolerable, [for example, has been] progressively reduced: A level of work arduousness that substantially impedes the enjoyment of leisure time is, in many cases, no longer accepted" (Baldamus, 1960: 43–44). Until the end of the 19th century only the physical effort was compensated for by the wages. Today, far more subtle factors also weigh in, such as job insecurity, health hazards, the dullness or sustainability of the task. In short, any compensation for work arduousness in the form of wages is governed by a just and reasonable relation between pay and burdens

## The Empirical Evidence

Social scientists interested in the societal distribution of wealth and incomes have spent disproportionate amounts of energy on examining the *concentration* of wealth and *wage inequality/polarization* (since the late 1970s) in advanced societies but have displayed considerably less interest in changes in the average level of economic well-being *over time*.

Special statistical measures of dispersion, such as the Gini coefficient or the Lorenz curve and share of labor's income as a proportion of the GDP, have been deployed to reduce the empirical pattern of inequality to a single figure. The Gini coefficient, for example, can range from 0 to 1. A low figure represents a more equal distribution of household incomes, a high figure a significantly one-sided concentration of prosperity. Countries with low Gini coefficients are the Scandinavian societies. In Sweden, for instance, the Gini coefficient as a measure of income inequality stood at 0.25 in 2005. In the same year, the Gini coefficient for Portugal was 0.41. In Europe, at least, Gini coefficients have remained almost constant between 1995 and 2005. Significantly higher concentrations of income may be found in African and Latin American countries. In the United States, the coefficient in 2007 stood at 0.45 and in 2013 at 0.41. A less sophisticated measure of the income that goes to labor and capital is the labor and capital share of the GDP. We will discuss this measure and its changes in over time in the next section. But interest in the price of labor has been much less pronounced among social scientists.

In Europe and the United States, average real wages and standards of living have rapidly grown in the post-World War II decades, an unprecedented phenomenon since the onset of the industrial revolution.[102] The economic boom differed in its timing from country to country but, as Alan Milward (1992: 21; see also Judt, 2005: 324–353) has succinctly stated:

> By the end of this period the perpetual possibility of serious economic hardship which had earlier always hovered over the lives of three-quarters of the population now menaced only about one fifth of it. Although absolute poverty still existed in even the richest countries, the material standard of living for most people improved almost without interruption and often very rapidly for thirty-five years. Above all else, these are the marks of the uniqueness of the experience.

The emancipation from economic vulnerability and subjugation, unforeseen by Marx and Engels, but anticipated by Keynes ([1930] 1935) amid the global slump in the late 1920s, does not occur to the same extent and at a similar pace in all industrialized countries. As it is, it provides the basis not only for the material foundation of new forms of inequality (see Stehr, 1999), but also for morally coded markets.

The gains in real wages are difficult to measure and, in any event, typically do not include information about gains that are most significant for individuals, for example, their health, flexibility of working conditions including retirement options, life expectancy, or improvements in the general comforts of daily existence such as electricity, air-conditioning or the internet.

The growth of average nominal wages over time can be represented in a fairly straightforward way. But the trend in nominal wages, of course, does not show whether these changes are at the same time real-wage increases. Converting nominal-wage trends into real-wage trends means that price indexes must be calculated, for example, a cost-of-living index covering a range of years or even decades for a basket of consumer goods and services. Such a translation of nominal into real wages is immensely difficult. Any result achieved through complex calculations would give us an approximate idea of the evolution of the average price of labor over time. It would not provide us with any insights into the relative value of the different components of the price of labor.

As William Nordhaus (1996: 29–30) has pointed out, the difficulty of constructing "valid" price indices over time, last but not least because what is typically consumed today, can differ sharply from what was typically consumed only a few years let alone a century ago. In order to capture the impact of new technologies, for example, one would have to engage in a very elaborate construction and reconstruction of the basket of goods and services consumed. Now "we travel in vehicles that were not yet invented that are powered by fuels not yet produced, communicate through devices not yet manufactured. Enjoy cool air on the hottest days, are entertained by electronic wizardry that was not dreamed of and receive medical treatments that were unheard of." In order to arrive at valid estimates of changes in real wages we would have to somehow construct price indexes that reflect this evolution of consumption patterns; indeed, a monumental task.

In a small but pioneering step, William D. Nordhaus tries to reconstruct the price of *lighting* in order to arrive at a "true" estimate of advances in real living standards (in terms of expenses for lighting). He argues "traditional price indexes of lighting vastly overstate the increase in lighting prices over the last two centuries, and the true rise in living standards in this sector has consequently been vastly understated" (Nordhaus, 1996: 30). Using data on lighting efficiency, he attempts to develop a true price of light and to contrast these prices with conventional techniques.

If the results for lighting are representative, since lighting belongs to that category of more than one-third of consumer goods that has undergone the most dramatic changes due to technological developments—then the "growth of real wages and real incomes in conventional estimates might be understated by a very large margin" (Nordhaus, 1996: 64).

As many empirical studies in most countries of the world have aptly demonstrated education and training are among the most important if not the most important correlate of a person's earnings. According to the *canonical model* earnings are a function of human capital and hence what are generally also called skills (cf. Borghans, Ter Weel and Weinberg, 2014). But the dominant analysis of the economic value of skills which follows the human capital model treats the supply and the demand side of skills in general and the kind of skills required and available among employees in particular as a black box. In order to answer these foundational questions one not only "requires a conceptual framework that links the tasks and activities that workers perform on the job to the skills needed to carry out these activities" (Autor and Handel, 2013: 560) (demand side),[103] but also an understanding of the acquired skills brought to the world of work by employees (supply side), in the first instance.

Gary Becker (1994: 17) points to the validity of his human capital theory by stressing that "high school and college education in the United States greatly raise a person's income, even after netting out direct and indirect costs of schooling, and after adjusting for the better family backgrounds and greater abilities of more educated people. Similar evidence is now available for many points in time from over one hundred countries with different cultures and economic systems." The exact nature of the monetary advantages that can be attributed to educational achievements are not stable but vary from time to time, country to country and the composition of the labor force. The ratio of women in the labor force has increased rapidly since the 1970s in most Western societies. Whether or not such secular and other changes impacted the price of labor is a highly contentious issue.

Moreover, the human capital theory is not without its distracters who prefer to emphasize the impact of diplomas, degrees, and education as signals that convey information about skills, abilities and other productive traits of individuals. The theory of "credentialism" (cf. Blaug, 1976) denies that schooling or the education level is a helpful proxy for any enhanced productivity that is associated with schooling or, for that matter, skill.[104] Gary Becker (1994: 20) is not convinced; though credentialism exists "many kinds of evidence suggest that credentialism does not explain most of the positive association between earnings and schooling." The contest between human capital theory and credentialism as sources of differential earnings, in the end, to do not assist much in arriving a price of labor and in specifying what elements of the price of labor make of the total price of labor.

In addition to the methodological difficulties of measuring the exact price of the work, another methodological problem arises, namely to determine each of the multiple attributes of the price of the work. There is extensive empirical information on a number of characteristics of a person or company, such as gender, place of birth, education, age, vocational training, informal learning and experience or the size of a company, but little information on a person's specific work tasks.[105] The lack of empirical information on the moral components of the price of work is even more extensive.

In view of the widespread assumption that a person's work tasks are changing significantly due to technical change, this is an important research gap. Researchers have so far often come to terms with such an information deficit by hypothetically accepting and assuming certain typical work tasks or job skills of an occupation, but not those of a specific employee.[106] This procedure does not allow for a distinction to be made among employees who have the same occupational title but are engaged in different activities and perform different job skills. For example, medical doctors can carry out completely different professional activities.[107] In other words, it is necessary to collect information on precise professional work experience in order to relate this information to the price of the work.

David Autor and Michael Handel (2013: S62), using parts of the Princeton Data Improvement Initiative (PDII), have made a first attempt to overcome[108] "a lack of conceptual structure for analyzing the wage "returns" to tasks and a lack of data for analyzing the person-level relationship between tasks, education, and wages." Their data show (1) that work activities within occupations or classes of occupations differ and that these differences correlate with a variety of personal attributes, such as gender, ethnicity or English language skills (Autor and

Handel, 2013: S90). (2) Not surprisingly, there is a link between work activities and the price of work: „The tasks that workers perform on the job are significant predictors of their hourly wages, both between and within occupational, demographic, and education groups." These findings provide an important indication of the complexity of the differences between nominal and real values of work and underscore once again the considerable need for additional research on individual, societal and cultural determinants of labor remuneration.

## The Price of Labor Since the Financial Crisis

Evidence collected for trends in nominal wage remuneration in most advanced economies indicates that nominal wage growth has been strikingly lower compared to wage growth prior to the financial crisis 2008–2009. Even more pertinent, wages have not been rising in many countries including the Scandinavian countries, in the United States, Japan and Britain. Hand in hand with the stagnation of wages in many OECD countries comes a decline of the measured productivity growth over the past decade in the same set of nations. At the same time optimistic expectations among venture capitalists and technologist but also fears in other business areas regarding a perceived acceleration of changes in the world of work brought about by new technological advances, improvements of artificial intelligence (AI) and machine learning are being asserted.

As in the past, the promise of the new technologies should have greatly increased productivity. But unexpectedly, productivity has been cut by more than half compared to the previous decade (Syverson, 2017). In other words, the data

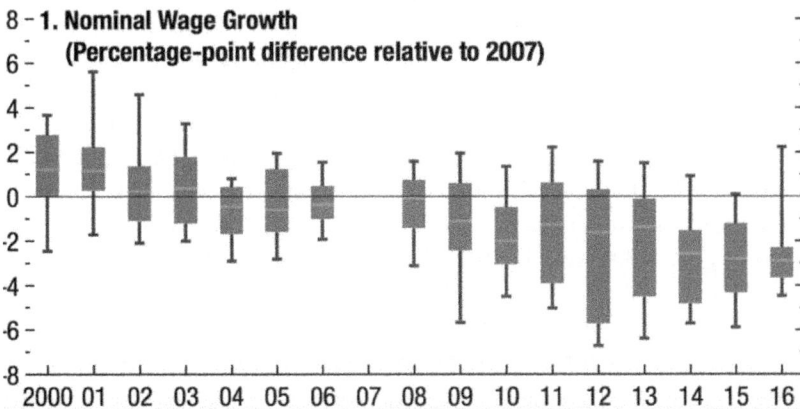

**FIGURE 4.9**  Nominal Wage Growth (Percentage-Point Difference Relative to 2007)

*Source:* Eurostat; national statistics; Organization for Economic Co-operation and Development; IMF

*Note:* Baltic countries are exempt. Wage per hour without self-employed. Horizontal line indicates median; top and bottom of boxes indicate quartiles; markers indicate top and bottom deciles.

appear to show a repetition of the so-called *productivity paradox* (also known as the Solow paradox) of a few decades ago that occurred during the height of business investments into computer and communications technologies. Today, the productivity paradox is linked to investments in digital technology—for example cloud computing, e-commerce, mobile internet, artificial intelligence, machine learning, and the Internet of Things resulting in new products and features (digital books and live location tracking), new ways to deliver them (for example, drones, streaming video), and new business models (for example, Uber or Lyft). In recent years, we may be witnessing therefore a new version of the Solow Paradox: while significant investments in digital technologies are carried out, they have yet to fuel productivity growth. Let us examine the productivity paradox linked to massive investments in information and communication technologies in more detail.

Yet when it comes to the economic affluence of a nation and the ability of a country's economy to improve the standard of living of its workers and citizens more generally and compete internationally, social scientists are in an unusual agreement that productivity "in the long run is almost everything" (Krugman, 1994: 13). In the initial discussion of a productivity paradox in the 1980s and 1990s, economists in particular had been puzzled and even irritated about the apparent lack of measurable productivity gains in goods producing and services industries in OECD countries in response to or in conjunction with the immense investments in information and communication technologies. The choice of labeling this phenomenon the "productivity paradox" results from the disjuncture between the huge economic expectations and promises that have been engendered by the "computer age," on the one hand, and the apparent lack of sustainable economic payoffs resulting from the enormous investments by corporation and the state in information and communication technologies, on the other.

In 1990 alone, American businesses invested US\$ 61 billion in hardware, US\$ 18 billion in software and US\$ 75 billion in data processing and computer services. Paul Attewell (1994: 24) sums up the research on the productivity paradox by affirming its existence and adds that "no study documents substantial IT effects on productivity." Although conceptual, methodological and data difficulties that extend to the very definition of productivity do exist in the information that is typically utilized in generating these findings (also Brynjolfsson, Rock and Syverson, 2017: 7–8; Syverson, 2017), they do not appear to invalidate the results entirely.[109]

Given the excessive and often repeated claims about the transformative capacity of information and communication technologies (ICTs) for the world of work one could even be tempted to ask, why have productivity gains that can be attributed to ITCs not been even more spectacular?[110] By the early 1990s some economists signaled that the danger has passed, and that the productivity paradox disappeared (e.g. Brynjolfsson and Hitt, 1996; Sichel, 1999). The main reason for the gap between investments in new technology and attributable productivity gains is to refer to the time it takes to economically harness the benefits of new technology.

Erik Brynjolfsson and colleagues (2017: 1) designate the renewed slowdown in productivity growth in the last decade as the *modern productivity paradox* and offer the first resolution. Investments by corporations into AI have accelerated. Once more, there is no evidence that these transformative technological developments and investments are not concurrently paying off in terms of an observed productivity growth. The question, therefore, is once more how does one account for the slowdown in productivity growth in recent years? As in the case of the earlier productivity paradox, the explanation of the modern paradox revolves around the time lag between measurable gains and investments made. The impact of the new digital technologies of the so-called fourth industrial revolution on productivity has not as yet occurred or remains more or less invisible (cf. Soete, 2018: 40).[111] Erik Brynjolfsson and his colleagues (2017: 34) conclude

> The breakthroughs of AI technologies already demonstrated are not yet affecting much of the economy, but they portend bigger effects as they diffuse. More importantly, they enable *complementary innovations* that could multiply their impact. Both the AI investments and the complementary changes are costly, hard to measure, and take time to implement, and this can, at least initially, depress productivity as it is currently measured. Entrepreneurs, managers and end-users will find powerful new applications for machines that can now learn how to recognize objects, understand human language, speak, make accurate predictions, solve problems, and interact with the world with increasing dexterity and mobility
>
> *(our emphasis).*

Unemployment rates have decreased significantly (not taking into consideration that such statistics tend to be highly politicized measures, see Stehr, 2001) in some countries (but continue to be elevated in other countries) since the financial crisis but without benefits in terms of higher wages for employees. The decline in unemployment is mostly the outcome of job creation (see (IMF, 2017: 76). Job skills that require specialized abilities are in demand and so are low-paying, low-skill jobs. The large number of positions in between those highly-skilled and low-skilled jobs mainly account for the statistics showing the stagnation of wages.

Explanation for the stagnation of the price of labor since the financial crisis in 2008/2009 list a number of interrelated factors (cf. IMF, 2017; Goodman and Soble, 2017):

- The persistent consequences of the worst economic downturn since the Great Depression of 1929
- The loss of the collective bargaining power of employees, that is, the decline of labor union membership and labor market deregulation
- The increase in the involuntary and voluntary temporary employment and of part-time workers[112] and a reduction in the number of hours per worker.

Both represent a challenge to the existing social insurance systems bases as it were on the binary opposition of either full-time employed or unemployed.

- The growing deployment of robots and other forms of automation of the work place[113] and the rise of digital innovations that benefits mainly the upper income groups[114]
- Declining potential economic growth (cf. IMF, 2017: 87)
- Globalization and the intensified competitive pressure experienced in North America and Europe from factories in Asia, Latin America and Africa

In addition to the overall stagnation of the price of labor since the financial crisis, the distribution of income has changed nonetheless. Income inequalities have increased in most OECD countries while there has been no growth for the bottom fifty percent of the income pyramid. The greatest beneficiaries were in the top one percent category of the income distribution.

In general, however, it should be noted that all forecasts of the impact of technological change, including the possible impact of AI on the number of socially necessary workers, are characterized by a restricted perspective. A shortened perspective that disregards a number of important societal processes in its calculation of job losses (or gains) or excludes these social processes from the outset and is due to a largely technology-centric perspective.

A technology-centered perspective means concentrating exclusively on the alleged "power" of technology. The new technology, for example, eliminates the need to move a vehicle from one place to another or to have a haircut done by a hairdresser. If both abilities are replaced by a technique, a machine or a software, one calculates corresponding job losses attributed to the new technique. What is not taken into account, of course, is that other social changes can make up for the loss of these jobs. This includes, for example, the reactions of demand, in particular its elasticity,[115] preference shifts, a change in values, generational structural changes, etc., which in turn determine whether new technologies, as in the past in the case of the textile, steel or automotive industries, have absorbed job losses. Whether this will actually be the case remains a matter for the future.

## The Falling Rate of Labor's Share

The *collective* share of labor-based income (LS) in relation to the share that goes to the stock of capital has, as noted earlier, declined in a number of countries with developed economies according to a number of recent studies. However, the aggregate labor share as a portion of the gross domestic product varies when considered over a longer period of time (see Piketty, [2013] 2014: 8–16). Periods of a decline are typically followed by years and decades of an increase in inequality. The magnitude of the secular shifts in the capital/labor ratio can be quite significant and falsify the assumption that labor's share is a constant feature of the distribution of income in developed countries (cf. Kaldor, 1957). The forces that produce such shifts are distinct economic, political and societal processes as well as the presence or absence of strong labor unions and the development of the cost of living. Comparing labor's share across countries is made difficult by virtue of distinct methods of computing national shares of capital and labor.

In the aggregate, economic growth that benefits all not always represents a tide that lifts everyone. The causes for shifts in the aggregate labor share have to include non-economic factors. For example, the "resurgence of inequality after 1980 is due largely to the political shifts of the past several decades, especially in regard to taxation and finance" (Piketty, [2013] 2014: 20). Figures like those quoted by Piketty differentiate between the value added by those who do not own the means of production and the class that does. A declining share of labor signals an economy's value-added is distributed less to those who produce it and more to those who own the means of production. What exactly are the forces that assure above and beyond secular shifts in the pattern of inequality an asymmetric allocation of the fruits of production? One truly cannot dismiss the core Marxian insight that ownership of the means of production plays a decisive role.

The strict differentiation between labor and capital income hides a range of important features of inequality. It is for example the case that households in modern economies are recipients of both capital and labor-based income, be as owners of capital or, indirectly, though an insurance policy and similar assets, or simply as self-employed individuals. And it is of course also true that poor households rarely own assets (for example, in the United States, the poorest fifty percent of households own 0,5 percent of all shares).

Equally important is a decomposition of labor income over time. As Piketty ([2013] 2014: 24) for instance notes „the spectacular increase in inequality [in the United States in the 1980s until 2000] largely reflects an unprecedented explosion of very elevated incomes from labor, a veritable separation of the top managers of large firms from the rest of the population."[116] Dongya Koh and her colleagues (2015: 2) advance the discussion about the forces that shape labor's share in modern economies by introducing "intellectual property products" (IPP) into the calculation of the distribution of income. Their findings indicate that "the shift in the speed at which aggregate capital accumulates and depreciates due to the increasing importance of IPP capital in the US economy fully accounts for the observed decline of the LS."

The possibility to take IPP capital into account follows a revision in US national accounts in classifying (or decomposing) capital to extend to the category of intangible assets. Intangible assets (IPP) with its high depreciation rate incorporate investment in R&D, software, and artistic originals. Overall, the revisions in national accounts "capture the increasingly important role of IPP in the US economy: The share of IPP in aggregate investment has increased from 8% in 1947 to 26% in 2013" (Koh, Santaeulàlia-Llopis and Zheng, 2015: 3). The investment in tangible capital allows for a calculation of the income generated by such investments. The results show that a decline in labor's share is highest in industries with high investments in intangible goods while manufacturing has not experienced any decline in LS since the mid-1980s in the absence of IPP investments. In other words, labor's share in industries with a traditional stock of capital remains trendless.

## Cognitive Abilities

> The great idea of investigating the relationship between wage differences and differences in ability opens a vast perspective. The new trail is steep and stony, but it must be followed.
>
> —*Joseph Schumpeter (1916: 68)*

Joseph Schumpeter encouragement addressed to his fellow social scientists is more than a century old. However, it continues to be valid and remains a most difficult challenge.[117] There is no consensus to begin with on whether cognitive or noncognitive skills have a greater impact on the price of work. Nevertheless, it can be assumed that in an intangible economy, cognitive skills are particularly rewarded. Tim Kautz and his colleagues (2015: 3) argue that non-cognitive skills could be more important in the labor market and at work than cognitive skills: "Non-cognitive skills—personality traits, goals, traits and motivations that are highly valued in the labor market, at school and elsewhere—are not covered by intelligence and performance tests. But in many ways their predictive power is just as great, if not greater than that of cognitive abilities." However, the question of the significance of non-cognitive skills for the price of work has not yet been answered.

A number of empirical studies from the past two decades have shown that cognitive skills are additionally rewarded. Although different measurement methods or indices of cognitive skills in different occupations and sectors of the economy have an influence on their results, overall, they suggest that the influence of the moral component embodied within "cognitive skills" on the overall price of work is not very high.

## Conclusion: Determining the Price (and Value) of Labor

The price of labor is a multifaceted concept. A range of highly heterogeneous factors and the result of a multiplicity of variables that vary across time and space, i.e. across societies and world regions, influence it. Many of the variables that co-determine the price of labor may be found in almost all societies and regions; they are subject to secular structural changes such as, for example, the long-term decline in importance of the industrial sector (deindustrialization; see also Rodrik, 2016), diminishing trade union coverage, long-term demographic transformations of the age structures of societies, technological changes or, overall societal trends toward, for instance, smaller households (single mother households).

The price of labor varies as a function of the prevailing legal frameworks for action and current power relations, both of which have repercussions on the labor market. Another important dimension of the price of labor are moral determinants such as, for instance, nominal income and wage differentials, a worker's race or gender, whether one lives in the northern or the southern hemisphere, or whether or not the factor "labor" is mobile.

The specific individual and collective attitudes toward work are unlikely to be firmly fixed over generations. At the same time, shifting attitudes toward work should affect the price of labor. Such shifts may oscillate between securing and emphasizing material-existential needs or emphasizing work as a meaningful pursuit that makes life worthwhile. The two functions of labor are not necessarily mutually exclusive, but the importance of either purpose of work may depend on the societal circumstances, be it on the ascendency or in decline. In either case, attention to work as central-life interest stresses attributes of the supply-side of labor for the price of work.

Finally, and importantly, the price of labor does not fall easily. Due to efforts of the individuals and groups involved, the structure of economic relations as well as action originating outside the world of work, especially due to interventions of the government and secular changes within and across societies, there is a significant amount of downward price rigidity of labor. The "gains from rigid wages are greater than the gains from flexible wages" (Thurow, [1980] 1981: 59).

It is easy to see from the multitude of influencing factors that it is impossible to arrive at a general definition of the price of labor. The difficulty of determining the price of labor is further complicated by the following facts (see Bowles, Gintis and Osborne, 2001: 1137–1139): (1) The income of different people, who otherwise differ little in many occupational characteristics from each other, receive different wages; (2) success in the world of work is a function of social origin (e. g. Björklund and Jäntti, 2012) and (3) seemingly irrelevant attributes of a person (for example, her height, appearance and/or weight) influence the price of labor.

Given the heterogeneity and variety of the factors that co-determine the actual market-based earnings, the price of labor, although by no means a random parameter, defies any more general determination. And there are more factors in addition to those discussed above that co-determine the price of labor, namely the heterogeneity of work processes and the cognitive and social skills that are needed to produce immaterial goods, for instance.[118] Given these considerations, André Gorz ([2003] 2010: 36) therefore concludes that

> the heterogeneity of the work activities termed 'cognitive' and of the material products they create and of the capacities and knowledge they involve, render the value of both the labour-powers and their products non-measurable [. . .] The impossibility of calibrating and standardizing all the parameters of the required work gives rise to vain efforts to quantify its qualitative dimension and the definition of performance standards.

What importantly remains, then, is our suggestion that the price of labor is composed of two factors: a part to ensure a sustainable livelihood and a part of moral compensation, neither of which, however, lends itself to standardization. Beyond the differentiation of the material and the moral component of the price of labor what can be stated with confidence is that the most effective and certain way to increase the income of individual wage earners (and in the process reduce wage inequalities) is to enhance the education level, the skills and the capacities of the working population (cf. Piketty, [2014] 2014: 313).

At the same time, this analysis of growing wage differentials and how to avoid them corresponds to our emphasis on a supply-oriented view of the major changes in the world of work. It is the skills and competences that employees bring with them and not the skills that employers anticipate for a future world of work and its supposed requirements that will be decisive. Whether and to what extent automation and robotization will lead to a loss or even an increase in the necessary work for society is therefore a question that will be determined not least by the people aspiring to the labour market and their skills.

## Notes

1. Karl Polanyi ([1944] 2001: 49) summarizes the findings of ethnographers of the characteristics of earlier civilizations: „The absence of the motive of gain; the absence of the principle of laboring for remuneration; the absence of the principle of least effort; and, especially, the absence of any separate and distinct institution based on economic motives." Polanyi's observation is at the same time a helpful reference to the "law" of the simultaneity of the non-simultaneous: Much of the work in modern societies is the unpaid immaterial and emotional work done primarily by women (cf. Weeks, 2011). An analysis of the value or price of genuine immaterial and emotional labor goes beyond the scope of our investigation.
2. The elementary distinction between manual and mental labor already signals how difficult it will be to reduce to and combine the diverse attributes of labor to a quantitative single unit.
3. It is worth noting that the terms "work" and "labor" are now used almost interchangeably (for a history of the terms, see Komlosy, [2014] 2000) Labor, in contrast to work, was seen as based on circumstances under another person's direction and control (toilsome activity); while *work* referred to an activity that directly maintains a person's livelihood and is carried out with relative autonomy (including the redemption linked to a created product)
4. For a more extensive, general and enlightening discussion of the origins and the nature of work in industrial society, see André Gorz ([1988] 1989: 13–88).
5. Given the terminology that speaks of a fourth industrial revolution, the prior technological changes for most part based on microelectronics and the evolution of integrated circuits in turn form the foundation for the fourth step in industrial revolutions, e.g. robotics and AI.
6. The demand-based perspective, as long as it is not simply describing the quantity of labor in demand by employer's speaks for example to the "secular growth in the *demand* for more educated workers, females and 'more-skilled' workers" as necessary to "interpret the observed changes in the relative wages as changes in competitive

skill prices" (Katz and Murphy, 1992: 76; our emphasis). Demand growth accounts according to Katz and Murphy for thee observed price and quantity changes in the wage structure while fluctuations in supply do not help to illuminate for example the differences in male/female differential.

7. However, the use of robots can also be interpreted as a change in labor supply, as Borjas and Freeman (2019: 1) do in their study of the substitution of industrial workers by robots. Their approach comes to the following conclusion on the basis of actual: "we estimate that an additional robot reduces employment and wages in an industry by roughly as much as an additional 2 to 3 workers and by 3 to 4 workers in particular groups."

8. "The effects of demographic change on investment in robots are robust and quantitatively sizable. For example, differential aging alone accounts for about 40% of the cross-country variation in investment in robotics" (Acemoglu and Restrepo, 2018b: 32–33).

9. Moreover, Acemoglu and Restrepo (2018a: 33) demonstrate "using data on intermediate exports and patents that demographic change not only encourages the adoption of automation technologies *but also their development*" (our emphasis).

10. The confidence with which employer organizations and management deliver forecasts about the kind of skills needed in the future world of work is remarkable. The influence of such visions on educational policy is equally remarkable as is the failure to critically deconstruct such forecasts.

11. Among professional economist, Jan Tinbergen (1956, 1975) is one of the early proponents of at least considering the relevance of supply-side attributes for the determination of labor income. In particular, Tinbergen (1975) synthesized demand and supply components and he opened up the black box of the demand focus of the educational planning literature and stressed a continuum of skills (cf. Heckman, 2018).

12. Please note that our more intensive and critical discussion of the theory of human capital can be found in our discussion of the "Price of Knowledge" in Chapter 5. We interpret the notion of human capital as a proxy for estimating the value of knowledge. However, the volume of individual human capital can of course also be interpreted to offer information about the price of labor. Hence it is worth reading our discussion of human capital theory in the later chapter as a contribution to the analysis of the value of labor.

13. The *New York Times* developed the so-called "Marx ratio." The Marx ratio does not provide an empirically based answer to the question of a change in the relative income of labor or capital in the course of recent technological developments in the world of work. The question that is raised is: „Who benefits the most when a company is successful: its shareholders or its employees? Capital or labor?." The Marx ratio "captures the relationship between a company's profits—the return to capital, on a per-employee basis—and how much its median employee is compensated, a rough proxy for the return to labor." The figures for US companies show that companies with a large proportion of highly qualified employees (e.g. in the pharmaceutical industry) or active in the financial sector (e.g. in real estate companies) show comparatively high returns on investment. However, it also becomes clear that a number of other factors influence the scope of the Marx ratio. Compare this with Irwin 2018.

14. One of the analytical tools employed in the literature, perhaps even unconsciously in an effort to remove the essential uncertainty about future aspects of the "work society" is to give the impression that the most recent data, for example about the present volume of socially necessary labor is not only the present state of affairs but is the future. It is our impression that this tool kit applies to Ulrich Beck's ([1999] 2000: 2–3) liberal extension of his description of present labor market trends as indicative not only of a past but a future trend. As a result, such an analysis is arrested by unanticipated (economic and/or political) changes that fail to confirm the trend objectified by available

data as a future trend. The temptation to consider the present as foretelling the future is a fallacy that can be observed only too frequently.

15. However, as Maestas et al. (2018: 2) point out, systematic evidence for such preferences are lacking: "it has been difficult to assess to what extent differences in the incidence and valuations of non-wage job characteristics shape persistent wage differentials in the labor market. In the United States, there currently is no survey of a representative sample of workers about a broad range of job attributes. Moreover, it has proven very difficult to estimate willingness no-pay for job amenities based on observational data alone. While the theoretical relationship between job characteristics and wages is clear . . . the empirical literature documenting the existence and magnitude of such tradeoffs has faced substantial challenges given multiple sources of selection."

16. Daniele Checci and Herman G. van de Werfhorst (2017: 155) report that the inequality of the *quality* of education (that is, student performance on standardized tests) has a greater impact on income inequality than inequality in *quantity* of education

17. For example, Lin, Lutter and Ruhm (2016), Acemoglu and Autor (2011: 1044–1095), Autor (2017). It should be noted at the outset that the prevailing measurement of the "skill level" of employees is restricted to the proxy of the educational level of the worker. The skill premium, the ratio of the income of unskilled to skilled employees, has been for the most part been defined as the difference between "low-skilled workers are defined as those with up to lower-secondary education, middle-skilled as those with upper-secondary or postsecondary nontertiary education, and high-skilled as those with tertiary education (IMF, 2017: 91).

18. In much the same sense, Max Weber ([1956] 1978: 110) counts work as a central life interest among the decisive motivations of economic activity under the condition of a market economy: Individuals „in varying degrees subjectively . . . value economically productive work as a *mode of life* (our emphasis)."

19. Borrowing Karl Polanyi's ([1944] 2001: 71) term of fictitious commodities, hybrid attributes of labor represent labor as a fictitious commodity. Labor is not a commodity since it is not produced for sale. The commodity description of labor is entirely fictitious. But in the course of the development of market organization, the fiction of money, land and labor "being so produced [as a commodity] became the organizing principle [of a market] society. . .; a network of measures and policies was integrated into powerful institutions designed to check the action of the market relative to labor, land and money" (Polanyi, [1944] 2000: 79). The price of fictitious commodities extends to hybrid (market and non-market) attributes.

20. Perhaps one of the best examples of hybrid qualities would be the volume of social capital an individual is able to mobilize. Agust Arnorsson and Gylfi Zoega (2016) for example find significant differences of social capital between and within European regions and surmise that these differences in the capacity of individuals to be independent, imaginative and tolerant may account for variations in unemployment, male labor participation and average hours of work.

21. Nathan Wilmers (2017: 178) reports findings, valid for the USA indicating that industries more dependent on high-income *consumers* have greater income inequalities. The segmentation of consumers contributes to wage inequality patterns among corporations and the economy in general. The large scale statistical study of David Autor (2014: 36) and his colleagues concludes "workers who in 1991—prior to China's rapid growth—were employed in an industry that was subsequently exposed to greater import competition from China experienced over the 1992 to 2007 period lower cumulative earnings, weakly lower cumulative employment, lower earnings per year worked, and greater reliance on Social Security Disability Insurance. . . . Reductions in cumulative earnings are concentrated among workers with low initial wages, workers with low tenure at their initial firm, workers with weak attachment to the labor force, and those employed at large firms with low wage levels."

22. For Luis Garicano and Esteban Rossi-Hansberg (2014: 6), an employee's salary is *the* indicator or definition of the extent of her knowledge or skills.
23. As Francis Teal (2011: S8) emphasizes "the central fact about the price of labour is that its price is much more closely correlated with where the person lives than with what they know. In other words, geography matters far more than human capital" (also Treffler, 1993).
24. In this context, David Autor (2015a: 16) points out "if demand for the output of abstract task-intensive activities is inelastic, these productivity gains might work to lower expenditure on these outputs, which could mitigate wage gains. However, all outward evidence suggests that as technology has boosted the output of the professions, demand for their services has more than kept pace. Health care is an obvious example, but one can readily make similar arguments about finance, law, engineering, research, and design."
25. The discussion among policy makers and social scientists about the impact of a changing age structure on the labor market, productivity and economic growth has become more intensive in recent years in the „developed" world as their populations age; see for example an early discussion of this set of issues in Murphy and Welch (1992) and present-day contribution in Acemoglu and Restrepo (2017) and Maestas, Mullen and Powell (2016). The more recent contributions begin to center on the impact of robots and Artificial Intelligence on the volume of socially necessary labor.
26. As Acemoglu and Restrepo (2018d: 1489) specify based on new occupational titles "today, as industrial robots, digital technologies, computer-controlled machines, and artificial intelligence replace labor, we are again witnessing the emergence of new tasks ranging from engineering and programming functions to those performed by audio-visual specialists, executive assistants, data administrators and analysts, meeting planners, and social workers. Indeed, during the last 35 years, new tasks and new job titles have accounted for a large fraction of US employment growth."
27. For example, in a *Guardian* essay (Saval 2017) on the disadvantages of globalization for the price of labor one finds the following observation summarizing the consequences of the "integration" of the global economy: "Over and over, [the workers] would be held hostage to the possibility that their business would up and leave, in order to find cheap labour in other parts of the world; they had to accept restraints on their salaries—or else. Opinion polls registered their strong levels of anxiety and insecurity, and the political effects were becoming more visible."
28. Not to be confused with the notion of the *just price* a now somewhat obscure notion in economics that signals for the most part the *market price* as an expression of the just price (de Roover, 158: 422).
29. The moral component of the price/value of labor is not necessarily *without calculation*. For example, the cost of additional free time instead of wages can be computed by the employer. But if the moral component is subjected to calculation, calculation is a minor even disliked element of the value of labor. Calculation destroys the specificity of the moral component of the price of labor. The moral component of the price of labor points to the value of labor *in-itself* and not *for-itself*.
30. Our distinction between a moral and a material (existential) component of the price of labor resonates with the difference between a *vita contemplativa* and a *vita activa*; a distinction, as Hannah Arendt (1987: 24) observes, which "we encounter in our tradition of philosophical and religious thought up to the threshold of the modern age" and "that when we speak of contemplation and action we speak not only of certain human faculties but of two distinct ways of life." Active life is the condition for the possibility of contemplation; or, as Arendt (1987: 24) underlines as well, active life "is not only what most men are engaged in but even what no man can escape altogether. For it is in the nature of the human condition that contemplation remains dependent upon all sorts of activities—it depends upon labor to produce whatever is necessary to keep the

human organism alive, it depends upon work to create whatever is needed to house the human body, and it needs action in order to organize the living together of many human beings in such a way that peace, the condition for the quiet of contemplation is assured." The moral component of the price of labor makes possible and enhances opportunities of a *vita contemplativa*.

31. The data used in the study by De Neve und Ward are mainly based on the Gallup World Poll. The Gallup World Poll covers over 150 countries and is representative of 98% of the world's population.

32. It is in this context that the analysis of the origin, distribution and differentiation of economic preferences carried out by Anne Becker, Benjamin Enke and Armin Falk (2018) is of relevance.

33. The economist Chinhui Juhn and his colleagues (2017: 30) using firm-level data in manufacturing, retail and selected service industries and for workers that are *continuing* with the firm find that "in the 2000s, very little of the volatility in firm performance is passed through to workers." The authors speculate that firms "are more likely to lay off workers [than in the European context we would add] in adverse circumstances and employment risk has increased for American workers."

34. Peter Drucker (1999: 89) offers a significant example of the price of labor as an *incentive*: "The Ford Motor Company . . . increased the pay of skilled workers from eighty cents a day to $5.00 a day on January 1, 1914. It did so because its turnover had been so excessive as to make its labor costs prohibitively high; it had to hire 60,000 people a year to keep 10,000. Even so, everybody (including Henry Ford himself, who had at first been bitterly opposed to this increase) was convinced that the higher wages would greatly reduce the company's profits. Instead, in the very first year, profits almost doubled. Paid $5.00 a day, practically no workers left—in fact, the Ford Motor Company soon had a waiting list."

35. The personal/individual attribution of the moral components and existential parts of wages, as well as their evaluation, is of course not least a function of the person's own values (see for example Frank, Wertebroch and Maddux, 2015).

36. Note that the elucidation of social inequality in this statement is accompanied by its exclusion of women.

37. Joseph Schumpeter's (1954: 311) judgment of Adam Smith's theory of value is harsh and uncompromising: "To this day, it has remained difficult to make the philosophy-minded see that all this is completely irrelevant for a theory of value—considered not as a phenomenon of faith or as an argument in social ethics, but as a tool of analysis of economic reality."

38. Adam Smith ([1976] 2012: 111) already recognizes the existence of the *professions* and the relevance of what later became the *human capital theory*; on both grounds, the social trust extended towards such individuals (their functional importance) and their exceptional educational accomplishment explain why professionals command a higher wage: "We trust our health to the physician: our fortune and sometimes our life and reputation to the lawyer and attorney. Such confidence could not safely be reposed in people of a very mean or low condition. Their reward must be such, therefore, as may give them that rank in the society which so important a trust requires. The long time and the great expense which must be laid out in their education, when combined with this circumstance, necessarily enhance still further the price of their labour."

39. As has become evident, we are refraining from elaborating Karl Marx's theory of labor value since it has significant intellectual linkages to the theory of labor value developed by Adam Smith (and David Ricardo). Hence the Marxian perspective on the price of labor does not add significantly to the theory just outlined. For Karl Marx ([1875] 1981: 18), in his *Critique of the Gotha Program*, "labour is *not the source* of all wealth. *Nature* is just as much the source of use values . . . as labour itself is only the manifestation of a force of nature." The standard interpretation of Marx's theory

of wage determination is to point out that wages are on average equal to the value of labor power (for example, the cost of their production). We will point to an exception later that suggest that Marx had an inkling about the notion of the moral component of wages. Marxian analysis maintains that profits arise from the exploitation of labor. It follows that labor-intensive production should be more profitable than profits generated by corporations that use little labor. Is that the really the case?

40. John Maynard Keynes ([1936] 1961: 17) points out that in an economy with a given organization, equipment and technique "real wages and the volume of output (and hence of employment) are uniquely correlated, so that, in general, an increase in employment can only occur to the accompaniment of a decline in the rate of real wages."

41. Compare the notion of *immaterial labor* as discussed by Maurizio Lazzaroto (1996) and André Gorz ([2003] 2010). Lazzarato (1996: 133) defines immaterial labor as labor „that produces the informational and cultural content of the commodity." In contrast, Michael Hardt and Antonio Negri (2004: 108) support a much more comprehensive approach. According to them, immaterial labor "creates immaterial products, such as knowledge, information, communication, a relationship, or an emotional response."

42. It should be noted that in tracing the evolution of the capitalist mode of production, Karl Marx always took considerable care to include both the "negative" and the "emancipating" effects of the forces of production. However, as long as the advances of science and technology occur within the frame of capitalist relations of production, their development fosters the profits of the owners of the means of production, at the expense of the workers. After all, for Marx, socialist modes of production do not involve scrapping modern technological means of production (cf. Sohn-Rethel, 1978). As to whether it is possible to respond to the contentious idea that what Marx suggests is an exemplary form of technological determinism, see both the affirmative and the negative answers provided by Heilbroner, 1965; Dickson, 1974; MacKenzie, 1984.

43. There is a strong measure of ambivalence in the Marxian set of metaphors designed to capture the nature of the greatest productive force to displace direct labor. Besides the power of agencies, Marx ([1939–1941] 1973: 705–706) refers to the general state of science, general social knowledge, or the general powers of the human mind.

44. The question of the foundations of the growth of knowledge workers has been discussed first in Nico Stehr (2000). We are drawing on these observations regarding the societal basis of the productivity paradox, that is, the change in the supply (the composition of the labor force) rather than the demand side of the world of work.

45. Among the surprising even amazing properties of the transformation of the labor market is that the American economy was able to "satisfy the expectations of all these people with long years of schooling. . . . As a result of the change in supply, we now have to create genuine knowledge jobs, whether the work itself demands it or not. For a true knowledge job is the only way to make highly schooled people productive. . . . That the knowledge worker came first and knowledge work second—that indeed knowledge work is still largely to come—is a historical accident. From now on, we can expect increasing emphasis on work based on knowledge, and especially skills based on knowledge" (Drucker, [1968] 1992: 285).

46. Claudia Goldin and Lawrence Katz (2008: 119) reject the stipulated supply-side thesis as not consistent with the evidence. However, there is conflation of demand and supply issues in their own discussion of the issue.

47. John Kenneth Galbraith dismisses Drucker's argument out of hand. He affirms the orthodox view about the relation between education and the labor market and considers Drucker's perspective as evidence for the typical self-complacency and pretension of the educator misreading the real power balance in society in the process. Galbraith (1967: 238) suggests it is the "vanity of educators that they shape the educational system to their preferred image. They may not be without influence but the decisive

force is the economic system. What the educator believes is latitude is usually latitude to respond to economic need." In other words, Galbraith insists that the *demand*-side explanation generally favored by economists (as well as employers, educators and educational policy makers one should add) primarily accounts for the increase in skilled work.

48. The degree of technology intensity in individual firms was measured by the authors of the study by counting the number of technical processes or devices such as computer driven machines, robots and so on found in the plants (see Doms, Dunne and Troske, 1997: 287–288 for a detailed description of the different processes and devices).

49. In concrete terms, "the positive relationship between technology use and the percent of skilled workers is primarily due to a dramatic increase in the percent of scientists and engineers in the most technologically advanced plants" (Doms, Dunne and Troske, 1997: 263).

50. Observations and at times, of course, concerns that the quality of the available jobs may not be compatible with rising educational levels (Harman, 1978: 209) correspond to exactly the opposite perspective, namely that the basic transformations of the world of work are primarily driven by the nature of the *demand*.

51. Thibault Darcillon (2015: 499) reports that he found "robust results suggesting that the process of financialization has gradually contributed to a weakening of workers' bargaining power in the direction of an erosion/decentralization: most OECD countries have experienced an erosion of collective bargaining power since the early 1970s with the decline in union density and union coverage. Second, economies with traditional centralized collective bargaining institutions evolve toward a decentralization of the industrial relations. Similarly, I find strong evidence that the process of financialization affects employment protection institutions. I find results showing that financialization is associated with a reduction in the level of employment protection legislation."

52. The countries in question are: Australia, Austria, Belgium, Canada, the Czech Republic, Denmark, Finland, France, Germany, Greece, Hungary, Island, Italia, Luxemburg, Holland, New Zealand, Norway, Portugal, Slovenia, Spain, Sweden, Switzerland, Great Britain, and the United States.

53. These numbers are the result of an extrapolation (see Dobbs et al., 2016) based on a detailed study in six countries (where data were available, namely France, Italy, Holland, Sweden, Great Britain and the USA) to these 25 countries.

54. "Using panel data on individual labor income histories from 1957 to 2013," Guvenen et al. (2017: 1) document "the *distribution of lifetime income in the United States*. . . . From the cohort that entered the labor market in 1967 to the cohort that entered in 1983, median lifetime income of men declined by 10%–19%. . . . For women, median lifetime income increased by 22%–33% from the 1957 to the 1983 cohort, but these gains were relative to very low lifetime income for the earliest cohort" (our emphasis).

55. James Bessen (2018: 14) present a model in which "the responsiveness of demand is key to understanding whether major new technologies will decrease or increase employment in affected industries"; for example, if "productivity-enhancing technology will increase industry employment if product demand is sufficiently elastic. If the price elasticity of demand is greater than one, the increase in demand will more than offset the labor saving effect of the technology." Missing from Bessen's model that stresses changes in the demand function are considerations about the nature of any changes in the demand; for example, changing preferences of the consumer that could be quite independent from the price of the service or the commodity.

56. Our reference here is to Martin Ford's (2015) monograph entitled *When Robots Rise: Technology and the Threat of a Jobless Future*.

57. The answer for many observers is in the affirmative though vague: For example, the Bank of England's Chief Economist Andy Haldane warned on Monday, August 20, 2018 "that the rise of artificial intelligence (AI) threatens to replace a huge number of jobs" (Browne 2018).

58. As Daron Acemoglu and Pascual Restrepo (2018b: 32–33) explain "the adjustment process is likely to be slower and more painful than this account of balance between automation and new tasks at first suggests. This is because the reallocation of labor from its existing jobs and tasks to new ones is a slow process, in part owing to time-consuming search and other labor market imperfections. But even more ominously, new tasks require new skills, and especially when the education sector does not keep up with the demand for new skills, a mismatch between skills and technologies is bound to complicate the adjustment process."

59. Cf. *Automation and Technological Change*: Hearings Before the United States Joint Committee on the Economic Report, Subcommittee on Economic Stabilization, Eighty-Fourth Congress, First Session, on Oct. 14, 15, 17, 18, 24–28, 1955 (United States, 1955).

60. A partial exception is a study by the International Monetary Fund (IMF) published in 2018. The IMF forecasts that approximately 180 million women and 150 males around the globe, with particular emphasis on Asia, will lose their jobs due to the automation of industry in the next two decades (see "180 Millionen 'weibliche' Arbeitsplätze in Gefahr," *Frankfurter Allgemeine Zeitung, October 10, 2018, p. 17*).

61. David Autor (2015b: 5) refers in this context to a paradox of abundance: "The paradox is that the threat to social welfare posed by technological change is the threat of excess rather than the threat of scarcity." The (growing) prosperity of society is seen as a threat to the well-being of society, since the (technological) source of this growing prosperity may result in rising unemployment.

62. According to Peter Drucker (1955a: 41) the term "automation" originated with the Ford Company's manufacturing vice-president Del Harder in 1945 describing the technological revolution of the second half of the 20th century and defining it as machines run by machines.

63. The concept of robots can first be found in discussions about the future of industrial society in the 1920s and 1930s. The 1920 stage play by Karel Capek (Rossum's Universal Robots) plays an important role. As Tobias Higbie (2013: 103) points out, robots at that time, as uniform entities and obedient servants to their boss, were in conflict with the workers' sense of freedom. Over the decades, the concept of the robot has expanded to become a symbol of modern technology and rarely as an indication of workers' rebellion.

64. Business Insider, March 16, 2016: www.businessinsider.com/carls-jr-wants-open-automated-location-2016-3.

65. In spite of the generally optimistic outlook about the long-term impact of technological change, especially automation on employment the 1964 "[US] Blue-Ribbon National Commission on Technology, Automation, and Economic Progress recommended "a guaranteed minimum income for each family; using the government as the employer of last resort for the hard core jobless; two years of free education in either community or vocational colleges; a fully administered federal employment service, and individual Federal Reserve Bank sponsorship in area economic development free from the Fed's national headquarters" (as quoted by Autor, 2015a: 3). A proposal that resonates with this idea continues to be discussed until this day now generally under the heading of a guaranteed minimum income or basic income guarantee.

66. Technological unemployment according to Keynes ([1930] 1963: 325) refers to "unemployment due to our discovery of means of economising the use of labour outrunning the pace at which we can find new uses for labour." Involuntary unemployment is a category of unemployment *classical* economic theory does not recognize. John Maynard Keynes ([1936] 1961: 15) definition of involuntary unemployment refers to "*men [that] are involuntarily unemployed if, in the event of a small rise in the price of wage-goods relatively to the money-wage, both the aggregate supply of labour willing to work for the current money-wage and the aggregate demand for it at that wage would be greater than the existing volume of employment.*" For Keynes ([1930] 1963: 325) technological unemployment

will be "a temporary phase of maladjustment [if] in the long run. . . *mankind is solving its economic problem.*"

67. The OECD measure of hours worked, as displayed in the next graphic may actually underestimate the decline in hours worked per job because individuals now accumulate working hours across multiple jobs more often than in the past (IMF, 2017: 78). The number of individuals who hold multiple jobs in the developed economies has increased significantly in the last years. The evidence indicates, "hours declined more in sectors with higher shares of low- and middle-skilled workers, suggesting that factors were at play beyond workers preferences (IMF, 20§7 78–79).

68. Citing an Austrian study from 1976, Leontief (1982: 204) remarks that unemployment in the country would by 1990 reach ten percent, that is, if state-of-the-art labor-saving technology would be fully applied. We now know that at least this projection did not come true. The actual unemployment rate in Austria was quite low in the 1990s (in 1990 close to 3 percent) demonstrating how difficult it is to make such projections.

69. Source: https://ec.europa.eu/research/industrial_technologies/pdf/robotics-ppp-roadmap_en.pdf; The political purpose on the report "Robotics 2020" is clearly expressed in the document: "The strategy presented in this document promotes collaboration between partners in the wider European robotics community, the stimulation of investment and the creation of an innovation climate, all of which are critical to ensuring that advances in technology are brought to market in time to increase European competitiveness and establish Europe as a global supplier in key robotic markets."

70. Interview with Andrew McAfee, "Eine Welt ohne Plackerei," *Der Spiegel* 25. August 2014, p. 69.

71. An overview article in the *New York Times* by Kim Tingley (2017) points out after visiting a laboratory that produces robots, "At the M.I.T. Media Lab, researchers have programmed a 'growth mind-set' into robots that have enough personality to engage preschoolers in puzzle games. An initial study showed that playing with these robots, which respond to adversity with statements like 'I will do better next time,' increased the likelihood of children's believing that they can improve with practice: The robot was a teacher but also an experimental control for testing theories of mind. Across the street, Julie Shah is designing robots that can shadow people in highly instinctual jobs, like head nurses, and detect patterns in how they make decisions. This would enable the nurses to use them to help train rookies."

72. David Autor (2015: 27) points to additional job descriptions, who's primarily manual tasks will likely be subject to automatization in the coming decade: "I anticipate that we will see fewer housekeepers and janitors, fewer waiters and busboys, fewer vehicle operators, fewer assembly line workers, fewer store stockers and warehouse workers, and fewer salespersons—even in 'brick and mortar' shops."

73. See Editorial Board, 2017.

74. As cited in the same *New York Times* editorial of February 21, 2017.

75. See the draft report by the member of the European parliament Mady Delvaux from the committee on legal affairs published in May of 2016.

76. See Naughton 2017.

77. A rigid economic division of society will no doubt have consequences for its political order. Drutman and Mounk (2016) anticipate the following serious political consequences: "Devoid of the middle class that has historically sustained it, democracy is unlikely to survive. At some point, deep inequality will undermine elites' support for democracy. They will simply have too much to lose from policies that help the growing ranks of the poor. Given elites' considerable resources, and their dwindling need for the human labor (or force) that the masses provide, they are likely to coopt the democratic process to serve their own ends in an even more radical way than they do now—or to dispense with the pretense of democracy altogether. Without a

middle class between the rich and the poor, it seems unlikely that popular democratic institutions can survive. As sociologist Barrington Moore put it: 'no bourgeois, no democracy'."

78. The difficulties experienced in exactly defining the economic effects of technological advances did not extend to the notion of technological progress itself. As a matter of fact, the conception of technological progress that prevailed at the time was strictly instrumental, and limited to advances made in the processes of exchange with nature designed to enhance the efficiency of man's domination of nature or, as one might characterize the same idea today, to more effectively exploit nature (cf. Ott, 1971: 9).

79. The assertion, frequently voiced, that the amount of employment growth can be calculated once the rate of technological change is known fails to take into consideration a number of relevant factors and processes such as, for instance, the impact of real wages, prices, interest rates and profits on the gross national product, the volume of work and the rate of technological "progress."

80. Cf. for example Günter Friedrichs (1963), who summarizes and interprets the findings of a number of studies regarding the impact of automation and other technological advances on the labor force.

81. See "Wettrüsten der Anlageroboter. Der Erfolg computergestützter Anlageprogramme für Privatanleger hat die Wertpapierbranche aufgeschreckt [The arms race of the robot investors. The success of computer-assisted investment programs for private investors has frightened the securities industry]," *Frankfurter Allgemeine Zeitung*, June 16, 2016, p. 30.

82. Nick Srnicek and Alex Williams (2015: 126) suggest that labor should no longer be the only credible issue on the political agenda of the left: "A twenty-first century left must seek to combat the centrality of work to contemporary life. . . . Work must be refused and reduced, building on synthetic freedom in the process." The abolition of much of socially necessary work requires, as a logical consequence, "full automation; the reduction of the working week; universal basic income and the diminishment of the work ethic" (Srnicek and Williams, 2015: 127).

83. See Tabuchi 2017.

84. See Coldewey and Lardinois 2017.

85. PwC UK (2017) "*Consumer spending prospects and the impact of automation on jobs*," www. pwc.co.uk/services/economics-policy/insights/uk-economic-outlook.html

86. Jean-François Lyotard ([1979] 1984: 53) anticipates that "professors" will eventually no longer be needed; much of the labor professors currently perform can and will be taken over by computerized data network systems.

87. See for example: "Wir werden Götter sein," interview with the historian Yuval Noah Harari; *Der Spiegel* Nr. 12, March 18, 2017, p. 106.

88. The cautious, if not deliberately vague formulation of Nancy Stokey's (2016: 36) study of the relationship between technology, work skills and wage structure underscores our conclusion: "Wage inequality has displayed large and long-lived shifts over the last century . . . and many of these shifts are surely due to changes in technology."

89. The unabbreviated reference in Marx's *Critique of the Gotha Program* reads as follows: "In a higher phase of communist society, after the enslaving subordination of the individual to the division of labor, and therewith also the antithesis between mental and physical labor, has vanished; after labor has become not only a means of life but life's prime want; after the productive forces have also increased with the all-around development of the individual, and all the springs of co-operative wealth flow more abundantly—only then can the narrow horizon of bourgeois right be crossed in its entirety and society inscribe on its banners: From each according to his ability, to each according to his needs."

90. The idea of a just price seems to resonate with the moral component of the price of labor. The contested (and mainly banished from economics) notion of a just price,

however, is in its main core quite different from what we describe as moral pay. The idea of a just price is often at the core of regulations of economic affairs and their justification such as the minimum wages, laws against loan shaking, dumping, or anti-trust legislation. The just price philosophy is therefore often seen as detrimental to the unfettered operation of the market. In this sense, a just price is the current market price. As Robert Skidelsky (2010: 145–146) notes, John Maynard Keynes opted in favor of operating in economics with the idea of a just price. Just prices for Keynes are "those which correctly reward talents and efforts."

91. The idea that labor alone produces wealth has to be extended as to Karl Marx (1875: 18) himself insisted in his *Critique of the Gotha Program*: "labour is not the source of all wealth. Nature is just as much the source of use values . . . as labour, which itself is only the manifestation of a force of nature."

92. Universal basic income experiments are carried out in a number of countries at the present time, for example, in Finland, Kenya, USA and Canada. The amount of money made available, the number of individuals involved, and the length of the experiments varies, of course. The results that are reported to date are insufficient to pass judgment about the advantages or flaws of the universal basis income (cf. Carrie Arnold, "The Anti-Poverty Experiment," *Nature* 557: 626–628).

93. At the present time, an individual in Germany is permitted to hold on to Euro 1133,80 that are exempt from seizure; additional family members—up to a maximum of five—add to the total monies not subject to seizure. A couple with two children for example is able to set aside a total of Euro 2035,97.

93. The text of the *The Fair Labor Standards Act* of 1938 as amended can be found here: www.dol.gov/whd/regs/statutes/FairLaborStandAct.pdf; it should be noted that "the Fair Labor Standards Act excludes any business with gross annual revenue less than $500,000 whose employees do not engage in "interstate commerce." It also contains a variety of smaller occupational exclusions, such as those for telephone switchboard operators, private investigators, and babysitters" (The Economic Policy Institute: www.epi.org/minimum-wage-tracker/?gclid=EAIaIQobChMI2v6Hu_202wIVcyjTCh1K YgZ_EAAYAiAAEgJsoPD_BwE.

95. See the FAQ on their website: https://poverty.ucdavis.edu/faq/what-history-minimum-wage.

96. The discussion of a fair price can be traced back to medieval discourses. The determination of the just price by scholars of this period was the result of the sum of economic and ethical aspects (cf. Hamouda and Prices, 1997).

97. The irrelevance of the certain means of orientation (for example, this business is reliable; this salesperson is not knowledgeable; this customer is trustworthy; I have always shopped well in this store, and so on) for the conduct of market participants, together with an understanding of the attributes of other individuals or corporate actors, enhances the complexity of decision-making. But in practice, as Niklas Luhmann ([1970] 1982: 199) for example stresses this complexity is likely to be reduced or undercut by reverting to these very means of orientation: "In more complex markets, where organizations rather than individuals make exchanges, and where personalization is thus not possible, other functionally equivalent 'mollifications' replace it—above all agreements about limiting competition. By such means, the complexity and risks of the market are reduced to practicable and secure forms."

98. Social "tolerance" and acceptance of the specific rules of economic code and conduct, however, can only be expected "if there is a guarantee that economic decisions do not *eo ipso* fulfill political, familial, educational, and military functions and that changes in the economy not be automatically carried over into other functional domains of the society, but instead be perceived by them as changes in their environment that can be worked over adaptively" (Luhmann, [1970] 1982: 201).

99. In much the same sense, Niklas Luhmann ([1970] 1982: 203) emphasizes that the "communication of set prices [in particular] requires no further discussion. Through this lack of ambiguity, economic communication becomes indifferent to circumstances, to biographical details, and to personal acquaintances. People do not need to know each other and to size up each other morally in order to come to an understanding."

100. Frank Knight's (1950) examination of "just wages" is mainly concerned with incomes from two sources, capital and labor power; as a consequence, the issue is whether unequal incomes in the form of profit and wages can be considered just. For Wilhelm Baldamus (1960: 79), approaching the issue of just wages with a focus on wages and profits, however, is representative of a 19th century perspective with its concern with the functional distribution of national incomes.

101. We relied on the German edition of Baldamus' analysis. The English edition carried the title *Efficiency and Effort* (Baldamus, 1961).

102. See Morgan Housel, "How this all happened," www.collaborativefund.com/blog/how-this-all-happened/ which is a short story about what occurred to the economy in the United States since the end of World War II. Robert Gordon (2016) has written an economic history of the United States that covers the period where real wages rose rapidly. He calls the time between 1870 and 1979 "the special century." His conclusion about the future of economic growth is more circumspect. Gordon does not expect a repeat performance.

103. For some years now, a number of theoretical and empirical studies have been carried out investigating the question of specific occupational skills and, on the basis of this information, examine the demand side of occupational tasks. For example, Author, Levy and Murnane (2003) coined the term "task framework" (working activities) to help answer the question of the skills that are actually required in the individual jobs (see also Author and Thorn, 2013). However, as Autor and Handel (2013: 561) point out self-critically, the question of the relationship between occupational activities and human capital is an unfinished desideratum: "This disjuncture between tasks and human capital is particularly relevant to the analysis of *the wage returns to job tasks*" (our emphasis).

104. Using the educational level as a proxy for skills, middle-skill employees are individuals with some postsecondary education, low-skill level workers are defined as individuals with a high-school degree or less and high-level employees refer to those with a bachelor's or advanced degree (cf. Monestino, 2016).

105. Ina Elisabeth Rüber and Thijs Bol (2017: 774) report for the German case that informal learning (life-long learning) on the job, that is "self-initiated acquisition of knowledge" though it assumes both a core role in political and scientific discussions about skill formation in the contemporary world of work and in the (dynamic) human capital perspective has no impact on wages.

106. As Michael Handel (2016: 178) points out, "a longstanding problem was that most of these studies used either rough proxy measures of job skill demands available in nationally representative data sets (broad occupation group, personal education, average education within occupations), occupation-level job measures from individual cross-sections . . . or, more rarely, case-level measures created for unique surveys administered to restricted samples."

107. A *New York Times* article describes the fear of a practicing physician that his profession could soon be to transformed into an appendix of machines; the threat, more precisely refers to "electronic health records and machine learning pose to the physician's clinical judgment," in fact, turning medical doctors into clerical workers. www.nytimes.com/interactive/2018/05/16/magazine/health-issue-what-we-lose-with-data-driven-medicine.html?hp&action=click&pgtype=Homepage&clickSource=story-head

108. The information from the PDII survey covers work activities and therefore allow an analysis of different characteristics of identically named occupations.

109. Nico Stehr (2000) has pointed out that the productivity paradox coincides with a substantial change in the composition of the labor force. The workforce at the time shifted increasingly to more educated workers. In other terms, the explanation for the productivity paradox old and new should not only involve economic or technical dimensions and processes but extend to societal (secular) changes as well. For example, James Manyika and Myron Scholes, 2018) offer such an account of the recent (digital) paradox identifying "historically low growth in capital intensity, digitization, and a weak demand recovery. Together these features help explain why annual productivity growth dropped 80%, on average, between 2010 and 2014, to 0.5%, from 2.4% a decade earlier."

110. Dale Jorgenson (1997: 4) sees the productivity paradox as arising from the prevailing identification of "productivity growth with technological change." Technological change and productivity gains are distinct. Productivity growth is but a minor component to growth. Technological change occurs, he argues, as a result of investments; economic growth also is due to capital investment. Capital investments can be categorized into investments into tangible assets, human and intellectual capital. The purchase of computers constitutes an investment into tangible assets. But the key concept in this context, intellectual capital remains but a vague and perhaps even more irritating to economists an unmeasured and immeasurable concept.

111. In response to the prediction by Andy Haldane, the chief economist of the Bank of England that large "swathes" of jobs will disappear once AI takes over. The columnist of *The Guardian* replied on the same day affirming and specifying that many jobs done by humans will not disappear: "The latest cliche, the 'fourth industrial revolution,' supposedly describes a new algorithmic age. If there is to be a fourth revolution it will be the complete opposite, a reversion to the economy of human experience. The digital age will satisfy the mundanities of life, releasing leisure time for activities that are already soaring in demand. These cover everything from health, beauty, travel, food, the arts and entertainment to psychotherapy, social work, the care of children and the elderly. These service industries essentially involve human relationships. They cannot be done by robots or machines. They are labor-intensive and they are costly, whether in the private or public sector. They are also booming. Leisure and travel are second in value only to financial services" (Source: www.theguardian.com/commentisfree/2018/aug/20/robots-stealing-jobs-digital-age).

112. Temporary and part-time workers are more common now than in pre-recession years (cf. IMF, 2017: 78).

113. The International Monetary Fund (2017: 90) suggests that in recent years "Automation (proxied by the relative price of investment goods) appears to have made a small contribution to subdued wage dynamics following the Great Recession due to a limited decline in the relative price of investment goods in recent years compared with the previous downward trend. The analysis suggests that automation could weigh on wage growth more substantially in the future if the decline in the relative price of investment goods were to pick up again."

114. In their paper, Dominique Guellec and Caroline Paunow (2017: 1) argue that "the increasing importance of digital innovation (which are new products and processes based on or embodied in software code and data, in and beyond IT industries) is magnifying innovation-based (and possibly bigger) rents that contribute to increasing the income share of the top income groups. Specifically the paper focuses on inequality coming from market rents accruing to top executives, key employees and shareholders, but little to the average worker."

115. James Bession (2017: 34) emphasizes as a result of his research into the relationship between automation and workload: If the demand for an industry's products is highly elastic, technological change will lead to more jobs in the industry in question.

116. Thomas Piketty ([2013] 2014: 24) offers a possible explanation for the statistics, suggesting that "the skills and productivity of od these top managers rose suddenly in relation to those of other workers." A different account would emphasize the impact of financialization and the size of *boni* (partially self-allocated). As a matter of fact, in the United Kingdom boni are counted as labor's share.

117. We are using Hans Staehle's (1943) translation of the original German Schumpeter quote.

118. The best we are able to conclude about the magnitude and the shifting relevance of attributes of individuals that influence the price paid for labor at any given time are for example observations such as those found in a study by Catherine Weinberger (2014), who reports that in the United States employment in and the premium paid for *both* high levels of social and cognitive skills grew substantially in the last decade of the 20th century compared to occupations hat require only one or none of these skills.

# References

Acemoglu, Daron and Pascual Restrepo (2018a), "Demographics and automation," *NBER Working Paper* No. 24421.

Acemoglu, Daron and Pascual Restrepo (2018b), "Artificial intelligence, automation and work," *NBER Working Paper* No. 24196.

Acemoglu, Daron and Pascual Restrepo (2018c), "Low-skill and high-skill automation," *Journal of Human Capital* 12: 204–232.

Acemoglu, Daron and Pascual Restrepo (2018d), "The race between man and machine: Implications of technology for growth, factor shares, and employment," *American Economic Review* 108: 1488–1542.

Acemoglu, Daron and Pascal Restrepo (2017), "Robots and jobs. Evidence form the U.S. labor market," *NBER Working Paper* No. 23285.

Acemoglu, Daron and David Autor (2012), "What does human capital do? A review of Golding and Katz's *The Race between Education and Technology*," *Journal of Economic Literature* 50: 426–463.

Acemoglu, Daron and David Autor (2011), "Skills, tasks and technologies: Implications for employment and earnings," pp. 1043–1171 in David Card and Orley Ashenfelter (eds.), *Handbook of Labor Economics, Volume 4*. Amsterdam: Elsevier.

Acemoglu, Daron (2002), "Technical change, inequality, and the labor market," *Journal of Economic Literature* 40: 7–72.

Alarcon, Diana (2018), "Comments on the report of the international panel for social progress, Chapter 7: The future of work, good jobs for all," *Economics & Philosophy*. DOI:10.1017/S0266267118000251

Arendt Hannah (1987), "Labor, work, action," pp. 24–49 in S. J. W. Bernauer (ed.), *Amor Mundi. Boston College Studies in Philosophy*. Dordrecht: Springer.

Arnorsson, Agust and Gylfi Zoega (2016), "Social capital and the labor market," *Capitalism and Society* 11 (1): Article 1.

Arntz, Melanie, Terry Gregory and Ulrich Zierahn (2016), "The risk of automation for jobs in OECD countries: A comparative analysis," *OECD Social, Employment and Migration Working Papers*, No. 189. Paris: OECD Publishing.

Aßländer, Michael S. (2008), "Was ist ein gerechter Lohn? Philosophisch-historische Anmerkungen zu einer zeitlosen Frage," *Forum Wirtschaftsethik* 16(4): 7–17.

Attewell, Paul (1994), "Information technology and the productivity paradox," pp. 13–53 in Douglas H. Harris (ed.), *Organizational Linkages. Understanding the Productivity Paradox*. Washington, DC: National Academy Press.

Autor, David H. (2017), "How long has this been going on? A discussion of 'recent flattening in the higher education wage premium: Polarization, skill downgrading, or both?" by Robert G. Valletta. National Bureau of Economic Research, Conference on Research and Income in Wealth.

Autor, David, David Dorn, Lawrence F. Katz, Christina Patterson and John Van Reenen (2017), "Concentrating on the fall of the labor share," *NBER Working Paper*.

Autor, David H., David Dorn, Gordon H. Hanson and Jae Song (2014), "Trade adjustment: worker-level evidence," *The Quarterly Journal of Economics* 129: 1799–1860.

Autor, David H. and David Dorn (2013), "The growth of low skill service jobs and the polarization of the U.S. labor market," *American Economic Review* 103: 1553–1597.

Autor, David (2015a), "Why are there still so many jobs? The history and future of workplace automation," *Economic Perspectives* 29: 3–30.

Autor, David H. (2015b), "Paradox of abundance," *Oxford Scholarship Online*, DOI:10.1093/acprof:oso/9780198744283.001.0001

Autor, David H., David Dorn and Gordon H. Hansen (2015), "Untangling trade and technology: Evidence from local labor markets," *Economic Journal* 125(584): 621–646.

Autor, David H. and Michael J. Handel (2013), "Putting tasks to the test: Human capital, job tasks, and wages," *Journal of Labor Economics* 31: S59–S91.

Autor, David H., Frank Levy and Richard J. Murnane (2003), "The skill content of recent technological change: An empirical investigation, *Quarterly Journal of Economics* 118: 1279–1333.

Avent-Holt, Dustin and Donald Tomaskovic (2010), "The relational basis of inequality: Generic and contingent wage distribution processes," *Work and Organizations* 37: 162–193.

Baecker, Dirk (2007), "Arbeiten ist gefährlich," pp. 56–72 in Dirk Baecker, *Studien zur nächsten Gesellschaft*. Frankfurt am Main: Suhrkamp.

Baldamus, Wilhelm (1984), "Efficiency and effort revisited," Paper to be presented to the Annual Conference of the British Sociological Association, Bradford, April. (unpublished).

Baldamus, Wilhelm (1961), *Efficiency and Effort*. London: Tavistock Publikations.

Baldamus, Wilhelm (1960), *Der gerechte Lohn. Eine industriesoziologische Analyse*. Berlin: Duncker & Humblot.

Barth, Erling, James C. Davis, Richard B. Freeman and Andrew J. Wang (2017), "The effects of scientists and engineers on productivity and earnings at the establishment where they work," *NBER Working Paper* No. 23484.

Beaudry, Paul, David A. Green and Benjamin M. Sand (2013), "The great reversal in the demand for skill and cognitive skills," *NBER Working Paper* No. 18901.

Beck, Ulrich ([1999] 2000), *The Brave New World of Work*. Cambridge: Polity Press.

Becker, Anke, Benjamin Enke and Armin Falk (2018), "Ancient origins of the global variation in economic preferences," *NBER Working Paper* No. 24291.

Becker, Gary S. (1994), *Human Capital: A Theoretical and Empirical Analysis with Special Reference to Education*, 3rd ed. Chicago, IL: University of Chicago Press.

Bell, Daniel (1973), *The Coming of Post-Industrial Society. A Venture in Social Forecasting*. New York: Basis Books.

Bendix, Reinhard ([1956] 1959), *Herrschaft und Industriearbeit. Untersuchungen über Liberalismus und Autokratie in der Geschichte der Industrialisierung*. Stuttgart: Europäische Verlagsanstalt.

Benjamin, Walter ([1938] 2006), "A chronicle of Germany's unemployed," pp. 126–134 in Walter Benjamin, *Selected Writings. Volume 4: 1938–1940*. Cambridge, MA: Harvard University Press.

Ben-Porath, Yoram (1967), "The production of human capital and the life cycle of earnings," *Journal of Political Economy* 75: 352–365.

Berger, Johannes (2004), "Über den Ursprung der Ungleichheit unter den Menschen," *Zeitschrift für Soziologie* 33: 354–374.

Berman, Eli, John Bound and Zvi Geliches (1994), "Changes in the demand for skilled labor within U.S. manufacturing industries: Evidence from the annual survey of manufacturing," *Quarterly Journal of Economics* 59: 367–398.

Bernard, Andrew B. and J. Bradford Jensen (1997), "Exporters, skill upgrading and the wage gap," *Journal of International Economics* 42: 3–31.

Bessen, James (2018), "AI and jobs: The role of demand," *NBER Working Paper* No. 24235.

Bessen, Janes (2017), "Automation and jobs: When technology boosts employment," Boston University School of Law. *Law & Economics Paper* No. 17–09.

Björklund, Anders and Markus Jätti (2012), "How important is family *background* for labor-economic outcomes?" *Labour Economics* 19: 465–474.

Blau, Francine D. and Lawrence M. Kahn (2017), "The gender wage gap: Extent, trends, and explanations," *Journal of Economic Literature* 55: 789–865.

Blaug, Mark (1976), "The empirical status of human capital theory: A slightly jaundiced survey," *Journal of Economic Literature* 14: 827–855.

Block, Fred and Larry Hirschhorn (1979), "New productive forces and the contradictions of contemporary capitalism," *Theory and Society* 17: 363–395.

Bonacich, Edna (1976), "Advanced capitalism and black/white race relations in the United States: A split level labor market interpretation," *American Sociological Review* 41: 34–51.

Borghans, Lex, Bas Ter Weel and Bruce A. Weinberg (2014), "People skills and the labor-market outcomes of underrepresented groups," *Industrial and Labor Relations Review* 67: 287–334.

Borjas, George J. and Richard B. Freeman (2019), "From immigrants to robots: The changing locus of substitutes for workers," *NBER Working Paper* No. 25438.

Bourguignon, François (2015), *The Globalization of Inequality*. Princeton, NJ: Princeton University Press.

Bourguignon, François (2014), "Inequality trends in the world: Common forces, idiosyncrasies and measurement errors," presented at the *Economic Research Forum*. Cairo. URL: https://www.slideshare.net/erf_latest/bourg-erf-2014 (accessed 15 July 2019).

Bowen, Harold R. (1966), *Report of the National Commission on Technology, Automation, and Economic Progress, Volume 1*. Washington, DC: U.S. Government Printing Office.

Bowles, Samuel, Herbert Gintis and Melissa Osborne (2001), "The determinants of earnings: A behavioral approach," *Journal of Economic Literature* 39: 1137–1176.

Braudel, Fernand ([1979] 1992), *The Structures of Everyday Life. The Limits of the Possible*. Berkeley: University of California Press.

Breza, Emily, Supreet Kaur and Yogita Shamdasani (2016), "The morale effects of pay inequity," *NBER Working Paper* No. 22491.

Browne, Ryan (2018), "Bank of England's chief economist warns A.I. could threaten 'large' amount of jobs," *CNBC.com* August 20. https://www.cnbc.com/2018/08/20/bank-of-england-haldane-ai-could-threaten-large-amount-of-jobs.html.

Brynjolfsson, Erik, Daniel Rock and Chad Syverson (2017), "Artificial intelligence and the modern productivity paradox—A clash of expectations and statistics," *NBER Working Paper* No. No. 24001.

Brynjolfsson, Erik and Andrew McAfee (2014), *Race Against the Machine. How the Digital Revolution is Accelerating Innovation, Driving Productivity, and Irreversibly Transforming Employment and the Economy*. Lexington, MA: Digital Frontier Press.

Brynjolfsson, Erik and Lorin Hitt (1996), "Paradox lost? Firm-level evidence on the returns to information systems spending," *Management Science* 42: 541–558.

Cappelli, Peter and J. R. Keller (2013), "Classifying work in the new economy," *Academy of Management Review* 38: 575–596.

Castells, Manuel ([1996] 2000), *The Information Age. Economy, Society and Culture. Volume 1: The Rise of the Network Society*, 2nd ed. Oxford: Blackwell.

Checci, Daniele and Herman G. van de Werfhorst (2017), "Policies, skills and earnings: How educational inequality affects earnings inequality," *Socio-Economic Review* 16: 137–160.

Chui, Michael, James Manyika and Mehdi Miremadi (2016), "Where machines could replace human—And where they can't (yet)," *McKinsey Quarterly* (June). URL: www.mckinsey.com/business-functions/business-technology/our-insights/where-machines-could-replace-humans-and-where-they-cant-yet (accessed 14 July 2019).

Clemens, Jeffrey, Lisa B. Kahn and Jonathan Meer (2018), "The minimum wage, fringe benefits, and worker welfare," *NBER Working Paper* No. 24635.

Clemens, Michael A. and Jennifer Hunt (2017), "The labor market effects of refugee waves: Reconciling conflicting results," *NBER Working Paper* No. 23433.

Coldewey, Devin and Frederic Lardinois (2017), "DeepL schools other online translators with clever machine learning," *Techcrunch.com*. techcrunch.com/2017/08/29/deepl-schools-other-online-translators-with-clever-machine-learning/.

Cushen, Jean (2013), "Financialization in the workplace – Hegemonic narratives, performative interventions and the angry knowledge worker," *Accounting, Organization and Society* 38: 314–331.

Czarnitzi, Dirk, Bronwyn H. Hall and Raffaele Oriani (2006), "Market valuation of US and European intellectual property," pp. 111–131 in Derek Bosworth (ed.), *The Management of Intellectual Property*. Cheltenham: Edward Elgar.

Dahrendorf, Ralf (2000), "Die globale Klasse und die neue Ungleichheit," *Merkur* 54: 1057–1068.

Dahrendorf, Ralf (1968), "On the origins of inequality among men," pp. 151–178 in Ralf Dahrendorf, *Essays in the Theory of Society*. London: Routledge & Kegan Paul.

Darcillon, Thibault (2015), "How does finance affect labor market institutions? An empirical analysis in 16 OECD countries," *Socio-Economic Review* 13: 477–504.

Dauth, Wolfgang, Sebastian Findeisen, Jens Suedekum and Nicole Woessner (2017), "German robots—the impact of industrial robots on workers," *Discussion Paper* No. DP12306, Centre for Economic Policy Research 33 Great Sutton Street, London EC1V 0DX, UK.

Davenport, Thomas H. and Julia Kirby (2016), *Only Humans need Apply. Winners and Losers in the Age of Smart Machines*. New York: HarperCollins.

Davenport, Thomas H. (2005), *Thinking for a Living. How to Get Better Performance and Results from Knowledge Workers*. Boston, MA: Harvard Business School.

Dekker, Fabian, Anna Salomons and Jeroen van der Waal (2017), "Fear of robots at work. The role of economic self-interest," *Socio-Economic Review* 15: 539–562.

Dencker, John C. and Chichun Fang (2016), "Rent seeking and the transformation of employment relationships: The effect of corporate restructuring on wage patterns, determinants, and inequality," *American Sociological Review* 81: 467–487.

Deming, David J. (2017), "The growing importance of social skills in the labor market," *The Quarterly Journal of Economics* 132: 1593–1640.

De Neve, Jan-Emanuel and George Ward (2017), "Happiness at Work," *CEP Discussion Paper* No. 1474. The Centre for Economic Performance. London School of Economics.

De Roover, Raymond (1958), "The concept of the just price: Theory and economic policy," *The Journal of Economic History* 18: 418–434.

Dickson, David (1974), *Alternative Technology and the Politics of Technical Change*. New York: Fontana.

Dingwall, Robert (1999), "Professions and social order in a global society," *International Review of Sociology* 9: 131–140.

Dobbs, Richard, Anu Madgavkar, James Manyika, Jonathan Woetzel, Jacques Bughin, Eric Labaye and Pranav Kashyap (2016), *Poorer than Their Parents? A New Perspective on Income Inequality*. McKinsey Global Institute Analysis. URL: www.mckinsey.com/global-themes/employment-and-growth/poorer-than-their-parents-a-new-perspective-on-income-inequality (accessed 14 July 2019).

Doms, Mark, Timothy Dunne and Kenneth Troske (1997), "Workers, wages and technology," *The Quarterly Journal of Economics* (February): 253–290.

Drucker, Peter (1999), "Knowledge-worker productivity: The biggest challenge," *California Management Review* 41: 79–94.

Drucker, Peter (1998), "Worker and work in the metropolis," *Daedalus* 97: 1243–1262.

Drucker, Peter F. (1994), *Post-capitalist Society*. London: Routledge.

Drucker, Peter ([1968] 1992), *The Age of Discontinuity. Guidelines to Our Changing Society. With a New Introduction by the Author*. New Brunswick, NJ: Transaction Books.

Drucker, Peter F. (1955a), "America's next twenty years I: The coming labor shortage," *Harper's Magazine* March 1: 27–32.

Drucker, Peter F. (1955b), "America's next twenty years II: The promise of automation," *Harper's Magazine* April 1: 41–47.

Drutman, Lee and Yascha Mounk (2016), "When the robots rise," *The National Interest*. URL: http://nationalinterest.org/feature/when-the-robots-rise-16830 (accessed 14 July 2019).

Dubin, Robert, Joseph E. Champoux and Lyman W. Porter (1975), "Central life interests and organizational commitment of blue-collar and clerical workers," *Administrative Science Quarterly* 20: 411–421.

Dubin, Robert (1956), "Industrial workers' worlds: A study of the 'central life interests' of industrial workers," *Social Problems* 3: 131–142.

Editorial Board (2017), "No, robots aren't killing the American dream," *New York Times* February 20. www.nytimes.com/2017/02/20/opinion/no-robots-arent-killing-the-american-dream.html?action=click&pgtype=Homepage&click Source=story-heading &module=opinion-c-col-left-region&region=opinion-c-col-left-region&WT. nav=opinion-c-col-left-region&_r=0.

Eichhorst, Werner, André Portela de Souza Pierre Cahuc, Didier Demazière, Colette Fagan, Nadya Araujo Guimarães, Huiyan Fu, Arne Kalleberg, Alan Manning, Frances McGinnity, Hillel Rapoport, Phil Scranton, Johannes Siegrist, Kathleen Thelen, Marie-Anne Valfort and Jelle Visser (2018), *The Future of Work. Good Jobs for All. Chapter 7 of International Panel on Social Progress*. Geneva: International Panel on Social Progress. URL: www.ipsp.org/download/chapter-7-future-work-pdf (accessed 14 July 2019).

Engel, Ernst (1857), "Die Produktions- und Cosumptionsverhältnisse des Königreichs Sachsen," *Zeitschrift des statistischen Bureaus des Königleich Sächsischen Ministeriums* 8–9, 28–29.

Eucken, Walter (1949), "Die Wettbewerbsordnung und ihre Verwirklichung," pp. 1–99 in Walter Eucken and Franz Böhm (eds.), *Ordo. Jahrbuch für die Ordnung von Wirtschaft und Gesellschaft*. Würzburg: De Gruyter.

Falk, Armin, Fabian Kosse, Ingo Menrath, Pablo E. Verde and Johannes Siegrist (2017), "Unfair pay and health," *Management Science*. DOI:10.1287/mnsc.2016.2630

Feher, Michel (2009), "Self-appreciation: Or, the aspirations of human capital," *Public Culture* 21: 21–41.

Festinger, Leon (1954), "A theory of social comparison processes," *Human Relations* 7: 117–140.

Ford, Martin (2015), *When Robots Rise. Technology and the Threat of a Jobless Future*. New York: Basic Books.

Frank, Douglas H., Wertenbroch, Klaus and William W. Maddux (2015), "Performance pay or redistribution? Cultural differences in just-world beliefs and preferences for wage inequality," *INSEAD and WHARTON Alliance Working Paper Series*.

Frey, Carl B. and Michael A, Osborne (2013), *The Future of Employment: How Susceptible Are Jobs to Computerisation?* URL: http:// www.oxfordmartin.ox.ac.uk/downloads/ academic/The_Future_of_Employment.pdf (accessed 21 July 2017).

Friedrichs, Günter (1963), 'Technischer Fortschritt und Beschäftigung in Deutschland," pp. 80–132 in Günter Friedrichs (ed.), *Automation und technischer Fortschritt in Deutschland und den USA. Ausgewählte Beiträge zu einer internationalen Arbeitstagung der Industriegewerkschaft Metall für die Bundesrepublik Deutschland*. Frankfurt am Main: Europäische Verlagsanstalt.

Fulmer, Ingrid Smithey and Robert E. Ployhart (2014), "'Our most important asset': A multidisciplinary/multilevel review of human capital valuation for research and practice," *Journal of Management* 40: 161–192.

Galbraith, John Kenneth (1967), *The New Industrial State*. Boston, MA: Houghton Mifflin.

Gallaway, Lowell and Richard K. Vedder (1987), "Wages, prices, and employment: Von Mises and the progressives," *The Review of Austrian Economics* 1: 33–80.

Garicano, Luis and Esteban Rossi-Hansberg (2014), "Knowledge-based hierarchies: Using organizations to understand the economy," *NBER Working Paper* No. 20607.

Gissis, Snait (2002), "Late nineteen century Lamarckism and French sociology," *Perspective on Science* 1: 69–122.

Goldfield, Michael (1989), *The Decline of Organized Labor in the United States*. Chicago, IL: University of Chicago Press.

Goldin, Claudia and Lawrence F. Katz (2008), *The Race between Education and Technology*. Cambridge, MA: Harvard University Press.

Goldin, Claudia and Lawrence F. Katz (2007), "Long-run changes in the wage structure: Narrowing, widening, polarizing," *Brookings Papers on Economic Activity* 2: 135–165.

Goodman, Peter S. and Jonathan Soble (2017), "Global economy's stubborn reality: Plenty of work, nor enough pay. Even as job markets are tight in many major economies, low unemployment is failing to spur robust increases in wages, leaving workers angry," *New York Times*, 7 October. URL: https://www-nytimes/2017/10/07/business/unemployment-wages-economy.html?partner=bloomberg (accessed 14 July 2019).

Goos, Maarten and Alan Manning (2007), "Lousy and lovely jobs: The rising polarization of work in Britain," *Review of Economics and Statistics* 89: 118–133.

Goos, Maarten, Alan Manning and Anna Salomons (2014), "Explaining job polarization: Routine-biased technological change and offshoring," *American Economic Review* 104: 2509–2526.

Gottschalk, Peter (1997), "Inequality, income growth and mobility," *Journal of Economic Perspectives* 11: 21–40.

Gordon, Robert J. (2016), *The Rise and Fall of American Economic Growth: The US Standard of Living since the Civil War*. Princeton, NJ: Princeton University Press.

Gorz, André ([2003] 2010), *The Immaterial. Knowledge, Value and Capital*. London: Seagull.

Gorz, André ([1988] 1989), *Critique of Economic Reason*. London: Verso.

Grace, Katja, John Salvatier, Allan Dafoe, Baobao Zhang and Owain Evans (2017), "When will AI exceed human performance? Evidence from AI experts," arXiv:1705.08807v2 [cs.AI] 30 May 2017.

Graeber, David (2018), *Bullshit Jobs*. New York: Simon & Schuster.

Graetz, Georg and Guy Michaels (2015), "Robots at work," Economics Department, Uppsala University, Uppsala, Sweden.

Guerreiro, Joao, Sergio Rebelo and Pedro Teles (2017), "Should robots be taxed?" *National Bureau Working Paper* No. 23806.

Guellec, Dominique and Caroline Paunov (2017), "Digital innovation and the distribution of income," *NBER Working Paper* No. 23987.

Guvenen, Faith, Greg Kaplan, Jae Song and Justin Weidner (2017), "Lifetime incomes in the United States over six decades," *NBER Working Paper* No. 23371.

Hamouda, O.F. and B. B. Price (1997), "The justice of the just price," *Journal of the History of Economic Thought* 4: 191–216.

Handel, Michael (2016), "What do people do? A profile of U.S. jobs from the survey of workplace Skills, Technology, and Management Practices (STAMP)," *Journal of Labor Marker Research* 49: 177–197.

Handel, Michael J. (2005), "Trends in perceived job quality, 1989 to 1998," *Work and Occupations* 32: 66–94.

Harari, Yuval Noah (2016), *Homo Deus. A Brief History of Tomorrow*. London: Vintage.

Hardt, Michael and Aantonio Negri (2004), *Multitude: War and Democracy in the Age of Empire*. New York: Penguin Press.

Harman, Willis W. (1978), "Chronic unemployment: An emerging problem of postindustrial society," *Futurist* 12: 209–214.

Heckman, James J. (2018), "The race between demand and supply: Tinbergen's pioneering studies of earnings inequality," *NBER Working Paper* No. 25415.

Heilbroner, Robert (1965), "Men and machines in perspective," *Public Interest* 1: 27–36.

Helpman, Elhanan (2016), "Globalization and wage inequality," *NBER Working Paper* No. 22944.

Hicks, John ([1932] 1963), *Theory of Wages*. London: Palgave Macmillan.

Higbie, Tobias (2013), "Why do robots rebel? The labor history of a cultural icon," *Labor Studies in Working Class history of the Americas* 10: 99–121.

Hirschi, Caspar (2017), "Die Automatisierung der Angst. Wir brauchen mehr Grundwissen in Technologiegeschichte: Die Rede von der digitalen Massenarbeitslosigkeit ist aufgewärmt, unglaubwürdig und lenkt von echten Problemen ab," *Frankfurter Allgemeine Zeitung*, 26 May, 9.

Hirschman, Albert O. (1982), "Rival interpretations of market society: Civilizing, destructive, or feeble?" *Journal of Economic Literature* 20: 1363–1484.

Hobbes, Thomas ([1651] 1985), *Leviathan*. London: Penguin Classics.

International Monetary Fund [IMF] (2017), *World Economic Outlook. Seeking Sustainable Growth: Short-Term Recovery, Long-Term Challenges*. Washington, DC: IMF.

Irwin, Neil (2018), "Is capital or labor winning at your favorite company? Introducing the Marx ratio," *New York Times* May 21. www.nytimes.com/interactive/2018/05/21/upshot/marx-ratio-median-pay.html?module=WatchingPortal&region=c-column-middle-span-region&pgType=Homepage&action=cl.

Iversen, Torben, and Soskice, David W. (2019). *Democracy and Prosperity: Reinventing Capitalism through a Turbulent Century*. Princeton, NJ.: Princeton University Press.

Johnson, George F. (1997), "Changes in earnings inequality: The role of demand shifts," *Journal of Economic Perspectives* 11: 41–54.

Jorgenson, Dale (1997), "Computers and productivity," Paper presented to the Centre for the Study of Living Standards Confererence on Service Sector Productivity and the Productivity Paradox, 11–13 April, Ottawa, Canada.

Judt, Tony (2005), *Postwar. A History of Europe since 1945.* London: William Heinemann.

Juhn, Chinhui, Kristin McCue, Holly Monti and Brooks Pierce (2017), "Firm performance and the volatility of workers earnings," *NBER Working Paper* No. 23102.

Kaldor, Nicholas (1957), "A model of economic growth," *The Economic Journal* 67: 591–624.

Kaldor, Nicholas (1932), "A case against technical progress?" *Economica* 36: 180–196.

Kalleberg, Arne L. (2011), *Good Jobs, Bad Jobs: The Rise of Polarized and Precarious Employment Systems in the United States, 1970s to 2000s.* New York: Russell Sage Foundation.

Kaplan, Greg and Sam Schulhofer-Wohl (2018), "The changing (dis-)utility of work," *NBER Working Paper* No. 24738.

Katz, Lawrence F. and Kevin M. Murphy (1992), "Changes in relative wages, 1963–1987: Supply and demand factors," *The Quarterly Journal of Economics* 107: 35–78.

Kautz, Tim, James J. Heckman, Ron Diris, Bas ter Weel and Lex Borghans (2015), "Fostering and measuring skills: Cognitive and non-cognitive skills to promote lifetime success," *OECD Education Working Paper* No. 110.

Kautz, Tim, James J. Heckman, Ron Diris, Bas ter Weel and Lex Borghans (2014), "Fostering and measuring skills: Cognitive and non-cognitive skills to promote lifetime success," *NBER Working Paper* No. 20749.

Kehrig, Matthias and Nicolas Vincent (2018), "The micro-level anatomy of the labor share decline," *NBER Working Paper* No. 25275.

Keynes, John Maynard (1939), "Relative movements of real wages and output," *The Economic Journal* 49: 34–51.

Keynes, John Maynard ([1936] 1961), *The General Theory of Employment, Interest and Money.* London: Macmillan & Co.

Keynes, John M. ([1930] 1963), "Economic possibilities for our grandchildren," pp. 358–373 in John M. Keynes, *Essays in Persuasion.* New York: W.W. Norton.

Kleinman, Daniel Lee and Steven P. Vallas (2001), "Science, capitalism, and the rise of the 'knowledge worker': The changing structure of knowledge production in the United States," *Theory and Society* 30: 451–492.

Kniesner, Thomas J., W. Kip Viscusi, Christopher Woock and James P. Ziliak (2012), "The value of a statistical life: Evidence from panel data," *Review of Economics and Statistics* 94: 74–87.

Knight, Frank H. (1950), "The determination of just wages," pp. 467–511 in Donald Anthony Walker (ed.) *Twentieth Century Economic Thought.* New York: Philosophical Library.

Koh, Dongya, Raül Santaeulàlia-Llopis and Yu Zheng (2015), "Labor share decline and intellectual property products capital," *EUI Working Papers* Eco 2015/05.

Komlosy, Andrea ([2014] 2018), *Work. The Last 1000 Years.* London: Verso.

Kramarz, Francis (2017), "Offshoring, wages, and employment: Evidence from data matching imports, firms, and workers," in Lionel Fontagne and Ann Harrison (eds.), *The Factory Free Economy.* URL: https://www.researchgate.net/ publication/ 303374155 The Factory Free Economy (accessed 14 July 2019).

Krugman, Paul and Anthony J. Venables (1995), "Globalization and the inequality of nations," *The Quarterly Journal of Economics* 110: 857–880.

Krugman, Paul (1994), *The Age of Diminished Expectations. U.S. Economic Policy in the 1990s.* Revised and updated ed. Cambridge, MA: MIT Press.

Laurison, Daniel and Sam Friedman (2016), "The class pay gap in higher professional and managerial occupations," *American Sociological Review* 81: 668–695.

Lazzarato, Maurizio (1996), "Immaterial labour," pp. 133–147 in Paolo Virno and Michael Hardt (eds.), *Radical Thought in Italy: A Potential Politics.* Minneapolis: University of Minnesota Press.

Lederer, Emil H. (1938), *Technological Progress and Unemployment. An Inquiry into the Obstacles to Economic Expansion.* Geneva: International Labour Office.

Leontief, Wassily (1982), "The distribution of work and income," *Scientific American* 247: 188–204.

Leontief, Wassily (1952), "Machines and man. What about the economic and social impact of automatic control systems? Can industry afford to buy them, and will they cause widespread technological unemployment?" *Scientific American* 187: 150–160.

Levy, Frank and Richard J. Murnane (2005), "How computerized work and globalization shape human skill demands," *MIT IPC Working Paper* No. IPC-05-006

Lewis, W. Arthur (1954), "Economic development with unlimited supplies of labour," *The Manchester School* 22: 139–191.

Lin, Dajun, Randell Lutter and Christopher J. Ruhm (2016), "Cognitive performance and labor market outcome," *NBER Working Paper* No. 22470.

Lin, Ken-Hou and Donald Tomaskovic-Devey (2013), "Financialization and US income inequality, 1970–2008," *American Journal of Sociology* 118: 1284–1329.

Lindley, Robet M. (2002), "Knowledge-based economies: The European employment debate in a new context," pp. 95–145 in Maria João Rodrigues (ed.), *The New Knowledge Economy in Europe. A Strategy for International Competitiveness and Social Cohesion.* Cheltenham: Edward Elgar.

Lindqvist, Erik and Roine Vestman (2011), "The labor market returns to cognitive and noncognitive ability: Evidence from the Swedish enlistment," *American Economic Journal: Applied Economics* 3: 101–128.

Lordan, Grace and David Neumark (2017), "People versus machines: The impact of minimum wages on automatable jobs," *NBER Working Paper* No. 23667.

Lübker, Malte and Thorsten Schulten (2018), *WSI Minimum Wage Report 2018.* Hans-Böckler-Stiftung: Economic and Social Research Institut.

Luhmann, Niklas (1993), "Wirtschaftsethik—als Ethik?" pp. 134–147 in Josef Wieland (ed.), *Wirtschaftsethik und Theorie der Gesellschaft.* Frankfurt am Main: Suhrkamp.

Luhmann, Niklas ([1970] 1982), "The economy as a social system," pp. 190–225 in Niklas Luhmann, *The Differentiation of Society.* New York: Columbia University Press.

Luhmann, Niklas (1970), "Wirtschaft als soziales System," pp. 204–231 in Niklas Luhmann, *Soziologische Aufklärung. Aufsätze zur Theorie sozialer Systeme. Band 1.* Köln and Opladen: Westdeutscher Verlag.

Lyotard, Jean-François ([1979] 1984), *The Postmodern Condition: A Report on Knowledge.* Minneapolis: University of Minnesota Press.

Machin, Amanda and Nico Stehr (2016), *Understanding Inequality. Social Benefits and Social Costs.* Wiesbaden: Springer VS.

MacKenzie, Donald (1984), "Marx and the machine," *Technology and Culture* 25: 473–502.

Maestas, Nicole, Kathleen J. Mullen and David Powell (2016), "The effect of population aging on economic growth," Santa Monica: Rand Corporation. URL: www.rand.org/pubs/working_papers/WR1063-1.html (accessed 14 July 2019).

Maestas, Nicole, Kathleen J. Mullen, David Powell, Till von Wachter and Jeffrey B. Wenger (2018), "The value of working conditions in the United States and implications for the structure of wages," *NBER Working Paper* No. 25204.

Manyika, James and Myron Scholes (2018), "Solving the productivity puzzle," URL: www.project-syndicate.org/commentary/solving-the-productivity-puzzle-by-james-manyika-and-myron-scholes-2018–05 (accessed 14 July 2019).

Marchak, Jacob (1925), "Wages," pp. 291–302 in Erwin R. A. Seligman (ed.), *Encyclopedia of the Social Sciences. Volume 15.* New York: Macmillan.

Marcuse, Herbert (1955), *Eros and Civilization.* Boston, MA: Beacon Press.

Marx, Karl ([1890] 1976), *Capital: A Critique of Political Economy, Volume 1.* London: Penguin Books.

Marx, Karl ([1939–1941] 1973), *Grundrisse.* New York: Vintage.

Marx, Karl ([1875] 1881), *Critique of the Gotha Program.* Worldside Press.

Mas, Alexandre and Amanda Pallais, A., (2017), "Valuing alternative work arrangements," *American Economic Review* 107: 3722–3759.

Milward, Alan S. (1992), *The European Rescue of the Nation-State.* Berkeley: University of California Press.

Modestino, Alicia Sasser (2016), "The importance of middle-skill jobs," *Issues in Science and Technology* 33(1).

Mortensen, Dale T. (2005), *Wage Dispersion: Why Are Similar Workers Paid Differently?* Cambridge, MA: MIT Press.

Mokyr, Joel, Chris Vickers and Nicolas L. Ziebarth (2015), "The history of technological anxiety and the future of economic growth: Is this time different?" *Economic Perspectives* 29: 31–50.

Mulligan, Casey B. (2015), "Fiscal policies and the price of labor: A comparison of the U.K and U.S.," *NBER Working Paper* No. 21358.

Murphy, Kevin M. and Finis Welch (1992), "The structure of wages," *Quarterly Journal of Economics* 107: 285–326.

Nagl, Wolfgang, Gerlinde Titelbach and Katarina Valkova (2017), *Digitalisierung der Arbeit: Substituierbarkeit von Berufen im Zuge der Automatisierung durch Industrie 4.0.* Institut für Höhere Studien, Wien. URL: www.ihs.ac.at/fileadmin/public/2016_Files/Documents/20170412_IHS-Bericht_2017_Digitalisierung_Endbericht.pdf (accessed 14 July 2019).

Naughton, John (2017), "If the robots are coming for our jobs, make sure they pay their taxes," *Guardian* February 26. www.theguardian.com/commentisfree/2017/feb/26/robots-make-sure-pay-taxes (accessed 14 July 2019).

Negt, Oskar (2001), *Arbeit und die menschliche Würde.* Göttingen: Steidl Verlag.

Nell-Breuning, Oswald von (1960), *Kapitalismus und gerechter Lohn.* Freiburg: Herder.

Nordhaus, William D. (1996), "Do real-output and real-wage measures capture quality? The history of lighting suggests not," pp. 29–70 in Timothy F. Bresnahan and Robert J. Gordon (eds.), *The Economics of New Goods.* Chicago, IL: University of Chicago Press.

Ott, Alfred E. (1971), "Zur ökonomischen Theorie des technischen Fortschritts," pp. 7–28 in Verein Deutscher Ingenieure (ed.), *Wirtschaftliche und gesellschaftliche Auswirkungen des technischen Fortschritts.* Düsseldorf: VDI-Verlag.

Person, Harlow S. (1932), "Labor, methods of remuneration," pp. 677–682 in Erwin R. A. Seligman (ed.), *Encyclopedia of the Social Sciences. Volume 8.* New York: Macmillan.

Phillips, Alban W. (1958), "The relation between unemployment and the rate of change of money wage rates in the United Kingdom, 1861 1957," *Economica* 25: 283–299.

Pigou, Arthur Cecil (1933), *Theory of Unemployment*. London: Macmillan.

Piketty, Thomas ([2013] 2014), *Capital in the Twenty-First Century*. Cambridge, MA: Harvard University Press.

Pinto, Sanjay and Jason Beckfield (2011), "Organized labor in European countries, 1960–2006: Persistent diversity and shared decline," pp. 153–179 in David Brady (ed.) *Comparing European Workers Part B: Policies and Institutions*. Emerald Group Publishing Limited.

Polanyi, Karl ([1944] 2011), *The Great Transformation. The Political and Economic Origins of Our Time*. Boston, MA: Bacon Press.

Pold, Henry and Fred Wong (1990), "The price of labour," *Perspectives on Labour and Income* 2: 42–49.

Pratt, Gill A. (2015), "Is a cambrian explosion coming for robotics?" *Economic Perspectives* 29: 51–60.

Reese, Byron (2018), *The Fourth Age. Smart Robots, Conscious Computers, and the Future of Humanity*. New York: Atria Books.

Ricardo, David ([1821] 1973), *The Works and Correspondence of David Ricardo, Vol. 1: On the Principles of Political Economy and Taxation*, 3rd ed. Royal Economic Society.

Ricardo, David ([1817] 1911), *The Principles of Political Economy and Taxation*. London.

Rifkin, Jeremy (1995), *The End of Work: The Decline of the Global Labor Force and the Dawn of the Post-market Era*. New York: J.P. Putnam's Sons.

Rodrik, Dani (2016), "Premature deindustrialization," *Journal of Economic Growth* 21: 1–33.

Rousseau, Jean Jacques ([1794] 1984), *Diskurs über die Ungleichheit*. Paderborn: Schöningh.

Rüber, Ina Elisabeth and Thijs Bol (2017), "Informal learning and labour market returns, evidence from German Panel data," *European Sociological Review* 33: 765–778.

Sachs, Jeffrey (2012), *The Price of Civilization. Reawakening Virtue and Prosperity after the Economic Fall*. London: Viking Books.

Sachs, Jeffrey D. and Lawrence J. Kotlikoff (2012), "Smart machines and long-term misery," *NBER Working Paper*, 18629.

Saval, Nikil (2017), "Globalisation: the rise and fall of an idea that swept the world," *Guardian* July 14. https://www.theguardian.com/world/2017/jul/14/globalisation-the-rise-and-fall-of-an-idea-that-swept-the-world.

Schelsky, Helmut (1975), *Die Arbeit tun die anderen. Klassenkampf und Priesterherrschaft der Intellektuellen. Zweite Auflage*. Opladen: Westdeutscher Verlag.

Schelsky, Helmut ([1957] 1965), "Die sozialen Folgen der Automatisierung," pp. 105–130 in Helmut Schelsky, *Auf der Suche nach der Wirklichkeit*. Gesammelte Aufsätze. Düsseldorf-Köln: Eugen Diederichs.

Schiller, Robert (2017), "Why robots should be taxed if they take people's jobs," *Guardian* March 22. www.theguardian.com/business/2017/mar/22/robots-tax-bill-gates-income-inequality.

Schneck, Stefan (2014), "My wage is unfair! Just a feeling or comparison with peers?" *Review of Behavioral Economics* 1: 245–273.

Schumpeter, Joseph A. (1954), *History of Economic Analysis*. New York: Oxford University Press.

Schumpeter, Joseph A. (1916), "Das Grundprinzip der Verteilungstheorie," *Archiv für Sozialwissenschaft und Sozialpolitik* 42: 1–88.

Sichel, Daniel E. (1999), "Computers and aggregate economic growth: An update," *Business Economics* 34: 18–24.

Simmel, Georg ([1900] 2004), *The Philosophy of Money*. London: Routledge and Kegan Paul.

Skidelsky, Robert (2010), *Keynes. The Return of the Master*. New York: Public Affairs.

Smith, Adam ([1776] 2012), *An Inquiry into the Nature and Causes of the Wealth of Nations*. Ware: Wordworth Editions Limited.

Soete, Luc (2018), "Destructive creation: Explaining the productivity paradox in the digital age," pp. 29–46 in Max Neufeind, Jacqueline O'Reilly and Florian Ranft (eds.), *Work in the Digital Age: Challenges of the Fourth Industrial Revolution*. London: Roman & Littlefield.

Sohn-Rethel, Alfred (1978), *Warenform und Denkform: mit 2 Anhängen*. Frankfurt am Main: Suhrkamp.

Solow, Robert M. (1965), "Technology and unemployment," *Public Interest* 1: 17–26.

Srnicek, Nick and Alex Williams (2015), *Inventing the Future. Postcapitalism and a World without Work*. London: Verso.

Staehle, Hans (1943), "Wages, and income," *The Review of Economics and Statistics* 25: 77–87.

Stehr, Nico (2002), *Knowledge and Economic Conduct: The Social Foundations of the Modern Economy*. Toronto, ON: University of Toronto Press.

Stehr, Nico (2001), "Politische Arithmetik," *Merkur* 265: 453–456.

Stehr, Nico (2000), "The productivity paradox: ICTs, knowledge and the labour market," pp. 255–272 in John de la Mothe and Gilles Paquet (eds.), *Information, Innovation and Impacts*. Boston, MA: Kluwer Academic Publishers.

Stehr, Nico (1999), "The future of inequality," *Society* 36: 54–59.

Stehr, Nico (1992), *Practical Knowledge. Applying the Social Sciences*. London: Sage.

Stehr, Nico (1991), *Praktische Erkenntnis*. Frankfurt am Main: Suhrkamp.

Stephens, Jr., Melvin and Desmond J. Toohey (2018), "The impact of health on labor market outcomes—Experimental evidence from MRFIT," *NBER Working Paper* No. 24231.

Stokey, Nancy L. (2018), "Technology, skill and the wage structure," *Journal of Human Capital* 12: 343–384.

Stokey, Nancy L. (2016), "Technology, skill and the wage structure," *NBER Working Paper* No. 22176.

Syverson, Chad. (2017), "Challenges to mismeasurement explanations for the US productivity slowdown," *Journal of Economic Perspectives* 31: 165–186.

Tabuchi, Hiroko (2017), "Coal mining jobs Trump would bring back no longer exists," *New York Times* March 29. https://nyti.ms/2nBM2r4.

Teal, Francis (2011), "The price of labour and understanding the causes of poverty," *Labour Economics* 18: S7–S15.

Tenbruck, Friedrich H. ([1980] 1996), "Arbeit—Existenzsicherung und Lebenswert," pp. 235–250 in Friedrich H. Tenbruck, *Perspektiven der Kultursoziologie*. Gesammelte Aufsätze. Wiesbaden: Westdeutscher Verlag.

Thurow, Lester C. ([1980] 1981), *The Zero-Sum Society. Distribution and the Possibilities for Economic Change*. New York: Penguin.

Tinbergen, Jan (1956), "On the theory of income distribution," *Weltwirtschaftliches Archiv* 77: 155–173.

Tinbergen, Jan (1975), *Income Distribution: Analysis and Policies*. New York: North-Holland Publishing Company.

Tingley, Kim (2017) "Learning to love our robot co-workers," *New York Times* February 23. www.nytimes.com/2017/02/23/magazine/learning-to-love-our-robot-co-workers.html?_r=0.

Tomaskovic-Devey (2014), "The relational generation of workplace inequalities," *Social Currents* 1: 51–73.

Tomaskovic-Devey, Melvin Thomas and Kecia Johnson (2005), "Race and the accumulation of human capital: A theoretical model and fixed-effects application," *American Journal of Sociology* 111: 58–89.

Touraine, Alain ([2010] 2014), *After the Crisis*. Cambridge: Polity Press.

Treffler, Daniel (1993), "International factor price differences: Leontief was right," *Journal of Political Economy* 101: 961–987.

United States (1955), *United States. Congress. Joint Committee on the Economic Report. Subcommittee on Economic Stabilization*. Washington, DC: U.S. Government Printing Office.

Voigt, Andreas (1892), "Der ökonomische Wert der Güter," *Zeitschrift für die gesamte Staatswissenschaft* 48: 193–250.

Weber, Max ([1956] 1978), *Economy and Society*. Edited by Guenther Roth and Claus Wittich. Berkeley: University of California Press.

Weber, Max ([1922] 1976), *Wirtschaft und Gesellschaft. 5. revidierte Ausgabe*, Tübingen: J.C.B. Mohr (Paul Siebeck).

Weber, Max ([1921] 1972), *Wirtschaft und Gesellschaft: Grundriss der Verstehenden Soziologie*, 5th ed. Tübingen: J.C.B. Mohr.

Weber, Max ([1918] 1994), "Socialism," pp. 272–303 in Max Weber, *Political Writings*, edited by Peter Lassman and Ronald Spiers. Cambridge: Cambridge University Press.

Weinberger, Catherine J. (2014), "The increasing complementarity between cognitive and social skills," *The Review of Economics and Statistics* 96: 840–861.

Weeks, Kathi (2011), *The Problem with Work. Feminism, Marxism, Antiwork Politics, and Postwork Imaginaries*. Durham, NC: Duke University Press.

Welsch, Johann (1983), "Auf dem Weg in eine technologische Arbeitslosigkeit? Technischer Fortschritt und Beschäftigung als Problem der 80er Jahre," pp. 408–441 in Universität Bremen (ed.), *Arbeit und Technik. Analyse von Entwicklungen der Technik und Chancen in der Gestaltung von Arbeit*. Bremen: Universität Bremen.

Wetzel, James R. (1995), "Labor force, unemployment, and earnings," pp. 59–105 in Reynolds Farley (ed.), *State of the Union. America in the 1990s. Volume One: Economic Trends*. New York: Russell Sage Foundation.

Wilmers, Nathan (2018), "Wage stagnation and buyer power: How buyer-supplier relations affect U.S. workers' wages, 1978 to 2014," *American Sociological Review* 83: 213–242.

Wilmers, Nathan (2017), "Labor unions as activist organizations: A union power approach to estimating union wage effects," *Social Forces* 95: 1451–1478.

Wolf, Jean-Claude (1996), "Arbeit, Ausbeutung und gerechter Lohn," *Studia Philosophica* 54: 245–261.

Woytinsky, Wladimir (1925), "Wages: History and statistics. Methods of wage statistics," pp. 302–320 in Edwin R.A. Seligman (ed.), *Encyclopedia of the Social Sciences. Volume 15*. New York: Macmillan.

# 5

# THE PRICE OF KNOWLEDGE[1]

There are some things which cannot be purchased with wealth, and knowledge is one of them. Wealth can purchase houses, lands, adherents, and bauble honors, and a man may sit down and enjoy these things at once. An heir to an empire may be born, he may be the legal successor to thrones, armies, and navies; over these he may exercise dominion and be their possessor, but no man was ever born an heir to *knowledge*.

—*Scientific American, 1851*[2]

This chapter addresses the question of how to assess and measure the price and value of knowledge—a conundrum that seems to be sufficiently answered already as the quote from the 1851 issue of the *Scientific American* suggests. We will nevertheless probe this pertinent issue from a variety of social scientific and practical perspectives. Against the background of a *sociological* concept of knowledge, economic, political, social and juridical perspectives are discussed that may lead us to a price of knowledge.

We observe at the outset, as is widely assumed by social science and policy that knowledge plays an ever-greater role within as well as across economies and politics.[3] The embodiment of knowledge makes it difficult to divorce it from its carriers, if at all; knowledge is deeply entrenched in questions of social relations and stratification, about the uncertainties of future conditions (Nordhaus and Popp, 1996) and last but not least it is subject to depreciation, decay or obsolescence.

Our inquiry stresses the function of knowledge in economic relations. Our focus on the functions of knowledge therefore differs from what has been the main preoccupation of classical social scientific investigations of knowledge within the traditions of the sociology and philosophy of knowledge, namely the social context, the creation and development of knowledge (e.g. Mannheim, [1929] 1936);

Fleck, [1935] 1979; Cohen and Schnelle, 1986). We share the constitutive idea with the classical sociology of knowledge that knowledge cannot be separated from the social collectivities who develop, share and communicate it. However, the problem of the genesis of knowledge, epistemological issues or sociotechnical networks of knowledge production, often the focus in contemporary sociology of science studies are of secondary importance in this context.

In our introduction in Chapter 1, we already referred to a number of important characteristics, functions and consequences of knowledge. These attributes of knowledge stand in radical contradiction to the observation that knowledge is a non-economic category. That this is not the case and that it can therefore make eminent sense to ask about the price of knowledge can already be determined by the fact that knowledge, as well as other factors of production but also other social phenomena, for example, violence, can be *monopolized*.

If one follows a suggestion by Norbert Elias ([1984] 2005) and replaces the concept of knowledge with the expression "sense of orientation," which is the essence of knowledge, it quickly becomes clear that knowledge can be monopolized[4] and may be scarce.[5] The state and the distribution of knowledge as a capacity to act are "a necessary and irreducible condition in the explanation of social change" (Barnes, 1977: 81) and of course economic change.

To begin with, the aging of knowledge should have an impact on its value. That is so say, the impact aging may have on knowledge does not necessarily result in a depreciation of the "price" of knowledge. A decline or an increase in the price of knowledge may signal a reduction or an enhancement in the value of knowledge. Knowledge may be criticized as out-of-date or located at the research front. Such a critique or praise of knowledge therefore offers an insight into what in this example makes knowledge more or less valuable.

In general, the obsolescence of knowledge is an important but not well understood process. It is evident that the pace with which knowledge ages, that the parts of knowledge that become obsolete or how outdated knowledge is related to emerging knowledge all should impact in some fashion on the price and value of knowledge. For example, the impact of obsolete knowledge on the wages and earning of employees that are carriers of such knowledge is one of the accompanying but poorly understood issues of the worth of knowledge over time (cf. Rosen, 1975; Welch and Ureta, 2002).

There are at least two general conceptual dimensions that are both linked to the obsolescence of knowledge, the time perspective as indicated and what Robert K. Merton famously called the process of the "obliteration of incorporation" that also contains a reference to elapsing time. In his study of the benefits of knowledge, Fritz Machlup (1979: 66) refers to a time dimension that is part of the evaluation of knowledge, namely the "usual" value of knowledge, which *ex ante* is linked to certain expectations and the value *ex post*, for example, should expectations in the worth of new knowledge not have been fulfilled or even exceeded.

Robert K. Merton introduced the concept of "obliteration by incorporation" in 1949 in his *Social Theory and Social Structure* ([1949] 1968: 27–28, 35–37). The concept refers, as Merton observes, to gradual loss of information about the origins of a *scientific* idea, its initial formulation or its inventors. As Merton points out such a phenomenon is more common in the natural rather than the social sciences. Knowledge in natural science fields of inquiry is seen to evolve like a spiral. Knowledge becomes part of the common or standard intellectual heritage of a discipline (the paradigm or in text book of a scientific field) and as part of the shared understanding of many of its practitioners is no longer attributed to its originators or the issues that prompted the research in the first instance.[6]

Whether any determination of the value of knowledge may be related to the loss of information about the genesis of the findings to be assessed is a difficult question that we cannot decide at this point. However, it is quite conceivable that with the destruction by incorporation relevant information for the evaluation of knowledge will be lost. This includes, for example, information about the nature and amount of resources that were necessary for the discovery of capacities for action, but remain unknown and possibly would require extensive resources to unearth any missing information. In addition, there is another obstacle to the general assessment of the value of knowledge, namely, the future oriented, logical difficulty of measuring the value of prospective knowledge that is not yet quite known to the "user" (Machlup, 1979: 66).[7] The future value of knowledge presumably cannot be captured in a straightforward manner, using either market-based tools or non-market evaluations especially given the persistent standoff between its individual, economic, and public relevancies and benefits.

At this point, we can already emphasize the cautionary observation that a simple arithmetic of the price of knowledge fails as the reference to Machlup's idea of the future value of knowledge shows. Indeed, what stipulations could be employed in order to calculate the possible future price of knowledge? Whether establishing an "economics of knowledge" in analogy to an economics of real estate is reasonable and feasible becomes equally doubtful.[8]

## Point of Departure

We begin our examination of the ways in which knowledge may be priced by pointing to some of the pitfalls one encounters in establishing exactly what theorists and practitioners are referring to when they define the phenomenon to be valued in the first instance, especially as observers attempt do so from an economist's perspective:

First, can knowledge actually be measured, and if so, is knowledge really the referent?[9]

Second, we deal with attempts to specify and quantify "human capital" as forms of knowledge assets by examining various prominent approaches especially within this field of economics that have attended to the nature and the role of human capital.

Third, we turn to a more sociological viewpoint in determining the value of *symbolic* knowledge and knowledge *capital*. Of particular relevance in this context is Pierre Bourdieu's notion of cultural capital as a form of symbolic *capital*. We find that Bourdieu's idea is insufficient to capture the ambivalent role knowledge plays in the processes of economic relations, social stratification and empowerment.

Fourth, in a next step toward encircling the price on knowledge, we deal with patents and other forms of intellectual property rights (IPR) that play an increasing role in today's economies.

Fifth, in an attempt to find yet another proxy for evaluating the price of knowledge, we turn to the world of politics and the question of taxation, in particular the public funding of education. Based on John Dewey's classic question of how much knowledge a democracy requires of its citizens, we use the case of a political-legal dispute to approach the question of what knowledge is worth and how much of it we should afford.

Sixth, we discuss the notion of *additional* knowledge, starting out from the assumption that added (new) knowledge should have a specific value that perhaps can more readily be assessed compared to knowledge that has been available for a time.

Seventh, we turn to the idea that knowledge may be a public good. Public goods tend to be defined as *free* goods.[10] It is often an essential attribute of the concept of public goods (clean air, ideas, public heath, national security) that for those who consume them the price of public goods (commodified collective goods, for instance, drinking water) may at times be negligible or altogether absent. Knowledge as a public good may come closest to the idea of a *just price* for knowledge, at least in the eyes of those who are strongly committed to the idea that knowledge should not carry a price label. Moreover, it is commonly accepted among economists that markets operating on their own are an efficient allocation mechanism for public resources (cf. Stiglitz, 2017: 4). The canonical economic theory states that (pure) public goods in contrast to private goods are non-excludable and non-rival.[11]

Eighth, and finally, we examine the idea found in the economics literature that commodities constitute embedded knowledge.

## Measuring Knowledge

> Unlike general social labour, knowledge is impossible to translate into—or measure in—simple abstracts units. It is not reducible to a quantity of abstract labour of which it can be said to be the equivalent, the outcome or the product.
> —*André Gorz ([2003] 2010: 35)*

The economist Herbert Simon (1999: 24) is much more buoyant than André Gorz about our ability to develop robust measures of knowledge. Simon emphatically stresses that all aspects of knowledge

> can be (and have been) analyzed with the tools of economics. Knowledge has a price and a cost of production; there are markets for knowledge, with their supply and demand curves, and marginal rates of substitution between one form of knowledge and another.

However, Simon (1999: 24) at least partly retracts his strong endorsement about the rigor with which the tools of economics can be applied to measure the value of knowledge by pointing out that knowledge "is simply one among the many commodities in which our economy trades, albeit one of large and rapidly growing importance. It requires *special* treatment only because of its special properties" (our emphasis).[12] Let us take a closer look at how these "special properties" of knowledge are dealt with in economic discourse.

Our examination of the economics literature[13] that proclaims to deal with the value or price of knowledge as an asset and the monetary return to knowledge exemplifies two assertions:

First, our search of the literature of economics confirms once more our observation (cf. Adolf and Stehr, 2014: 25f) that the terms of knowledge and information are liberally conflated (e.g. Hess and Ostrom, 2003; World Bank, 1999). Gary Becker (1994a: 53),[14] for example, notes that increased *knowledge* raises the real income of individuals and specifies his hypothesis by saying: "*information* about the prices charged by different sellers would enable a person to buy from the cheapest, thereby raising his command over resources; information about the wages offered by different firms would enable him to work for the firm paying the highest" (our emphasis).[15]

Second, we find that efforts by economists that are genuinely concerned with the value of knowledge, for example in the sense of knowledge assets as "intangibles," for the most part display a strongly ambivalent idea of the value of knowledge and also display strong self-doubts about the very possibility of arriving at a price of knowledge. Such ambivalence contrasts of course with the massive affirmation in the economics literature that human resources of an organization as well as investments into human resources—at a rate close to the investment in tangibles—in R&D, software, brands, and other intangibles are the key to sustainable competitive advantages in the modern economy. As a result, measures of the Gross National Product (GDP) that do not include all intangible investments misrepresent the actual changes in output (cf. McGrattan, 2017). Yet, little has been done to actually capture the value of intangible assets for the purpose of accounting for the GNP of a country.

Although human resources are deemed as critically important properties for firms in the contemporary competitive economic environment, the very definition of intangibles as "unseen wealth" (Blair and Wallman, 2001; Leadbeater, 1999; Teece, 1998; Brynjolfsson, Rock, and Syverson, 2018)[16] already indicates the difficulties of devising ways of measuring the monetary value of copyrights, patents, trade secrets, brand loyalty, organizational capabilities—let alone *knowledge skills* (see Fulmer and Ployhart, 2014; Popp, 2017), *human capital* or the value of "early" knowledge[17] (cf. Nordhaus and Popp, 1996: 3).[18]

Moreover, at least in the United States, the widely accepted accounting principles (GAAP) that govern the reporting of financial information to external sources prohibit companies from recording the value of human capital resources as assets.[19] Instead, human capital expenses are recorded as expenditures (cf. Tan, 2014). Since the expenditures for and the values of human capital might not correspond, the actual price of human capital assets remains a mystery. Given the essential difficulties in determining the exact value of intangible assets, it follows that the validity and comparability of national indicators of macroeconomic performance, labor productivity or asset allocation are uncertain or even questionable (cf. McCulla, Holden and Smith, 2013; Feldsein, 2017).

Such ambivalence or lack of precision (how profitable is private investment in R&D?) satisfies numerous critics who are convinced that knowledge does not or should not carry a price tag and instead be part of the "public domain" (cf. Boyle, 2003), or that it is particularly ill suited for a conversion to private property and market pricing.[20] To begin with, therefore, we are able to assert that there is—as in the case of the social phenomenon of power—no standardized or objective approach to quantify the value of knowledge (or information).

Even assuming that one is able to specify a price, the value of knowledge will not be a constant but in all likelihood increase or decay (become obsolete), depending on relevant circumstances such as the time that has passed since the discovery of a product, the difficulty of keeping it from other agents (cf. the case of generic drugs) or the assets that have to be mobilized to transmit it (cf. Pakes and Schankerman, 1979).

The theoretical and empirical accounts that are of interest to us either gain insight into the value of knowledge by treating knowledge as a form of *input*, for example, in the production process, and as one of the factors of production such as human capital or as a form of *output*, for example in the sense of patents, copyright restrictions and the like.

Many of the studies and discussions that can be found in the economics literature claiming to deal with the price of knowledge actually are about the price of *information* (e.g. Rosewall, 2005). This is most notable in consumer behavior research, which examines the impact of consumers' knowledge of the price of a product/commodity on the decisions made by them in supermarkets (e.g. Olavarrieta et al., 2012; Dickson and Sawyer, 1990), the effect the product price has on consumer satisfaction (e.g. Homburg, Koschate-Fischer and Wiegner, 2012), the level of price knowledge that children hold (cf. Damay, Guichard and Clauzel (2014) or the impact of the price of tertiary education on decisions made by university students (e.g. Junor and Usher, 2004/2005).

Most other efforts aiming to arrive at a price of knowledge can be subsumed under some form of a critique of the so-called *commodification* process of knowledge. These efforts recognize but are critical of the idea that knowledge carries a price and is sold on markets on the ground that scientific and economic activities are embedded in distinct functional subsystems of modern society and therefore should treated or in fact become a commodity.

A prominent exemplar of the critical observation that our age is characterized by a growing commodification of knowledge may be found in Jean-François Lyotard's ([1979]: 1) *La condition postmoderne*. Lyotard point of departure is in agreement with the leading thrust of views about the growing importance of knowledge in modern society. The status of knowledge has been beginning in the 1950s altered "as societies enter what is known as the postindustrial age and cultures enter what is known as the postmodern age." Lyotard refers for support of his observation about the amplified societal role of knowledge to the standard text by Daniel Bell or Alain Touraine about the emergence of post-industrial economies. Lyotard ([1979] 1984: 4) offers the following specific comments about the fortune of knowledge in the modern age:

> We may . . . expect a thorough exteriorisation of knowledge with respect to the "knower," at whatever point he or she may occupy in the knowledge process. The old principle that the acquisition of knowledge is indissociable from the training (*Bildung*) of minds, or even of individuals, is becoming obsolete and will become ever more so. The relationships of the suppliers and users of knowledge to the knowledge they supply and use is now tending, and will increasingly tend, to assume the form already taken by the relationship of commodity producers and consumers to the commodities they produce and consume—that is, the form of value. Knowledge is and will be produced in order to be sold, it is and will be consumed in order to be valorised in a new production: in both cases, the goal is exchange.

Knowledge loses its early dominant "use-value" and its value is reduced to its "exchange-value," that is, the commercialization of knowledge. The point of departure in discussions about the commodification of knowledge, then, tends to be the observation that a growing volume of scientific activities especially in the field of genetics and biochemistry is no longer curiosity-driven but carried out in the laboratories of private corporations; as a result, knowledge increasingly takes on the characteristics of a *commodity*.

The economization of science is often criticized (Balzer, 2003), for example, in the case of efforts to patent genes (see Matthijs, 2004; Resnik, 2004). Lyotard does not, however, offer any hint of the effect of the commodification of knowledge on the price of knowledge except perhaps in the most general and conventional sense that market forces will be responsible in setting prices.

Both of the approaches we discussed, knowledge as input or as output and knowledge as a commodity confirm how awkward claims are that knowledge comes with a price tag. But knowledge is simply a much too "valuable," "special" and uniquely human or "largely unobservable"[21] resource for it to be measured in any strictly monetary sense.[22] Is the aim therefore to price knowledge an effort to "price the priceless"? After all, knowledge in many ways resembles wisdom, insight, good judgment or "nature" (cf. Fourcade, 2011) and therefore properties that are not at home in the market place.[23] Hence the often-repeated assertion that what cannot be counted or quantified (such as unpaid work) is not necessarily without value. We will return to this observation in our discussion of patents.

Nonetheless, according to some of the most influential international organizations—the World Bank (e.g. 2011) and the United Nations (e.g. UNU-IHDP and UNEP, 2014)—ask whether "human capital" as a proxy for the knowledgeability of individuals for most countries in the modern world is the *most significant component* of human wealth. Economic growth requires capable workers. In other words, there is widespread agreement among social scientists, union leaders, educators, parents and policy makers that knowledge is the core determinant of economic growth and work-related success in modern societies.

For example, Claudia Goldin and Lawrence Katz (2008) show how human capital has been the defining factor for the economic identity of the industrialized world of the 20th century (also Acemoglu and Autor, 2012).[24] However, there also is widespread disagreement about the exact terms of analysis. The expressions "human capital," "skills," "information," "capacities" and "knowledge" that can be applied to all occupations, jobs, tasks and sectors of the economy are widely conflated in many of the empirical studies researching the role of intellectual abilities in the world of work. It is in general often also unclear how exactly human capital attributes are related to job performance and hence to rewards that might accrue to different values/components that constitute human capital of individuals.

Since human capital is seen to be virtually identical with the knowledge acquired and commanded by (mainly isolated) *individuals*, it would appear to be self-evident that the value human capital represents one promising pathway for an assessment of the value or even price of knowledge. However, this is not the case, as we will show in the next section. Such a calculus if it exists at all must of course recognize from the beginning that any evaluation of individual human capital is in practice dependent on the external judgments and estimates of other individuals (cf. van Doorn, 2014: 358). It does not make sense either to assume that human capital represents an entirely individual achievement. The human capital of a single person is always decisively determined by the social context in which such capital is acquired (cf. Tomaskovic-Devey, Thomas and Johnson, 2005).

For the economist, human capital theory also affirms their conviction, at least as put forward by members of the Chicago school as major contributors to human capital theory that the system-theoretic distinction between economic and social system should be rejected. Every aspect of human conduct can be represented in terms of economic theory and driven by economic choices. Hence the choice to attain or forego the acquisition of human capital is an economic choice, last but not least because knowledge comes with a price.

## Human Capital

Among the theoretical approaches and concepts that might be regarded as a proxy for the price of knowledge, *cultural capital* and *human capital* theories stand out.[25] Efforts abound by economists to estimate the value of the "most valuable asset most people own [which] is their human capital" (Haggett and Kaplan, 2015: 1). By the same token, corporations (at times universities) are quick to endorse the slogan "our employees are our best and most important asset." For the state, corporations and the economy information about the value of human capital becomes a resource for political decision-making, financial reporting, fiscal management and managerial decision-making (for universities in efforts to shift priorities and values).

The contest among the relative weight of those shares of collective income that are generated by different forms of capital has significant repercussions for the formation of social inequality in a society. Thomas Piketty ([2013] 2014: 21) for example notes, "the progress of technological rationality is supposed to lead automatically to the triumph of human capital over financial capital and real estate, capable managers over fat stockholders, and skill over nepotism." But, as he adds in a cautionary remark, "inequalities would thus become more meritocratic and less static (though not necessarily smaller): economic rationality would then in some sense automatically give rise to democratic rationality" (Piketty, [2013] 2014: 21).

In the course of the emergence of the knowledge-based economy, the linkage and the dependence of economic capital on cultural capital—and as we would specify, *knowledge capacities*—is significantly enhanced. Strata and individuals effective in mobilizing knowledge capacities, for example, exploiting discretionary opportunities or the ability to generate new and persuasive ideas, are more likely to accumulate and defend financial gains within the frame of the knowledge economy (see Stehr, 2016: 101–108).

The notion of human capital that is modeled on the valuation of fixed capital has been developed and deployed primarily within *economic* discourse (Schultz, 1961; Becker, 1964; Tan, 2014)[26] and, more specifically, the economics of education.[27] Human capital theory places the working person (as a presumed rationally acting subject motivated by future returns) at the center of its considerations. A variant of human capital theory, or its development in terms of incorporating empirical indicators of skills (for example, cognitive skills such as math, science, and literacy skills across countries), is what Eric Hanushek and Ludger Woessman (2015: 16) call *knowledge capital theory*. In any case, in human capital theory education plays a crucial role.

As Gary S. Becker (1994b: 16) in a subsequent revisit of human capital theory therefore summarizes, "expenditures on education, training, medical care, etc., are investments in capital. However, these produce human, not physical or financial, capital because you cannot separate a person from his or her knowledge, skills, health, or values the way it is possible to move financial and physical assets while the owner stays put."[28]

My human capital, in more extensive sense than Becker's definition, and as Michel Feher ([2007] 2009: 26) describes it succinctly "is me, as a set of skills and capabilities that is modified by all that affects me and all that I affect. . . . [Human capital] now refers to all that is produced by the skill set that defines me. Such that everything that I earn—be it salary, returns on investment, booty, or favors I may have incurred—can be understood as the return on the human capital that constitutes me." Thus, it is not only formal education that counts as the input of a person's human capital, but also influences of a societal nature, such as the kind of family background and the social strata of origin (cf. Gould, Simhon and Weinberg, 2019).

It is within the context of human capital theory that the *value* of knowledge, skills and capabilities of active economic agents and their *costs* rather than their intrinsic good becomes the relevant consideration. Not all the returns to human capital investment are necessarily monetary in nature; "a person's appreciation of literature over much of his or her lifetime" may also be a return to investment (Schultz, 1962: 7). But as the typical usage of the human capital theory in economics indicates what counts above all is the *income* generated by one's human capital assets. In the world of symbolic economy valued income includes income from or the appreciation of financial products.

If however we extend the consideration of the price of labor both comparatively across different societies or regions within societies (cf. Teal, 2011: S8), then the price of labor is much more determined by *where* the person lives rather than the volume of human capital (held constant across nations or regions) an individual commands; and when we enlarge the time frame historically, then *when* a person lived is much more significant for the price of labor than her human capital (held constant over time). History and geography do matter. And as Francis Teal (2011: S8) concludes, "the central fact about the price of labour is that its price is much more closely correlated with where the person lives than with what they know."

Just as physical capital is created by changes in the means of production brought about by new instruments and artifacts that facilitate production, human capital rests on the transformation of *individuals* who impart skills and capacities[29] that allow them to contribute to productive processes.[30] In contrast to other forms of capital, human capital is embodied in its owner. In its most simplified variety, human capital theory expects *income differences* to be a strict reflection of acquired skill differentials of occupations. You earn what you deserve, as David Ricardo among others have argued.

The acquisition of skills is a form of durable investment rather than consumption. The acquisition of human capital is fostered by the desire of the individual agent to maximize utilities, a future-oriented perspective, constant rational conduct and stable preferences. The choices of the individual are constrained by market forces, time, income, and available opportunities (Becker, 1993) and thus depend on the conduct or judgment of others.

Skills can be acquired by attending school and job training. Learning and training of course also happen outside formal educational institutions, especially on the job (cf. Becker, 1994b: 20). In research on human capital, the number of years of schooling and job training is typically taken as a proxy for differential skills (for an example with historical data, see de Pleijt, 2016). Existing estimates of the rate of return rely almost exclusively on school attainment as a substitute for various skills relevant to occupational achievement (typically focusing on early career workers) rather than on any *direct* measures of cognitive skills and capacities over the full occupational history of workers such as ongoing learning (see Hanushek, Schwerdt, and Wiederhold, 2015). A cautionary note would therefore include, as Peter Cappelli (2014: 31) stresses: "Using education as a proxy for the "skill" that employers want should be interpreted with caution as well given that the extensive literature in job analysis shows that the knowledge, skills, and abilities that are used in jobs have at best only a partial overlap with what is taught in typical college courses."

These estimates indicate indirectly at least that the price of knowledge taken to mean the skills of an employee is what makes the employee more productive. Louis Garicano and Esteban Rossi-Hansberg (2015: 5) offer the observation that it is not merely an estimate of the value of educational achievement that allows for a calculation of the value of human capital: "Perhaps the best measure of the marketable knowledge and skills of an agent is his or her wage." In the end, the close correlation between wages and education ensures that every analysis of human capital value arrives at the same (tautological) conclusion independent of its point of departure, be it education or wages. Educational attainment as such is of course not irrelevant to occupational success; and, as internationally comparative studies have indicated, both the quality and quantity of education contribute to country differences in income and economic growth (e.g. Schoellman, 2012).

An initial reduction in consumption or the abandonment of other investment opportunities by economically *rational*, motivated individuals should pay off at a later time in their lives in the form of higher levels of income. Indeed, it is one of the governing assumptions of human capital discourse in economics that differential earnings are in fact closely related to the individual (atomistic) capital at hand and that this interdependence between capital and wages is observable in an unambiguous fashion and based on constant motives across time and space (for a competing, sociological perspective see Fevre, Rees and Gorard, 1999; Hilmer and Hilmer, 2012).

It is on the basis of these assumptions that estimates of the price of skills (Mincer, 1974) and the rate of returns on investments into human capital are calculated (e.g. Blaug, [1965] 1968). What proportions of the returns to skills will be appropriated by the individual who has invested in these skills is a contentious matter. The corporation expects benefits (e.g. Barney, 1991; Becker and Gerhart, 1996) and may even *appropriate* most of the returns to the skills of the individual worker (as the classical Marxist labor theory of value for example stipulates).

As long as labor market competition is presumed free especially from extraneous constraints, and competition therefore approaches perfect competition, human capital theory assumes that income differentials among individuals directly reflect differential investments in the acquisition of the relevant skills. Human capital theory, then, amounts to a theoretical perspective that *explains* equality rather than inequality. "Unearned income" can only be generated by competitive distortions (see Atkinson, 1983: 104; Berger, 2004: 367–368). From a macro-perspective an increasing supply of human capital to the economy will reduce—assuming a demand for human capital that is lower than the supply—the skill premium or the value commanded by human capital (cf. Acemoglu and Autor, 2012: 427).

Human capital is not homogeneous. For example, it is possible to distinguish among general human capital that is mobile, and specific context-sensitive human capital that is not mobile across boundaries. It is often argued that changes in the kinds of skills in demand in the labor market are the result of changes in technology. The standard assumption is that only the individual who makes the investment in the first place can, under most circumstances, appropriate returns on human capital. Human capital is embodied capital. Human capital cannot be separated from the individual, but the value of the investment depends also on the assessments made by other agents (see van Doorn, 2014) or on the network of social relations this individual is able to mobilize. The stock of human capital cannot be directly traded and transferred unless one trades and transfers the individual person. Human capital theory is silent on the influence of collective factors such as, for example, the societal reputation of post-secondary degrees that affect the successful acquisition of human capital or, correspondingly, the failure to do so.

Canonical human capital theory is equally opaque on the question of the depreciation of such capital and therefore how the earning streams may decline or, for that matter, continues to grow over time.[31] Unlike the impact on capital invested in the plants and the equipment of a corporation, the impact of recessionary economic times, for example, on the value of human capital (does it depreciate or even increase in value?) is an unexplored question (see Stiglitz, 2015: 6–10).[32]

By the same token, human capital theory tends to be silent on the impact of socio-structural features of society and the nature of the economic system that may enhance or reduce payoffs in return for the individual investments made. Finally, human capital theory is quit "on what factors determine the skills that are demanded. . . . [E]mpirical analysis of the return to education is not directly informative about what skills workers use on the job, why these skills are required, and how these skill requirements have changed over time" (Autor and Handel, 2009: 1).

Human capital theories as well as efforts to apply this perspective empirically remain hamstrung by a superficial stylized notion of how human capital manifests itself in social reality. Mark Granovetter's (1985: 486; also, Williamson, 1975: 255–258) criticism of standard economic discourse that it fails to recognize the importance of social relationships also applies to the typical exposition of the theory and empirical study of human capital: "The interpersonal ties described in their arguments are extremely stylized, average, 'typical'- devoid of specific content, history, or structural location."

The empirical representation of human capital is for the most part seen as we have pointed out, to reflect the number of years of schooling; schooling being taken to represent a homogeneous variable and a valid indication of the differential skills and knowledge of the individual. Dajun Lin and his co-authors follow the convention of quantifying human capital by relating

> cognitive performance as measured by the end of secondary schooling in relation to labor market outcomes of 20 through 50-year-old individuals. The labor market outcomes taken into consideration in relation to cognitive performance are annual labor incomes and work hours and hourly wage rates as well as a measure of total (discounted) lifetime labor income. The cognitive performance was measured from scores of the Armed Forces Qualification Test (AFQT): "AFQT scores are calculated using information from four of the ten Armed Services Vocation Aptitude Battery (ASVAB) of tests—word knowledge, paragraph comprehension, math knowledge and arithmetic reasoning."
>
> *(Lin, Lutter and Ruhm, 2016: 14)*[33]

Their analysis finds that "cognitive performance is positively associated with future labor market outcomes at all ages" (Lin, Lutter and Ruhm, 2016: 4, 24). Moreover, the "cognitive skill effect on income is universally larger for women than men, although the differences are not always statistically significant, with particularly pronounced gaps at young ages." The effect of early life human capital investment of cognitive performance (exempting non-cognitive abilities in reaching adult outcomes) increases with age. The relationship continues to be observable after controlling for non-cognitive characteristics. The reported relations between an early-life cognitive achievement test and income could be the outcome of a number of different intervening factors and social processes including for example the social status of the family of the individual subjects.

The Becker-Tomes (1986) model of the intergenerational transmission of human capital recognizes the impact of previous generations on the individual's acquisition of human capital. Specifically, the Becker-Tomes model proposes that the level of human capital and the abilities of parents matter for the human capital of their children when credit constraints limit the parents' ability to invest in the human capital formation of their offspring. Whether or not the rational understanding of economic constraints or opportunities by parents, let alone their educational attainment, plays a role in the intergenerational transmission of human capital is a contested issue. A similar unresolved question is the influence of grandparents on the transmission of human capital (see Lindahl et al., 2014). In the final analysis, however, human capital theory tends to treat the complex dimension of cognitive capacities and skills and the intergenerational transmission of these abilities as a black box.

Eric Hanushek and his colleagues (2015) have tried to partly fill this gap by providing information about the returns to *cognitive skills* across the entire labor force, using data from the *Programme for the International Assessment of Adult Competencies* (PIAAC) for 23 countries. How do earnings (expressed in pre-tax and pre-transfer wages) of full-time workers between 35 and 54 years of age differ depending on a direct measure of cognitive skills?[34] The results obtained in this analysis of the PIAAC data focus on numeracy skills, that is, the "ability to access, use, interpret, and communicate mathematical information and ideas in order to engage in and manage the mathematical demands of a range of situations in adult life," which the authors of the study considered comparable across countries.

The results "consistently indicate that better skills are significantly related to higher labor-market earnings, . . . a one-standard-deviation increase in numeracy skills is associated with an average increase in hourly wages of 17.8 percent across the 23 countries" (Hanushek, Schwerdt and Wiederhold, 2015: 108). The returns to skills, measured across numeracy, literacy and problem-solving domains, however, vary significantly from country to country. Returns to skills are twice as high in the United States as in the Scandinavian countries.

Nevertheless, in spite of many efforts, the conclusion remains that we are not able to find a reliable method of determining the exact monetary value of human capital, for example for (isolated) pupils, students, corporations or society (Machlup, 1979: 70). Georg Simmel ([1900] 2004: 420) summarizes one of the significant criticisms of the human capital theory with its emphasis on the individual as follows, "all qualified labour as such in no way rests solely upon the higher education of the worker but rests equally upon the higher and more complicated structure of the objective conditions of work, of materials and the historical-technical organization."

## Symbolic and Knowledge Capital

In contrast and in addition, the theory of cultural, symbolic and social capital mainly explicated by Pierre Bourdieu within *sociological* discourse, and the idea of knowledge capital proposed by André Gorz ([2003] 2010: 1–2) begin to open up the black box of symbolic capital and alert us to the existence of immaterial forms of capital and the complex ways of its context-sensitive acquisition. Pierre Bourdieu ([1983] 1986: 241; see also Michels, [1908] 1987: 140–141) explicates his insights into the role of immaterial capital that can be translated into economic capital (that is "immediately and directly convertible into money") with the economic perspective, particularly a Marxist approach, very much in mind.

Pierre Bourdieu ([1983] 1986: 243) first encountered the usefulness of the notion of "cultural capital" in social inequality research. This origin of Bourdieu's theory of the reproduction of privilege has a considerable impact on the ways in which the notion of cultural capital designed to enlarge the orthodox concept of class is strategically deployed in discourse. Bourdieu's research was designed to explain the unequal academic achievement of children from different social classes in France; unequal academic achievement, or the "specific profits" (failures) students are able acquire in the academic market, are related to the existing stratified distribution of cultural capital among social classes and the unequal chances of acquiring such capital at home (cf. Bourdieu and Passeron, [1964] 1979). Cultural capital is added to existing cultural capital stocks, thereby reproducing the structure of the distribution of cultural capital between social classes (cf. Bourdieu, [1971] 1973: 73). It can therefore be argued that the benefits that derive from the unequal distribution of cultural capital represent a form of *unearned income*. Given its intellectual origins, Bourdieu's theory of cultural capital is fundamentally about societal power and domination. As a result, Bourdieu's main concern is with the role this capital plays in the reproduction of social hierarchies.

Although the educational system is of course not the only social site where cultural capital may be acquired, education not only fulfills a role in converting academic into social hierarchies but has a function also in the legitimation and perpetuation of the social *status quo*. The pretensions of "merit," "gifts," skills, equal opportunities and democratic selection that appear to put the chances of acquiring cultural capital in the educational systems onto an equal footing are weakened by virtue of the fact that "the ruling classes have at their disposal (to begin with) a much larger cultural capital than the other classes" (Bourdieu, [1971] 1973: 85). The modern educational system canonizes privilege by ignoring it.

Bourdieu distinguishes between different forms of cultural capital: its embodied or symbolic form as internalized culture, its objectified form in material objects and media, and its institutionalized form (for example, as academic certificates).[35] These distinctions signal the ways in which cultural capital is stored and passed on by way of becoming an integral habitus of the individual. Bourdieu identifies two additional forms of capital, economic capital and social capital. Social capital refers to the gain's individuals may derive from their network of social relations (also Coleman, 1988).[36] The various forms of capital correlate highly with each other and form what could be called capital "repertoires." One form of capital "comes to be added, in most cases" to other forms of capital, for example, cultural to economic capital (Bourdieu, [1971] 1973: 99).

We will focus on Bourdieu's concept of cultural capital (or informational capital) since it resonates, at least on the surface, more closely with our concept of knowledge, that is, *knowledge as a capacity to act*.[37] In Bourdieu's understanding, cultural capital as a form of *symbolic capital* is much broader but also less tangible than the concept of human capital favored by economic discourse.[38] In contrast, the idea of knowledge capital as developed by André Gorz[39] is a form of knowledge that is not acquired in settings of formal education but in everyday life and belongs to everyday culture. As a matter of fact, the notion of knowledge capital resonates closely with the concepts of *knowledge skills* that we have explicated elsewhere (Stehr, 2016).

As we have seen, modern economic human capital theory relates deliberate and measurable educational investments (and achievements) in the acquisition of useful skills and knowledge to the *monetary* gains or losses they generate, and therefore to the value of knowledge. As one of the originators of the idea of human capital, Theodore W. Schultz (1961), contends that skills and knowledge have grown in Western societies at a much faster rate than nonhuman capital. Schultz suggests that investment in human capital embodied in human beings has driven much of the growth in the real wages of income-earning individuals in recent decades, as well as economic growth in general (cf. Benhabib and Spiegel, 1994).[40]

In strong contrast, cultural capital theory does not proceed from the assumption of a kind of *tabula rasa* that allows all individuals to enter and participate in the competitive market where human capital is allocated and where success or failure is most affected by unequal natural aptitudes. Cultural capital theory not only acknowledges the preexisting unequal access to the distributional channels for its accumulation but also the different ways in which the "market" promotes the chances of particular players from the very beginning. In a largely undifferentiated society or community, of course, culture does not function as a vehicle for the emergence of differential cultural capital. As the societal division of labor increases, however, the social conditions of the transmission of cultural capital tend to be much more disguised than those that govern the transmission of economic capital. The portion of individual lives that can be afforded for the acquisition of cultural capital is highly significant. Cultural capital yields benefit of distinction for its owner.

Even though the analysis of the acquisition and transmission of cultural capital is situated within what Bourdieu calls "social fields" (see Wacquant, 1989: 39), one of the most evident drawbacks of Bourdieu's explication of cultural capital theory is, first, its strong individualistic bias, that is, the extent to which he stresses the fusion of cultural capital with the personality of its individual owner. Cultural capital is not a homogeneous phenomenon. Not all cultural capital is equal. Cultural capital is fragile. Fashion and the demand for novelty change the value of specific forms of cultural capital.

With Bourdieu, the emphasis remains for the most part on cultural capital as an inherent attribute of the individual carrier. Cultural capital in the form of educational credentials, for example, declines and dies with its carrier since it has the same biological limits as its carrier. Bourdieu's individualistic conception of cultural capital appears to be linked to his determination not to dispossess cultural capital theory of the ability to calculate and attribute investment gains that derive from cultural capital. And such returns of investment are seen to accrue primarily to the investor. In this sense, cultural capital theory continues to resonate with human capital theory. It contains crucial residues of the economic discourse.[41] Frequent references to the marketplace, to supply and demand, to costs, investments and profits would be examples of such a conflation of perspectives. It is important to recognize that cultural capital is embodied in collective processes and structures; hence the benefits typically do not accrue only to those who have invested resources, which raises the free-rider issue. The production as well as consumption of such capital is not charged to the individual. It is borne by the collectivity. At one extreme, such capital can even be seen to be entirely free in that its use by certain individuals does not diminish its utility for or availability to others. Cultural capital is human-made capital and as such subject to limits and dynamics applicable to all human products and creations, especially in modern societies.

Second, and as we have emphasized already, Bourdieu discovers and utilizes the concept of cultural capital in the context of social inequality research. The concept derives much of its coherence and its critical tone from this context, a context in which the persistence of distinction, of processes of inclusion and exclusion, domination and subordination play a decisive role. Bourdieu thereby retains a strong reference to the objective and inescapable presence and constraint of the social, economic and political presence of social class in modern society.[42] Cultural capital, in the end, is merely derivative and closely mirrors the objective realities of class. As John R. Hall (1992: 257) therefore observes, "the dazzling variety and endless differences of culture obtain surprising coherence when we look at them through the lens of social stratification."

Cultural capital becomes a peculiar entity that is apparently acquired and transmitted (*reproduced*) almost mechanically though in a selective fashion with great ease, considerable precision and success. The risks of failure appear to be at a minimum while the possibility of a perpetuation of the cultural and socio-structural patterns is at a maximum. Whether such a description conforms to reality is questionable, as is the idea that there is a close correspondence between particular manifestations of culture and class membership (see Halle, 1992: 134– 135). Culture is much more fluid and leaves "much opportunity for choice and variation" (DiMaggio, 1997: 265).

Access, at least today, is much more open than a theory of cultural capital that stresses the stratification of power and domination in society would suggest. Pierre Bourdieu's distinction and the openness for change, resistance and innovation accorded to the capacities of individuals and groups are limited (cf. Garnham and Williams, 1986: 129). But cultural frames and meaning production as well as re-production in an immense and creative variety of ways is the hallmark of the work that cultural capital conceived of in a less mechanical fashion may well accomplish for individuals and collectivities. It must also be asked if the relevance of class divisions is not undermined or even eliminated by virtue of the transformation of economic realities. In such a society, distinctions and advantages that are linked to cultural processes are not merely derivative and subordinate but foundational (Stehr, 2002). The extent to which the educational system in modern societies actually fails to faithfully reproduce the existing system of social inequality (Boudon, 1974) is testimony not only to the dynamic character of modern society but also to profound changes in inequality regimes in which knowledge and knowledge skills play a more significant and independent role (see Stehr, 1999, Stehr and Adolf, 2017).

Third, although the notion of human cultural capital is not employed in a fully a historic manner, it is for the most part devoid of historical specificity, lacks linkage to various major societal formations such as industrial society, the state or science and is at times also used not unlike the notion of years of education in human capital theory (e.g. Bourdieu, [1984] 1988: 230–232). Bourdieu does not explore the socio-historical conditions under which different strategies and regimes of inequality formation become possible. In principle it would seem that the idea of different forms of capital was universally applicable although the extent and the ease of their convertibility—for example the extent to which parental labor at home can be translated into status attainment for their children— varies within historical contexts (see Calhoun, 1995: 139–141).

New "structures of consciousness" (to use a term coined by Benjamin Nelson, 1973) cannot be captured by Bourdieu's theory of cultural capital. In many ways, the structure of consciousness of knowledge societies is, of course, not novel. It resonates with the consciousness of modernity that dates—although this, too, is a highly contested issue—at least from the more immediate socio-historical origins of the French Revolution. In other respects, the *conscience collective* in knowledge societies is at variance with the belief systems and mental sets that are usually identified as uniquely modern and therefore warrants to be called a new structure of consciousness. In any event, the notion of cultural capital seems ill designed to capture such transformations. Given its close reliance on the assertion that cultural capital is about power and domination, it cannot capture the opposite phenomenon, namely the extent to which knowledge is strategically deployed to *soften* and *undermine* authority, power and domination.

We have already noted that little has been done in accounting to actually capture the value of such intangible assets.[43] Nonetheless, it is worth reviewing existing attempts to arrive at a price of intangibles as another avenue to gain insight into the value of knowledge. What tangible and intangible assets share are that they are *not used up* in the process of conducting business. But as far as most national accounts are concerned what is measured and becomes part of quantifying the volume of the economic activity of a country are tangible in contrast to immaterial investments. But what exactly are intangible investments and assets, how to determine their value, how productive such investments happen to be or how to recognize intangibles in the balance sheets of a company are currently largely open and unresolved questions.

## The Value of Intangible Investments

Not surprisingly, assertions about the proportion of the market value of a corporation that stems from its intangible assets are all over the place. Estimates range from a small percentage to significant proportions such as 75 percent to corporations who value consists only of intangible assets. However, and as we have stressed, concurrence can be found among observers of the modern economy that the significance of intangible assets such as knowledge and information, employees' capabilities, databases, platforms, brand, customer goodwill, and R&D for the competitive success of a company are growing rapidly. More agreement may also be found when it comes to ways of measuring and therefore of incorporating intangible assets into the balance sheet of a company. The agreement is that there is no agreement. A brief enumeration of some of the intangibles identified in the economics literature only strengthens an ambivalent conclusion. In the case of retail firms' intangibles extend to brand values, the design of supply and distribution networks, advertising, logistical and organizational changes (cf. Crouzet and Eberly, 2018).

The discovery of the *productivity paradox* in the 1960s and in later years ignited the interest among social scientists in exploring the role of apparently non-tangible investments on the balance sheet of corporations and the national economy.[44] As Robert Solow (1987) famously put it, the impact of the growing reliance on computers are in evidence everywhere except in the productivity statistics. Yet when it comes to the economic affluence of a nation and the ability of a country's economy to improve the standard of living of its citizens and compete internationally, social scientists are in an unusual agreement that productivity "in the long run is almost everything" (Krugman, 1994: 13). Manuel Castells (1996: 80) throughout his extensive study of modern society as a network society seconds this observation and concludes, "productivity is the source of the wealth of nations." In this light, Krugman (1994: 17) comments somewhat despairingly, the slowdown of "American productivity growth since the early 1970s becomes the most important single fact about our economy."

Economists in particular have been puzzled and even irritated about the apparent lack of measurable productivity gains in goods producing and services industries in OECD countries in response to or in conjunction with the immense investments in recent years in information and communication technologies. The choice of labeling this phenomenon the "productivity paradox" resulted from the disjuncture between the immense economic expectations and promises that have been engendered by the "computer age," on the one hand, and the apparent lack of sustainable economic payoffs resulting from the considerable investments by corporations and the state in information and communication technologies, on the other hand. The variety of research and accounts of the productivity paradox exemplify the growing and deepening division of labor in social science and its essentially contested nature. For some observers, the productivity paradox does not exist in reality. The productivity puzzle is a measurement construct or indicative of a mismeasurement of outputs that conceals real gains that are made (cp. Quinn, 1996; Diewert and Fox, 1997). But even if the puzzle does exist, the magnitude of the problem is small upon first examination since investments in computers form a relatively minor part of all capital input. For others, the paradox represents but a transitory phase not unlike the productivity lag produced by the transition to technological systems in the past such as the diffusion of electric power. And as is the case for other learning processes, it takes a protracted period of time before the economic benefits show up (cf. David, 1990; Petit and Soete, 1997; Davenport, 1997). Still other observers see the productivity paradox not as a gap that reflects economic realities. Rather, its persistence is an indicator of intellectual or theoretical deficits in economic discourse (cf. Jorgenson, 1997).[45] Last but not least, some economists have signaled that the danger has passed and that the productivity paradox disappeared by 1991 (e.g. Brynjolfsson and Hitt, 1996; Sichel, 1999).

What becomes clear in the wake of the perplexing productivity paradox is that an effort is needed to measure the contribution of the assets represented by information technologies. The initial approach consisted in taking the (quality adjusted) price of computers into account. But computers represented a tangible good. But that does not apply to the software on which computers run: information embedded in codes that have at times a lasting usefulness. In 1999 United State Bureau of Economic Analysis introduced software as an investment item in the calculation of the US GDP. Similarly, the OECD proposed to developed frameworks in an effort to count intangible investments (Young, 1998).

As shown in the information provided by the OECD for the 14 countries in Figure 5.1, there is currently no internationally comparable methodology for collecting data on the importance of intangible investments. The aggregation of different components of intangible investments does not reveal the value of knowledge as a whole or as part of one of the elements of intangible factors. As a matter of fact, the term "knowledge" does not appear at all in the list of individual parts of intangible investments.

## Patents[46]

Patents represent a legal grant (a category in law) by (typically) a state or bundle of states such as the European Patent Office (EPO) or a series of corresponding patents (Triadic Family of patents at the EPO, the United States Patent and Trademark Office (USPTO and the Japan Patent Office). A simple definition of a patent would be that the inventor is granted property rights for a specified time (17 years in the United States) and space in analogy to the general legal rules governing property in general. The owner of the invention acquires a legal title that prevents others from making, using, or selling the invention while granting the owner the right to sell her "intangible" asset for a price. A patent—often acquired

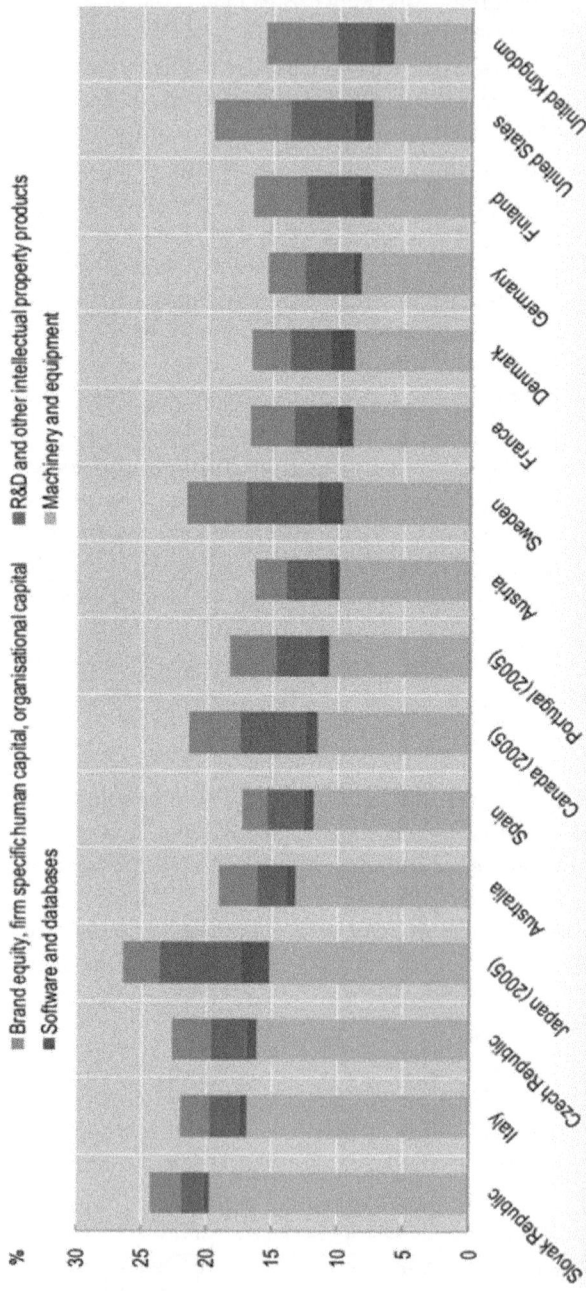

**FIGURE 5.1** Investment in Tangible and Intangible Assets as Share of GDP, 2006

*Source:* MSEE (https://cordis.europa.eu/docs/projects/cnect/0/284860/080/deliverables/001-MSEED221AnalysisofintangibleassetmgmtV10.pdf)

*Note:* What is included in intangible assets? Using as their basis a seminal paper by C. Corrado, Hulten and Sichel (2006), researchers in 14 countries have computed aggregates for intangible investment. Software and databases provide a measure of computerized information. Scientific R&D, mineral exploration, copyright and license costs, and other product development, design and research are a measure of innovative property. Brand equity, firm-specific human capital and organizational capital are taken as measures of economic competencies. Some of these intangibles—software and, more recently, R&D—are now recognized by the international statistical community as capital assets and will be accounted for in the System of National Accounts (see the OECD Handbook on Deriving Capital Measures of Intellectual Property Products, 2010). More work is needed to harmonize the definition of intangible assets and collect data on an internationally comparable basis so as to better identify and measure new sources of growth.

in a lengthy administrative process involving highly specialized experts—grants the owner the right to practice the invention described in the patent. Thus, patents convert knowledge into private property[47] and knowledge becomes scarce in a legal sense. It is the owner of the patent who must ensure that the patent is not misused. Under the conditions of globalization such control can be most difficult. A patent may come with strict or weaker restrictions of its use by other actors. The policy challenge is to find the right mix (cf. Forey, 2000: 76–77).

Since the 1980s, policies with regard to the legal protection of intellectual property (patents, trademarks, copyrights) have changed radically, and litigation about patent infringements has risen (for example, the patent struggle between Apple and Samsung about the design of the smart phone).[48] With the World Trade Organization's (WTO) Agreement on Trade-Related Aspects of Intellectual Property (TRIPS), stringent und unprecedented obligations have been enacted for all members of the WTO with respect to their national intellectual property policies. In order to take part in international trade and access foreign markets, every member country has to adopt legal frames that conform to patent laws in the economically dominant countries of the world. Moreover, the transnational integration of the major patent offices in the United States, Europe and Japan has created a global network of knowledge governance that results in a "concealed" harmonization of patent laws (Drahos, 2010).[49]

But patent protection is not just a technical or economic matter. Patent laws have social, political as well as economic implications. IPR are intended to offer incentives to stimulate innovation (Stiglitz and Greenwald, 2014: 429–456).[50] The counterpart to IPR is the public domain. William Landes and Richard Posner (2003: 14–15) note that even the strongest defenders of property rights "acknowledge the economic value of preserving public domains—that is, of areas in which property is available for common use rather than owned—even in regard to physical property and a *fortiori* in regard to intellectual property."

A debate surrounding IPR that is just starting (cf. Li, MacGarvie and Moser, 2015) but is getting more intense concerns the extent to which scientific texts, for example, are made freely available by companies (such as Google, Academia or Research Gate) or libraries, to the dismay of publishers and authors.[51] Opponents to *free access* see these developments as a one-sided privilege favoring the "consumers" of texts and neglecting the rights of the "producers" of the respective intellectual accomplishments. Supported by law and court decisions, libraries in Germany, for example, are permitted to scan textbooks and make them available for students to save on sticks—which of course allows them to pass them on without restrictions.[52]

Critical issues surrounding patents involve the question whether patents actually stimulate innovation (cf. Williams, 2016 for an empirical investigation of the issue in the health care market), the extent to which patents add to the price the consumer has to pay (for example, for pharmaceuticals), the meaning of a fencing-in of knowledge, in the first place, which we have discussed, or the scope and the degree of novelty demanded for granting a parent. Answers to these issues are highly contestable. Every invention that is granted legal protection for a limited period of time of course relies on previously accumulated knowledge (cf. Stiglitz, 1999: 314–316; Stiglitz, 2012: 78). "Because patent lawyers are masters of obfuscation," as the *Economist* ("Time to fix patents," August 8, 2015) argues, patents in fact tend to slow innovation by slowing the dissemination of knowledge; patents tend to lock in the advantages of the patent holders. Hence the conclusion that follows from critical questions about the role of patents would seem to be that the patent system should not be enhanced but reduced in its impact, if not abolished (see Boldrin and Levine, 2013).[53]

Private IPR now widely employed by law-makers at international (cf. Fink and Maskus, 2005), national and regional levels are not restricted to patents but also extend to copyrights (which, in contrast to patents, are acquired almost instantly upon creation), databases (David, 2000), trademarks, designs, software (see Harison, 2008; Bonaccorsi, Calvert and Joly, 2011), plant varieties, and trade secrets (in the sense of information and knowledge held by a business that is kept out of the public domain through agreements with employees or other firms).[54]

It is not surprising therefore to observe that there are many types of IPR and many types of institutions that deal with their administration. The variety of IPR and the ways they interrelate with law, markets, corporations and individuals makes it most difficult if not impossible to gain a robust general insight into the value of (distinctive) ideas, inventions, knowledge and copyrights.[55] The propensity to attempt to patent an invention or, on the contrary, to make ideas freely available depends on the social context in which new knowledge is discovered. For example, "using data collected by the National Research Council within the US National Academies from their survey of firms that received National Institutes of Health Phase II Small Business Innovation Research awards between 1992 and 2001, [Link and Ruhm, 2009] find that entrepreneurs with academic backgrounds are more likely to publish their intellectual capital compared to entrepreneurs with business backgrounds, who are more likely to patent their intellectual capital" (Link and Ruhm, 2009: 1).

The benefits that accrue to intellectual property may arrive in many ways, depending on the nature of the invention (such as a license granted or the signal a patent sends to others, see Long, 2002). After all, R&D efforts are inherently heterogeneous, sometimes successful, at other times without valuable results and "there is a large variance in the value of individual patents, rendering patents counts an extremely noise indicator of R&D success" (Czarnitzki, Hall and Oriani, 2006: 124). At best, we will be able to arrive at an indirect and ambivalent assessment, especially with respect to quantity, of the value and costs associated with intellectual proper rights.[56]

In the strict sense of the term, knowledge tends to be embedded only in patents and not in trademarks. Trademarks are names affixed by a company to their products or similar attributes; hence, based on our definition of information, trademarks convey information. From an economic perspective, a patent—if well enforced—represents a monopoly that offers a rent to the owner. In the context of examining the value of knowledge, we are interested in the rent patents may generate.[57]

As Margaret Blair and Steven Wallman (2001: 73) in their report on "unseen wealth" point out, "once an intangible [such as a copyright] has been defined by law as a piece of property, and the rights associated with that property have been delimited, it becomes easier to estimate a value associated with those property rights and to sell, or transfer, or enter into other transactions involving that piece of property." Assigning property rights to an invention, a text, a musical score or software does, as such, not immediately allow for an assessment of the value of intellectual property. In fact, the value of intellectual property could be zero or even negative if the investment afforded for generating the invention is never returned. Presumably, not all patents are successful. The value will be a function of the many additional features related to the activity of the owner, for example his willingness to invest in activities protecting the monopoly or, last but not least, of the nature of the intellectual property itself.

From an economic perspective, a patent enshrined in law represents a capacity to act and a solution to the "appropriability problem" (a protective function for new knowledge) or is seen to offer an answer to the free-rider issue since knowledge is viewed as "non-excludable." Patent protection translates non-rival goods into excludable goods. Only the patent holder is legitimized to appropriate the benefits of the invention. Others are excluded from enjoying the profits of the knowledge in question. In addition, from an economic point of view, patents are seen to serve as an incentive to produce socially and economically desirable innovations.

Patent laws are powerfully influenced by assumptions about knowledge and innovation from neo-classical economics (see Dempsey, 1999). But a comprehensive theory of the economic effects of patents must also take into account that legal intellectual property protections can restrain rather than encourage innovation, the growth of knowledge and socio-economic development. If knowledge is defined as a *public good* (Stiglitz, 1995; cf. Zhou, 2015), that is, as non-rival in use and non-excludable in consumption, the ideas associated with knowledge claims "may even stimulate others to have an idea with large commercial value" (Stiglitz, 1999: 309).[58] On the other hand, profit-oriented actors would not be interested in entering into the production of public goods because they could not make a profit (Archibugi and Filippetti (2015: 481). André Gorz ([2003] 2010)[59] defends the desirability of treating knowledge as a common good on the basis of a couple of considerations: (1) Knowledge is from the outset the product of collective labor, (2) knowledge does not have the attributes of commodities that escape the owner's control upon being sold or losing legal control and (3) privatization would restrict the societal utility of knowledge. But as Charlotte Hess and Elinor Ostrom (2007: 5) warn, a common good lead to conduct "such as competition for use, free riding and over-harvesting"; and "[t]ypical threats to knowledge commons are commodification or enclosure, pollution and degradation, and non-sustainability." Even if you declare and understand that knowledge is a common good, what remains is the difficult task to devise and learn effective ways with the help of which knowledge can be shared.[60] Such a demand is of course at the core of every educational effort.

In a "well-functioning" economy the monetary value of an individual good should be represented by its price. Many efforts have been made to accomplish exactly this. Most often efforts to establish the value of intellectual property are based on the use of *proxies*.[61] For example, the value of IPR are inferred from the value of the prices of shares of a company listed on the stock exchange, thus establishing IPR as part of the "unseen wealth" of a corporation. Intangibles "can be related to brand names, process or product innovations, advertising, managerial skill, human capital in the workforce, and other aspects of the firm" (Greenhalgh and Rogers, 2007: 551; also, Van Eckelen, 2015).[62] Such arithmetic indicates that highly contentious figures could result from such an effort. It is virtually impossible to arrive at a robust conclusion regarding whether such an accounting under- or overestimates the value of the intellectual property of a firm. In short, "the eventual returns to individual patents or trademarks can vary enormously: most returns are very small, but a few generate huge returns."

What is possible, however, is to revert to the broad collective income and the expenditures of royalty and license fees received and paid by entire nations. The World Bank[63] offers such statistics for a wide range of countries. And as recent data from the "2014 World Development Indicators" show, the "Balance of Technology Trade" is heavily tilted in favor of a few countries whose expenditures on R&D, as percentages of the national Gross National Product (GNP), have been high (also Ganguli, 2000).

Large expenditures on R&D in a country appear to ensure that the balance of royalty and license fees received is positive (e.g. in the case of Finland, Germany, Japan, Sweden, the United Kingdom and the United States) while comparatively low R&D expenditures correlate with a negative balance (e.g. in the case of Brazil, Canada, Ireland, Portugal and Russia). But there are cases where this correlation does not hold, for example in the case of Austria where high R&D expenditures coexist with a negative balance of royalty and license fees both in 2007 and 2014. In many instances of nations with a significant balance of inter-nation technology trade, the gap has increased in recent years (e.g. Canada, Austria, India, Italy and Korea).[64]

The statistic of the inter-nation technology trade balances does not allow for a precise inference of relevant data regarding the value and costs of IPR. It provides only a very broad indication that such rights are translated into national monetary advantages; that both payments and receipts of royalty and license fees tend to increase in more recent years; that disadvantages and benefits are unequally distributed across the globe; and about the size of the receipts and payments. The conclusion that can be drawn is that the economic role of IPR is increasing measurably, signifying the transformation of national economies into what is at times designated as knowledge-based economies.

## Taxation, or the Price of Education[65]

It is not only the professional but also the common-sense view that citizens of democratic societies should be knowledgeable and well informed. Being knowledgeable and well informed comes at a price. One avenue that is open to social scientists interested in the question of the price of knowledge is to examine specific contested cases in which the question of the price of knowledge plays a role, if only an indirect one. We will describe such a conflict about the resources that should be mobilized by the state to ensure that its citizens acquire the level of knowledge and information that is deemed desirable for a democratic society.[66]

During the last century the relation between education and democracy had become almost conventional wisdom. John Dewey ([1916] 2005), for example, views broad if not high levels of educational attainment as a precondition for democracy; while in the post-war era, Seymour Martin Lipset's (1959: 80) cross-national empirical study concludes that "high" levels of educational achievement are a necessary condition for the existence and stability of a democratic society. Even more recent empirical work tends to support this conclusion (e.g. Barro, 1999; Przeworski et al., 2000). An examination of the role and experience of science advising and science policy formation in the United States in the late 1950s (last but not least in the wake of the launch of the first manmade satellite, Sputnik, by the Soviets in the fall of 1957) emphatically concludes that "a democratic nation can only cope with the scientific revolution if thoughtful citizens know what it truly entails" (Dupré and Lakoff, 1962: 181).

However, it is also John Dewey ([1916] 2005: 108–110) who warns against treating education as a *black box*. High levels of formal education are indeed compatible—as the case of Germany demonstrates—with an authoritarian personality and an elevated deference to the state. Dewey ([1916] 2005: 57) notes that in the case of the German educational system, "the educational process was taken to be one of disciplinary training rather than of personal development . . . only in and through an absorption of the aims and meaning of the organized institutions does [the individual] attain true personality." In other words, the philosophy of education and the aims of the educational system "required subordination of individuals to the superior interests of the state." The subservient personality as the primary goal to be realized by educational policies not only in imperial Germany but for decades to come required a "thoroughgoing 'disciplinary' subordination to existing institutions." Dewey's observations are a useful reminder that a high formal level of education in a society does not necessarily lead to support for democratic values and conduct. The association between formal educational achievement and democracy is a complex relationship that requires careful attention to the nature of the actual education system.

This raises the question of how much knowledge and information the citizen of modern societies needs to acquire, and the related issue of the volume of the resources the state has to invest to accomplish such an outcome. There can be little doubt that these questions are highly complex and contentious, as the long-lasting conflict between the State of New York and the City of New York over educational finances readily demonstrates.[67]

For over a decade, the State of New York and the City of New York were entangled in a legal battle over the question of whether the State of New York provided fair and sufficient financial means for the gigantic public school system of the City of New York.[68] The legal dispute ran its course parallel to the so-called "educational standards movement" which has been fighting for the continual improvement of the expectations and standards attached to a high school diploma. In a number of American states, for example Kentucky, courts have indeed pre-scribed much higher, clearly defined standards.

At first glance, this is apparently one of those everyday rhetorical disputes between different political jurisdictions over contested questions of revenue shar-ing between various political levels—a familiar occurrence in any democratic society. The State of New York provides approximately half of the school budget for the City of New York. One of the most recent judgments in this legal action, however, has made reference to a fundamental philosophical or constitutional problem: Which skills, information and proficiencies should the modern state be *minimally* obligated to successfully convey to students in its schools; and to which students; and how expensive must an education system be that guarantees stand-ards of this type? The developments in the New York dispute make it evident that this conflict over how to answer the question under debate is ultimately based on a problem that must be decided within the political system.

The constitution of the State of New York stipulates that the State is obligated to guarantee "the maintenance and support of a system of free common schools wherein all the children of this state may be educated." The interpretation of this constitutional norm as an obligation for the state to make possible a "sound, basic" education is concretized by the Court of Appeals of the State of New York, in a 1995 judgment. This court further ruled that the public school system must be in a position to guarantee that students "function productively as civic participants capable of voting and serving on a jury." In a later judgment of 2001, a judge of the Constitutional Court of the State of New York ruled that as jurors, citizens are required to answer complex questions: Jurors "must determine questions of fact concerning DNA evidence, statistical analysis and convoluted financial fraud, to name only three topics." The State successfully appealed this judgment.

In June 2002, however, the Appellate Division of the State Supreme Court of New York defined a restrictive interpretation of this constitutional norm: On the basis of relevant constitutional standards, the State is not obliged to finance more than a *minimal* education. More concretely, after eight or nine years, students should be able to read political parties' campaign literature; serve the courts as jurors; and fulfill the requirements of an employment that makes minor demands on them. The high school diploma should only ensure that the student had acquired the ability "to get a job, and support oneself, and thereby not be a charge on the public fiscus."

The court's decision was variously received: In some quarters, this minimal educational requirement was understood as a kind of capitulation on the part of the State. In others, the judges were praised for their wise decision, since (more) money was not necessarily an adequate solution to the educational dilemma—other factors also influenced students' opportunities of acquiring cultural capital. The court emphasized that its task had been only to determine the citizen's minimum rights to education as laid out in the constitution; this minimum demand is indeed met by the schools of the City of New York. A claim for compensatory education, for instance, is therefore untenable. And to the extent that the citizens disagree with these minimum goals, they will have to replace the responsible politicians by electoral means. The plaintiff, The Campaign for Fiscal Equity, filed an appeal.

Could this ruling by one of the highest courts of the State of New York be an arbitrary verdict that reflects the spirit of the industrial rather than the knowledge society, that is, what matters is that its citizens are able to find their way to the voting booth and function as a juror?

The legal dispute finally ended (with no possibility of further appeal) on November 20, 2006, with a verdict by the highest court of the State of New York, the Court of Appeals, in which the State of New York was ordered to provide an additional US$ 1.93 billion annually for the city school system. This sum is considerably lower than the US$ 4.7 billion that a lower court had ruled to be appropriate. The final judgment was based on the recommendation of a commission appointed by New York State Governor Pataki in 2004. In a dissenting opinion from that of the majority of the court, one of the two judges in the minority states that "a sound basic education will cost approximately US$ 5 billion in additional annual expenditure. I remain hopeful that, despite the court's ruling today, the policymakers will continue to strive to make schools not merely adequate, but excellent, and to implement a statewide solution." The four judges responsible for the court's majority verdict were all appointees of then New York Governor George Pataki (1995–2006).

## Additional Knowledge

Additional knowledge enlarges our capacity to act; thus, novel or additional knowledge may be of particular value. We may consider "breakthrough" (rare and valuable) knowledge as a subset of additional knowledge that may well have (higher) value (see Park, Howard and Gomulya, 2017). Whether additional knowledge constitutes breakthrough knowledge can only be determined *ex post facto*. It is unavoidable that knowledge has *political as well as economic* attributes. Knowledge as a capacity to act contributes to what is constitutive for politics: to change or to preserve and perpetuate. In general, therefore, knowledge is a medium of social control because once *deployed* it may structure and restructure social formations. In the context of the knowledge-based economy in modern societies (cf. Stehr, 2002), knowledge becomes as we have maintained a force of production, displacing the forces of production typical of industrial society, namely property and capital, and therefore a source of *additional* value, economic growth and productivity including, of course, the possibility of a transition to a sustainable economic system.

The science system in modern societies is by definition a core part of the set of societal institutions that generates additional knowledge. The prestige, the exceptional social, economic and intellectual importance of scientific knowledge is firmly associated with the capacity of the social system of science within which it is embedded to fabricate *additional knowledge* claims. In modern societies, scientific and technical knowledge is uniquely important because it produces *incremental* capacities for social and economic action, or an *increase* in the ability of "how-to-do-it" that may be "privately appropriated," at least temporarily.[69] In social institutions other than science, routinized, habitual conduct and the interpretation and defense of established intellectual perspectives are constitutive. In science, invention and therefore the production of knowledge beyond what already exists is the prime function of the social system of science.

Contrary to neoclassical assumptions, in the case of the economic importance of knowledge in general and additional knowledge in particular the unit price for knowledge-intensive commodities and services decreases with increased production, reflecting "progress down the learning curve" (cf. Schwartz, 1992; see also the economic implications of learning by doing, Arrow, 1962). Incremental knowledge is just as heterogeneous as is socially widely accessible knowledge. Thus, it is entirely conceivable that incremental knowledge may, at any given time, include "key findings" that will prove to be especially valuable in many respects, as for example in economic, military or political contexts. Which knowledge will become key knowledge can only be determined empirically (see Stehr, 2000).

Knowledge constitutes a *basis* for power. Knowledge excludes. As John Kenneth Galbraith (1967: 67) stresses with justification, power "goes to the factor which is hardest to obtain or hardest to replace . . . it adheres to the one that has greatest inelasticity of supply at the margin." But knowledge as such is not a scarce commodity, though there is one feature of some knowledge claims that may well transform knowledge from a plentiful into a scarce resource: what is scarce and difficult to obtain is not access to knowledge *per se*, but access to *incremental knowledge*, to a "marginal unit" of knowledge. The greater the *tempo* with which incremental knowledge ages or decays, the greater the potential influence of the social system within which additional knowledge is produced and the greater the social importance and prestige of those who manufacture or augment knowledge; and, correspondingly, of those who transmit (moderate) such increments to other social systems.

If sold, knowledge enters the domain of others; yet it remains within the domain of the producer and can be spun off once again. This signals that the transfer and the absorption of knowledge do not necessarily include the transfer of the cognitive ability to generate such knowledge, for example, the theoretical apparatus, the technological regime or the required infrastructure that yields such knowledge claims in the first place and is the basis for them to be calibrated and validated. Cognitive *skills* of this kind, therefore, are scarce. Economists often take it for granted that the fabrication of knowledge is expensive whereas its dissemination is virtually without cost. This view is further supported by the common conviction that technological knowledge is nothing but a blueprint that is readily usable, at nominal cost, for all.

However, the acquisition of the kinds of cognitive skills needed to comprehend knowledge and technology can be quite expensive. For example, in many cases, only the rough outlines of technical knowledge are objectified or codified by non-personal means of communication (cf. Berrill, 1964). As a result, some economists suggest that the dissipation and absorption of knowledge, or at least some forms of knowledge, is costlier than its production (see Stigler, 1980: 660–641). Such a conclusion, as well as evidence supporting this observation (Teece, 1977), raises the question of whether the fabrication of knowledge can be easily separated from its dissemination, in terms of reproduction, in the first place.

The progressive elimination of time and space as relevant elements in the production of knowledge has paradoxically injected the importance of time and location into the interpretation and use of (objectified) knowledge. Since the mere understanding and the validation process of knowledge cannot, except in rare circumstances, refer back to the original author(s) of the claim, the separation of social roles makes the interpretive tasks carried out by "experts" more crucial. Knowledge must be made available, interpreted, and linked to local, contingent circumstances. The complexity of the linkages and the volume of the resources required to enact capacities for action delineate the limits of the power of scientific and technical knowledge. Such limits are an inevitable part of the fabrication of scientific knowledge and explain why, generally speaking, the knowledge work performed by the stratum of experts in knowledge-based occupations attains greater and greater centrality in advanced societies. The social prestige, authority and influence of experts are heightened, moreover, if their claim to expertise is uniquely coupled with access to additional knowledge (see Grundmann and Stehr, 2012).

The centrality of knowledge-based occupations or, to use a narrower term, of experts in knowledge societies does not mean that we are on the way, as social theorists have feared in the past, to a technocratic society or a technical state. A technocratic model of society and its major social institutions, which "sees technicians dominating officials and management, and which sees the modern technologically developed bureaucracies as governed by an exclusive reliance on a standard of efficiency" (Gouldner, 1976: 257), be it a nightmare or a utopia, is a counterintuitive scenario. It is doubtful whether the crucial choices that modern societies will be forced to make are more about the technical means and less about the competing ends of social action.

Quite a number of arguments can be deployed to demystify the threat of technocracy and a new ruling class made up of faceless experts. The most persuasive argument is social reality itself, which has failed to support the transformation of society in this direction. The long-predicted emergence of technocratic regimes has not materialized. The diagnosis of an imminent and menacing technocratic society was greatly overdrawn.

Michel Crozier offers a less obvious argument about the limits of the power of experts, counselors and advisors in his study of the bureaucratic phenomenon. Crozier ([1963] 1964: 165) argues that the power of an expert is self-curtailing and self-defeating:

> The rationalization process gives him power, but the end results of rationalization curtail his power. As soon as a field is well covered, as soon as the first intuitions and innovations can be translated into rules and programs, the expert's power disappears. As a matter of fact, experts have power only on the front line of progress—which means that they have a constantly shifting and fragile power.

The objectification and routinization of incremental knowledge curtails the power of knowledge. Yet knowledge assimilated to power is most likely incremental knowledge. Crozier's vision of the "natural" limits of the power of experts, however, is still animated, if only implicitly, by the idea that experts—temporarily and exclusively—command uncontested knowledge, that their clients fully trust expert knowledge, and that experts therefore do not get enmeshed in controversies.

But the growing importance of knowledge-based occupations in modern society does not mean that the trust of the public in experts, advisers and consultants (cf. Miller, 1983: 90–93) is growing at the same pace or is not contingent on relationships (Wynne, 1992). On the contrary, we believe less and less in experts, although we employ them more and more. Yet without some element of trust in experts exhibited by ordinary members of society, expertise would vanish.

Nonetheless, experts today are constantly involved in a remarkable number of controversies. The growing policy field of setting limits to the presence of certain ingredients in foodstuffs, of safety regulations, risk management, and hazard control has had the side effect of ruining the reputation of experts. As long as an issue remains a contested matter, especially a publicly contented matter, the power and influence of experts and counter-experts is limited (see Nelkin, 1975, 1987); once a decision has been made and a question has been settled, the authority of experts also becomes almost uncontested. The work required to transform a contested matter into an uncontested matter is linked to the ability of experts to mobilize social and cultural resources in *relevant* contexts (see Limoges, 1993).

How knowledge and its role are defined in a particular context is determined by individual actors as well as by the legal, economic, political, or religious constructs that have gained authority. Moreover, the nature of the interaction, whether private or public (see van den Daele, 1996), the issue or practices at hand, and the audiences concerned are crucial in deciding what knowledge is mobilized and how it is enacted. Defining the role of knowledge is increasingly the job of experts, counselors, and advisors. The group of occupations designated here as experts, counselors and advisors is required to mediate between the complex distribution of knowledge that keeps changing and those who seek for knowledge. Ideas tend to travel as the baggage of people, as it were, whereas skills, in the sense of know-how and rules of thumb, are embodied or inscribed in them. Studies of innovation processes have shown how important the close coupling of social networks is for knowledge transfer as well as for the ultimate success of innovations in economic contexts; the studies indicate that the traffic of *people* within and among firms, for example, is crucial to the process of knowledge transfer (e.g. DeBresson and Amesse, 1991; Freeman, 1991; Callon, 1992; Faulkner, Senker and Velho, 1995).

A chain of interpretations must come to an "end" in order for knowledge to become relevant in practice and effective as a capacity for action. This function of putting an end to the process of reflection—or of healing the lack of immediate practicability that is inherent to scientific and technical knowledge as it emerges from the scientific community—for the purpose of action is largely performed by various groups of experts in modern society. Their societal prominence today is intimately related to the central role of knowledge for contemporary society.

But aside from the question of the nature of practical and additional knowledge, it is important to briefly reflect about what can only be called the uneven development of knowledge. For example, while we may well have a surplus of knowledge in fields such as bioengineering, weapons know-how, or psychological knowledge designed to manipulate and persuade by hidden means, there are pressing social, political or health issues that remain unsolved due to our lack of knowledge.

The differentiation between common-sense or everyday knowledge and expert or scientific knowledge is the most frequent difference among forms of knowledge that one typically encounters both in everyday life and in the scientific community. The difference is most often asymmetrical. Objective knowledge enhances and embellishes itself by pointing to the deficiencies of common-sense knowledge. The deficits of non-scientific knowledge are legion. Everyday knowledge is superficial, if not unreflective and false. In many analyses, as a result, the elevated *social role* of scientific and technological knowledge is almost invariably tied to its superior attributes. The deficiencies of common-sense knowledge, in turn, account for its inferior, if not declining, status and function in modern societies. But one certainly must wonder how it is that everyday knowledge, given such inherent deficiencies, has managed to survive in modern societies. In response, we do not want to collapse or dispense with the difference between everyday and scientific knowledge (see Shapin, 2001). But in contrast to the common-sense distinction between lay and expert knowledge, we want to make the case that the many characteristics that justify the rise of scientific knowledge above the multiple insufficiencies of common-sense knowledge are helpful in accounting for what is undoubtedly the greater social, intellectual and economic importance of scientific knowledge in modern societies.

## Practical Knowledge

The definition of practical knowledge and other forms of knowledge that differ from practical knowledge are linked to specific analytical interest such a definition is supposed to fulfill. Some of the major definitions of practical knowledge are connected to a science of science perspective (e.g. Bourdieu, [1972] 1977), the functions knowledge may serve (Baecker, 1998) or the likely effectiveness knowledge under constraints of practical action (Grundmann and Stehr, 2012).

Although it would appear that much effort has been extended over the decades to arrive at meaningful set of categories of knowledge, in fact, scientific discourse developed a quasi-natural attitude toward its own knowledge. For this reason, the number of well-explicated categories of knowledge in social science has been limited. Later explications of different forms of knowledge tend to be similar to Max Scheler's ([1924] 1960) early categories of knowledge, though that Schelerian ancestry is not often acknowledged or otherwise recognized, namely (1) knowledge of salvation, (2) cultural knowledge, or knowledge of pure essences, as well as (3) knowledge that produces effects.

The most widely employed conceptions of different forms of knowledge are dichotomies. Dominant is the distinction between scientific and everyday or non-scientific (common-sense) knowledge. This distinction was taken for granted for such a long period of time in the social sciences that it has not really been elaborated for decades, except in the sense that everyday or non-scientific knowledge became a residual form of knowledge. In addition, the dichotomy between specialized and everyday knowledge has been widely used in sociological discourse, whereby specialized knowledge was often seen as identical with scientific and technical knowledge. The almost self-explanatory distinction between theoretical and practical knowledge can also be found frequently in the literature on the social role of knowledge.

How can we more specifically define the difference between practical and theoretical knowledge, especially in relation to our main interest the value of knowledge? Theoretical knowledge would appear to distinguish itself by its distance to practical purposes. Practical knowledge would claim for itself to be close to serving functions of enacting practical action.

One definition of practical knowledge refers to such knowledge as a form of knowing that precisely excludes the question of the conditions of its own possibility. Practical knowledge in this sense refers to all that is "inscribed in the relationship of *familiarity* with the familiar environment, the unquestioning apprehension of the social world which, by definition, does not reflect on itself" (Bourdieu, [1972] 1977: 3). Reflexive forms of knowledge, depending on the degree of self-reflection are phenomenological and objectivist knowledge. One of the immediate examples of practical knowledge *within* scientific research extends perhaps to the demand or claim that knowledge generated in *biomedical research* should conform to the guiding principle of "socially valuable knowledge." The apparent vagueness of its conception makes it most difficult if not impossible, so it seems, to deploy it in the task of assessing the value of practical knowledge. However, it would appear to be evident that a robust identification of what makes for practical knowledge would go a long way to estimate its value/price, especially in contrast to purely theoretical forms of knowledge.

## The Social Value of Knowledge

Narrative on the social value of knowledge is a prominent construct with biomedical research and refers to the claim or demand that decisions about future biomedical research involving human subjects are to be calibrated against the guiding principle that the outcome of such research enhances the social value of knowledge. As a matter of fact, the principle of socially valuable knowledge is enshrined in the 2016 guidelines of the Council for International Organizations of Medical Sciences (CIOMS) along with converging principles in other guidelines (such as the Nuremberg code or the Helsinki principle). Acting on behalf of society in which it is assumed the value of socially valuable knowledge is legitimate, Bioethicists pursue the difficulty tasks to glance into the future.

According to the Council, biomedical research involving human subjects demands prior to setting out to carry of the work the prospect that the research outcomes protects and promotes the health of humans and human welfare. In other terms, the guidance stipulates that research generates a *potential* instrumental value that can be ascribed to the knowledge gained in the research and that the clinical trials for example must benefit a specified cohort of individuals by improving their health or disease prevalence (cf. Holzer, 2017: 559–560). Once such a narrative about the social value of the expected knowledge is accepted the research may proceed.

It is almost self-evident that the bioethical demand for a socially valuable outcome of knowledge production raises critical questions that extend well beyond the border of the biomedical research community even after that community has set new administrative and institutional structures designed to insulate itself to some degree from society and execute decision about the ethics of future research. Bioethical decisions demand knowledge about knowledge especially anticipatory knowledge about knowledge in the face of the widespread conviction that the future of knowledge is unknown or at least uncertain.

However, we are less interested in the epistemological, moral or political pitfalls of claims that undoubtedly can be ascribed in a most general sense to the position of arriving at a calculus for socially beneficial knowledge than we are intrigued by the claim that the value of knowledge can somehow be calculated even if the reference for such an estimate is linked to but a small group of individuals who may suffer from a rare disease.

The value of knowledge perspective allows for the determination of but a *dichotomous* estimate of the value of yet unknown knowledge. The knowledge expected to be generated by research may either be of value or it lacks such a benefit. Hence the calculative ability of the approach is narrow and fails to substantially contribute to the puzzle of the value of knowledge.

## Knowledge as a Public Good

> Knowledge is perhaps the quintessential public good.
>
> —*Peter Drahos (2004: 321)*

One additional consideration in our search for the price of knowledge relates to the claim that knowledge is, in the end, actually a public good. Should Peter Drahos' thesis as quoted above that knowledge is an essentially public good be correct, then the question of the price of knowledge as such a product can be answered promptly and, of course, correctly: Knowledge is without a price.

And if there is answer to the question that interests us also in the context of our study, whether there can be a *just price* for knowledge, this answer should be: The lack of a price tag for knowledge as a public resource may be the best indication of a just price for knowledge. In order to escape the possibility that any stratified access to knowledge offers huge advantages to those with such privileged opportunities and therefore enhances social inequality formations in society not only through its role as an economic resource but also as a foundation for social power and authority, knowledge should be without a price. In other words, the rewards that accrue to the use of knowledge should be impartially distributed throughout society while the benefits that follow from the discovery of knowledge might be dispersed according to contribution or merit.[70] Joseph Stiglitz (1999) enlarges the thesis that knowledge is a public good in a dual sense. He describes why knowledge is not merely a public good but a *global* public good. In addition, Stiglitz designates human rights, political, economic and environmental goals as public goods.[71]

Most if not all discussions about knowledge as a public good are normative or political in nature. Economists tend to strongly defend either the idea that knowledge should be available to all (for different reasons, obviously) or the idea that knowledge, for example additional knowledge, needs to be protected and hence carry a price tag (again for difference reasons but mainly to ensure that the propensity to generate additional knowledge is not discouraged).

But first, we need to inquire in more detail into what exactly is a *public good* and why the idea of a public good is related to the issue of the price of knowledge? As we have already seen in the case of the definition of a public good by Joseph Stiglitz, public goods can refer to rather diverse phenomena. Economists consider products, knowledge, services, ideas, and information that are produced or available in a society to be public goods if access to them is not regulated and can in principle be shared by all members of a community. In other terms, public goods are goods which nonpaying people cannot be kept from using (Machlup, 1979: 74): Street names, social trust or safety are public goods. Public goods, therefore, emerge as a result of certain social norms (such as, for instance, peace, civic order, environmental safety and good governance) or are physical phenomena (such as, for instance, carbon-absorbing forests, algae or air).

Environmentalists prefer to distinguish public goods from "Commons" goods (*Gemeingüter*). The difference between public goods and commons resources is considered to be significant with respect to access and governance of goods (cf. Hess and Ostrom, 2007; Quilligan, 2012). Commons goods are as a rule *not* freely accessible and available for use. Commons goods, for example, solar energy cooperatives or the lobster fishing industry in Maine (see Acheson, 2003) is (can be made) subject to rules and formal and cultural norms negotiated freely among the individuals who use these goods collectively (user communities). In a "constructed commons" much of the value pertains to embedded knowledge and information such as patented discoveries. However, neither the extent, the nature nor the value of knowledge and information in constructed commons goods is readily transparent and available. The focus of constructed Commons analysis has focused on the social organization of such associations rather than the value constructed by such communities. The intellectual interest in carrying out these studies was, after all, driven by the desire to promote the establishment of Commons communities, for example, in contrast, and opposition to the institution of private property (Madison, Frischmann and Strandberg, 2010).

The price of *private* in contrast to public goods is negotiated in the market place. Market places are also seen as the most efficient context for furthering the propensity to produce private goods. The propensity to produce is further secured by conditions extraneous to the market, for example, property or intellectual rights; but producers for markets rely also on public goods or non-market goods such as the air to breathe, the climate, national defense, a tax system or gravity.

Public goods are freely available by definition, they are not subject to property rights, and their burdens or benefits cannot be restricted to an individual or a collectivity. As far as their use or utility is concerned public goods are *non-excludable*. Moreover, the consumption of a public good is non-excludable if unauthorized actors (free-riders) cannot be prevented from enjoying the benefits or incurring the costs of being exposed to it. The non-excludability of a good, a service or an environmental condition is a contingent matter; for example, "it is easier to exclude individuals from the use of a bike than it is from national defense" (Drahos, 2004: 324).

If many individuals and organizations can enjoy a public good without depleting it and if its consumption or enjoyment does not come at another person's expense, a public good is *non-rival*. From an individual perspective, the consumption of public goods carries no restrictions. A mathematical theorem "satisfies both attributes: if I teach you the theorem, I continue to enjoy the knowledge of the theorem at the same time that you do" (Stiglitz, 1999: 308). Once the theorem is published, no one can be excluded, anyone can utilize it.

Joseph Stiglitz (1999: 309) also makes the point that the nonrivalrousness of knowledge implies, for example, that there is zero marginal cost for an additional individual or organization that benefits from available knowledge. Even if it would be possible to prevent someone from taking such knowledge on board, it would be undesirable to impose restrictions since there are no marginal costs associated with sharing the benefits that come with the knowledge in question.

Conflating knowledge and information, Stiglitz (1999: 309) argues that "if information is to be efficiently utilized, it cannot be privately provided because efficiency implies charging a price of zero—the marginal cost of another individual enjoying the knowledge." However, as Stiglitz is quick to add, "at zero price only knowledge that can be produced at zero cost will be produced." In this case, private markets "would not provide them at all or would do so at deficient levels relative to those demanded by citizens" (Maskus and Reichman, 2004: 284). Hence, the probability that additional knowledge will be generated is also close to zero. If additional knowledge is without price, the supply of new knowledge will dry up. The idea that the acquisition of new knowledge comes at no cost of course describes an ideal typical condition. After all, the actual transmission and acquisition of additional knowledge requires some resources, however small or significant.

Nonexcludability also has implications for the price of knowledge. Since such knowledge is available to everyone, the price would approach zero. We have already discussed patents and IPR as ways of restricting the number of users. Depending on the legal frame of patenting, the patent application makes a considerable "amount" of the relevant innovation publicly accessible. Whether this knowledge can in fact be appropriated is not dependent on its mere availability, however.

The probability of fabricating incremental knowledge and enjoying the economic advantages that flow from such knowledge is, of course, a stratified and contingent process. Within technological regimes, techno-economic networks (cf. Freeman, 1991; Callon, 1992)[72] or theoretical "paradigms," the advantage goes to those who already have produced, and therefore command, significant elements of incremental knowledge. Technological regimes or paradigms may be embedded within a company or in a network of firms, research institutes, etc. In analogy to Robert Merton's (1995) observations about the operation of the Matthew effect in the process of accumulating standing and prestige in science, it is possible to stipulate a similar principle for the stratification of incremental knowledge.

Generating incremental knowledge is likely to be easier for those who can disproportionately benefit from what they already know; for example, due to the capacity of combining local and global knowledge (cf. Stiglitz, 1999: 317–318).

The competitive advantages that may accrue to individuals or firms that generate and manage to control incremental knowledge is, without question, limited in terms of time, especially but not only due to the time limits of the protection granted by patents or copyrights. Thus, such companies must continuously strive to stay ahead in the fabrication of knowledge:[73] "Once their intellectual advantages are imitated and their outputs standardized, then there are downward wage and employment pressures" (Storper, 1996: 257) as well as a decline in profitability.[74]

In contrast to incremental knowledge, the general, mundane and routinized stock of knowledge consists mostly of knowledge that is non-rival as well as non-excludable; that is, these forms of knowledge may very well constitute public goods.[75] But even the general mundane stock of knowledge is hardly ever completely excludable or without rivalry. Such protection may be based either on legal norms or on some other apparatus in which knowledge may be inscribed, preventing its use by others. Once a certain capacity to act has been discovered it usually can be used again and again and at relatively low transaction cost, if any. From a collective point of view, for example from the perspective of all consumers or a community, the use of public goods, as noted early (see Hume, [1739] 1961; Hardin, 1968), may give rise to the free-rider problem.

It might be useful to distinguish between pure public goods and quasi-public or impure public goods. Quasi-public goods would refer to conditions of action, for example, from which a consumer or an employer benefits even though she has not incurred any of the cost of the discovery and the explication of the intangible asset. The publicly accessible infrastructure of a country would be an example, or an employee's training and education that is not entirely paid for by the employer but nonetheless of great benefit to the corporation.

As Inge Kaul, Isabelle Grunberg and Marc Stern (1999: xx) point out, financial stability has "public good qualities. A bank or financial institution can generate much profit through risky lending. All it stands to lose is its capital if fails. But in a complex and interdependent financial system, the cost of a single institution defaulting is much higher—often a multiple—because one default can lead to more failures and defaults." Technically, such a possibility is known as a case of negative externalities. But it is better known as a way of socializing costs. In the case of what is seen as global public goods, the risks, costs and benefits, the externalities, are shared or borne across the world.

## Capital as Embodied Knowledge

A final pathway in our exploration of finding a way of measuring the price of knowledge is to turn to the prominent idea within economics asserting that capital goods as opposed to financial or human capital are embodied knowledge (see Baetjer, 2000: 148).

However, the idea that capital, especially in the form of investment goods, represents knowledge or at least partly embodied knowledge and that capital goods *differ* from financial and human capital in this respect is questionable. The generation and hence the constitution of financial and human capital also embodies knowledge. In many cases, it is even possible to underline that the nature of financial and human capital embodies knowledge to a far greater extent than is likely to be the case with many investment goods. Derivatives as financial assets are knowledge-based, just like an employee's intellectual abilities. Accordingly, Gary Becker and colleagues (Becker, Murphy, and Tamura, 1994: 326) define human capital as "[people] embodied knowledge and skills, and economic development depends on advances in technological and scientific knowledge, development presumably depends on the accumulation of human capital."

The idea that capital represent embodied knowledge can already be found in a plausible example in Adam Smith's *An Inquiry into the Nature and Causes of the Wealth of Nations*. In this volume, Adam Smith ([1776] 2012: 14) offers a plausible example of how an idea enters into the construction of capital equipment ("frozen knowledge" [Boulding, 1966: 6–7]), in this instance the early development of the steam engines. Precisely, what Smith has in mind are insights that become a part of the design and hence the production of the steam engine; a design feature that makes the steam engine as a tool more efficient:

> a boy was constantly employed to open and shut alternately the communication between the boiler and the cylinder, according as the piston either ascended or descended. One of those boys, who loved to play with his companions, observed that, by tying a string from the handle of the valve which opened this communication to another part of the machine, the valve would open and shut without his assistance, and leave him at liberty to divert himself with his playfellows.

The observation by Adam Smith is generalized by members of the Austrian School of Economics. Carl Menger ([1871] 1981: 74) for example emphasizes: "The quantities of consumption goods at human disposal are limited only by the extent of human knowledge of the causal connections between things, and by the extent of human control over these things." From the basic observation of knowledge as knowledge incorporated into capital goods to a determination of the value of embodied knowledge, it is obviously a distant and complicated path which may not in the end lead to the desired goal.

If one follows the conventional terminology of economic theory it rather easy so it seems to infer, as for example R. Harrod (1939: 18) underlines that the value of the capital can be determined relatively easily: the "actual saving in a period . . . is equal to the addition to the capital stock." Joan Robinson (1979:

100) in contrast is equally convinced that "no one ever makes it clear how capital is to be measured."

Without wishing to extend this particular line of reasoning any further, one must conclude with Howard Baetjer (2000: 169) that the value of capital and thus the value of capital goods ultimately is not exactly measurable. And as long as it is difficult to determine the exact value of capital assets, it is evident that the value of the frozen knowledge (as a part of such assets or products) is also not sufficiently determinable or quantifiable.

General conclusions of the failure to discover the price of knowledge or the set of open issues can be specified more precisely: (1) Incorporated knowledge can not only be very heterogeneous but also "invisible" (tacit knowledge). (2) Is it necessary to ask if knowledge stands in a symmetrical manner to other resources that constitute a capital good? (3) How to establish a relationship between other resources (or products) and knowledge in order to determine how much the share of knowledge is in the aggregate product? (4) How do we assess knowledge that has been incorporated at different temporal phases into production? (5) What is the value of knowledge given the loss of value of knowledge over a certain period of time and how can the loss of value (or profit) be determined? (6) If the value of a capital good is set in relation to its production output, these questions cannot be solved. (7) What is the effect of the complementary interaction of investment goods in production on the value of knowledge? (8) What is the importance of learning processes, including the learning of learning for the valuation of the capital goods, for example, in the case of software and thus knowledge? (9) Labor and capital form a (hybrid) unity in many economic contexts. What significance does this unit have for the value of knowledge?

## Conclusion: Determining the Price (and Value) of Knowledge

Our investigation of how to put a "price" on knowledge interrogated various social science and practical perspectives for their usefulness in arriving at some arithmetic for determining the value of knowledge. Even if one tries to stick to established, manifest proxies of this difficult problem, it becomes increasingly clear how formidably obfuscated the matter presents itself, thus perhaps only emphasizing the strong suspicion of many observers that knowledge simply cannot have or does not come with a price. It is not surprising therefore that the OECD (2006: 5) concludes its elaborate search for a way to quantify and measure "intangible assets" with the sensible recommendation that such assets including of course knowledge are "best dealt with through *narrative* financial reporting" (our emphasis).

We hope to have demonstrated, along the lines of our prior work toward a sociological conception of knowledge, that knowledge and its possible price, unless it is, as is often the case conflated with the category of information, is (1) embodied and thus most difficult to divorce from its carriers or products;

(2) deeply entrenched in questions of social relations and thus stratification, both as a resource for other "goods" as well as a "product" of social circumstances; (3) does indeed play an ever greater role within as well as across (national) economies and societies, but unfortunately for the observer of the knowledge of knowledge in a manner that is anything but straight-forward; and that (4) the situation becomes even more complicated once these three dimension of our inquiry become entangled in a stand-off between individual, economic and public relevancies regarding the role and the value of knowledge.

Most of the theoretical approaches of value of knowledge we have examined are based on the assumption that efforts in arriving at a price for knowledge has the best chance to succeed if based on considerations that revolve around the *use* of knowledge. Whether one follows the human capital approach, the discussion of intangibles, patents, or tax law, it is the exploit of knowledge, as a capacity to act that should determine its price.

Heather Rimes, Jennie Welch and Barry Bozeman (2014: 154) follow this rule and stipulate "that the true value of *scientific knowledge* (emphasis added) lies in how often and how widely it is applied—information that is not captured in its market price. In other words, the value of knowledge derives from the *intensity and range of its use*."[76] The differentiation created in their advice on how to arrive at a (qualitative) price for knowledge is one between the market price (market-based strategies, or the economic value of knowledge) and a non-economic value evaluation of knowledge (including the use of knowledge in the context of knowledge creation) that the economic calculus it is claimed ignores.

## Notes

1. On a number of occasions, Nico Stehr has discussed the broad theme of the "knowledge of knowledge" resulting in different publications. These publications form a relevant background to our present examination of the price of knowledge (e.g. Stehr, 1994, 2002 and 2016). An earlier version of our chapter on the value of knowledge may be found in Adolf and Stehr (2017: 207–236).
2. "Knowledge is democratic," in *Scientific American* 6, 253–253 (26 April 1851) doi:10.1038/scientificamerican04261851–253.
3. The production of new knowledge and thus the satisfaction of the demand for knowledge is promoted in many societies through a variety of policy measures; these include tools such as "intellectual property rights aimed at increasing the levels of appropriability, public subsidies to R&D expenditures aimed at compensating private investors for the missing revenues, a public research infrastructure including Universities and public research institutions aimed at generating upstream scientific knowledge that could support the downstream generation of knowledge by the business sector" (Antonelli, 2017: 184).
4. This applies, for example, through a monopolization of language in which a sense of direction can be expressed and developed.
5. However, once a thought is expressed, make public, it is impossible to recapture and monopolize it: "The thought that has been once expressed can no longer be captured again by any amount of power in the world; its content is irrevocably the public

property of all who apply the mental energy necessary to recall it" (Simmel, [1900] 2004: 415).

6. Robert Merton's ([1965] 1985) expression "obliteration by incorporation" is strongly reminiscent of another famous Mertonian metaphor that also refers to social processes of accumulative scientific knowledge, namely "standing on the shoulders of giants," a study first published in 1965.

7. See also our discussion of the "social value of knowledge" developed with respect to biomedical ethics later in this chapter.

8. For an explicit effort by economists to develop an economics of knowledge see Stiglitz and Greenwald (2014).

9. Heather Rimes and her colleagues (2014: 154) argue that a market-based price of knowledge cannot correspond to the "true" value of knowledge; the true or objective price of knowledge "lies in how often and how widely is it applied—information that is not captured in market price . . . the value of knowledge derives from the *intensity and the range of its use*." This is a helpful reference in some respects, yet it only increases the significant obstacles that lead to a possible evaluation of past and present knowledge. Nor does their suggestion resolve the difficulties we will describe in quantifying the price of knowledge.

10. Whether a public good is necessarily socially beneficial is a contested matter. In any event, a public good cannot as a result of its attributes of non-excludability and non-rivalry be privatized. Hans Radder (2017: 439) argues, "a *common* good should be in the public interest and should not be privatized, independently of whether it can or cannot be privatized for economic reasons" (our emphasis). Critical questions about the usefulness of the very notion of common goods may be found in Claus Offe, ([2001] 2012).

11. However, whether the canonical economic perspective does apply in the strict sense of the definition of non-rival and non-excludable to complex ideas or scientific knowledge is doubtful. After all, the acquisition of knowledge requires at times considerable transaction costs. The idea that knowledge is, on the other hand, a free good is a notion defended by Kenneth Arrow (2014: 507); however, it implies, as Arrow also stresses that "the biggest cost in its transmission is not in the production or distribution of knowledge, but in its assimilation."

12. Kenneth Boulding, like Herbert Simon, believes that knowledge can be a commodity. However, Boulding (1966: 2) is more reluctant in pressing the case that knowledge may become a commodity. He points to a number of fundamental difficulties, which we will discern as well in treating knowledge as a commodity: "It is a little hard to put [the label commodity] on it because of the difficulties of measuring the quantity of the commodity itself. . . . The absence of any unit of knowledge itself, however, and perhaps the intrinsic heterogeneity of its substance, make it very difficult to think of a price of knowledge as such, and indeed has probably contributed to a certain resistance of thinking of knowledge as a commodity."

13. Samuli Leppälä (2015) summarizes the intellectual origins and the defining characteristics of the economic analysis of knowledge, employing the "standard epistemological definition" of knowledge as "justified belief." It is also noteworthy that Leppälä does not raise the issue of the price or value of knowledge in his survey of the diverse economics literature that attends to the *economic* role of knowledge.

14. The conceptual discussion of the so-called data-information-knowledge-wisdom hierarchy (DIKW) in the social systems literature (for example, Ackoff, 1989) explicitly offers to separate the phenomena in the form of a pyramid by referring to progressively smaller layers until one reaches the state of wisdom. For instance, as one "processes" data you get information and so on. Since the various steps within the pyramid are far from clear-cut, in the end the proposal amounts to another conflation of the various parts that make up the DIKW pyramid.

15. On the other hand, Olivier Gossner (2010: 95) matter-of-factly states: "'knowledge' refers to the information possessed by the agent."
16. In his discussion more than a century ago of "the nature of capital," Thorstein Veblen ([1908] 1919: 325–326) refers to part of the capital of a collectivity as "immaterial equipment" or "intangible assets." Intangible assets according to Veblen mainly consist of knowledge and information that "in the early days at least, . . . is far and away the most important and consequential category of the community's assets or equipment."
17. William Nordhaus and David Popp (1996: 3) define the value of early knowledge compared to the cost of improving our knowledge in the case of global warming as follows: "The value of early knowledge is the improvement in our consumption possibilities that comes from avoiding wasteful decisions because we are too ignorant about future possibilities." In other words, the difference between the anticipated value of damages from global warming with good information and that of poor information is the value of the information (Nordhaus and Popp, 1996: 16). Note the ready conflation of knowledge and information in the paper by Nordhaus and Popp. Obviously such a calculation process itself must rely or defer on many uncertainties.
18. Carol Corrado and her colleagues (Corrado et al., 2006: 3) generally emphasize "the factors typically associated with the growth of the 'knowledge economy' assume a greater importance once intangibles are included." Corrado and colleagues observe that "the inclusion of intangibles makes a significant difference in the measured pattern of economic growth: the growth rates of output and of output-per worker are found to increase at a noticeably more rapid rate when intangibles are included than under the baseline case in which intangible capital is completely ignored, and capital deepening (when expanded to include both tangibles and intangibles) becomes the unambiguously dominant source of growth in labor productivity" (Corrado, Hulten und Sichel, 2006: 3).
19. But why are human capital resources not recognized by US accounting standards as accountable for the purpose of financial statements? As pointed out in Sollosy, McInerney, and Braun (2016: 23) the US Financial Accounting Standards Board "requires, among other things, that in order for an asset to be recognized for financial statement purposes, the future benefits of the resource must be under the control of the organization and that they be reliably measurable." This position is not without its strong critics (e.g. Fulmer and Ployhart, 2014 or Lim et al., 2010). What remains is the persistent appeal by accounting specialist's, "has not the time come to seriously consider how to best reflect the value of intangible assets in a manner that allows for the comparison of competing organizations within an industry?" (Sollosy, McInerney, and Braun (2016: 224). For the time being, it accurate to conclude the case that "in the wake of the growth of intangible assets the ultimate measure of firm value, share prices, has become largely divorced from (historical) accounting measures" (Bryan, Rafferty and Wigan, 2017: 63).
20. The doubt expressed about efforts to monetarize knowledge at times even refers to Socrates who taught his students without demanding any monetary compensation. Socrates expressed nothing but malice for teachers who claimed to be able to generate a lofty income from their wealthy students. But what was the reason for Socrates to refuse to take money in return for knowledge? If he charged for his teaching, Socrates maintained, he would be forced to teach students he did not appreciate; in other words, he wanted to protect his liberty in choosing his students (see Bertram Schefold, "Die Ökonomisierung der Wissenskultur [The economisation of the culture of knowledge]," *Frankfurter Allgemeine Zeitung*, April 12, 2010).
21. Dominique Forey (2006: 9), for example, emphasizes that "knowledge is largely unobservable" and "most phenomena relating to knowledge are largely unmeasurable."
22. Motherhood is seen in very similar terms (thanks to Susan McDaniel for pointing this out).

23. "Where is the wisdom we have lost in knowledge? Where is the knowledge we have lost in information?" T. S. Eliot, *Choruses from "The Rock," 1934, I.*
24. Daron Acemoglu and David Autor (2012: 427) summarize the historical and econometric evidence of Goldin and Katz's (2008) study: "Human capital is a central determinant of economic growth, both in general and in the specific case of economic growth in the United States during the twentieth century." In addition, the study demonstrates according to their reviewers that the steady accumulation of human capital is a major *equalizing* force in the labor market of the United States. It follows that rising inequality is a function of a slowing rate of accumulation of human capital in light of a growing demand for skilled-based occupations (Acemoglu and Autor, 2012: 456).
25. The *World Bank* (2019) has issued a *Human Capital Index* for 157 nations based on the national investment in people. The bank's index is constructed from data on child survival and growth, years of primary and secondary school and health. The assumption of the bank following human capital theory is that a country's productivity and prosperity is closely tied the knowledge and the capabilities of its citizens. The top scorers include the usual culprits, Singapore, South Korea and Japan while African nations are found at the bottom of the list.
26. In sociology there are many precursors and parallel perspectives in which the importance of education for social stratification is emphasized. At this point, reference is made only to one of Max Weber's observations ([1917] 1994: 103–104): "the way the modern state and economy are organised ensures that a privileged position is permanently given to *specialsed training* and thereby to 'education' (*Bildung*) which is not identical with specialised training but promoted by it for purely technical educational reasons, this being one of the most powerful factors in status group (*ständisch*) differentiation in modern society."
27. An early critique of the image of the individual within human capital theory that views individuals not as moral or ethical beings but driven by the logic of rational economic discourse, may be found in Shaffer (1961). Harry Shaffer objects that the term "investment" is not really applicable to the issue of human capital; "investment" in individual employees should not be used as a basis for policy formation. A fundamental criticism of the human capital theory is therefore also prompted by the (implicit?) idea that a more comprehensive school education is associated with productivity gains and that a higher income of these groups is seen as a function of these productive gains (for example, Gouldner, 1979: 108). Randall Collins (1971) refers, as Gouldner (1979: 108) emphasizes that "the main activity of schools . . . is to teach status cultures, this socializing persons to gain admission to status groups and their privileges" (see also Stehr, 2000).
28. Human capital theory has a strong intellectual affinity to the notion of "knowledge capital." The idea of knowledge capital (for economic development) was promoted by the *World Bank* beginning in 1996 as it began to promote itself the Knowledge Bank. The World Bank conceived of the *right* form of knowledge as a form of capital that could be leveraged in the developing world for economic growth (cf. World Bank, 1999: 2; Enns, 2015).
29. An exceptional, deviant definition of human capital that extends to so-called *innate abilities* of individual agents is rarely found in economic discourse; but see Laroche and Mérette (1999: 88) for such a conceptualization.
30. Human capital theory resonates strongly with post-war mainstream sociological theories of social stratification, for example, Talcott Parsons' ([1949] 1954: 327) theory of social stratification: "the status of the individual must be determined on grounds essentially peculiar to himself, notably his own personal qualities, technical competence, and his own decisions about his occupational career and with respect to which he is identified with any solidary group. . . . It is nevertheless fundamental that status and role allocation and the processes of mobility from status to status are in terms of

the individual as a unit and not of solidary groups, like kinship groups, castes village communities etc."

31. Based on considerations of this kind, Michel Feher ([2007] 2009: 27) argues that "an investor in his or her human capital is concerned less with maximizing the returns on his or her investments—whether monetary or psychic—than with appreciating, that is, increasing the stock value of, the capital to which he or she is identified. In other words, insofar as our condition is that of human capital in a neoliberal environment, our main purpose is not so much to profit from our accumulated potential as to constantly value or appreciate ourselves—or at least prevent our own depreciation."

32. See also the discussion of the creative class typology of occupations by Gabe, Florida and Mellender (2013: 39) who assert that "in contrast to the educational-based human capital measure, the Creative Class occupational typology takes into account what people actually do (and related skill requirements) in their current jobs, rather than the amount of schooling they have completed." The empirical evidence the authors (Gabe, Florida and Mellender, 2013: 51) consulted for the US labor market between 2006–2011 indicates that "that having a Creative Class occupation lowers an individual's probability of being unemployed—in fact, the effect is larger than the marginal effect associated with having a four-year college degree (compared to someone with only a high school diploma)—and that the impact of having a creative occupation became more beneficial in the two years following the recession."

33. The dollar amounts reported as the outcome of the cognitive performance an individual's life-time income are calculated as follows: "A 0.1 standard deviation increase in AFQT is associated with a rise of 2.15 percent, or $11,846, in lifetime income through 65 for the average NLSY79 respondent, which translates into an increase of $19,545 for an infant born in 2014. The predicted effect is somewhat larger in absolute terms for men than women ($20,724 versus $16,778 for 2014 births) but since women earn less than men, the percentage growth is substantially larger for females (2.62 percent versus 1.71 percent)."

34. PIAAC attempted to measure the cognitive and workplace skills that are needed to advance both on the job and in society. In 23 countries, a representative sample of adults was interviewed. Information about three fields of cognitive skills was collected: literacy, numeracy and problem solving in a high-technology environment. Literacy, for example, was defined as the "ability to understand, evaluate, use and engage with written texts to participate in society, to achieve one's goals, and to develop one's knowledge and potential" (Hanushek, Schwerdt, and Wiederhold, 2015: 108).

35. It might be pointed out that Bourdieu's discussion of cultural capital resonates strongly with Georg Simmel's observations ([1907] 1978: 439–440) in *The Philosophy of Money* about the role of the "intellect" in modern society. Simmel notes "the apparent equality with which educational materials are available to everyone interested in them is, in reality, a sheer mockery. The same is true for other freedoms accorded by liberal doctrines which, though they certainly do not hamper the individual from gaining goods of any kind, do however disregard the fact that only those already privileged in some way or another have the possibility of acquiring them. For just as the substance of education—in spite of, or because of its general availability—can ultimately be acquired only through individual activity, so it gives rise to the most intangible and thus the most unassailable aristocracy, to a distinction between high and low which can be abolished neither (as can socio-economic differences) by a decree or a revolution, nor by the good will of those concerned. . . . There is no advantage that appears to those in inferior positions to be so despised, and before which they feel so deprived and helpless, as the advantage of education."

36. For James Coleman (1988: 100–101) social capital "comes about through changes in the relations among persons that facilitate action. . . . Just as physical capital and human capital facilitate productive activity, social capital does as well. For example, a group

within which there is extensive trustworthiness and extensive trust is able to accomplish much more than a comparable group without that trustworthiness and trust." Coleman's definition of social capital indicates that is impossible to quantify the value of individual social capital.

37. See Adolf and Stehr (2014) and Stehr and Adolf (2015) for an extensive discussion of the concept of knowledge as a "capacity to act."

38. More specifically, symbolic capital represents a social process and accomplishment; symbolic capital refers to intellectual or cognitive capacities; symbolic capital "is made . . . by those who are submitted to it but if, and only if, the objective structure of its distribution is at the basis of the cognitive structures that they bring into play in order to produce it—as, for example, with such structuring oppositions as masculine/feminine, young/old, noble/common, rich/poor, white/black, etc." (Bourdieu, 1999: 336).

39. André Gorz's ([2003] 2004: 9) notion of knowledge capital or, rather, the knowledge that counts in the modern knowledge economy can be found in his introduction to the German edition of his book on *The Immaterial. Knowledge, Value and Capital* ([2003] 2010). However, Gorz's idea is closely linked to economics: what is required in all branches of the economy is knowledge and, due to the growing "informatization," knowledge not in the forms that are acquired in formal education but, rather, "non-formalized forms of knowledge. . . . What is required is empirical knowledge, judgment, coordination, self-organization and communication ability, i.e. forms of living knowledge that can be acquired in everyday social dealings and is part of popular culture." It is only on the basis of Gorz' specification of the relevant knowledge forms that the proximity to our concept of knowledge capability becomes evident.

40. Mara Squicciarini and Nico Vogtlaender (2014) demonstrate that human capital (in the sense of worker skills) is a strong predictor for economic development not only today but was so already at the beginning of the industrial revolution (also Mokyr, 2005).

41. In Bourdieu's defense one has to recognize that however strongly the quantity of capital acquired may depend on, for example, the stock of capital already accumulated in the family of an individual, its actual acquisition is ultimately—as Simmel ([1907] 1989: 439) already observed—an individual activity. Moreover, Bourdieu (Wacquant, 1989: 41–42) defends himself against the charge of a narrow "economism"; his choice of the term "capital," for example, does not mean that he also adopts the narrow, economic conception of interests manifest in a single universal interest.

42. Sympathetic critics of Bourdieu's capital theory have pointed to other attributes of his approach as problematic; for example, reference is made to the holistic presupposition as a general theoretical assumption. Bourdieu tends to postulate cultural capital as a generalized medium of accumulation and distinction that is not suited for the analysis of a society with multiple cleavages and divisions (see Lamont and Lareau, 1988; Halle, 1992).

43. The lack of standard accounting for the value of intangibles or intellectual property likely contributes to the reluctance of banks to consider such resources as collateral against loans which could mean that "interest rate cuts by a central bank have less power to generate increased investment spending" (Neil Irwin, "Are superstar firms and Amazon effects reshaping the economy?" (*New York Times* August 26, 2018; www. nytimes.com/2018/08/25/upshot/big-corporations-influence-economy-central-bank.html?action=click&module=Top%20Stories&pgtype=Homepage.

44. Nico Stehr (2000) investigated the productivity paradox from a sociological perspective and suggested that the phenomenon has to do last but not least with societal changes linked to the significance of (supply) the higher educational achievements of those entering the labor force at the time. We are drawing on the perspective developed in this examination of the productivity paradox.

45. Dale Jorgenson (1997: 4) sees the productivity paradox as arising from the prevailing identification of "productivity growth with technological change." Technological

change and productivity gains are distinct. Productivity growth is but a minor component to growth. Technological change occurs, he argues, as a result of investments; economic growth also is due to capital investment. Capital investments can be categorized into investments into tangible assets, human and intellectual capital. The purchase of computers constitutes an investment into tangible assets. But the key concept in this context, intellectual capital remains but a vague and perhaps even more irritating to economists an unmeasured and immeasurable concept.

46. An informative discussion and description of intellectual property concepts and procedures including a brief reference to patent law systems may be found in Knight (2013: 1–48). A history of the idea of IPR may be found in Long (1991) and Hesse (2002).

47. On the sociological definition of private property rights and its implicit ban on a utilization by other individuals, see Heinrich Popitz, (1986: 111–112). For a discussion of the various advantages identified in the literature on patents see Budish, Roin and Williams (2016). Of course, patents also involve costs. "The average U.S. patent costs an estimated $20,000 to obtain and thousands more to keep from expiring before its term, which is 20 years from the application date" (Farre-Mensa, Hegde and Ljungqvist, 2017).

48. As the *Guardian* (February 12, 2013) reported, "the agricultural giant Monsanto has sued hundreds of small farmers in the United States in recent years in attempts to protect its patent rights on genetically engineered seeds that it produces and sells"; a report by the Center for Food Safety and the Save Our Seeds campaigning groups "has outlined what it says is a concerted effort by the multinational to dominate the seeds industry in the US and prevent farmers from replanting crops they have produced from Monsanto seeds."

49. The resistance by NGOs to TRIPS-inspired legislation is chronicled in Matthews (2011).

50. Economic or innovation-centered perspectives have indeed dominated the discussion about patents. More recently, a broader view relies on a "rights-based" perspective. As Stephen Hilgartner (2002: 945) argues, "decisions about intellectual property are about much more than simply finding ways to stimulate and reward innovation; they are also about accountability, control, and governance" leading to a politics of patents conception.

51. Consider the following recent example: "During the past few years, as the cost of TV rights for sporting events has escalated apparently without limit, so has the ease by which conventional broadcast methods can be circumvented. Despite the best efforts of global authorities, including the City of London Police's Intellectual Property Crime Unit (PIPCU), the proliferation, accessibility and reliability of sport streaming sites have only increased. 'Historically, most arrests and attempted prosecutions are made under the provision of the Copyright, Designs and Patents Act 1988, which prohibits the broadcast of material without the license of the copyright owner. However, in February 2012, during a case between the Premier League and a pub landlady from Portsmouth named Karen Murphy, the European Court ruled that live sporting events could not be regarded as 'intellectual creations'. They were instead 'subject to rules of the game, leaving no room for creative freedom'. The court decided that 'accordingly, those events cannot be protected under copyright'." See www.theguardian.com/football/2015/aug/01/faster-easier-free-illegal-football-streams (accessed August 1, 2015) and www.theguardian.com/media/2012/feb/24/pub-landlady-karen-murphy-premier-league (accessed August 1, 2015).

52. See Roland Reiss, "Eine Kriegserklärung an das Buch" [A declaration of war on books], *Frankfurter Allgemeine Zeitung*, October 13, 2015.

53. Michele Boldrin and David Levine (2013: 3) sum up their case against the economic efficacy of patents as follows: "There is no empirical evidence that [patents] serve to increase innovation and productivity, unless productivity is identified with the number

of patents awarded—which, as evidence shows, has no correlation with measured productivity."

54. We have to recognize—although this attribute of the concept of intellectual property is not part of our analysis of the value of knowledge—that the notion of intellectual property is an essentially contested concept across different cultures, for example, in cultures that mainly rely on oral or written transmission (cf. Garmon, 2002) or in societies that recognize hybrid ownership between strictly individual and strictly collective (public domain) ownership (e.g. Strathern, 2005; Ghosh and Soete, 2006; for the case of software, see Ghosh, 2005).

55. For this reason, one may infer, the European Commission and the other international organizations in their report *System of National Accounts 2008* (2009: 263) conclude, „originals of intellectual property products, such as computer software and entertainment, literary or artistic originals should be entered at the written down value of their initial cost, revalued to the prices of the current period. Since these products will have often been produced on own account, the initial cost may be estimated by the sum of costs incurred including a return to capital on the fixed assets used in production. If value cannot be established in this way, it may be appropriate *to estimate the present value of future returns* arising from the use of the original in production" (our emphasis).

56. 157 US universities responding to a 2011 survey of the Association of University Technology Managers reported an earned income of "more than $1.8-billion from commercializing their academic research in the 2011 fiscal year, collecting royalties from new breeds of wheat, from a new drug for the treatment of HIV, and from longstanding arrangements over enduring products like Gatorade." See "Universities Report $1.8-Billion in Earnings on Inventions in 2011," Chronicle of Higher Education August 28, 2012.

57. Whether or not monopolies are a burden on value-adding activities or even encourage desirable innovations or lead to overpricing and undersupply, is not at issue in our examination of patents (but see Nordhaus, 1969; Boldrin and Levine, 2005; Crampes and Langinier, 2009).

58. As a matter of practical considerations, the strength, the design and the range of IPR has a strong influence on the "extent to which innovation adds or subtracts from the pool of ideas that are available to be commercially exploited, i.e. to technological opportunities" (Stiglitz, 2010, 2014: 1).

59. Interview with André Gorz, "Entsinnlichung des Wissens [The loss of meaning of knowledge]," *Die Tageszeitung*, August 8, 2003.

60. As Alfredo Macias Vazquez and Pablo Alonso Gonzalez (2016: 46–47) note in general terms, „it would be crucial to organize cooperative and relational processes grounded in non-exclusionary and non0divisible principles, Likewise, it would be necessary to development mechanisms of ownership regulation that are not solely underpinned by anonymous criteria supported by legal provisions that have a single set of terms to all users."

61. There are of course legal means for enforcing the rights inherent in a patent, trademark and copyright. The recognition of the considerable economic value and perhaps also economic power and prestige has led to an increase in litigation activities in the context of IPRs (cf. Hoti and McAleer, 2006).

62. Bregie van Eckelen (2015: 447) investigates "what conditions need to be met for knowledge to be incorporated as a new category of value, and whether these conditions (such as separability, commensurability and appropriability) differ from the accounting requirements for more tangible capital."

63. See http://databank.worldbank.org/data//reports.aspx?source=2&Topic=14.

64. In the 2009 publication of the *System of National Accounts,* one finds the follow cautionary note, "the value of research and development (R&D) [which does not include the value of human capital] should be determined in terms of *the economic benefits it*

*is expected to provide in the future.* This includes the provision of public services in the case of R&D acquired by government. In principle, R&D that does not provide an economic benefit to its owner does not constitute a fixed asset and should be treated as intermediate consumption. Unless the market value of the R&D is observed directly, it may, by convention, be valued at the sum of costs, including the cost of unsuccessful R&D" (European Commission et al., 2009: 206; our emphasis).

65. An initial discussion of the taxation-regime perspective on the price of knowledge can be found in Stehr (2015).

66. The discussion in the scientific and legal literature of the "direct" taxation of knowledge or intangible resources is in its infancy (see Simkovic, 2015). The only discussion we could find of the practice of taxation, in the United States in this case, is a brief article by Luscombe (1996).

67. A comparable and equally drawn-out legal dispute between the State of New Jersey and plaintiffs who argued that the state provided inadequate funding to some school districts in order to ensure the "provision of educational services sufficient to enable pupils to master the Core Curriculum Content Standards" was settled by the Supreme Court of New Jersey on May 24, 2011 in favor of the plaintiffs. The court enjoined the State of New Jersey to increase state education aid by $500 million in the coming school year, distributed among 31 school districts in historically poor cities. The Court concluded that the State failed to meet its constitutional burden to make sure that a "thorough and efficient education" was provided. The New Jersey constitution indeed charges the State with the fundamental responsibility to educate schoolchildren: "The Legislature shall provide for the maintenance and support of a thorough and efficient system of free public schools for the instruction of all the children in the State between the ages of five and eighteen years" (N.J. Const. art. VIII, § 4, 1.). The fundamental right to an adequate education extends to all children in the State. The court relied in its decision on Special Master's Opinion/Recommendations to the Supreme Court, submitted by Judge Peter E. Doyne (source www.judiciary.state.nj.us/opinions/index.htm and Winnie Hu and Richard Pérez-Peña, "Court orders New Jersey to increase aid to schools," *New York Times,* May 25, 2011).

68. We rely on the accounts of the conflict between the State of New York and the City of New York found in the *New York Times,* especially the article dated June 30, 2002 ("Johnny can read, not well enough to vote?"); and subsequent coverage in the same newspaper, especially "School financing case argued before State's highest court," *New York Times,* October 11, 2006 (see also Scherer, 2004–2005).

69. Peter Drucker (1993: 184) observes that the initial economic advantages gained by the application of (new) knowledge become permanent and irreversible. What this implies, according to Drucker, is that imperfect competition becomes a constitutive element of the economy. Knowledge can be disseminated or sold without leaving the context from which it is disseminated or sold. The edge that remains is perhaps best described as an advantage based on cumulative learning. The matter is even more complicated by virtue of the possibility that the acquisition of incremental knowledge may mean that "the buyer does not know what she is buying, and not need the product when she knows" (Eggertsson, 2009: 138).

70. For as John Maynard Keynes argues, a just price is a matter of equity not equality. Just prices "are those which correctly reward talents and efforts" (see Skidelsky, 2010: 145–146).

71. Joseph Stiglitz (1995) specifically identifies a total of five global public goods: "international economic stability, international security (political stability), the international environment, international humanitarian assistance and knowledge." A definition of global public good that is not merely confined to identifying examples of global public goods but also considers their availability concludes that "global public goods might usefully be defined as those goods (including policies and infrastructure) that are systematically

underprovided by private market forces and for which such under-provision has important international externality effects" (Maskus and Reichman, 2004: 284).

72. Michel Callon (1992: 73) defines techno-economic networks as a "coordinated set of heterogeneous actors—for instance, public laboratories, centres for technical research, companies, financial organizations, users and the government—who participate collectively in the conception, development, production and distribution or diffusion of procedures for producing goods and services, some of which give rise to market transactions."

73. Existing or new companies can bring innovative products to the market and thus displace the products of competitors; or companies active in the market can improve their own products. A study by Daniel Garcia-Macia and colleagues (2016) shows that the much greater increase in employment (in the USA) is the result of the innovative activities of existing companies, in particular through the improvement of products. The improvement of production is therefore at least in this respect (and relatively short term) more important than the creative destruction of products.

74. William Starbuck's (1992: 716) definition of a knowledge-intensive firm resonates with these observations about the function of incremental knowledge since he stresses "exceptional and valuable expertise" rather than the possession of knowledge per se as constitutive of knowledge-intensive firms: "If one defines knowledge broadly to encompass what everybody knows, every firm can appear knowledge-intensive." However, these broad designations do not as yet represent operational measures of incremental knowledge or exceptional expertise.

75. These characteristics of knowledge allow for a decoupling of the "cost" of the fabrication of knowledge from the benefits that accrue to those who use it. As a result, the non-rival and non-excludable attributes of knowledge constitute a disincentive to invest in the production of knowledge (see Dosi, 1996: 83). Geroski (1995: 94–100) discusses various strategies that might be instrumental in overcoming the appropriability problem of incremental knowledge.

76. The practical uses on the basis of which the value of knowledge may be calculated are assumed to be non-transitive. It is not possible to rank or weigh different uses (Bozeman and Rogers, 2002: 773). Moreover, the use value is dependent on the capacity of knowledge to achieve some kind of transformation; the transformation is envisioned as a cycle, that is, transforming information into knowledge and knowledge into information. These considerations underline partly our conclusion that it is an impossible task to arrive at a rational and judicious arithmetic of the (quantitative) value of the means of production called "knowledge."

# References

Acemoglu, Daron and David Autor (2012), "What does human capital do? A review of Goldin and Katz's the race between education and technology," *Journal of Economic Literature* 50: 426–463.

Acheson James (2003), *Capturing the Commons*. Lebanin, New Hampshire: University Press of New England.

Ackoff, Russell L. (1989), "From data to wisdom," *Journal of Applied Systems Analysis* 16: 3–9.

Adolf, Marian and Nico Stehr (2014), *Knowledge. Key Ideas Series*. London: Routledge.

Antonelli, Christiano (2017), "The derived demand for knowledge," *Economics of Innovation and New Technology* 26: 183–194.

Archibugi, Daniele and Andrea Filippetti (2015), "Knowledge as global public good," pp. 479–503 in Andrea Filippetti and Daniele Archibugi (eds.), *The Handbook of Global Science, Technology, and Innovation*. New York: John Wiley.

Arrow, Kenneth J. (2014), "Commentary," pp. 504–508 in Joseph E. Stiglitz and Bruce C. Greenwald (eds.), *Creating a Learning Society. A New Approach to Growth, Development, and Social Progress*. New York: Columbia University Press.

Arrow, Kenneth J. (1962), "The economic implications of learning by doing," *Review of Economic Studies* 29: 155–173.

Atkinson, Anthony B. (1983), *The Economics of Inequality*, 2nd ed. Oxford: Clarendon Press.

Autor, David H. and Michael J. Handel (2009), "Putting tasks to the test: Human capital, job tasks and wages," *NBER Working Paper* No. 15116.

Baecker, Dirk (1998), "Zum Problem des Wissens in Organisationen," *Organisationsentwicklung* 17: 4–21. Reprinted in Dirk Baecker, *Die Organisation als System*. Frankfurt am Main: Suhrkamp, pp. 68–101.

Baetjer, Howard Jr. (2000), "Capital as embodied knowledge: Some implications for the theory of economic growth," *Review of Austrian Economics* 13: 147–174.

Balzer, Wolfgang (2003), "Wissen und Wissenschaft als Waren," *Erkenntnis* 58: 87–110.

Barney, Jay B. (1991), "Firm resources and sustained competitive advantage," *Journal of Management* 17: 99–120.

Barro, Robert (1999), "The determinants of democracy," *Journal of Political Economy* 107: 158–183.

Becker, Gary S. and Barry Gerhart (1996), "The impact of human resources management on organizational performance: Progress and prospect," *Academy of Management Journal* 39: 779–801.

Becker, Gary S. (1994a), *Human Capital: A Theoretical and Empirical Analysis, with Special Reference to Education*, 3rd ed. New York: National Bureau of Economic Research.

Becker, Gary S. (1994b), "Human capital revisited," pp. 15–28 in Gary S. Becker (ed.), *Human Capital: A Theoretical and Empirical Analysis, with Special Reference to Education*, 3rd ed. New York: National Bureau of Economic Research.

Becker, Gary S., Kevin M. Murphy and Robert Tamura (1994), "Human capital, fertility, and economic growth," pp. 323–350 in Gary S. Becker (ed.), *Human Capital: A Theoretical and Empirical Analysis with Special Reference to Education*, 3rd ed. Chicago, IL: The University of Chicago Press.

Becker, Gary S. (1993), "The economic way of looking at behavior," *Journal of Political Economy* 101: 385–409.

Becker, Gary S. (1964), *Human Capital*. New York: National Bureau of Economic Research.

Becker, Gary S. and Nigel Tomes (1986), "Human capital and the rise and fall of families," *Journal of Labor Economics* 4: 1–39.

Benhabib, Jess and Mark M. Spiegel (1994), "The role of human capital in economic development. Evidence from aggregate cross-country data," *Journal of Monetary Economics* 34: 143–173.

Berger, Johannes (2004), "Über den Ursprung der Ungleichheit unter den Menschen," *Zeitschrift für Soziologie* 33: 354–374.

Berrill, Kenneth (ed.) (1964), *Economic Development with Special Reference to East Asia*. New York: St Martin's Press.

Blair, Margaret M. and Steven H.M. Wallman (2001), *Unseen Wealth*. Report of the Brookings Task Force on Intangibles, Washington, DC: Brookings Institution.

Blaug, Mark ([1965] 1968), "The rate of return on investment in education," pp. 215–259 in Mark Blaug (ed.), *Economics of Education 1*. Harmondsworth: Penguin.

Boldrin, Michele and David K. Levine (2013), "The case against patents," *Journal of Economic Perspectives* 27: 3–22.

Boldrin, Michele and David K. Levine (2005), "The economics of ideas and intellectual property," *PNAS* 102: 1252–1256.

Bonaccorsi, Andrea, Jane Calvert and Pierre-Benoit Joly (2011), "From protecting texts to protecting objects in biotechnology and software: A tale of changes of ontological assumptions in intellectual property protection," *Economy and Society* 40: 611–639.

Boudon, Raymond (1974), *Education, Opportunity and Social Inequality*. New York: Wiley.

Boulding, Kenneth E. (1966), "The economics of knowledge and the knowledge of economics," *The American Economic Review* 56: 1–13.

Bourdieu, Pierre (1999), "Scattered remarks," *European Journal of Social Theory* 2: 334–340.

Bourdieu, Pierre ([1984] 1988), *Homo Academicus*. Oxford: Polity Press.

Bourdieu, Pierre ([1983] 1986), "The forms of capital," pp. 241–258 in John G. Richardson (ed.), *Handbook of Theory and Research for the Sociology of Education*. New York: Greenwood.

Bourdieu, Pierre and Jean-Claude Passaron ([1964] 1979), *The Inheritors: French Students and their Relation to Culture*. Chicago, IL: University of Chicago Press.

Bourdieu, Pierre ([1972] 1977), *Outline of a Theory of Practice*. Cambridge: Cambridge University Press.

Bourdieu, Pierre ([1971] 1973), "Cultural reproduction and social reproduction," pp. 71–112 in Richard Brown (ed.), *Knowledge, Education, and Cultural Change*. London: Tavistock.

Boyle, James (2003), "The second enclosure movement and the construction of the public domain," *Law and Contemporary Problems* 66: 33–74.

Bozeman, Barry and Juan D. Rogers (2002), "A churn model of scientific knowledge value: Internet researchers as a knowledge value collective," *Research Policy* 31: 769–794.

Bryan, Dick, Michael Rafferty and Duncan Wigan (2017), "Capital unchained: Finance, intangible assets and the double life of capital in the offshore world," *Review of International Political Economy* 24: 56–86.

Brynjolfsson, Erik, Daniel Rock and Chad Syverson (2018), "The productivity j-curve: How intangibles complement general purpose technologies," *NBER Working Paper* No. 25148.

Brynjolfsson, Erik and Lorin Hitt (1996), "Paradox lost? Firm-level evidence on the returns to information systems spending," *Management Science* 42: 541–558.

Budish, Eric, Benjamin N. Roin and Williams, Heidi (2016), "Patents and research investments: Assessing the empirical evidence," *NBER Working Paper* No. 21889.

Calhoun, Craig (1995), *Critical Social Theory. Culture, History, and the Challenge of Difference*. Oxford: Blackwell.

Callon, Michel (1992), "The dynamics of techno-economic networks," pp. 132–161 in Rod Coombs, Paolo Saviotti and Vivien Walsh (eds.), *Technological Change and Company Strategies*, London: Academic Press.

Cappelli, Peter (2014), "Skill gaps, skill shortages and skill mismatches: Evidence for the US," *NBER Working Paper* No. 20382.

Castells, Manuel (1996), *The Information Age: Economy, Society and Culture. Volume I: The Rise of the Network Society*. Oxford: Blackwell.

Cohen. Robert S. and Thomas Schnelle (1986), *Cognition and Fact. Materials on Ludwik Fleck*. Dordrecht: D. Reidel.

Coleman, James S. (1988), "Social capital in the creation of human capital," *American Journal of Sociology* 94: 95–120.

Collins, Randall (1971), "Functional and conflict theories of educational stratification," *American Sociological Review* 1002–1019.

Corrado, Carol, A., Charles R. Hulten and Daniel E. Sichel (2006), "Intangible capital and economic growth," *NBER Working Paper* No. 11948.

Crampes, Claude and Corinne Langinier (2009), "Are intellectual property rights detrimental to innovation?" *International Journal of the Economics of Business* 16: 249–268.

Crouzet, Nicolas and Janice Eberly (2018), "Intangibles, investment and efficiency," Memo: Kellogg School of Management, Northwestern University, Evanston, IL.

Crozier, Michel ([1963] 1964), *The Bureaucratic Phenomenon*. Chicago, IL: University of Chicago Press.

Czarnitzki, Dirk, Bronwyn H. Hall and Raffaele Oriani (2006), "The market valuation of knowledge assets in US and European firms," pp. 111–131 in *The Management of Intellectual Property*. Cheltenham Glos.: Edward Elgar.

Damay, Cornelia, Nathalie Guichard and Amélie Clauzel (2014)," Children's price knowledge," *Young Consumers* 15: 167–177.

Davenport, Paul (1997), "The productivity paradox and the management of information technology," Paper presented to the Centre for the Study of Living Standards Conference on Service Sector Productivity and the Productivity Paradox, 11–13 April, Ottawa, Canada.

David, Paul A. (2000), "The digital technology boomerang: New intellectual property rights threaten global 'open science'," *World Bank Conference Paper*.

David, Paul (1990), "The dynamo and the computer. An historical perspective on the modern productivity paradox," *American Economic Review* 80: 355–361.

DeBresson, Christian and Ferdinand Amesse (1991), "Networks of innovators: A review and introduction to the issue," *Research Policy* 20: 363–379.

Dempsey, Gillian (1999), "Revisiting intellectual property policy: Information economics for the information age," *Prometheus* 17: 33–40.

de Pleijt, Alexandra M. (2016), "Human capital formation in the long run: Evidence from average years of schooling in England, 1300–1900," *Cliometrica* 1–28.

Dewey, John. ([1916] 2005), *Democracy and Education*. Stilwell, KS: Dickson.

Dickson, Peter R. and Alan G. Sawyer (1990), "The price knowledge and search of supermarket shoppers," *Journal of Marketing* 54: 42–53.

Diewert, Erwin and Kevin Fox (1997), "Can measurement error explain the productivity paradox?" Paper presented to the Centre for the Study of Living Standards Conference on Service Sector Productivity and the Productivity Paradox, 11–13 April, Ottawa, Canada.

DiMaggio, Paul (1997), "Culture and cognition," *Annual Review of Sociology* 23: 263–287.

Dosi, Giovanni (1996), "The contribution of economic theory to the understanding of a knowledge-based economy," pp. 81–92 in Organisation for Economic Co-Operation and Development (ed.), *Employment and Growth in the Knowledge-Based Economy*. Paris: OECD.

Drahos, Peter (2010), *The Global Governance of Knowledge: Patent Offices and Their Clients*. Cambridge: Cambridge University Press.

Drahos, Peter (2004), "The regulation of public goods," *Journal of International Economic Law* 7: 321–339.

Drucker, Peter (1993), *Post-Capitalist Society*. New York: Harper Business.

Dupré, J. Stefan and Sanford Lakoff (1962), *Science and the Nation. Policy and Politics*. Englewood Cliffs, NJ: Prentice-Hall.

Eggertsson, Thráinn (2009), "Knowledge and the theory of institutional change," *Journal of Institutional Economics* 5: 137–150.

Elias, Norbert ([1984] 2005), "Knowledge and power: An interview with Peter Ludes," pp. 202–242 in Nico Stehr and Volker Meja (eds.), *Society & Knowledge. Contemporary Perspectives in the Sociology of Knowledge & Science*. New Brunswick, NJ: Transaction Publishers.

Enns, Charis (2015), "Knowledges in competition: Knowledge discourse at the World Bank during the Knowledge for Development Era," *Global Social Policy* 15: 61–80.

European Commission, International Monetary Fund, Organisation for Economic Co-operation and Development, United Nations and World Bank (2009), *System of National Accounts 2008*. New York: European Commission, International Monetary Fund, Organisation for Economic Co-operation and Development, United Nations and World Bank.

Farre-Mensa, Joan, Deepak Hegde and Alexander Ljungqvist (2017), "What is a patent worth? Evidence from the U.S. patent 'lottery'," *NBER Working Paper* No. 23268.

Faulkner, Wendy, Jacqueline Senker and Lea Velho (1995), *Knowledge frontiers: Industrial Innovation and Public Sector Research in Biotechnology, Engineering Ceramics, and Parallel Computing*. Oxford: Oxford University Press.

Feher, Michel ([2007] 2009), "Self-appreciation; or, the aspirations of human capital," *Public Culture* 21: 21–41.

Feldstein, Martin S. (2017), "Underestimating the real growth of GDP, personal income and productivity," *NBER Working Paper* No. 23306.

Fevre, Ralph, Gareth Rees and Stephen Gorard (1999), "Some sociological alternatives to human capital theory and their implications for research on postcompulsory education and training," *Journal of Education and Work* 12: 117–140.

Fink, Carsten and Keith E. Maskus (2005), "Why we study intellectual property rights and what we have learned," pp. 1–15 in Carsten Fink and Keith E. Maskus (eds.), *Intellectual Property and Development. Lessons from Recent Economic Research*. Washington, DC: The World Bank.

Fleck, Ludwik ([1935] 1980), *Entstehung und Entwicklung einer wissenschaftlichen Tatsache. Einführung in die Lehre vom Denkstil und Denkkollektiv*. Frankfurt am Main: Suhrkamp.

Foray, Dominique (2006), *The Economics of Knowledge*. Boston, MA: MIT Press.

Foray, Dominique (2000), "Intellectual property and innovation in the knowledge-based economy," No. CEMI-REPORT-2005–010.

Fourcade, Marion (2011), "Cents and sensibility: Economic valuation and the nature of nature," *American Journal of Sociology* 116: 1721–1777.

Freeman, Chris (1991), "Networks of innovators: A synthesis of research issues," *Research Policy* 20: 499–514.

Fulmer, Ingrid Smithey and Robert E. Ployhart (2014), "'Our most important asset': A multidisciplinary/multilevel review of human capital valuation for research and practice," *Journal of Management* 40: 161–192.

Gabe, Todd, Richard Florida and Charlotta Mellander (2013), "The creative class and the crisis," *Cambridge Journal of Regions, Economy and Society* 6: 37–53.

Galbraith, John K. ([1967] 1971), *The New Industrial State*. Boston, MA: Houghton Mifflin.

Ganguli, Prabuddha (2000), "Intellectual property rights. Imperatives for the knowledge industry," *World Patent Information* 22: 167–175.

Garcia-Macia, Daniel, Chan-Tai Hsieh and Peter J. Klenow (2016), "How destructive is innovation?" *NBER Working Paper* No. 22953.

Garicano, Luis and Esteban Rossi-Hansberg (2015), "Knowledge-based hierarchies: Using organizations to understand the economy," *Annual Review of Economics* 7: 1–30.

Garmon, Cecile W. (2002), "Intellectual property rights," *American Behavioral Scientist* 45: 1145–1158.

Garnham, Nicholas and Raymond Williams (1986), "Pierre Bourdieu and the sociology of culture: An introduction," pp. 209–223 in Richard Collins (ed.), *Media, Culture and Society*. London: Sage.

Geroski, Paul (1995), "Markets for technology: Knowledge, innovation and appropriability," pp. 90–131 in Paul Stoneman (ed.), *Handbook of the Economics of Innovation and Technological Change*. Oxford: Blackwell.

Ghosh, Rishab A. and Luc Soete (2006), "Information and intellectual property: The global challenges," *Industrial and Corporate Change* 15: 919–935.

Ghosh, Rishab A. (2005), *CODE: Collaborative Ownership and the Digital Economy*. Cambridge, MA: MIT Press.

Golding, Claudia and Lawrence F. Katz (2008), *The Race between Education and Technology*. Cambridge, MA: Harvard University Press.

Gorz, André ([2003] 2010), *The Immaterial. Knowledge, Value and Capital*. Chicago, IL: University of Chicago Press.

Gorz, André ([2003] 2004), *Wissen, Wert und Kapital. Zur Kritik der Wissensökonomie*. Berlin: Rotpunktverlag.

Gossner, Olivier (2010), "Ability and knowledge," *Games and Economic Behavior* 69: 95–106.

Gould, Eric, Avi Simhon and Bruce A. Weinberg (2019), "Does parental quality matter? Evidence on the transmission of human capital using variation in parental influence from death, divorce, and family size," *NBER Working Paper* No. 25495.

Gouldner, Alvin W. (1979), *The Future of Intellectuals and the Rise of the New Class*. New York: Continuum.

Gouldner, Alvin W. (1976), *The Dialectic of Ideology and Technology: The Origins, Grammar and Future of Ideology*. New York: Seabury Press.

Granovetter, Mark (1985), "Economic action and social structure: The problem of embeddedness," *American Journal of Sociology* 91: 481–510.

Greenhalgh, Christine and Mark Rogers (2007), "The value of intellectual property rights to firms and society," *Oxford Review of Economic Policy* 23: 541–567.

Grundmann, Reiner and Nico Stehr (2012), *The Power of Scientific Knowledge. From Research to Public Policy*. Cambridge: Cambridge University Press.

Haggett, Mark and Greg Kaplan (2015), "How large is the stock component of human capital," *NBER Working Paper* No. 21238.

Hall, John R. (1992), "The capital(s) of cultures: A nonholistic approach to status situations, class, gender, and ethnicity," pp. 257–285 in Michèle Lamont and Marcel Fournier (eds.), *Cultivating Differences. Symbolic Boundaries and the Making of Inequality*. Chicago, IL: University of Chicago Press.

Halle, David (1992), "The audience for abstract art: Class, culture and power," pp. 131–181 in Michèle Lamont and Marcel Fournier (eds.), *Cultivating Differences. Symbolic Boundaries and the Making of Inequality*. Chicago, IL: University of Chicago Press.

Hanushek, Eric A., Guido Schwerdt and Simon Wiederhold (2015), "Returns to skill around the world: Evidence from PIAAC," *European Economic Review* 73: 103–130.

Hanushek, Eric A. and Ludger Woessmann (2015), *The Knowledge Capital of Nations*. Cambridge, MA: MIT Press.

Hardin, Garrett (1968), "The tragedy of the commons," *Science* 162: 1243–1248.

Harison, Elad (2008), "Intellectual property rights in knowledge-based economy: A new frame-of-analysis," *Economic Innovation New Technology* 17: 377–400.

Harrod, Roy F. (1939), "An essay in dynamic theory," *The Economic Journal* 49: 14–33.

Hess, Charlotte and Elinor Ostrom (2007), *Understanding Knowledge as a Commons: From theory to practice*. Cambridge, MA: MIT Press.

Hess, Charlotte and Elinor Ostrom (2003), "Ideas, artifacts and facilities: Information as a common-pool resource," *Law and Contemporary Problems* 66: 111–148.

Hesse, Carla (2002), "The rise of intellectual property, 700 B.C.—A.D. 2000: An idea in the balance," *Daedalus* 131(2): 26–45.

Hilgartner, Stephen (2002), "Acceptable intellectual property," *Journal of Molecular Biology* 319: 943–946.

Hilmer, Michael J. and Christiana E. Hilmer (2012), "On the relationship between student tastes and motivations, higher education decisions, and annual earnings," *Economics of Education Review* 31: 66–75.

Holzer, Felicitas S. (2017), "Defending the social value of knowledge as a safeguard for public trust," *Bioethics* 31: 559–567.

Homburg, Christian, Nicole Koschate-Fischer and Christian M. Wiegner (2012), "Customer satisfaction and elapsed time since purchase as drivers of price knowledge," *Psychology and Marketing* 29(2): 76–86.

Hoti, Suhejla and Michael McAleer (2006), "Intellectual property litigation activity in the USA," *Journal of Economic Surveys* 20: 715–729.

Hume, David ([1739] 1961), *A Treatise of Human Nature*. Garden City, NJ: Dolphin Books.

Jorgenson, Dale (1997), "Computers and productivity." Paper presented to the Centre for the Study of Living Standards Conference on Service Sector Productivity and the Productivity Paradox, 11–13 April, Ottawa, Canada.

Junor, Sean and Alex Usher (2004/2005), "The price of knowledge," *Policy Options* 61–66.

Kaul, Inge, Isabelle Grunberg and Marc A. Stern (1999), "Introduction," in Inge Kaul, Isabelle Grunberg and Marc A. Stern (eds.), *Global Public Goods. International Co-operation in the 21st Century*. New York: Oxford University Press, pp. xix–xxxviii.

Knight. H. Jackson (2013), *Patent Strategy for Researchers and Research Managers*, 3rd ed. New York: John Wiley.

Krugman, Paul (1994), *The Age of Diminished Expectations. U.S. Economic Policy in the 1990s*. Revised and updated ed. Cambridge, MA: MIT Press.

Lamont, Michèle and Annette Lareau (1988), "Cultural capital: Allusions, gaps and glissandos in recent theoretical developments," *Sociological Theory* 6: 153–168.

Landes, William M. and Richard A. Posner (2003), *The Economic Structure of Intellectual Pproperty Law*. Cambridge, MA: Harvard University Press.

Laroche, Mireille and Marcel Mérette (1999), "On the concept and dimensions of human capital in a knowledge-based economy context," *Canadian Public Policy* 25: 87–100.

Leadbeater, Charles (1999), "New measures for the new economy," *International Symposium on Measuring and Reporting Intellectual Capital: Experience, Issues and Prospects*, Amsterdam: OECD.

Leppälä, Samuli (2015), "Economic analysis of knowledge: The history of thought and the central themes," *Journal of Economic Surveys* 29: 263–286.

Li, Xing, Megan MacGarvie and Petra Moser (2015), "Dead poet's property: How does copyright influence price?" *NBER Working Paper* No. 21522.

Lim, Lynn L., Christopher C. Chan and Peter Dallimore (2010), "Perceptions of human capital measures: From corporate executives and investors," *Journal of Business and Psychology* 25: 673–688.

Limoges, Camille (1993), "Expert knowledge and decision-making in controversy contexts," *Public Understanding of Science* 2: 417–426.

Lin, Dajun, Randell Lutter and Christopher J. Ruhm (2016), "Cognitive performance and labor market outcome," *NBER Working Paper* No. 22470.

Lindahl, Mikael, Mårten Palme, Sofia Sandgren-Massih and Anna Sjögren (2014), "A test of the Becker-Tomes model of human capital transmission using microdata on four generations," *Journal of Human Capital* 8: 80–96.

Link, Albert and Christopher Ruhm (2009), "Public knowledge, private knowledge: The intellectual capital of entrepreneurs," *NBER Working Paper* No. 14797.

Lipset, Seymour M. (1959), "Some social requisites of democracy: Economic development and political legitimacy," *American Political Science Review* 53: 69–105.

Long, Clarisa (2002), "Patent signals," *University of Chicago Law Review* 69: 625–679.

Long, Pamela O. (1991), "Invention, authorship, 'intellectual property,' and the origin of patents: Notes toward a conceptual history," *Technology and Culture* 32: 846–884.

Luscombe, Mark A. (1996), "Taxation of knowledge," *Taxes* 74: 183.

Lyotard, Jean-François ([1979] 1984), *The Postmodern Condition: A Report on Knowledge.* Minneapolis: University of Minnesota Press.

Machlup, Fritz (1979), "Uses, value and benefits of knowledge," *Knowledge: Creation, Diffusion, Utilization* 1: 62–81.

Madison, Michael J., Brett M. Frischmann and Katherine J. Strandburg (2010), "Constructing Commons in the cultural environment," *Cornell Law Review* 95: 657–709.

Mannheim, Karl ([1929] 1936), *Ideology and Urtopia.* London: Routledge.

Maskus, Keith E. and Jerome H. Reichman (2004), "The globalization of private knowledge goods and the privatization of global public goods," *Journal of International Economic Law* 7: 279–320.

Matthews, Duncan (2011), *Intellectual Property, Human Rights and Development: The Role of NGOs and Social Movements.* Cheltenham: Edward Elgar.

Matthijs, Gert (2004), "Patenting genes: May slow down innovation, and delay availability of cheaper genetic tests," *British Medical Journal* 329: 1358.

McCulla, S., Holden, A. and Smith, S. (2013), *Improved Estimates of National Income and Product Accounts: Results of the 2013 Comprehensive Revision.* Washington, DC: Bureau of Economic Analysis.

McGrattan, Ellen R. (2017), "Intangible capital and measured productivity," *NBER Working Paper* No. 23233.

Menger, Carl ([1871] 1981), *Principles of Economics.* New York: New York University Press.

Merton, Robert K. (1995), "The Thomas theorem and the Matthew effect," *Social Forces* 74: 379–424.

Merton, Robert K. ([1965] 1985), *On the Shoulder of Giants. A Shandiran Postcript.* New York: Harcourt Brace Jovanovich.

Merton, Robert K. ([1949] 1968), *Social Theory and Social Structure.* Revised and Enlarged ed. New York: Free Press.

Michels, Robert ([1908] 1987), "Die oligarchischen Tendenzen der Gesellschaft. Ein Beitrag zum Problem der Demokratie," pp. 133–180 in Robert Michels (ed.), *Masse, Führer, Intellektuelle.* Frankfurt am Main: Campus.

Miller, Jon D. (1983), *The American People and Science Policy.* New York: Pergamon.

Mincer, Jacob (1974), *Schooling, Experience, and Earnings*. New York: NBER Press.

Mokyr, Joel and Hans-Joachim Voth (2009), "Understanding Growth in Europe, 1700–1870: Theory and Evidence: Volume 1, 1700–1870," in S. Broadberry and K. H. O'Rourke (eds.), *The Cambridge Economic History of Modern Europe: Volume 1, 1700–1870*. Cambridge: Cambridge University Press.

Mokyr, Joel (2005), "The intellectual origins of modern economic growth," *Journal of Economic History* 65: 285–351.

Nelkin, Dorothy (1987), "The political impact of technical expertise," *Social Studies of Science* 5: 35–54.

Nelkin, Dorothy (1975), "The political impact of technical expertise," *Social Studies of Science* 5: 35–54.

Nelson, Benjamin (1973), "Civilizational complexes and intercivilizational encounters," *Sociological Analysis* 34: 79–105.

Nordhaus, William D. and Davod Popp (1996), "What is the value of scientific knowledge? An application to global warming using the Price model," *Cowles Foundation Discussion Paper* No. 1117. Yale University: Cowles Foundation for Research in Economics.

Nordhaus, Wilhelm D. (1969), *Invention, Growth and Welfare. A Theoretical Treatment of Technological Change*. Cambridge, MA: MIT Press.

OECD (2010), "Intangible assets," in *Measuring Innovation: A New Perspective*, OECD Publishing, Paris. DOI:10.1787/9789264059474-6-en

OECD (2006), *Intellectual Assets and Value Creation: Implications for Corporate Reporting*. Paris: OECD.

Offe, Claus ([2001] 2012), "Whose good is the common good?" *Philosophy & Social Criticism* 38: 665–684.

Olavarrieta, Sergio, Pedro Hidalgo, Enrique Manzur and Pablo Farias (2012), "Determinants of in-store price knowledge for packaged products: An empirical study in a Chilean hypermarket," *Journal of Business Research* 65: 1759–1766.

Pakes, Ariel and Mark Schankerman (1979), "The rate of obsolescence of knowledge, research gestation lags, and the private rate of return to the research resources," *NBER Working Paper* No. 346.

Park, Haemin Dennis, Michael D. Howard and David M. Gomulya (2017), "The impact of knowledge worker mobility through an acquisition on breakthrough knowledge," *Journal of Management Studies* 55. DOI:10.1111/joms.12320.

Parsons, Talcott ([1949] 1954), "Social classes and class conflict in the light of recent sociological theory," pp. 323–335 in Talcott Parsons (ed.), *Essays in Sociological Theory*. New York: Free Press.

Piketty, Thomas ([2013] 2014), *Capital in the Twentieth-First Century*. Cambridge: MA: Harvard University Press.

Petit, Pascal and Luc Soete (1997), "Is a biased technological change fuelling dualism." Paper presented to the Centre for the Study of Living Standards Confererence on Service Sector Productivity and the Productivity Pradox, 11–13 April, Ottawa, Canada.

Popitz, Heinrich (1986), *Phänomene der Macht. Autorität—Herrschaft—Gewalt—Technik*. Tübingen: J.C.B. Mohr (Paul Siebeck).

Popp, David (2017), "From science to technology: The value of knowledge from different energy research institutions," *Research Policy* 46: 1580–1594.

Przeworski, Adam, Michael Alvarez, José A. Cheibub and Fernando Limongi (2000), *Democracy and Development. Political Institutions and Material Well-being in the World, 1950–1990*. New York: Cambridge University Press.

Quilligan, James B. (2012), "Warum wir Commons von öffentlichen Gütern unterscheiden müssen," pp. 99–106 in Silke Helfrich and Heinrich-Böll-Stiftung (eds.), *Commons. Für eine neue Politik jenseits von Masrkt und Staat*. Bielefeld: Transcript.

Quinn, James B. (1996), "The productivity paradox is false: Information technology improves service performance," *Advances in Services Marketing and Management* 5: 71–84.

Radder, Hans (2017), "Which scientific knowledge is a common good?" *Social Epistemology* 31: 431–450.

Resnik, David B. (2004), *Owning the Genome: A Moral Analysis of DNA Patenting*. Albany, NY: State University Press of New York.

Rimes, Heather, Jennie Welch and Barry Bozeman (2014), "An alternative to the economic value of knowledge," pp. 154–164 in Cristiano Antonelli and Albert N. Link (eds.), *Routledge Handbook of the Economics of Knowledge*. New York: Routledge.

Robinson, Joan (1979), *The Generalisation of the General Theory and other Essays*. London: Macmillan.

Rosen, Sherwin (1975), "Measuring the obsolescence of knowledge," pp. 199–232 in F. T. Juster (ed.), *Education, Income and Human Behavior*. New York: Carnegie Foundation for the Advancement of Teaching & National Bureau of Economic Research.

Rosewall, Bridget (2005), "The knowledge of price and the price of knowledge," *Futures* 37: 699–710.

Scheler, Max ([1924] 1960), *Die Wissensformen und die Gesellschaft*. Bern and München: Francke.

Scherer, Bonnie A. (2004–2005), "Footing the bill for a sound education in New York City: The implementation of campaign for fiscal equity v. state," *Fordham Urban Law Journal* 32: 901–935.

Schoellman, Tod (2012), "Education quality and development accounting," *Review of Economic Studies* 79: 388–417.

Schultz, Theodor W. (1992), "Reflections on investment in man," *Journal of Political Economy* 70: 1–8.

Schultz, Theodore H. (1962), "Reflections on investment in man," *Journal of Political Economics* 70: 1–8.

Schultz, Theodore W. (1961), "Investment in human capital," *American Economic Review* 51: 1–17.

Schwartz, Jacob T. (1992), "America's economic-technological agenda for the 1990s," *Daedalus* 121: 139–165.

Shaffer, Harry G. (1961), "Investment in human capital: Comment," *American Economic Review* 52: 1026–1035.

Shapin, Steven (2001), "Proverbial economies how an understanding of some linguistic and social features of common sense can throw light on more prestigious bodies of knowledge, science for example," *Social Studies of Science* 31: 731–769.

Sichel, Daniel E. (1999), "Computers and aggregate economic growth: An update," *Business Economics* 34: 18–24.

Simkovic, Michael (2015), "The knowledge tax," *The University of Chicago Law Review* 82: 1981–2043.

Simmel, Georg ([1907] 2004), *The Philosophy of Money*. London: Routledge and Kegan Paul.

Simmel, Georg ([1900] 2004), *The Philosophy of Money*. London: Routledge and Kegan Paul.

Simmel, Georg ([1907] 1989), *Philosophie des Geldes. Gesamtausgabe Band 6*. Frankfurt am Main: Suhrkamp.

Simmel, Georg ([1907] 1978), *The Philosophy of Money*. London: Routledge and Kegan Paul.

Simon, Herbert (1999), "The many shapes of knowledge," *Revue d'Economie Industrielle* 88: 23–39.

Skidelsky, Robert (2010), *Keynes: The Return of the Master*. Philadelphia, PA: Perseus Books Group.

Smith, Adam ([1776] 2012), *An Inquiry into the Nature and Causes of the Wealth of Nations*. London: Wordworth Editions Limited.

Sollosy, Marc, Marjorie McInerney and Charles K. Braun (2016), "Human capital: A strategic asset whose time has come to be recognized on organizations' financial statements," *Corporate Accounting & Finance* 27: 19–27.

Solow, Robert M. (1987), "We'd better watch out," *New York Times Book Review* 12 July, 36.

Squicciarini, Mara P. and Nico Vogtlaender (2014), "Human capital and industrialization: Evidence from the age of enlightenment," *NBER Working Paper* No. 20219.

Starbuck, William H. (1992), "Learning by knowledge-intensive firms," *Journal of Management Studies* 29: 713–740.

Stehr, Nico and Marion Adolf (2017), *Knowledge. Is Knowledge Power?* London: Routledge.

Stehr, Nico (2016), *Information, Power, and Democracy. Liberty Is a Daughter of Knowledge*. Cambridge: Cambridge University Press.

Stehr, Nico and Marian Adolf (2015), *Ist Wissen Macht? Erkenntnisse über Wissen*. Weilerswist: Velbrück Wissenschaft.

Stehr, Nico (2002), *Knowledge and Economic Conduct: The Social Foundations of the Modern Economy*. Toronto, ON: University of Toronto Press.

Stehr, Nico (2000), "The productivity paradox: ICT's, knowledge and the labour market," pp. 255–272 in John de la Mothe and Gilles Paquet (eds.), *Information, Innovation and Impacts*. Norwell, MA: Kluwer.

Stehr, Nico (1999), "The future of inequality," *Society* 36: 54–59.

Stehr, Nico (1994), *Knowledge Societies*. London: Sage.

Stigler, George J. (1980), "An introduction to privacy in economics and politics," *The Journal of Legal Studies* 9: 623–644.

Stiglitz, Joseph E. (2017), "The revolution of information economics. The past and the future. *NBER Working Paper* No. 23780 w23780.

Stiglitz, Joseph E. (2015), "The measurement of wealth: Recessions, sustainability and inequality," *NBER Working Paper* No. 21327.

Stiglitz, Joseph E. and Bruce G. Greenwald (2014), *Creating a Learning Society. A New Approach to Growth, Development, and Social Progress*. New York: Columbia University Press.

Stiglitz, Joseph E. (2014), "Intellectual property rights, the pool of knowledge, and innovation," *NBER Working Paper*.

Stiglitz, Joseph E. (2012), *The Price of Inequality*. New York: Norton.

Stiglitz, Joseph E. (2010), "Intellectual property, dissemination of innovation, and sustainable development," *Global Policy* 1: 237–251.

Stiglitz, Joseph E. (1999), "Knowledge as a global public good," pp. 308–325 in Inge Kaul, Isabelle Grunberg and Marc A. Stern (eds.), *Global Public Goods. International Co-operation in the 21st Century*. New York: Oxford University Press.

Stiglitz, Joseph E. (1995), "The theory of international public goods and the architecture of international organizations," *United Nations Background Paper* No. 7. New York: United Nations.

Strathern, Marilyn (2005), "Imagined collectivities and multiple ownership," pp. 13–28 in Rishab A. Ghosh (ed.), *Code. Collaborative Ownership and the Digital Economy*. Cambridge, MA: MIT Press.

Storper, Michael (1996), "Institutions of the knowledge-based economy," pp. 255–283 in Organisation for Economic Co-Operation and Development (ed.), *Employment and Growth in the Knowledge-Based Economy*. Paris: OECD.

Tan, Emrullah (2014), "Human capital theory: A holistic criticism," *Review of Educational Research* 84: 411–445.

Teal, Francis (2011), "The price of labour and understanding the causes of poverty," *Labour Econnomics* 18: 7–15.

Teece, David J. (1998), "Capturing value from knowledge assets: The new economy, markets for know-how, and intangible assets," *California Management Review* 40: 55–79.

Teece, David J. (1977), "Technology transfer by multinational firms: The resource cost of transferring technological know-how," *The Economic Journal* 87: 242–261.

Tomaskovic-Devey, Melvin Thomas and Kecia Johnson (2005), "Race and the accumulation of human capital: A theoretical model and fixed-effects application," *American Journal of Sociology* 111: 58–89.

UNU-IHDP and UNEP (2014*), Inclusive Wealth Report 2014. Measuring Progress toward Sustainability*. Cambridge: Cambridge University Press.

Van Doorn, Niels (2014), "The neoliberal subject of value: Measuring human capital in information economies," *Cultural Politics* 10: 354–375.

Van den Daele, Wolfgang (1996), "Objektives Wissen als politische Ressource: Experten und Gegenexperten im Diskurs," pp. 297–326 in Wolfgang van den Daele and Friedhelm Neidhardt (eds.), *Kommunikation und Entscheidung*. Berlin: Sigma.

Van Eekelen, Bergie F. (2015), "Accounting for ideas: Bringing a knowledge economy into the picture," *Economy and Society* 44: 445–479.

Vazquez, Alfredo Macias and Pablo Alonso Gonzalez (2016), "Knowledge economy and the commons: A theoretical and political approach to postneoliberal common governance," *Review of Radical Political Economy* 48: 140–157.

Veblen, Thorstein ([1908] 1919), "The nature of capital," pp. 324–386 in Thorstein Veblen (ed.), *The Place of Science in Modern Civilisation and other Essays*. New York: The Viking Press.

Wacquant, Loic D. (1989), "Towards a reflexive sociology: A workshop with Pierre Bourdieu," *Sociological Theory* 7: 26–63.

Weber, Max ([1917] 1994), *Political Writings*. Edited by Peter Lassman and Ronald Spiers. Cambridge: Cambridge University Press.

Welch, Finis and Manuelita Ureta, (2002), "The obsolescence of skill," *Labor Economics* 21: 51–81. DOI:10.1016/S0147-9121(02)21005-5

Wenner, Danielle (2015), "The social value of knowledge and international clinical research," *Developing World Bioethics* 2: 76–84.

Williams, Heidi L. (2016), "Intellectual property rights and innovation: Evidence from health care markets," *Innovation Policy and the Economy* 16: 53–87.

Williamson, Oliver E. (1975), *Market and Hierarchies. Analysis and Antitrust Implications*. New York: The Free Press.

World Bank (2019), *The Human Capital Project*. Washington, DC: World Bank.

World Bank (2011), *The Changing Wealth of Nations—Measuring Sustainable Development in the New Millennium*. Washington, DC: World Bank.

World Bank (1999), *Knowledge for development: World development report 1998–99*. Washington, DC: The World Bank and Oxford University Press.

Wynne, Brian (1992), "Misunderstood misunderstanding: Social identities and public uptake of science," *Public Understanding of Science* 1: 281–304.

Young, Alison (1998), *Measuring Intangible Investment. Towards an Interim Statistical Framework: Selecting the Core Components of Intangible Investment*. Paris: OECD.

Zhou, Yi (2015), "The tragedy of the anticommons in knowledge," *Review of Radical Political Economics* 28: 158–175.

# CONCLUSIONS

There could not be any kind of social unity in which the converging directions of elements would not be permeated inextricably by the diverging ones.
—*Georg Simmel ([1908] 2009: 228)*

I am grateful to the circumstances for their contradictions.
—*Thomas Brasch, 1981*[1]

We have chronicled, interrogated and criticized the new master narrative that has shifted the attention of most observers of modern transformation processes from society to a mixture of technology and finance. And we did so with the explicit view to reinstitute the societal as the central focal point in the firm belief that this perspective was better suited to comprehend and influence the social functioning of modern society.

Contrary to the common-sense view that conflict poses a disintegrating social force, Georg Simmel in his classical essay on "Conflict" (*Streit*) argues that disagreement and divergence are an integrating element of collective relations. Simmel ([1908] 2009: 228) stresses that "society needs some quantitative ratio of harmony and disharmony, association and competition, good will and ill will, in order to arrive at a specific formation." Differences of opinion are not merely liabilities but promote social accord; dualistic divisions are part of the unity of collectivities. For example, when forming stable social and political coalitions "a certain measure of disagreements internal differences and outward controversies that, after all and in spite of everything, preserve the bond" (Simmel, [1908] 2009: 230).

Persistent collective strains and conflicts *on the societal time axis* represent the theoretical and methodological principle of the *simultaneity of the non-simultaneous* (see Mannheim, [1928] 1993; Lehnert, 2016). The emphasis on simultaneously non-simultaneous societal phenomena and processes helps us to embrace social complexity and avoid the fallacy of overgeneralization. Overgeneralization implies that phenomena and processes are regarded as self-contained and self-referential and thus as beyond the influence and control of any actors involved. André Gorz ([1997] 2000: 162), for instance, falls subject to overgeneralization when he describes the iron relationship between labor and digitalization: "The ubiquitous digitalization does not only abolish work . . . thus the physical and manual skills. It also abolishes the world that can be experienced by the senses." Digitalization overwhelms everything. Resistance against this practically insurmountable power seems hopeless.

However, as we have shown, such overgeneralization is not only a common fallacy in contemporary analyses of automation, digitalization, and artificial intelligence, but also widely accepted and recurrent in many social scientific discussions. When trying to make sense of fundamental societal transformation processes, we should not accept trivial, mutually exclusive dichotomies along concurrent collective and individual developments. This is the most fundamental lesson of the simultaneity of the non-simultaneous. In the analysis of social developments, it is paramount to respect the prohibition of a "synchronism of the incommensurable" (Max Frisch).

Our particular reference has been to the tensions between existential (rational) and moral interests in the economy, measured by the divergence between (market) *prices* and social *values* and applied to the four most elementary production factors land, capital, labor, and knowledge. We find that each of these multifaceted factors of production embodies conflicts that easily blend into other social institutions, in particular, everyday life, the churches, the family, or the state, amounting to massively-irritating discontinuities in modern society. For "Where one estimates the worth of everything solely according to its market price, one becomes uncertain and skeptical about all values for which there is no market price" (Simmel, 1915; our translation).

The multiple functions of the means of production, some are shared, others are unique to each one, make it very difficult if not impossible to establish an exact let alone "just" price. However, the realization alone that the *relative* relationship between price and value is increasingly divergent allows for important conclusions to be drawn regarding the functioning and, in particular, the transformation of modern societies.

The production factor *land* fulfils the functions typical of all production resources. In addition to its essential role in primary and industrial production, it is a source of income, but also serves aesthetic purposes and influences the formation of social inequalities. The price of land which used to be based exclusively on its utility value as a source of human livelihood, in modern financial capitalism is increasingly determined by speculative motives, which tend to consume, too, the environment and nature. This novel development has serious consequences.

Global processes such as *land grabbing* and *green grabbing* result in the comprehensive economic appropriation and expropriation of land and nature with devastating consequences for both, the environment and local populations. At the same time, the extensive rationalization, financialization, and quantification of nature seem to offer a system-conformist solution for reconciling environmental and climate protection with the objectives of capitalism.

But the sheer unbreakable urge of capital to commodify more nature in one place in order to (possibly) conserve it in others necessarily culminates in an entirely destructive zero-sum game. Admittedly, the need to justify land's green value in monetary terms can promote an unlikely alliance of environmentalists and financial managers. But it can never achieve its ultimate goal. For their hopes lie in the economic principle of scarcity, which at the same time constitutes ecology's most fundamental objective of prevention. In other words, applying a purely capitalist ratio, the law of scarcity always dominates the principle of diversity. With the rise of financialization, the value of land, nature, and the environment is reflected in their price in but a greatly diminishing degree.

*Capital*, on the other hand, is the basic ingredient of all productive action and thus comes with justifiable a price. There have been numerous attempts in the history of mankind to regulate or even prohibit entirely the price of capital. However, societies that exceed the size and complexity of archaic tribes have always found ways to create incentives to exchange capital in markets and enable productive action. We showed that the price of capital is essential to society and manifests itself above all in a constant competition between material and moral considerations. The rise of the immaterial economy, however, seems to be giving material efficiency the upper hand. With the rise of financialization, capital penetrates ever deeper into society, causing social individualization and forcing constant optimization through its compulsion to be permanently productive. At this early stage, we can only speculate about the social and political consequences of this fundamental development. But more recent political events in almost all modern societies clearly point to social radicalization and division resulting from significant inequality, individualization, commodification, political isolation, and alienation. All these phenomena are directly reflected in the unequal access to capital and its returns.

The production factor *labor* is also source of these problems and performs multiple functions. Labor is essential to production, represents a central aspiration in life, is a source of income for most social strata and, above all perhaps, essentially a bearer of individual and collective meaning. The rise of the immaterial economy, which knows no actual owners, is rewriting social structures and societal hierarchies. People who are able to mobilize and offer the complementary skills to remain useful and find work in the immaterial economy are the winners of new developments. Their income rises in relation to employees with only traditional skills. At the same time, however, the proportion of socially necessary work is falling, and formerly successful workers with traditional skills are increasingly the losers of modernity. They do not benefit from the added value of the immaterial economy. The sum of these developments reinforces the polarization of developed societies.

We showed that, contrary to conventional opinion, these fundamental transformations in the world of work are controlled neither by the demand side nor massive technological changes. The heretofore rather vaguely formulated human capital theory is one of the supply-oriented perspectives for determining the price of labor. The demand side (that is, the employer) may still be influential in managing the training of new professionals, but it is not in a position to anticipate or determine the cognitive and non-cognitive skills that will make a company successful in the immaterial economy in the long run. We simply do not know (see Knight, [1921] 1964; Keynes, 1937: 214) which special cognitive and non-cognitive abilities will be important in the future.

The price and value of work consists of a material and a moral part of remuneration. Both components and their exact relation cannot be clearly standardized or determined. What is certain, however, is that a society that defines its (moral) self-understanding and that of its dependents through the institution of employment faces considerable challenges in the transition to an immaterial economy.

How well a society is able to cope with these challenges ultimately depends on the question of the social and, in particular, economic handling of *knowledge*. Knowledge embodies a capacity to act; it is the foundation of cognitive and non-cognitive skills and is therefore indispensable for production processes. But knowledge has only recently been recognized as a factor of production. In the immaterial economy it is the basis for innovation, becomes the most important source of income, and increasingly contributes to disquieting imbalances in society. Politically, these social distortions manifest themselves in the inexorable rise of populist movements. (cf. Goodhart, 2017).

In our opinion, to avoid that stratified access to knowledge offers massive advantages and promotes social inequality—not least through its role as an economic resource—existing knowledge as a *public good* should not have a price. The rewards associated with the use of *existing* knowledge should be fairly distributed among society, while the benefits arising from the discovery of *new* knowledge should accrue according to contribution and merit. Similar to the price of labor, supply-side approaches to knowledge should be promoted, because in the immaterial economy's world of work, it is not specific skills but flexible knowledge-abilities that will determine well-being and woe, success and failure, ascent and descent.

Our analysis of the four most important factors of production has shown that the emerging *immaterial* economic system, next to climate change, constitutes, the most disruptive development in modern society. For with its core functions, *financialization* and economic *quantification*, it contributes to a massive acceleration and enhanced volatility of social conduct in all areas of social life. The immaterial economy is fast and capricious. Democracy is slow and unhurried. The conflict between the swift and precarious social institutions, such as the economy and social media, and the more ponderous and deliberate institutions of modern society, such as the political system and civil discourse, becomes strikingly apparent and poses a fundamental challenge for generations to come. Here, too, reigns the simultaneity of the non-simultaneous.

Modern societies are imbued with social phenomena that originate in different historical periods, the old and the new, phenomena that appear to be simultaneously on the ascent and on the decline, often in conflict with each other, and yet characterized by the common fact of defying resolution and closure with iron courage. Among such common problems is the aspiration to be a democracy. The simultaneity of the non-simultaneous combined with the tension-filled nature of the political assures that the democratic system remains complex, contentious, and assailable. This includes the persistent conflict between the collective and the individual, the state and civil society, and, as we have examined in particular, the fundamental discord between (economic) prices and (social) values; Idiosyncrasies resulting from historically unique developments and tensions of old and new, existing and emerging societal phenomena.

Against the background of our findings, our scrutiny of monies in modern societies is not merely an abstract sociology of money. For heretofore, a sociology of money concentrates on money as a reflexive social mechanism, as a medium and means of exchange, as the freedom to store or spend value, as a universal means of communication in the economic and social system, and more recently, as a crisis-inducing phenomenon. However, applied to our specific context of the emergence of the immaterial economy, and using Weberian terms, it is the persistent struggle between the substantive (moral) and existential (formal) rationality that remains as a lasting social problem of outstanding interest. Although, as Weber ([1956] 1978: 107) emphasizes, "formal rationality of money calculation is dependent on certain quite specific substantive conditions," moral and existential motives are distinguishable and remain in fierce competition. Since both, substantive and existential rationalities are distinct sources of motivation for economic conduct, in last analysis, there is an "unavoidable element of irrationality in economic systems." The charged relationship between moral and formal rationality "is one of the important sources of all 'social' problems" (Weber, [1956] 1978: 111). It is this ultimate lesson, which money embodies. We remain buoyant by the circumstances for their contradictions. The future is open even if uncertain, constrained, and contested, and one of the major trailblazing forces lies in the immaterial economy.

## Note

1. In 1981, Thomas Brasch (1945–2001), a film maker and writer received the Bavarian Film Price in the presence of Franz-Josef Strauss, the Bavarian premier at the time. Brasch, in his remarks accepting the reward, thanked the East German Film Academy for the training he received as a student of the Academy—to the evident dismay of his audience.

# References

Goodhart, David (2017), *The Road to Somewhere. The New Tribes Shaping British Politics.* London: Penguin.

Gorz, André ([1997] 2000), *Arbeit zwischen Misere und Utopie.* Frankfurt am Main: Suhrkamp.

Keynes, John Maynard (1937), "The general theory of employment," *Economic Journal* 51: 209–223.

Knight, Frank H. ([1921] 1964), *Risk, Uncertainty and Profit.* New York: Sentry Press.

Lehnert, Detlef (2016), "Ungleichzeitigkeit des Gleichzeitigen. Dynamiken und Paradoxien von Generationen," *Indes* 5(S1): 12–20.

Mannheim. Karl ([1928] 1993), "The problem of generations," pp. 351–395 in Kurt H. Wolff (ed.), *From Karl Mannheim.* New Brunswick, NJ: Transaction Books.

Simmel, Georg ([1908] 2009), *Sociology. Inquiries into the Construction of Social Forms.* Leiden: Brill.

Simmel, Georg (1915), "Geld und Nahrung," *Der Tag*, Nr. 74, 28. März 1915, Ausgabe A, Illustrierter Teil (Berlin).

Weber, Max ([1956] 1978), *Economy and Society.* Edited by Guenther Roth and Claus Wittich. Berkeley: University of California Press.

# INDEX